ANNOTATED READINGS IN THE HISTORY OF MODERN PSYCHOLOGY

C. JAMES GOODWIN
Western Carolina University

WILEY

JOHN WILEY & SONS, INC.

TO SUSAN

VP & EXECUTIVE PUBLISHER	Jay O'Callaghan
EXECUTIVE EDITOR	Christopher Johnson
SENIOR PRODUCTION EDITOR	Nicole Repasky
MARKETING MANAGER	Danielle Torio
DESIGNER	Madelyn Lesure
PRODUCTION MANAGEMENT SERVICES	Katie Boilard, Pine Tree Composition, Inc.
ASSISTANT EDITOR	Eileen McKeever
EDITORIAL ASSISTANT	Aaron Talwar
MEDIA EDITOR	Lynn Pearlman
COVER PHOTO	© Gary Gay/Alamy

This book was set in Times by Laserwords and printed and bound by Courier/Westford. The cover was printed by Courier/Westford.

The book is printed on acid-free paper. ∞

To order books or for customer service please, call 1-800-CALL WILEY (225-5945).

ISBN-13 978-0470-22811-1

Printed in the United States of America

10 9 8 7 6 5 4 3 2 1

CONTENTS

STRUCTURALISM AND FUNCTIONALISM

GESTALT PSYCHOLOGY

NATURE/NURTURE

ORIGINS OF BEHAVIORISM

EVOLUTION OF BEHAVIORISM

PSYCHOANALYSIS

CLINICAL PSYCHOLOGY

SEX AND RACE

INDUSTRIAL PSYCHOLOGY

MENTAL TESTING

PERSONALITY & SOCIAL PSYCHOLOGY

COGNITIVE PSYCHOLOGY

HUMANISTIC PSYCHOLOGY

PREFACE

It is not uncommon for instructors in the history of psychology course to ask students to read original writings by the great men and women in psychology's past. It is one thing to read about William James, the argument goes, but there is no substitute for reading William James himself. Traditionally, this strategy has meant assigning a book of readings or producing a list of readings for students to hunt down in the library. Today, the typical strategy is to direct students to original writings in psychology via the internet (e.g., electronic versions of articles via the university library's website), and this easy availability of original sources via electronic means has rendered the traditional book of readings obsolete. Both hard copies of readings and electronic versions of the same material share one serious drawback, however. For both, students are left on their own to read and comprehend what is often very difficult material for them. For one thing, the readings were not written for a student audience but for the professional peers of the writer, so the level of reading difficulty tends to be high. In addition, the materials were written at a particular time and place in psychology's history, and understanding the points made in the piece usually requires that the student know something of the historical context in which the article or book was written and something about the writer of the piece. Stylistic conventions in place at the time the material was written may also make comprehension difficult. This book of annotated readings is an attempt to solve these problems.

Each of the thirty-six chapters is this reader includes substantial excerpts from important books and papers in psychology's history, but the chapters also include my own narrative, interspersed with passages from the original source, designed to make it easier for students to comprehend the material. I will give the reader some information about the writer of the piece, describe the importance of the work for psychology's history, put the selection into its historical context, and try to explain or elaborate upon some of the more difficult passages. My narrative also serves to connect different segments of the selection.

The decisions about what to include in this annotated reader have been driven by two main considerations. The first, of course, is relevance—if students are only going to read a limited sample of the important writings in psychology's history, some care must be taken to choose important works. I cannot claim to have made the choices in an entirely systematic fashion, but I have taught this course for over twenty-five years, written a textbook for the course, and experience tells me that some choices are obvious (e.g., Ebbinghaus on memory, Watson's "behaviorist manifesto"). In addition, I examined tables of contents of textbooks other than my own to look for references to writings that might be close to universal (e.g., William James on emotion, something by Freud).

A second criterion that I used was readability. Some readings that I might have included were left out because they were either extremely tedious to read or, in my judgment, very difficult for students to understand (main criterion: I know that if I had trouble, then students would probably have even more difficulty).

This book could be used as a stand-alone text for a capstone course in psychology that focuses on history, for a first-year graduate seminar in psychology, or, most likely, as a supplement to a main text in the undergraduate history of psychology course. Cost considerations might make it difficult to justify using both this reader and a large history text, but there are several fine concise histories of psychology, most notably Ludy Benjamin's *A Brief History of Modern Psychology* (Wiley/Blackwell, 2007).

I would very much appreciate your feedback about this reader. I can be reached here: jgoodwin@wcu.edu.

ACKNOWLEDGMENTS

My graduate training was in the experimental psychology of memory, but I was fortunate enough to have a dissertation director, Darryl Bruce, with a true love of history. While teaching me to be a good scientist, he was also convincing me of history's great truth—you cannot understand the present without knowing the past. So, to my Canadian mentor Darryl, now retired in beautiful Nova Scotia, I owe a debt that I will never be able to repay.

I have come to think of myself as a "Wiley" author, this being my third book with them. Special appreciation goes to psychology editor Chris Johnson, who has been consistently supportive of all my projects; and assistant editor Eileen McKeever, whose enthusiasm, good cheer, and sharp mind have been largely responsible for this book being in your hands today. Thanks also go to Katie Boilard of Pine Tree Composition, Inc., who coordinated the production process with great skill and grace.

Finally, a tip of the hat to the reviewers for this reader, who included. Danny Benbassat, Ohio Northern University; Stewart W. Ehly, University of Iowa; Carlos A. Escoto, Eastern Connecticut State University; Paul M. Galvin, Framingham State College; Janet L. Kottke, California State University in San Bernadino; Paul Kulkosky, Colorado State University; Ronald B. McCarver, University of Alabama; Brady Phelps, South Dakota State University; John K. Robinson, Stony Brook University; Thomas H. Schilling, Fitchburg State College; Debra Swoboda, York College, and Andrew Jordan Wright, Columbia University.

CHAPTER PREVIEWS

RATIONALIST AND EMPIRICIST EPISTEMOLOGIES

CHAPTER 1 RENÉ DESCARTES (1596–1650): Mind-Body Interactionism
CHAPTER 2 JOHN STUART MILL (1806–1873): British Empiricism Firsthand

Included in this section are readings by the foremost advocate of the philosophical position called rationalism, René Descartes, and by the leading British empiricist of the nineteenth century, John Stuart Mill. The Descartes selection focuses on his argument for the validity of a rationalist strategy (the only way to certain knowledge is through the use of reason), his ideas on how the mind and body interact, and his famous model of reflex action. The Mill selection is from his autobiography, where he describes how his father (James Mill), also a well-known British empiricist, raised him. The empiricist tradition assumes an empty mind at birth, with the "blank slate" filled in with life's experiences. As you will learn from the reading, John Stuart Mill's childhood was spent having his blank slate filled daily.

NINETEENTH CENTURY STUDIES OF THE BRAIN

CHAPTER 3 FRANÇOIS MAGENDIE (1783–1855): The Bell-Magendie Principle
CHAPTER 4 PAUL BROCA (1824–1880): The Case of "Tan"

The readings in this section are prominent examples of nineteenth century physiological research on the workings of the brain and nervous system. The Bell-Magendie principle, which, as you will learn, should probably be called the Magendie principle, has to do with spinal cord functioning, and resulted from a brilliant series of surgical studies by the talented French surgeon, François Magendie. In the second reading, you will learn about a famous case study that led to the labeling of "Broca's area," that portion of the left frontal cortex that concerns the production of language.

THE "NEW PSYCHOLOGY" EMERGES

CHAPTER 5   WILHELM WUNDT (1832–1920): A New Scientific Psychology
CHAPTER 6   HERMANN EBBINGHAUS (1850–1909): On Memory

The official "founding" of modern psychology is said to have been in 1879, when the German scientist Wilhelm Wundt established a laboratory of experimental psychology at Leipzig. The first reading in this section is from an introductory text by Wundt, in which he outlined what this new psychology was and which methods it used to achieve its goals. The second selection is from a contemporary of Wundt's, Hermann Ebbinghaus, who was trained in philosophy but used experimental methods in the first systematic study of human memory. The reading highlights the Ebbinghaus method and some of his results, including a famous one on the time course of forgetting.

COMPARATIVE PSYCHOLOGY

CHAPTER 7   WILLARD S. SMALL (1870–1943): Inventing Maze Learning
CHAPTER 8   EDWARD L. THORNDIKE (1874–1949): Cats in Puzzle Boxes

One of the consequences of Darwin's theory of evolution was a strong interest in the study of animal behavior. "Comparative" psychology developed as an attempt to examine species differences in various abilities, with an eye toward making inferences about the evolution of ability, and this section includes two well-known studies. The first, by Willard Small of Clark University, was the first published study of rats learning a maze, a methodological tradition that later became standard in research in the behaviorist tradition. The Thorndike study also has become a classic, a systematic examination of learning, in which cats gradually learned to escape from crude puzzle boxes through trial and error.

AMERICAN PIONEERS

CHAPTER 9   WILLIAM JAMES (1842–1910): On Consciousness and Emotion
CHAPTER 10   MARY WHITON CALKINS (1863–1930): Experiments on
                 Association

In 1903, James McKeen Cattell surveyed psychologists, asking them to rank their peers for eminence. Not only did Harvard's William James of achieve the top ranking, he was ranked first on every ballot that Cattell received. James' most famous work, sometimes considered the most important book ever published in psychology, is his two-volume *Principles of Psychology*, which appeared in 1890. The first selection includes excerpts from two of the chapters of a briefer version of this famous book—the topics considered are consciousness and on emotion. Mary Calkins, a student (informally—Harvard did not officially admit women at the time) of James in the early 1890s, became the first woman president of the American Psychological Association (APA) in 1905. The second reading is from what would have been her doctoral dissertation, if Harvard granted them to women then. It is a memory study that examined the factors affecting association strength and developed the "paired associates" method, which later became a standard technique in memory research.

STRUCTURALISM AND FUNCTIONALISM

CHAPTER 11   E. B. TITCHENER (1867–1927): A Structural Psychology
CHAPTER 12   JAMES ROWLAND ANGELL (1869–1949): A Functional Psychology

Two so-called "schools" of psychology in the United States at the turn of the twentieth century were structuralism and functionalism. Structuralists were interested in analyzing mental processes in order to reduce them to their simplest elements (e.g., sensations). Functionalists, influenced by evolutionary thinking, were more concerned with how mental processes served to adapt the individual to the environment. The great structuralist was E. B. Titchener of Cornell and the first selection, from one of his textbooks, provides a good introduction to structuralist thinking. The second selection is from the APA presidential address of James Angell of the University of Chicago, which was a center of functionalist thinking. It became known as the first clear description of functionalist ideas.

GESTALT PSYCHOLOGY

CHAPTER 13   KURT KOFFKA (1886–1941): Gestalt Psychology and Perception
CHAPTER 14   WOLFGANG KÖHLER (1887–1967): Problem Solving in Apes

While structuralists and functionalists were arguing with each other, gestalt psychology was developing in Germany, under the leadership of Max Wertheimer (normally considered the founder of the movement), Kurt Koffka, and Wolfgang Köhler. It eventually reached the United States, in force, in the late 1920s and 1930s, when its leading exponents emigrated from Germany, in part because of the growing threat from Nazism. The famous gestalt catch phrase was "the whole is greater than the sum of its parts." The first reading is from a paper by Koffka that introduced most American psychologists to gestalt ideas when it first appeared in an American journal in 1922. The second selection is from a book on problem solving in apes. It summarized a classic series of studies by Köhler, who argued that apes were capable of insightful problem solving.

NATURE/NURTURE

CHAPTER 15   FRANCIS GALTON (1822–1911): The Inheritance of Mental Ability
CHAPTER 16   HENRY H. GODDARD (1866–1957): The Kallikak Study

One of psychology's enduring issues is the degree to which behavior is influenced by heredity or environment—the nature-nurture issue. In the first selection, Frances Galton (Darwin's cousin) took a firm stand on the side of heredity, arguing that human mental ability had little to do with upbringing and every-thing to do with heredity. On the basis of his beliefs, Galton became an advocate for eugenics (a term he created), the deliberate attempt to shape traits by such tactics as selective breeding. In the United States, Henry Goddard had a similar opinion about mental capacity and set about to investigate the inherited effects of disability by completing a genealogical study of a young institutionalized "feebleminded" woman given the pseudonym Deborah Kallikak. The second reading tells the story of the Kallikak family.

ORIGINS OF BEHAVIORISM

CHAPTER 17   IVAN PAVLOV (1849–1936): Conditioned Reflexes
CHAPTER 18   JOHN BROADUS WATSON (1878–1958): A Behaviorist Manifesto

The Russian physiologist Ivan Pavlov first became an international figure when he won a Nobel Prize in 1904 for his work on the physiology of digestion. Yet as every introductory psychology student knows, he became central to psy-chology's history by carefully studying what he called "psychical reflexes" (e.g., a dog salivating before the food was placed in its mouth), in the pro-cess creating a conditioning paradigm that became indispensable to behaviorist research. The first selection, from a translation of a set of lectures he gave in the 1920s, describes some of Pavlov's work. The second selection is one of psychology's most famous papers, delivered in 1913 by John Watson of Johns Hopkins University, in which he explicitly rejected both structuralist and functionalist psychologies in favor of a new approach—behaviorism. As much as any of his work, this paper earned Watson the title of "founder" of behaviorism.

EVOLUTION OF BEHAVIORISM

CHAPTER 19   EDWARD C. TOLMAN (1886–1959): Cognitive Maps
CHAPTER 20   B. F. SKINNER (1904–1990): An Experimental Analysis of Behavior

Following Watson, behaviorism evolved in the 1920s and 1930s and became a force in American experimental psychology. The best-known "neobehaviorists" were Edward Tolman, Clark Hull, Edwin Guthrie, and B. F. Skinner. This section includes a reading from Tolman, famous for his research on maze learning in rats and for arguing that rats do not just learn stimulus-response connections, a traditional behaviorist idea. Instead, he believed, they gradually develop a basic understanding of the spatial layout of the maze, what he called a cognitive map. As a vigorous promoter of behaviorist ideals, Skinner was the rightful heir to Watson. He became the center of a movement that remained strong at least up to his death in 1990, a "radical" behaviorism that, while recognizing the influence of genetic factors, argued that we are the way we are primarily because of our conditioning history. The second selection is from a Skinner text that outlined his basic views on what he called operant conditioning.

PSYCHOANALYSIS

CHAPTER 21   SIGMUND FREUD (1887–1967): The Clark Lectures on
Psychoanalysis
CHAPTER 22   KAREN HORNEY (1885–1952): Conflict, Anxiety, and Neurosis

Ask most people to name a psychologist and Sigmund Freud usually comes
to mind, even though he wasn't one (he was a physician, an M.D.). Freud's
ideas had a major impact on twentieth century thinking about the mind, and
his concepts of the unconscious, the Oedipal complex, dream analysis, and so
on, are widely (if not always accurately) known. The first selection is from a
set of lectures given by Freud on his only trip to the United States—he was
the centerpiece of a celebration of the twentieth birthday of Clark University in
1909. The second selection is from Karen Horney, a psychoanalyst trained in
the Freudian tradition, but with ideas of her own, including a strong rejection
of Freud's theories about female psychology. The excerpt is from one of her
books, in which she describes her ideas about anxiety and neurosis, and clarifies
her theoretical differences with Freud.

CLINICAL PSYCHOLOGY

CHAPTER 23   LIGHTNER WITMER (1867–1956): The Psychological Clinic
CHAPTER 24   MARY COVER JONES (1896–1987): Behavior Therapy

Lightner Witmer was trained as an experimental psychologist in Wundt's laboratory, but shifted his interests from pure laboratory work to using the lab
as a way to improve the academic performance of school children that were
experiencing various difficulties. He turned part of his lab into American psychology's first "clinic" and he invented the term "clinical psychology" (even
though his actual clinical work was more like what modern school psychologists do). The second selection is from Mary Cover Jones, a pioneer in what
eventually came to be called behavior therapy. Working in the 1920s, and under
the supervision of John Watson, she used behaviorist ideas to help alleviate
the fear that a young boy ("Peter") had of rabbits. Her successful technique
was in principle similar to a procedure that later became known as systematic
desensitization.

SEX AND RACE

CHAPTER 25   LETA STETTER HOLLINGWORTH (1886–1939): Sex Differences
in Aptitude
CHAPTER 26   KENNETH B. CLARK (1914–2005) and MAMIE PHIPPS CLARK
(1917–1983): The Doll Studies

Leta Hollingworth was one-half of a psychological dynamic duo. With her husband Harry, she pioneered a number of studies in applied psychology (e.g.,
testing the effects of the caffeine in coca-cola). On her own she investigated sex

differences in behavior, concluding that few important ones existed. The first reading, from a chapter in a book on vocational psychology by Harry Hollingworth, describes some of this research. The second selection has become known simply as the "doll study." It grew out of Mamie Phipps Clark's masters thesis at Howard University and eventually contributed to the historic 1954 *Brown* v. *Board of Education* Supreme Court decision that outlawed segregation in public schools. The doll studies documented the detrimental effects of segregation on school children.

INDUSTRIAL PSYCHOLOGY

CHAPTER 27 WALTER DILL SCOTT (1869–1955): Psychology and Advertising
CHAPTER 28 HUGO MÜNSTERBERG (1863–1916): Applying Psychology to Business

One major area of applied psychology in the United States is industrial psychology—the application of psychological principles to the world of business. Two important pioneers in this field were Walter Scott and Hugo Münsterberg. Like Witmer, both earned doctorates with Wundt, and both strayed from the straight and narrow of pure experimental psychology. In the early years of the twentieth century, Scott wrote extensively about applying psychology to advertising, and the first selection is from one of his books on the subject. In the second reading, Münsterberg, who was also a pioneer in forensic psychology, described how to use psychological principles to improve employee selection procedures.

MENTAL TESTING

CHAPTER 29 JAMES MCKEEN CATTELL (1860–1944): Mental Tests
CHAPTER 30 ALFRED BINET (1857–1911): The Binet-Simon Tests of Intelligence

In addition to industrial psychology, another important area of application in psychology involved the development of intelligence testing. The first selection describes an early attempt that, while known for coining the term "mental test," eventually failed to be a valid strategy for assessing ability. It was a strategy originated by Francis Galton and developed in the United States by James Cattell (yet another Wundt Ph.D.), sometimes known as the "American Galton." A second strategy, one that eventually led to modern IQ testing, developed in France with the work of Alfred Binet, who was commissioned to find a way to identify school children in need of special training. Binet's writing is featured in the second reading.

PERSONALITY & SOCIAL PSYCHOLOGY

CHAPTER 31   GORDON ALLPORT (1897–1967): The Uniqueness of Personality
CHAPTER 32   KURT LEWIN (1890–1947): The Leadership Studies

Two major subdisciplines in modern psychology are personality psychology and social psychology. Personality psychologists investigate individual differences in personality attributes and how best to measure these differences. Gordon Allport was an important pioneer, arguably the founder of modern personality psychology. The first selection is from a book that he wrote on the topic in 1937. Social psychologists investigate how behavior is influenced by social and societal factors, and Lewin is considered by many to be the founder of modern social psychology (some consideration also goes to Gordon Allport's brother Floyd). One of Lewin's famous studies compared different styles of leadership on the group behavior of young boys, and the second selection describes some of this research.

COGNITIVE PSYCHOLOGY

CHAPTER 33   FREDERICK C. BARTLETT (1886–1969): Constructive Memory
CHAPTER 34   JOHN JENKINS (1901–1948) and KARL DALLENBACH
(1887–1971): Interference and Memory

Modern cognitive psychology is the experimental study of such mental processes as memory, perception, attention, thinking, and language. When neobehaviorism weakened and began to lose strength in the late 1950s and early 1960s, cognitive psychology began to replace it as experimental psychology's main frame of reference. Yet even during the heyday of behaviorism, important pioneering projects in cognitive psychology appeared, two of them featured in this section. One was a 1932 book on memory by the British psychologist Frederick Bartlett, and the first selection is from that book. The second selection is from a study in the 1920s, to this day frequently found in general psychology books, showing that getting a good night's sleep before an exam might be a good idea.

HUMANISTIC PSYCHOLOGY

CHAPTER 35   ABRAHAM MASLOW (1908–1970): A Hierarchy of Needs
CHAPTER 36   CARL ROGERS (1902–1987): The Therapeutic Environment

In the 1960s, a time of turmoil and dissent in the United States, dissident movements also arose in psychology, and humanistic psychology was the major one. Said to be psychology's "Third Force" (psychoanalysis and behaviorism being the other two), it proposed an alternative model of human existence that focused on self-knowledge, personal responsibility, and moving toward what was called "self-actualization." The two leading proponents of this approach were Abraham Maslow, first trained as a behaviorist, and Carl Rogers, who had some early training in psychoanalysis. The first reading outlines Maslow's well-known hierarchy of needs model of motivation and the second describes Rogers' views on the ideal environment for therapeutic success.

CHAPTER 1

RENÉ DESCARTES (1596–1650): MIND-BODY INTERACTIONISM

The great French philosopher René Descartes (1596–1650) was a true Renaissance man—in addition to his importance to the history of philosophy, as a strong advocate for a rationalist position (a belief in the use of reason to arrive at truth), he made important contributions to mathematics, astronomy, meteorology, and, as you will learn here, to the physiology of the nervous system and to psychology. He was trained by Jesuits, but spent the majority of his life in the independent pursuit of knowledge, and he was often scornful of authority. He is perhaps best known for his *Discourse on Method* (Descartes, 1637/1960), which begins with an autobiographical chapter and includes a detailed description of his rationalist method of inquiry. In the year before his death, Descartes published *The Passions of the Soul* (1649/1969), which addressed issues that would eventually become important to physiologists and psychologists. A portion of that book is excerpted here.

Primarily a treatise on human emotions (and their rational control), *Passions* included an attempt to explain what we now call the *reflex*, and it included the description of a physiological model for Descartes' dualist position on the mind-body question. Descartes opened the book with an attack on the traditional, authority-based approach to the study of the emotions, arguing in his opening sentence that "[t]here is nothing in which the defective nature of the sciences which we have received from the ancients appears more clearly than in what they have written on the passions" (Descartes, 1649/1969, p. 331). He then began a discussion of the "bodily machine" which included (a) a direct reference to a contemporary, William Harvey, who had proposed, in 1628, a mechanical model of the heart-as-pump; (b) a description of the antagonistic action of the muscles; and (c) an opening discussion of the functioning of the nervous system.

> In order to render this more intelligible, I shall here explain in a few words the whole method in which the bodily machine is composed. There is no

Excerpts from: Descartes, R. (1969). The passions of the soul. In E. S. Haldane & G. R. T. Ross (Trans.), *The philosophical works of Descartes*. Vol. *I* (pp. 329–427). New York: Cambridge University Press. (Original work published 1649) one who does not already know that there are in us a heart, a brain, a stomach, muscles, nerves, arteries, veins, and such things. . . . Those who have acquired even the minimum of medical knowledge further know how the heart is composed. . . . Likewise all those whom the authority of the ancients has not entirely blinded, and who have chosen to open their eyes for the purpose of investigating the opinion of Harvey regarding the circulation of blood, do not doubt that all the veins and arteries of the body are like streams by which the blood ceaselessly flows with great swiftness. . . . We further know that all the movements of the members [e.g., arms and legs] depend on the muscles, and that these muscles are so mutually related one to another that when the one is contracted it draws toward itself the part of the body to which it is attached, which causes the opposite muscle to become elongated. . . . We know finally that all these movements of the muscles, as also all the senses, depend on the nerves, which resemble . . . little tubes, which all proceed from the brain, and thus contain like it a certain very subtle air or wind which is called the animal spirits. (pp. 333–334)

The *animal spirits* referred to by Descartes, a notion that traces to the ancient Greeks, were said to be derived from the "heat" of the blood and were the driving forces behind all movement. Descartes believed these spirits were tiny particles in constant motion and were found in the brain, the nerves, and the muscles.

[F]or what I here name spirits are nothing but material bodies and their one peculiarity is that they are bodies of extreme minuteness and that they move very quickly like the particles of the flame which issues from a torch. Thus it is that they never remain at rest in any spot, and just as some of them enter into the cavities of the brain, others issue forth by the pores which are in [the brain], which pores conduct them into the nerves, and from there into the muscles, by means of which they move the body in all the different ways in which it can be moved. . . .

For the sole cause of all the movements of the members is that certain muscles contract, and that those opposite to them elongate . . . and the sole cause of one muscle contracting rather than that set against it, is that there comes from the brain some additional amount of animal spirits, however little it may be, to it rather than to the other. Not that the spirits which proceed immediately from the brain suffice in themselves to move the muscles, but they determine the other spirits which are already in these two muscles, all to issue very quickly from the one of them and to pass into the other. (p. 336)

Muscle movement results from the action of animal spirits, but what determines which muscles will move? Two things, according to Descartes. First, the mind can initiate the movement of animal spirits in the brain by activating the nerves controlling certain muscles rather than others. That is, the mind can influence the body (more on this shortly). Second, certain muscles can move automatically in response to the results of specific sensory stimulation. That is, *reflexes* occur.

Descartes explained the relationship between sensation and the automatic motor (reflex) response by proposing the existence of thin, wire-like "filaments" that existed within the nerves and extended to the brain.

[T]here are three things to consider in respect of the nerves, i.e. first of all their marrow or interior substance, which extends in the form of little filaments from the brain, from which it originates, to the extremities of the other members [e.g., a hand] to which these filaments are attached; secondly the membranes which surround them, and which, being coterminus with those which envelope the brain, form little tubes in which these little filaments are enclosed; and finally the animal spirits which, being carried by these same tubes from the brain to the muscles, are the reason of these filaments remaining there perfectly free and extended, so that the least thing that moves the part of the body to which the extremity of any one of them is attached, causes by that same means the part of the brain from which it proceeds to move, just as when one draws one end of a cord the other end is made to move. (p. 337)

On the basis of his animal dissections and without the benefit of Anton van Leeuwenhoek's microscope, yet to be invented, Descartes believed the nerves to be hollow tubes (thus allowing for animal spirits to move through them) containing these thin filaments. Whenever our senses are stimulated, according to Descartes, these filaments move, causing certain "pores" in the brain to be opened. This in turn results in the flow of animal spirits that produces the reflex movement, as when we accidentally touch the stove and burn ourselves. The hand touches the burner on the stove, causing a tug on the filaments within the nerve in the hand. These filaments extend all the way to the brain where animal spirits are released into the nerve "tube." The spirits in turn are carried "partly to the muscles which pull back the [hand from the burner], partly to those which turn the eyes and the head in order to regard it, and partly to those which serve to advance the hands and to bend the whole body in order to shield itself" (Descartes, 1637, quoted in Fearing, 1930, p. 24). Descartes also stressed the idea that reflexes occur even if we deliberately (i.e., through the action of our "soul"—mind) try to avoid them. Note here the use of a "body as machine" metaphor frequently used by Descartes.

If someone quickly thrusts his hand against our eyes as if to strike us, even though we know him to be our friend, that he only does it in fun, and that he will take great care not to hurt us, we have all the same trouble in preventing ourselves from closing them; and this shows that it is not by the intervention of our soul that they close; seeing that it is against our will, which is its only, or at least its principle activity; but it is because the machine of our body is so formed that the movement of this hand toward our eyes excites another movement in our brain, which conducts the animal spirits into the muscles which cause the eyelids to close. (p. 338)

Descartes used the reflex concept to include not just motor reflexes, but all our automatic functioning (e.g., breathing, digesting). In yet another reference to the idea of the body as machine, he drew an analogy to the mechanics of a clock.

In this way all the movement which we make without our will contributing thereto (as frequently happens when we breathe, walk, eat, and in fact perform all those actions which are common to us and to the brutes), only depend on the conformation of our members, and on the course which the spirits, excited by the heat of the heart, follow naturally in the brain, nerves, and muscles, just as the movements of a watch are produced simply by the strength of the springs and the form of the wheels. (pp. 339–340)

In addition to resulting in reflex action, sensations can also give rise to the movement of animal spirits in the brain that lead to *deliberate* decisions to act; hence, the mind *by itself* can initiate action. How to explain the nature of this interaction between mind and body was a problem, however. It is one thing to say that the mind can directly affect bodily movement, but it is quite another thing to demonstrate just how this occurs. After careful analysis, Descartes

clearly ascertained that the part of the body in which the soul exercises its functions immediately is in nowise the heart, nor the whole of the brain, but merely the most inward of all its parts, to wit, a certain very small gland which is situated in the middle of its substance and so suspended above the duct whereby the animal spirits in its anterior cavities have communication with those in the posterior, that the slightest movements which take place in it may alter very greatly the course of these spirits; and reciprocally that the smallest changes which occur in the course of the spirits may do much to change the movements of this gland. (pp. 345–346)

The structure in question is the *pineal gland*, and Descartes selected it as the locus for mind-body interaction because he believed it was strategically located in a place where the flow of the animal spirits could be controlled. The pineal gland was also a brain structure that was not duplicated on both the left and right side of the brain. Because the mind (or soul) was considered to be unitary, Descartes reasoned, it must exert its effect through a structure that was also a single unit.

The reason which persuades me that the soul cannot have any other seat in all the body than this gland wherein to exercise its functions immediately, is that I reflect that the other parts of our brain are all of them double, just as we have two eyes, two hands, two ears, and finally all the organs of our outside senses are double; and inasmuch as we have but one solitary and simple thought of one particular thing at one and the same moment, it must necessarily be the case that there must somewhere be a place where the two images which come to us by the two eyes, where the two other impressions which proceed from a single object by means of the double organs of the other senses, can unite before arriving at the soul, in order that they may not represent to it two objects instead of one. And it is easy to apprehend how these images or other impressions might unite in this gland by the intermission of the spirits which fill the cavities of the brain; but there is no other place in the body where they can be thus united unless they are so in this gland. (p. 346)

It is worth noting that Descartes was not arguing that the pineal gland had its special function because it was a part of the brain found only in humans—he was well aware, on the basis of some of his own dissections, that other animals possessed the structure (Finger, 2000). What he was arguing was that the gland had a function in humans that would not be found in animals—the locus for mind-body interaction.

Descartes was not asserting that the mind was *in* the pineal gland, only that the gland serves as the place where mind and body influence each other. Thus, sensations produce a stretching of the small filaments that open pores in the brain, thereby moving the animal spirits. These movements are felt by the pineal gland and result in the mental event of a "sensation." The animal spirits also continue their movement back down the nerve fibers into the muscles, producing movement (i.e., as in a reflex). But muscle movements can also be created by the direct action of the will. The decision to move *causes* the pineal gland to move, which in turn produces the movements of the spirits that eventually move the muscles. In a similar fashion, our decision to think about something, or use our imagination, cause the pineal gland to move in such a way that animal spirits are directed to specific portions of the brain.

> Thus when we desire to imagine something we have never seen, this desire has the power of causing the gland to move in the manner requisite to drive the spirits towards the pores of the brain by the opening of which pores this particular thing may be represented; thus when we wish to apply our attention for some time to the consideration of one particular object, this desire holds the gland for the time being inclined to the same side. Thus, finally, when we desire to walk or to move our body in some special way, this desire causes the gland to thrust the spirits towards the muscles which serve to bring about this result. (pp. 350–351)

Furthermore, Descartes used his model to explain other mental processes such as memory, which he suggested was the result of animal spirits moving more easily along pathways that have been made more accessible by experience.

> Thus when the soul desires to recollect something, this desire causes the gland, by inclining successively to different sides, to thrust the spirits towards different parts of the brain until they come across that part where the traces left there by the object which we wish to recollect are found; for these traces are none other than the fact that the pores of the brain, by which the spirits have formerly followed their course because of the presence of this object, have by that means acquired a greater facility than the others in being once more opened by the animal spirits which come towards them in the same way. Thus the spirits in coming in contact with these pores, enter into them more easily than into the others, by which means they excite a special movement in the gland which represents the same object to the soul, and causes it to know that it is this which it desired to remember. (p. 350)

Of course, despite the noble effort, Descartes was wrong about the physiology. For example, the pineal gland, which secretes the hormone melatonin and remains poorly understood today, is not a mind-body Grand Central Station. A more important problem, one pointed out almost immediately by critics in his own day, was that his proposal of the pineal gland as the point of mind-body interaction really did not explain *anything*, but merely pushed the problem back by one step. If it is unclear how the unextended mind can influence and be influenced by an extended body in general, it is just as unclear how the unextended mind can influence, and be influenced by, the movements of a small, extended piece of the brain (Cottingham, 1986). For psychology, the significance of Descartes' work is not that he made a serious yet flawed effort to solve the mind-body problem, but that in so doing, he created the concept of reflex action, with its explicit distinction between sensory stimulus and motor response, and he tried to explain psychological concepts (e.g., memory) by using a physiological model. He was the first physiological psychologist.

Shortly after publishing *The Passions of the Soul* in 1649, Descartes was persuaded by Queen Christina of Sweden to move to Stockholm in order to tutor her. Christina had a keen mind, was fluent in five languages, and was determined to make Stockholm a center of learning in Europe. To accomplish her goal, she created a world-class library and began inviting scholars to her court, Descartes being among the first to be asked. He accepted with some misgivings and soon found himself conversing with and tutoring Christina for five hours a day, three days a week, beginning at 5 A.M., during a winter that was severe even by Swedish standards. He soon developed pneumonia and died on February 11, 1650.

CONCEPT REVIEW QUESTIONS

1. Use Descartes' model of the reflex to show how he was influenced by the mechanistic *Zeitgeist* of the day.
2. Why did Descartes pick the pineal gland as the place for the locus of mind-body interaction?
3. How did Descartes explain memory processes?

DISCUSSION QUESTION

1. Describe Descartes' solution to the mind-body problem. Does it make sense? Explain.

CHAPTER 2

JOHN STUART MILL (1806–1873): BRITISH EMPIRICISM FIRSTHAND

From the time of John Locke (1632–1704), a philosophical school of thought developed in Great Britain that came to be called British empiricism. Its central theme was the idea, dating back at least as far as Aristotle, that the contents of our minds are constructed from our experiences in the world—that we arrive at birth with our mind a *blank slate* (or white paper, to use Locke's analogy), and that during our lifetimes, experience writes on this blank slate. As Locke famously put it,

> Let us then suppose the mind to be, as we say, white paper, void of all characters, without any ideas; how comes it to be furnished? ... To this I answer, in one word, from experience; in that, all our knowledge is founded, and from that it ultimately derives itself. (Locke, 1690/1963, pp. 82–83)

John Stuart Mill was arguably the most important British empiricist of the nineteenth century. And what was remarkable about his life was that it represented what could be called "empiricism firsthand." This is because his father, James Mill (1773–1836), also a proponent of empiricist thinking, deliberately set about to apply its principles to the raising of his son. That is, the early life of John Stuart Mill became an experiment in how best to fill up a young boy's blank slate. The remarkable story of this experiment is told in a brief autobiography that Mill penned just before he died. This chapter's excerpt comes from this book.

Mill opened his autobiography by modestly wondering why anyone would be interested in reading it, and then by explaining why he wrote it. From the very beginning, he made it clear that a main focus would be his extraordinary early education.

> It seems proper that I should prefix to the following biographical sketch, some mention of the reasons which have made me think it desirable that I should leave behind me such a memorial of so uneventful a life as mine.

Excerpts from: Mill, J. S. (1989). *Autobiography*. New York: Penguin. (Original work published 1873)

I do not for a moment imagine that any part of what I have to relate can be interesting to the public as a narrative, or as being connected with myself. But I have thought that in an age in which education, and its improvement, are the subject of more, if not of profounder study than at any former period of English history, it may be useful that there should be some record of an education which was unusual and remarkable, and which, whatever else it may have done, has proved how much more than is commonly supposed may be taught, and well taught, in those early years which, in the common modes of what is called instruction, are little better than wasted. (p. 25)

James Mill's major accomplishment was the writing of a comprehensive history of India. His son was a great admirer, as can be seen here; after going through a long list of his father's responsibilities, Mill began a description of his early education.

And to this is to be added, that during the whole period, a considerable part of almost every day was employed in the instruction of his children: in the case of one of whom, myself, he exerted an amount of labor, care, and perseverance rarely, if ever, employed for a similar purpose, in endeavoring to give, according to his own conception, the highest order of intellectual education.

A man whom, in his own practice, so vigorously acted up to the principle of losing no time, was likely to adhere to the same rule in the instruction of his pupil. I have no remembrance of the time when I began to learn Greek. I have been told that it was when I was three years old. My earliest recollection on the subject, is that of committing to memory what my father termed Vocables, being lists of common Greek words, with their signification in English, which he wrote out for me on cards. . . . I learnt no Latin until my eighth year. At that time I had read, under my father's tuition, a number of Greek prose authors, among whom I remember the whole of Herodotus, and of Xenophon's *Cyropaedia* and *Memorials of Socrates*; . . . I also read, in 1813 [i.e., age 7], the first six dialogues of Plato. . . .

[M]y father, in all his teaching, demanded of me not only the utmost that I could do, but much that I could by no possibility have done. What he was himself willing to undergo for the sake of my instruction, may be judged from the fact that I went through the whole process of preparing my Greek lessons in the same room and at the same table at which he was writing; and as in those days Greek and English Lexicons were not [available], and I could make no more use of a Greek and Latin Lexicon than could be made without having yet begun to learn Latin, I was forced to have recourse to him for the meaning of every word which I did not know. This incessant interruption he, one of the most impatient of men, submitted to, and wrote under that interruption several volumes of his *History* and all else that he had to write during those years.

The only thing besides Greek that I learnt as a lesson in this part of my childhood, was arithmetic: this also my father taught me: it was the task of the evenings, and I well remember its disagreeableness. But the lessons were only a part of the daily instruction I received. Much of it consisted in the books I read by myself, and my father's discourses to me, chiefly during our walks. . . . My father's health required considerable and constant exercise, and he walked habitually before breakfast. . . . In these walks I

always accompanied him, and with my earliest recollections of green fields
and wild flowers, is mingled that of the account I gave him daily of what I
had read the day before. To the best of my remembrance, this was a voluntary rather than a prescribed exercise. I made notes on slips of paper while
reading, and from these, in the morning walks, I told the story to him; for
the books were chiefly histories, of which I read in this manner a great
number: Robertson's histories, Hume, Gibbon. . . . In these frequent talks
about the books I read, [my father] used, as opportunity offered, to give me
explanations and ideas respecting civilization, government, morality, mental
cultivation, which he required me afterwards to restate to him in my own
words. He also made me read, and give him a verbal account of, many books
which would not have interested me sufficiently to induce me to read them
of myself. . . . He was fond of putting into my hands books which exhibited
men of energy and resource in unusual circumstances, struggling against
difficulties and overcoming them. . . . Of children's books, any more than of
playthings, I had scarcely any, except an occasional gift from a relation or
acquaintance: Among those I had, *Robinson Crusoe* was preeminent, and
continued to delight me through all my boyhood. (pp. 27–30)

In addition to Greek, the study of Latin was added when young Mill was
age eight, and during the next few years he read and learned a wide range of
classic works that took him 2–3 pages to list. He made special note of Aristotle's
Rhetoric,

which, as the first expressly scientific treatise on any moral or psychological
subject which I had read, and containing many of the best observations
of the ancients on human nature and life, my father made me study with
peculiar care, and throw the matter of it into synoptic tables. During the same
years I learned elementary geometry and algebra thoroughly, the differential
calculus and other portions of the higher mathematics. . . .

As to my private reading, I can only speak of what I remember. History
continued to be my strongest predilection, and most of all ancient history.
(p. 32)

Mill's love of history led him to attempt writing one, a history of the
Roman government, which he began at age eleven. He wrote the equivalent of
a small book, but later destroyed it, "in my contempt of my childish efforts"
(p. 33). Meanwhile, his father kept up the relentless pressure on his son to
keep acquiring new learning. When young Mill was twelve, he began a systematic study of logic, with his father continuing to use his typical pedagogical
techniques.

Contemporaneously with the *Organon* [i.e., a collection of six books on
logic by Aristotle], my father made me read the whole or parts of several
of the Latin treatises on the scholastic logic; giving each day to him, in our
walks, a minute account of what I had read, and answering his numerous and
searching questions. (p. 36)

Mill found the study of logic immensely useful, because it provided the
ability to evaluate arguments, and it formed the foundation for acquiring other
knowledge.

My own consciousness and experience ultimately led me to appreciate quite as highly as he did, the value of an early practical familiarity with the school logic. I know of nothing, in my education, to which I think myself more indebted for whatever capacity of thinking I have attained. The first intellectual operation in which I arrived at any proficiency, was dissecting a bad argument, and finding in what part the fallacy lay: and though whatever capacity of this sort I attained was due to the fact that it was an intellectual exercise in which I was most perseveringly drilled by my father, yet it is also true that the school logic, and the mental habits acquired in studying it, were among the principle instruments of this drilling. I am persuaded that nothing, in modern education, tends so much, when properly used, to form exact thinkers, who attach a precise meaning to words and propositions, and are not imposed on by vague, loose, or ambiguous terms. (p. 37)

After a year of logic, the thirteen-year-old Mill began the study of political economy. The instruction included the usual drill and practice, but Mill also revealed another of his father's strategies—forcing his pupil to work through, and eventually master, difficult material without a great deal of guidance. The outcome, which Mill clearly valued, was an ability to think on his own, not just to retrieve knowledge that had been drilled into his head.

My father, therefore, commenced instructing me in the science [of political economy] by a sort of lectures, which he delivered to me in our walks. He expounded each day a portion of the subject, and I gave him next day a written account of it, which he made me rewrite over and over again until it was clear, precise, and tolerably complete. . . . I do not think that any scientific teaching ever was more thorough, or better fitted for training the faculties, than the mode in which logic and political economy were taught to me by my father. Striving, even in an exaggerated degree, to call forth the activity of my faculties, by making me find out everything for myself, he gave his explanations not before, but after, I had felt the full force of the difficulties; and not only gave me an accurate knowledge of these two great subjects, as far as they were then understood, but made me a thinker on both. I thought for myself almost from the first, and occasionally thought differently from him, though for a long time only on minor points, and making his opinion the ultimate standard. At a later period I even occasionally convinced him, and altered his opinion on some points of detail: which I state to his honour, not my own. It at once exemplifies his perfect candor, and the real worth of his method of teaching. (pp. 42–44)

The education of John Stuart Mill by his father was essentially complete by 1820, when the young pupil was age fourteen. He had acquired the equivalent of a university education. By any measure, it is quite clear that Mill was a child prodigy, and most descriptions of such children tend to accentuate the nature side of the nature-nurture issue. As you read how Mill summed up his experience, note that he would have disagreed vigorously with the argument that he was intellectually "gifted" right from the start. He thought virtually anyone was capable of achieving what he had achieved, given proper instruction.

At this point concluded what can properly be called my lessons. When I was about fourteen I left England for more than a year; and after my return, though my studies went on under my father's general direction, he was no longer my schoolmaster. I shall therefore pause here, and turn back to matters of a more general nature connected with the part of my life and education included in the preceding reminiscences.

In the course of instruction which I have partially retraced, the point most superficially apparent is the great effort to give, during the years of childhood, an amount of knowledge in what are considered the higher branches of education, which is seldom acquired (if acquired at all) until the age of manhood. The result of the experiment [shows] the ease with which this may be done. . . . If I had been by nature extremely quick of apprehension, or had possessed a very accurate and retentive memory, or were of a remarkably active and energetic character, the trial would not be conclusive; but in all these natural gifts I am rather below than above par. What I could do, could assuredly be done by any boy or girl of average capacity and healthy physical constitution: and if I have accomplished anything, I owe it, among other fortunate circumstances, to the fact that through the early training bestowed on me by my father, I started, I may fairly say, with an advantage of a quarter of a century over my contemporaries.

There was one cardinal point of this training . . . which, more than anything else, was the cause of whatever good it effected. Most boys or youths who have had much knowledge drilled into them, have their mental capacities not strengthened, but overlaid by it. They are crammed with mere facts, and with the opinions and phrases of other people, and these are accepted as a substitute for the power to form opinions of their own. And thus, the sons of eminent fathers, who have spared no pains in their education, so often grow up mere parroters of what they have learnt, incapable of using their minds except in the furrows created for them. Mine, however, was not an education of cram. My father never permitted anything which I learnt, to degenerate into a mere exercise of memory. He strove to make the understanding not only go along with every step of the teaching, but if possible, precede it. Anything which could be found out by thinking, I never was told, until I had exhausted my efforts to find it out for myself. . . . A pupil from whom nothing is ever demanded which he cannot do, never does all he can. (pp. 44–45)

Although Mill clearly believed that he profited from the highly rigorous education provided by his father, it is clear that there was a downside. One reason why Mill thought others could achieve what he had achieved was that he was never praised for his work, and never given the opportunity to compare himself with others when he was young (he was not allowed to go to school and he did not have playmates—"[Father] was earnestly bent upon my escaping not only the corrupting influence which boys exercise over boys, but the contagion of vulgar modes of thought and feeling." p. 47). Hence, Mill concluded that the outcome of this educational experiment did not reflect on his accomplishments, but on his father's skill as a teacher.

One of the evils most liable to attend on any sort of early proficiency, and which often fatally blights its promise, my father most anxiously guarded against. This was self-conceit. He kept me, with extreme vigilance, out of the way of hearing myself praised, or of being led to make self-flattering comparisons between myself and others. From his own intercourse with me I could derive none but a very humble opinion of myself; and the standard of comparison he always held up to me, was not what other people did, but what a man could and ought to do. He completely succeeded in preserving me from the sort of influences he so much dreaded. I was not at all aware that my attainments were anything unusual at my age.... I never estimated myself highly or lowly: I did not estimate myself at all. If I thought anything about myself, it was that I was rather backward in my studies, since I have always found myself so, in comparison with what my father expected from me.... I remember the very place in Hyde Park where, in my fourteenth year, on the eve of leaving my father's house for a long absence, he told me that I should find, as I got acquainted with new people, that I had been taught many things which youths of my age did not commonly know; and that many persons would be disposed to talk to me of this, and to compliment me upon it. What other things he said on this topic I remember very imperfectly; but he wound up by saying, that whatever I knew more than others, could not be ascribed to any merit in me, but to the very unusual advantage which had fallen to my lot, of having a father who was able to teach me, and willing to give the necessary trouble and time; that it was no matter of praise to me, if I knew more than those who had not had a similar advantage, but the deepest disgrace to me if I did not.... I felt no disposition to glorify myself upon the circumstance that there were other persons who did not know what I knew; nor had I ever flattered myself that my acquirements, whatever they might be, were any merit of mine: but, now when my attention was called to the subject, I felt that what my father had said respecting my peculiar advantages was exactly the truth and common sense of the matter, and it fixed my opinion and feeling from that time forward. (pp. 45–47)

John Stuart Mill survived his childhood and became a leading nineteenth century politician (e.g., three years in Parliament), philosopher, and activist for reform. Concerning the latter, for example, he became an ardent supporter of women's rights—his *The Subjection of Women* (Mill, 1869) is still considered an important treatise on the matter. As for psychology, although he never produced a book devoted to the topic, he believed that a scientific approach to psychology was possible, and a number of his writings place him firmly in the British empiricist camp. Also, his early rigorous training in logic led him to write *A System of Logic, Ratiocinative and Inductive, Being a Connected View of the Principles of Evidence, and the Methods of Scientific Investigation* (Mill, 1843/1987). In his *Logic*, Mill's descriptions of using logical analysis to evaluate evidence and to draw scientific conclusions are still quoted in research method texts today.

CONCEPT REVIEW QUESTIONS

1. Describe the methods used by James Mill to "fill up" his son's blank slate.
2. Today, John Stuart Mill might be considered a child prodigy, showing a high level of native ability. How would Mill reply to a claim that he was naturally gifted in his intellect?
3. Evaluate the strengths and weaknesses of James Mill's child-rearing strategy.

DISCUSSION QUESTION

1. What is the "blank slate" theory? What arguments can you produce both for it and against it?

CHAPTER 3

FRANÇOIS MAGENDIE (1783–1855): THE BELL-MAGENDIE PRINCIPLE

A drawing showing the cross-section of a spinal cord, common to introductory psychology textbooks, will typically display two pairs of nerve fibers entering the cord, one pair on the left side and one pair on the right. Two of those fibers, the ones closest to the surface of the body, are called the posterior or dorsal roots, and they are usually labeled "sensory" nerves in the text—they are part of the system that carries information from the senses to the spinal cord and brain. The other pair is usually labeled "motor" nerves; they lie below the posterior roots and are known as the anterior or ventral roots. The separate sensory and motor functions for these nerves were discovered in the early nineteenth century, and the principle that the posterior roots are sensory and the anterior are motor is called the Bell-Magendie Law. Two men are associated with the principle, Sir Charles Bell of England and François Magendie of France, because both worked on the problem at about the same time.

What follows is an excerpt from two 1822 articles by Magendie (translated from the French in 1965 by the daughter of psychology's most famous historian, E. G. Boring), documenting his meticulous study of the roles played by the anterior and posterior spinal roots (Magendie, 1822/1965). Bell's work will also be mentioned, but just briefly—his research lacked the experimental sophistication of Magendie's, and his conclusions about the functions of the anterior and posterior roots were incomplete (Sechzer, 1983).

Magendie opened his first paper by indicating that he had been interested in the problem of the spinal roots for some time, but faced a surgical difficulty in that it was hard to separate the roots from the spinal cord because of the hard bony structures of the spinal column ("vertebral canal"). A solution appeared

Excerpts from: Magendie, F. (1822). Expériences sur les functions des racines des nerfs rachidiens [Experiments on the functions of the spinal nerve roots]. *Journal de Physiologie Expérimentale et Pathologique, 2,* 276–279; Expériences sur les functions des racines des nerfs naissent de la moëlle épinière [Experiments on the functions of the nerve roots emanating from the spinal cord]. *Journal de Physiologie Expérimentale et Pathologique, 2,* 366–271. [1965 translation by Mollie D. Boring] in the form of puppies, whose "vertebral column was not yet ossified and thus could easily be separated to expose the spinal cord without injury" (Sechzer, 1983, p. 7).

> For a long time I have wanted to do the experiment of cutting the posterior roots of the nerves emanating from the spinal cord in an animal. I have made many attempts to do this, but without success, since it is difficult to open the vertebral canal without injuring the cord and causing the death of the animal, or at any rate gravely wounding it. But last month a litter of eight puppies, six weeks old, was brought to my laboratory; these animals seemed to me to be eminently suited for a new attempt at opening the vertebral canal. And, in fact, by using a very sharp scalpel I was able with a single stroke, so to speak, to lay bare the posterior half of the spinal cord within its envelopes. With this organ now all but bared, I had only to cut the surrounding *dura mater*, and this I did easily; I now had the lumbar and sacral pairs before my eyes and, lifting them successively, I was able to cut them on one side and leave the cord intact. I did not know what would result from this operation. I stitched up the wound by suturing the skin and observed the animal. At first I believed the limb corresponding to the cut nerves to be completely para-lyzed; it was insensitive to pricking and the hardest pressures and, further, it seemed immobile; but soon, to my very great surprise, I clearly saw it move, although sensibility remained completely absent. A second and third exper-iment gave me exactly the same result; it began to seem to me probable that the posterior roots of the spinal nerves could have different functions from the anterior roots and that these pertained most particularly to sensibility. (pp. 19–20, italics in the original)

At this point in the experiment, the surgery was relatively easy for Magendie—the posterior roots are close to the surface of the skin. Getting at the anterior roots presented a greater challenge, however.

> It naturally occurred to me now to cut the anterior roots while leaving the posterior ones intact, but such a project was easier to entertain than to carry out. How could one get around the posterior roots to get at the anterior part of the cord? I confess the problem at first seemed to me insurmountable; however, I kept thinking about it for two days, and I finally decided to use a sort of cataract knife, with a blade narrow enough to get in under the poste-rior roots and to cut the anterior roots by pressing them against the posterior surface of the vertebrae; but I was obliged to give up this tactic because of the large veins in the canal on the side that I opened with each movement forward. In making these attempts, I noticed that, by pulling up the vertebral *dura mater*, I could see the anterior roots joined into bundles at their points of entry into the membrane. I could not have asked for anything better, and in a few minutes I had cut all the pairs I wished to divide. As in the previous experiments, I made the section on one side only, so as to have a measure of comparison. You can imagine with what curiosity I followed the results of this section: there could be no doubt whatsoever; the limb was completely immobile and flaccid, although it retained an unequivocal sensibility. Finally, for completeness' sake, I cut both the anterior and the posterior roots; there was an absolute loss of feeling and movement.

> I repeated and varied these experiments on several species of animals;
> the results I have just described were verified in every way, both for the
> anterior and posterior limbs. I am continuing this research. . . . It is at present
> sufficient for me to be able to state here positively that the anterior and
> posterior roots of the nerves emanating from the spinal cord have different
> functions, that the posterior seem to pertain more particularly to sensibility,
> whereas the anterior seem especially linked with movement. (pp. 20–21,
> italics in the original)

Thus, Magendie was able to cut the posterior and then the anterior spinal cord roots separately, showing convincingly that the posterior roots perform sensory ("sensibility") functions, while the anterior roots have motor functions. In his second article, Magendie replicated and extended the research, using slightly different procedures. First, he was concerned about a side effect of his initial study, which involved cutting the dura mater, a tough membrane layer covering enclosing the brain and spinal cord. So he developed an alternative method that, he was pleased to discover, produced the same results.

> The discoveries I announced . . . are too important for me not to have tried
> clarifying them in further research.
>   First, I wanted to make sure it was possible to cut the anterior or posterior
> roots of the spinal nerves without opening the large canal of the vertebral
> *dura mater*; for in exposing the spinal cord to air and cold temperature, one
> appreciably weakens nervous action and, perforce, reaches one's conclusions
> in a roundabout manner.
>   The anatomical arrangement of these parts did not make the task impos-
> sible, for each bundle of spinal roots follows on for a little within a particular
> canal before rejoining and fusing with the other bundle. Hence, using scis-
> sors with damp points, I found it possible to remove enough of the vertebral
> lamina and lateral parts to expose the ganglion of each lumbar pair; it is then
> not too difficult—using a small probe—to separate the canal containing the
> posterior roots, and there is no further difficulty in making the section. This
> method of doing the experiment yielded the same results I had observed
> previously; but, as the experiment is much longer and more laborious than
> in the procedure of opening the large canal of the spinal *dura mater*, I see no
> reason to prefer it to the first method. (p. 21, italics in the original)

Magendie's next experiments involved using "nux vomica," an extract from an evergreen plant of the same name. Its other name is strychnine, a poison that produces violent muscle contractions ("tetanic convulsions") and can be deadly. Animals were given the drug after either the posterior or anterior roots had been severed. As expected, the convulsions did not occur when the anterior roots had been cut (no motor control), but remained vigorous when the posterior roots had been cut (affected sensation, not movement).

> I next wanted to submit my earlier results to a further proof. Everyone knows
> that nux vomica will cause very violent general tetanic convulsions in man
> and animals. I was curious to know whether these convulsions would take
> place in a limb in which the nerves of movement had been severed, and
> whether they would be just as violent with the nerves of feeling severed.

The results agreed completely with my earlier ones; that is to say, in an animal whose posterior roots had been cut the tetanus was complete and as intense as if the spinal roots were intact; on the other hand, with an animal in which I had cut the nerves of movement of one posterior limb, this limb remained supple and immobile at the moment when, under the influence of the poison, all the other body muscles showed the most pronounced tetanic contractions. (p. 21)

Next, having observed the effects of severing nerves, Magendie wondered what would be the effect of leaving them intact, but stimulating them. He first used a procedure to stimulate the nerves mechanically, and then used "galvanism," an electrical stimulation method. The outcome further strengthened his general conclusion about the functions of the spinal roots.

By irritating the nerves of feeling directly, or the posterior spinal roots, could one produce contractions? Would a direct irritation to the nerves of movement evoke pain? Such were the questions I asked myself, and experimentation alone could answer them.

With these in mind, I began by examining the posterior roots, the nerves of feeling. Here is what I observed: in pinching, plucking, or pricking these roots, the animal manifests pain; but this pain is nothing compared to the intensity that develops if one touches, even lightly, the spinal cord at the origin of these roots. Almost every time that the posterior roots are excited contractions are produced in the corresponding muscles; however, these contractions are not very marked and are infinitely weaker than if one touches the spinal cord itself. . . .

I repeated these operations on the anterior bundles and obtained analogous, though opposite, results: for here the contractions induced by pinching, jabbing, and the like are very strong and even convulsive, whereas the signs of sensibility are scarcely visible.

I had still another type of proof to which to submit the spinal roots: namely, galvanism. Therefore I excited the spinal roots by this method, at first leaving them in their normal state and then cutting them at the spine in order to isolate them. In these different cases, I obtained contractions with both sorts of roots; but the contractions that followed excitation of the anterior roots were in general stronger, more nearly total, than those which came when electric current was introduced into the posterior roots. The phenomena were the same whether one placed the zinc pole or the copper pole on the nerve. (pp. 21–22)

When Magendie published his research in 1822, it quickly caught the attention of Sir Charles Bell, a noted British anatomist. Bell immediately claimed priority, on the basis of a privately published paper that he had circulated among friends eleven years earlier. Thus began an acrimonious dispute over who should be given credit for the discovery. The final outcome was, of course, that both names are attached to the "law," but most historians believe that Magendie had a better claim—his research was more directly experimental, while Bell, for the most part, deduced function from anatomical structure. Furthermore, although Bell recognized that the posterior and anterior spinal roots had different functions, he did not differentiate those functions as clearly as had Magendie.

Magendie had not been aware of Bell's work (no surprise, given the manner of Bell's publication), but when he learned of it, he recognized the value of Bell's argument that the posterior and anterior spinal roots play different roles. As for the correct conclusions about those roles, however, Magendie made his feelings quite clear.

> In sum, Charles Bell had had, before me, but unknown to me, the idea of separately cutting the spinal roots; he likewise discovered that the anterior influences muscular contractility more than the posterior does. This is a question of priority in which I have, from the beginning, honored him. Now, as for having established that these roots have distinct properties, distinct functions, that the anterior ones control movement, and posterior ones sensation, this discovery belongs to me. (cited in Grmek, 1972, p. 9)

CONCEPT REVIEW QUESTIONS

1. Why would "puppies" solve a procedural problem faced by Magendie as he searched for the functions of the spinal roots?

2. What happened when Magendie severed the posterior roots and what did he conclude? Why did severing the anterior roots create a surgical problem for Magendie? When he severed these roots, what did he observe and what did he conclude?

3. Magendie followed his initial studies by using two other procedures that essentially replicated his findings. What did he do?

DISCUSSION QUESTION

1. Why is the principle discovered by Magendie usually called the Bell-Magendie Law and why might it be better to refer to it as the Magendie Law?

CHAPTER 4

PAUL BROCA (1824–1880): THE CASE OF "TAN"

When students first learn about the functions of the various parts of the brain, one location always included is *Broca's area*, which is located in the left frontal lobe and is responsible for speech production. It is named for the famous nineteenth century French neurologist Paul Broca, a pioneer in the clinical method. His technique was to examine individuals with specific kinds of behavioral or cognitive deficits, then, upon postmortem examination, determine if the problems correlated with some measurable brain damage.

An important issue in the nineteenth century concerned localization of function—the extent to which various areas in the brain had specific functions. The phrenologists argued for a highly specialized degree of localization, but the French physician Pierre Flourens (1846/1978), in a brilliant series of lesioning studies, succeeded in disproving at least some aspects of phrenology. Flourens argued that the brain functioned more as a coordinated whole, but other researchers thought some degree of specialization must occur. Broca fell into this latter category.

Broca's most famous case confronted him in April of 1861, when he encountered a very unusual patient, known to history as "Tan," for reasons that will soon be apparent. This patient had been in the Bicêtre hospital in Paris for twenty-one years, and had been incapacitated and in bed for the seven years prior to 1861, when a severe case of gangrene brought him to Broca's attention. What follows is an excerpt from Broca's description of this remarkable case (Broca, 1861/1965), as translated by Mollie Boring, who also translated the Magendie excerpt in the previous chapter. She was the daughter of E. G. Boring, psychology's most famous historian.

> On 11 April 1861 there was brought to the surgery of the general infirmary of the hospice at Bicêtre a man named Leborgne, fifty-one years old, suffering from a diffused gangrenous cellulitis of his whole right side, extending from the foot to the buttocks. When questioned the next day as to the origin of his disease, he replied only with the monosyllable *tan*, repeated twice in succession and accompanied by a gesture of his left hand. I tried to find out more about the antecedents of this man, who had been at Bicêtre for

Excerpts from: Broca, P. (1861). Remarques sur le siège de la faculté du langage articulé, suives d'une observation d'aphémie. *Bulletin de la Société Anatomique de Paris, 6*, 343–357. [1965 translation by Mollie D. Boring] twenty-one years. I questioned his attendants, his comrades on the ward, and those of his relatives who came to see him, and here is the result of this inquiry.

Since youth he had been subject to epileptic attacks, yet he was able to become a maker of lasts, a trade at which he worked until he was thirty years old. It was then that he lost his ability to speak and that is why he was admitted to the hospice at Bicêtre. It was not possible to discover whether his loss of speech came on slowly or rapidly or whether some other symptom accompanied the onset of his affliction.

When he arrived at Bicêtre he had already been unable to speak for two or three months. He was then quite healthy and intelligent and differed from a normal person only in his loss of articulate language. He came and went at the hospice, where he was known by the name of "Tan." He understood all that was said to him. His hearing was actually very good, but whenever one questioned him he always answered, "Tan, tan," accompanying his utterance with varied gestures by which he succeeded in expressing most of his ideas. If one did not understand his gestures, he was apt to get irate and added to his vocabulary a gross oath ("Sacré nom de Dieu!"). . . . Tan was considered an egoist, vindictive and objectionable, and his associates, who detested him, even accused him of stealing. These defects could have been due largely to his cerebral lesion. They were not pronounced enough to be considered pathological, and, although this patient was at Bicêtre, no one ever thought of transferring him to the insane ward. On the contrary, he was considered to be completely responsible for his acts.

Ten years after he lost his speech a new symptom appeared. The muscles of his right arm began to get weak, and in the end they became completely paralyzed. Tan continued to walk without difficulty, but the paralysis gradually extended to his right leg; after having dragged the leg for some time, he resigned himself to staying in bed. About four years had elapsed from the beginning of the paralysis of the arm to the time when paralysis of the leg was sufficiently advanced to make standing absolutely impossible. Before he was brought to the infirmary, Tan had been in bed for almost seven years. This last period of his life is the one for which we have the least information. Since he was incapable of doing harm, his associates had nothing to do with him any more, except to amuse themselves at his expense. This made him angry, and he had by now lost the little celebrity which the peculiarity of his disease had given him at the hospice. (pp. 224–225, italics in the original)

During the seven years in bed, Tan was more or less forgotten, and little information was available about him, except that his vision began to deteriorate. Because he remained continent, his linen was not changed regularly; thus, the gangrene that brought him to Broca's attention was not discovered until it had advanced considerably, infecting the whole leg. Broca reported that he hesitated examining Tan, because his general state "was so grave that it would have been cruel to torment him with long interviews" (p. 225). Nonetheless, Broca proceeded, both with a physical exam that confirmed the paralysis of the right arm and leg, and with an examination of Tan's mental capacities.

Tan's hearing remained acute. He heard well the ticking of a watch, but his vision was weak. When he wanted to see the time, he had to take the watch in his left hand and place it in a peculiar position about twenty centimeters from his right eye, which seemed better than his left.

The state of Tan's intelligence could not be exactly determined. Certainly he understood all that was said to him, but, since he could express his ideas or desires only by movements of his left hand, this moribund patient could not make himself understood as well as he understood others. His numerical responses, made by opening or closing his fingers, were best. Several times I asked him for how many days had he been ill. Sometimes he answered five, sometimes six days. How many years had he been at Bicêtre? He opened his hand four times and then added one finger. That made 21 years, the correct answer. The next day I repeated the question and received the same answer, but, when I tried to come back to the question a third time, Tan realized that I wanted to make an exercise out of the questioning. He became irate and uttered the oath, which only this one time did I hear from him. Two days in succession I showed him my watch. Since the second hand did not move, he could distinguish the three hands only by their shape and length. Still, after having looked at the watch for a few seconds, he could each time indicate the time correctly. It cannot be doubted, therefore, that the man was intelligent, that he could think, that he had to a certain extent retained the memory of old habits. He could understand even quite complicated ideas. For instance, I asked him about the order in which his paralyses had developed. First he made a short horizontal gesture with his left index finger, meaning that he had understood; then he showed successively his tongue, his right arm, and his right leg. That was perfectly correct, for quite naturally he attributed his loss of language to paralysis of his tongue.

Nevertheless there were several questions to which he did not respond, questions that a man of ordinary intelligence would have managed to answer even with only one hand. At other times he seemed quite annoyed when the sense of his answers was not understood. Sometimes his answer was clear but wrong—as when he pretended to have children when actually he had none. Doubtless the intelligence of this man was seriously impaired as an effect of his cerebral lesion or of his devouring fever, but obviously he had much more intelligence than was necessary for him to talk. (pp. 225–226)

Broca guessed that Tan had a cerebral lesion that for the first 10 years of the illness remained confined to a fairly limited area in the left side of the brain, but then had spread. He did not have long to wait in order to confirm the diagnosis.

The patient died on 17 April [1861]. The autopsy was performed as soon as possible—that is, after 24 hours. The weather was warm but the cadaver showed no signs of putrefaction. The brain was shown a few hours later to the Société d'Anthropologie and was then put immediately into alcohol. It was so altered that great care was necessary to preserve it. It was only after two months and several changes of the fluid that it began to harden. Today it is in perfect condition and has been deposited in the Musée Depuytren. (p. 227)

Remarkably, Tan's brain still resides in the Musée Depuytren, with the damage to the left frontal cortex clearly visible. It is labeled "Brain of a man LeBorgne called Tan aphasic. Chronic and progressive softening of the second and third left frontal convolution" (quoted in Schiller, 1979, p. 181). Broca's description of the extent of the damage was especially striking.

> The organs destroyed are the following: the small inferior marginal convolution of the temporal lobe, the small convolutions of the insula, and the underlying part of the striate body, and, finally, in the frontal lobe, the inferior part of the transverse frontal convolutions and the posterior part of those two great convolutions designated as the second and third frontal convolutions. Of the four convolutions that form the superior part of the frontal lobe, only one, the superior and most medial one, has been preserved, although not in its entirety, for it is softened and atrophied, but nevertheless indicates its continuity, for, if one puts back in imagination all that has been lost, one finds that at least three quarters of the cavity has been hollowed out at the expense of the frontal lobe. . . .
>
> Anatomical inspection shows us that the lesion was still progressing when the patient died. The lesion was therefore progressive, but it progressed very slowly, taking twenty-one years to destroy a quite limited part of the brain. Thus it is reasonable to believe that at the beginning there was a considerable time during which degeneration did not go past the limits of the organ where it started. We have seen that the original focus of the disease was situated in the frontal lobe and very likely in its third frontal convolution. Thus we are compelled to say, from the point of view of pathological anatomy, that there were two periods, one in which only one frontal convolution, probably the third one, was attacked, and another period in which the disease gradually spread toward other convolutions, to the insula, or to the extraventricular nucleus of the corpus striatum.
>
> When we now examine the succession of symptoms, we also find two periods, the first of which lasted ten years, during which the faculty of speech was destroyed while all other functions of the brain remained intact, and a second period of eleven years, during which paralysis of movement, at first partial and then complete, successively involved the arm and the leg of the right side.
>
> With this in mind it is impossible not to see that there was a correspondence between the anatomical and the symptomological periods. Everyone knows that the cerebral convolutions are not motor organs. Of all the organs attacked, the corpus striatum of the left hemisphere is the only one where one could look for the cause of the paralysis of the two right extremities. The second clinical period, in which the motility changed, corresponds to the second anatomical period, when the softening passed beyond the limit of the frontal lobe and invaded the insula and the corpus striatum.
>
> It follows that the first period of ten years, clinically characterized only by the symptom of aphemia, must correspond to the period during which the lesion was still limited to the frontal lobe. (pp. 228–229)

Broca's term for Tan's disorder was soon replaced with "aphasia" when it was pointed out that the Greek origin of "aphemia" refers to reputation or fame, while the root translation of "aphasia" is "without speech" (Ryalls, 1984). The disorder is now referred to as expressive or *motor aphasia*, and it is characterized by an inability to articulate ideas verbally, even though the vocal apparatus is intact and general intelligence is normal.

Over the next few years, Broca encountered several other aphasic patients like Tan, found the same general pattern of left frontal lobe damage, and concluded that the ability to produce speech was localized in the left frontal lobe. In his honor, the area is now known as Broca's area, although a close examination of history shows that others (e.g., Simon Auburtin) were arguing the same point about left frontal lobe function (Finger, 2000). As for Broca himself, he was also known for his research on the relationship between brain size and intelligence, which he believed confirmed the intellectual superiority of White, European males. On the basis of a series of comparative studies, and clearly influenced by his cultural biases, he concluded that the brain was

> larger in mature adults than in the elderly, in men than in women, in eminent men than in men of mediocre talent, in superior races than in inferior races. . . . Other things equal, there is a remarkable relationship between the development of intelligence and the volume of the brain. (quoted in Gould, 1981, p. 83)

Ironically, after his death in 1880, Broca's brain was examined and found to be no more than average in size.

CONCEPT REVIEW QUESTIONS

1. Describe the time frame—what was the progression of Tan's disorder over the twenty-one years spent at the Bicêtre hospital in Paris?

2. How did Broca determine that Tan, who could not communicate verbally, was nonetheless of reasonable intelligence?

3. Describe the outcome of the case, and what Broca concluded from it.

DISCUSSION QUESTION

1. Suppose you were Broca and had just finished the Tan case. As a scientist, what kind of follow-up research would you be likely to do over the next few years?

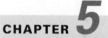
WILHELM WUNDT (1832–1920): A NEW SCIENTIFIC PSYCHOLOGY

It has become standard practice to identify modern psychology's "founder" as Wilhelm Wundt. As Boring (1950) argued, in his famous history text, founders might not be the first ones to make significant contributions to a discipline, but they are vigorous promoters of that discipline. Thus, others might have preceded Wundt in doing what today would be called "scientific psychology" (e.g., Gustav Fechner, who pioneered the study of sensory thresholds), but none of them had, as a goal, the creation of a new science. Wundt, however, made his purpose clear in the opening sentence of the Preface to his two-volume *Principles of Physiological Psychology*, published in 1873–1874, when he wrote that "[t]he book which I here present to the public is an attempt to mark out a new domain of science" (Wundt, 1874/1904, p. v).

Wundt was trained as a physician, earning an M.D. from the university at Heidelberg, Germany, in 1855. He was more interested in research than practice, however. After a productive six-year period working in the laboratory of Hermann Helmholtz (the nineteenth century's most prominent physiologist), Wundt held several academic positions and began publishing. Shortly after producing his *Principles*, he landed a position at Leipzig's university and, in 1879, established what came to be known as psychology's first laboratory of experimental psychology. He followed it two years later by creating a journal to publish the results of his and his students' research and, by the mid-1880s, students were coming regularly to Leipzig from Europe and the United States to learn about this "New Psychology" that took ancient philosophical questions about the human mind and tried to examine them in the laboratory.

Wundt's laboratory psychology involved the study of immediate conscious experience, focusing on basic sensory and perceptual processes. He also had a strong interest in higher mental processes, such as language, but he did not think that these more complex processes could be isolated and studied effectively in the laboratory (instead, they required other methods, such as direct observation). The excerpt here is from the first chapter of an 1897 introduction to psychology by Wundt, called *Outlines of Psychology*, translated by Charles Judd, a Yale

Excerpts from: Wundt, W. (1897). *Outlines of psychology* (C. H. Judd, Trans.). Leipzig: Wilhelm Engelmann.

University experimental psychologist who earned a Leipzig Ph.D. with Wundt in 1896. In his opening chapter, Wundt started by identifying "the problem of psychology," defining the field as the study of *immediate* conscious experience; this contrasted with the natural sciences (e.g., physics), defined as the study of *mediate* experience. Note that when he starts by referring to the "history of this science," he is using the term science loosely, and is in fact referring to the long history of the philosophical study of psychological issues.

1. Problem of Psychology

1. Two definitions of psychology have been the most prominent in the history of this science. According to one, psychology is the "science of mind", psychical processes being regarded as phenomena from which it is possible to infer the nature of an underlying metaphysical mind-substance. According to the other, psychology is the "science of inner experience"; psychical processes are here looked upon as belonging to a specific form of experience, which is readily distinguished by the fact that its contents are known through "introspection", or through the "inner sense" as it is called if one uses the phrase which has been employed to distinguish introspection from sense-perception through the outer senses.

   Neither of these definitions, however, is satisfactory to the psychology of today. The first or metaphysical definition belongs to a period of development that lasted longer in this science than in others. But it is here, too, forever left behind, since psychology has developed into an empirical discipline, operating with methods of its own; and since the "mental sciences" have gained recognition as a great department of scientific investigation, distinct from the sphere of the natural sciences, and requiring as a general groundwork an independent psychology, free from all metaphysical theories.

   The second or empirical definition, which sees in psychology a "science of inner experience", is inadequate because it may give rise to the misunderstanding that psychology has to do with objects totally different from the objects of so called "outer experience". It is, indeed, true that there are certain contents of experience which belong in the sphere of psychological investigation, and are not to be found among the objects and processes studied by natural science; such are our feelings, emotions, and decisions. On the other hand, there is not a single natural phenomenon that may not, from a different point of view, become an object of psychology. A stone, a plant, a tone, a ray of light, are, when treated as natural phenomena, objects of mineralogy, botany, physics, etc. In so far, however, as they are at the same time *ideas*, they are objects of psychology, for psychology seeks to account for the genesis of these ideas, and for their relations, both to other ideas and to those psychical processes, such as feelings, volitions, etc., which are not referred to external objects. There is then, no such thing as an "inner sense" which can be regarded as an organ of introspection, and as distinct from the outer senses, or organs of objective perception. The ideas of which psychology seeks to investigate the attributes, are identical with those upon which natural science is based; while the subjective activities of feeling, emotion, and volition, which are neglected in natural science, are not known through special organs but are directly and inseparably connected with the ideas referred to external objects.

2. It follows, then, that the expressions outer and inner experience do not indicate different objects, but *different points of view* from which we start in the consideration and scientific treatment of a unitary experience. We are naturally led to these points of view, because every concrete experience immediately divides into *two factors*: into a *content* presented to us, and our *apprehension* of this content. We call the first of these factors *objects of experience*, the second *experiencing subject*. This division points out two directions for the treatment of experience. One is that of the *natural sciences*, which concern themselves with the *objects* of experience, thought of as independent of the subject. The other is that of *psychology*, which investigates the whole content of experience in its relations to the subject and in its attributes derived directly from the subject. The standpoint of natural science may, accordingly, be designated as that of *mediate experience*, since it is possible only after abstracting from the subjective factor present in all actual experience; the standpoint of psychology, on the other hand, may be designated as that of *immediate experience*, since it purposely does away with this abstraction and all its consequences. (pp. 1–2, italics in the original)

Wundt followed this brief introductory section on the problem of psychology with a longer section called "general theories of psychology," in which he elaborated on the evolution of modern empirical (scientific) psychology from the earlier "metaphysical" (i.e., philosophical) psychology. He then discussed methodology.

3. Methods in Psychology

1. Since psychology has for its object, not specific contents of experience, but *general experience in its immediate character*, it can make use of no methods except such as the empirical sciences in general employ for the determination, analysis, and causal synthesis of facts. The circumstance, that natural science abstracts from the subject, while psychology does not, can be no ground for modifications in the essential character of the methods employed in the two fields, though it does modify the way in which these methods are applied.

The natural sciences, which may serve as an example for psychology in this respect, since they were developed earlier, make use of *two* chief methods: *experiment and observation. Experiment* is observation connected with an intentional interference on the part of the observer, in the rise and course of the phenomena observed. *Observation*, in its proper sense, is the investigation of phenomena without such interference, just as they are naturally presented to the observer in the continuity of experience. Wherever experiment is possible, it is always used in the natural sciences; for under all circumstances, even when the phenomena in themselves present the conditions for sufficiently exact observation, it is an advantage to be able to control at will their rise and progress, or to isolate the various components of a composite phenomenon. Still, even in the natural sciences the two methods have been distinguished according to their spheres of application. It is held that the experimental methods are indispensable for certain problems, while in others the desired end may not infrequently be reached through mere observation. If we neglect a few exceptional cases due to special relations, these two classes of problems correspond to the general division of natural phenomena into *processes* and *objects*. (pp. 18–19, italics in the original)

By "intentional interference" Wundt meant the deliberate manipulation of experimental conditions that are under the control of the scientist. In a modern research methods course, it is referred to as "manipulating the independent variable."

Experimental interference is required in the exact determination of the course, and in the analysis of the components, of any natural process such as, for example, light-waves or sound-waves, an electric discharge, the formation or disintegration of a chemical compound, and stimulation and metabolism in plants and animals. As a rule, such interference is desirable because exact observation is possible only when the observer can determine the moment at which the process shall commence. It is also indispensable in separating the various components of a complex phenomenon from one another. As a rule, this is possible only through the addition or subtraction of certain conditions, or a quantitative variation of them.

The case is different with *objects* of nature. They are relatively constant; they do not have to be produced at a particular moment, but are always at the observer's disposal and ready for examination. Here, then, experimental investigation is generally necessary only when the production and modification of the objects are to be inquired into. In such a case, they are regarded either as products or components of natural processes and come under the head of processes rather than objects. When, on the contrary, the only question is the actual nature of these objects, without reference to their origin or modification, mere observation is generally enough. Thus, mineralogy, botany, zoology, anatomy, and geography, are pure sciences of observation so long as they are kept free from the physical, chemical, and physiological problems that are, indeed, frequently brought into them, but have to do with processes of nature, not with the objects in themselves.

2. If we apply these considerations to psychology, it is obvious at once, from the very nature of its subject-matter, that exact observation is here possible only in the form of *experimental* observation; and that psychology can never be a *pure* science of observation. The contents of this science are exclusively *processes*, not permanent objects. In order to investigate with exactness the rise and progress of these processes, their composition out of various components, and the interrelations of these components, we must be able first of all to bring about their beginning at will, and purposely to vary the conditions of the same. This is possible here, as in all cases, only through experiment, not through pure introspection. Besides this general reason there is another, peculiar to psychology, that does not apply at all to natural phenomena. In the latter case we purposely abstract from the perceiving subject, and under circumstances, especially when favored by the regularity of the phenomena, as in astronomy, mere observation may succeed in determining with adequate certainty the objective components of the processes. Psychology, on the contrary, is debarred from this abstraction by its fundamental principles, and the conditions for chance observation can be suitable only when the same objective components of immediate experience are frequently repeated in connection with the same subjective states. It is hardly to be expected, in

view of the great complexity of psychical processes, that this will ever be the case. The coincidence is especially improbable since the very *intention to observe*, which is a necessary condition of all observation, modifies essentially the rise and progress of psychical processes. Observation of nature is not disturbed by this intention on the part of the observer, because here we purposely abstract from the state of the subject. The chief problem of psychology, however, is the exact observation of the rise and progress of subjective processes, and it can be readily seen that under such circumstances the intention to observe either essentially modifies the facts to be observed, or completely suppresses them. On the other hand, psychology, by the very way in which psychical processes originate, is led, just as physics and physiology are, to employ the experimental mode of procedure. A sensation arises in us under the most favorable conditions for observation when it is caused by an external sense-stimulus, as, for example, a tone-sensation from an external tone-vibration, or a light-sensation from an external light-impression. The idea of an object is always caused originally by the more or less complicated cooperation of external sense-stimuli. If we wish to study the way in which an idea is formed, we can choose no other method than that of imitating this natural process. In doing this, we have at the same time the great advantage of being able to modify the idea itself by changing at will the combination of the impressions that cooperate to form it, and of thus learning what influence each single condition exercises on the product. Memory-images, it is true, cannot be directly aroused through external sense impressions, but follow them after a longer or shorter interval. Still, it is obvious that their attributes, and especially their relation to the primary ideas through direct impressions, can most accurately be learned, not by waiting for their chance arrival, but by using such memory-ideas as may be aroused in a systematic, experimental way, through immediately preceding impressions. The same is true of feelings and volitions; they will be presented in the form best adapted to exact investigation when those impressions are purposely produced which experience has shown to be regularly connected with affective and volitional reactions. There is, then, no fundamental psychical process to which experimental methods can not be applied, and therefore none in whose investigation they are not logically required. (pp. 19–22, italics in the original)

When Wundt wrote that psychology could never be a "pure science of observation," and that the contents of the science are processes, not objects, what he meant was that experimental psychologists, when they examine their immediate conscious experiences, cannot separate ("abstract") themselves from the subject matter. When examining the physical characteristics of light from a light bulb, for example, physicists can separate themselves from the object being observed. Psychologists, however, when examining their experience of perceiving the light from a light bulb, are describing a process (of perception) that they are undergoing, rather than taking some independent measure from an instrument. The experimental method can be employed by, for example, manipulating the intensity of the light to see how it affects the perception of that light. Wundt next elaborated this point, and then began making a distinction between psychological phenomena that can be studied experimentally in the lab, and other "mental products" (e.g., "language, mythological ideas, and customs") that could not be controlled precisely in the laboratory, but could be observed as they occur naturally.

3. *Pure observation*, such as is possible in many departments of natural science, is, from the very character of psychic phenomena, impossible in *individual* psychology. Such a possibility would be conceivable only under the condition that there existed permanent psychical objects, independent of our attention, similar to the relatively permanent objects of nature, which remain unchanged by our observation of them. There are, indeed, certain facts at the disposal of psychology, which, although they are not real objects, still have the character of psychical objects inasmuch as they possess these attributes of relative permanence, and independence of the observer. Connected with these characteristics is the further fact that they are unapproachable by means of experiment in the common acceptance of the term. These facts are the *mental products* that have been developed in the course of history, such as language, mythological ideas, and customs. The origin and development of these products depend in every case on general psychical conditions which may be inferred from their objective attributes. Psychological analysis can, consequently, explain the psychical processes operative in their formation and development. All such mental products of a general character presuppose as a condition the existence of a mental *community* composed of many individuals, though, of course, their deepest sources are the psychical attributes of the individual. Because of this dependence on the community, in particular the social community, this whole department of psychological investigation is designated as *social psychology*, and distinguished from individual, or as it may be called because of its predominating method, *experimental* psychology. In the present stage of the science these two branches of psychology are generally taken up in different treatises; still, they are not so much different departments as different *methods*. So-called social psychology corresponds to the method of pure observation, the objects of observation in this case being the mental products. The necessary connection of these products with social communities, which has given to social psychology its name, is due to the fact that the mental products of the individual are of too variable a character to be the subjects of objective observation [i.e., experimentation]. The phenomena gain the necessary degree of constancy only when they become collective.

Thus psychology has, like natural science, *two* exact methods: the experimental method, serving for the analysis of simpler psychical processes, and the observation of general mental products, serving for the investigation of the higher psychical processes and developments. (pp. 22–24, italics in the original)

What Judd translated as "social psychology" has become well known as Wundt's "Völkerpsychologie," a major interest during the last twenty years of his professional life (Blumenthal, 1975). Most history of psychology texts concentrate on Wundt's experimental psychology, but the above excerpt makes it clear that Wundt considered both experimental and social psychology essential.

This final paragraph in Wundt's section on method explains why his 1873–74 book had the title it did—*Principles of Physiological Psychology*.

3a. The introduction of the experimental method into psychology was originally
due to the modes of procedure in physiology, especially in the physiology of the sense-organs and the nervous system. For this reason experimental psychology is also commonly called "physiological psychology";
and works treating it under this title regularly contain those supplementary facts from the physiology of the nervous system and the sense-organs,
which require special discussion with a view to the interests of psychology, though in themselves they belong to physiology alone. "Physiological
psychology" is, accordingly, an intermediate discipline which is, however,
as the name indicates, primarily *psychology*, and is, apart from the supplementary physiological facts that it presents, just the same as "experimental psychology" in the sense above defined. The attempt sometimes
made, to distinguish psychology proper from physiological psychology,
by assigning to the first the psychological interpretation of inner experience, and to the second the derivation of this experience from physiological processes, is to be rejected as inadmissible. There is only one kind of
causal explanation in psychology, and that is the derivation of more complex psychical processes from simpler ones. In this method of interpretation
physiological elements can be used only as supplementary aids, because
of the relation between natural science and psychology as above defined.
Materialistic psychology denies the existence of psychical causality, and
substitutes for this problem the other, of explaining psychical processes by
brain-physiology. This tendency, which has been shown to be epistemolog-
ically and psychologically untenable, appears among the representatives of
both "pure" and "physiological" psychology. (p. 24, italics in the original)

Wundt closed his introductory chapter by outlining his plan for the remainder of the book. He then followed with chapters on "psychical elements" ("pure
sensations" and "simple feelings") and "psychical compounds" (e.g., "spatial
ideas"). Next was a chapter called "interconnection of psychical compounds."
In this chapter he described the old philosophical concept of association and
elaborated on one of his key ideas, that of *apperception*. A major distinction
between associations and apperceptions is that associations occur passively—if
we always see Ed and Ted together, seeing Ed by himself brings Ted to our
mind (without deliberate effort) because of the association between the two.
Apperceptions, however, involve active attention and a purposeful attempt to
add meaning to an experience. In a later book Wundt (1912) evaluated association and apperception by comparing the incoherent ramblings of someone with
schizophrenia with the writing of Goethe's *Wilhelm Meister*. The former strings
together words that are clearly associated in the schizophrenic's experience, for
example, "school house garden build stones ... " (p. 124), but are not meaningfully "apperceived." One the other hand, Goethe's prose creates in the reader
a meaningful and organized whole.

Wundt concluded his book with brief chapters on "psychical developments" (e.g., discussion of the "psychical attributes" of animals and of
children) and "psychical causality and its laws" (e.g., a discussion of the
ancient mind-body problem, with Wundt arguing for a dualistic psychophysical
parallelism).

Following the publication of the 1897 *Outlines of Psychology*, Wundt remained active professionally for another 23 years, right up to his death in 1920. He continued revising his *Principles of Physiological Psychology*, completing a sixth edition in 1911; he produced a brief introductory book in 1912; he completed ten volumes of his *Völkerpsychologie*; and, just before his death, he published an autobiography. During his Leipzig years, from 1875 to 1920, Wundt directed the doctoral theses of 186 students (Tinker, 1980).

CONCEPT REVIEW QUESTIONS

1. Wundt would describe psychology and natural science (e.g., physics) as sciences that examine experience from different perspectives. Explain what he meant.

2. Wundt argued that laboratory psychology could never be a "pure science of observation." What did he mean?

3. Describe Wundt's distinction between association and apperception.

DISCUSSION QUESTION

1. Wundt described what amounted to two different kinds of psychology, experimental and social. What did they have in common and how did they differ?

CHAPTER 6

HERMANN EBBINGHAUS (1850–1909): ON MEMORY

Not much is known about the formative years of Hermann Ebbinghaus. He was born near Bonn, Germany, studied at several universities, and fought briefly for the German side in the Franco-Prussian War in the early 1870s. His academic interests shifted from history to philology (the historical study of language) to philosophy, and he eventually earned a doctorate in the latter from the University of Bonn in 1873. During the mid-1870s he traveled throughout England and France and, as legend has it, chanced upon a copy of Gustav Fechner's *Elements of Psychophysics* (1860/1966), a book on the measurement of sensory thresholds that many consider to have launched the experimental study of psychological phenomena. Fechner's demonstration that mental processes could be subjected to scientific methods inspired Ebbinghaus, who was wrestling with the philosophical problem of the association of ideas at the time.

As a philosopher, Ebbinghaus was thoroughly familiar with the British empiricist/associationists and their analysis of association processes. The British philosophers all considered association to be an essential component of the mind's organizational structure, but they argued over the basic laws of association (e.g., is contiguity sufficient or are other principles necessary?). For Ebbinghaus, Fechner's scientific approach to the mind apparently triggered a creative leap. If sensations could be measured with precision, why not other mental processes? Why not association? During the late 1870s, Ebbinghaus became resolved to study the formation and retention of associations scientifically. By the middle of the next decade, he had produced *Memory: A Contribution to Experimental Psychology* (1885/1964). This brief book (123 pages in a 1964 reprinting) inaugurated a research tradition that continues today and includes results still described in textbooks of general psychology.

Ebbinghaus opened his book by considering the various forms of memory and the difficulty of studying the process experimentally. He pointed out that what little was known about memory was known through common sense and from anecdotes about "extreme and especially striking cases" (p. 4). As for

Excerpts from: Ebbinghaus, H. (1964). *Memory: A contribution to experimental psychology* (H. A. Ruger & C. A. Bussenius, Trans.). New York: Dover. (Original work published 1885).

more fundamental questions about the exact relationships between our experiences and our memories, however, "[t]hese and similar questions no one can answer" (p. 5).

For Ebbinghaus, the only way to understand memory was through the "method of natural science" (p. 7). In his opening description of method, you will recognize the following as a description of the essential components of the experimental method: manipulating an independent variable, holding extraneous factors constant, and then measuring the outcome, the dependent variable.

> We all know of what this method consists: an attempt is made to keep constant the mass of conditions which have proven themselves causally connected with a certain result; one of these conditions is isolated from the rest and varied in a way that can be numerically described; then the accompanying change on the side of the effect is ascertained by measurement or computation. (p. 7)

Ebbinghaus recognized that keeping the "mass of conditions" under control was no easy task. In one of psychological science's more notable acts of creativity, he hit upon the idea of using materials that did not meaningfully relate to each other and were not especially meaningful in themselves. That is, he created *nonsense syllables*, three-letter units comprised of two consonants with a vowel in the middle, and produced lists of them for memorization.

> Out of the simple consonants of the alphabet and our eleven vowels and diphthongs all possible syllables of a certain sort were constructed, a vowel sound being placed between two consonants.
>
> These syllables, about 2,300 in number, were mixed together and then drawn out by chance and used to construct series of different lengths, several of which each time formed the material for a test.
>
> At the beginning a few rules were observed to prevent, in the construction of the syllables, too immediate repetition of similar sounds, but these were not strictly adhered to. Later they were abandoned and the matter left to chance. The syllables used each time [for a test] were carefully laid aside till the whole number had been used, then they were mixed together and used again.
>
> The aim of the tests carried on with these syllable series was, by means of repeated audible perusal of the separate series, to so impress them that immediately afterwards they could voluntarily just be reproduced. This aim was considered attained when, the initial syllable being given, a series could be recited at the first attempt, without hesitation, at a certain rate, and with the consciousness of being correct. (pp. 22–23)

Ebbinghaus realized that memorizing meaningful materials like poems or prose would be a problem; these materials would already carry with them innumerable meaningful associations that would affect how quickly they could be learned.

> The nonsense material, just described, offers many advantages, in part because of this very lack of meaning. First of all, it is relatively simple and relatively homogeneous. In the case of the material nearest at hand, namely

poetry or prose, the content is now narrative in style, now descriptive, or now reflective; it contains now a phrase that is pathetic, now one that is humorous; its metaphors are sometimes beautiful, sometimes harsh; its rhythm is sometimes smooth and sometimes rough. There is thus brought into play a multiplicity of influences which change without regularity and are therefore disturbing. Such are associations which dart here and there, different degrees of interest, lines of verse recalled because of their striking quality or their beauty, and the like. All this is avoided with our syllables. Among many thousand combinations there occur scarcely a few dozen that have a meaning and among these there are again only a few whose meaning was realized while they were being memorized. (p. 23)

Thus, Ebbinghaus recognized that some of the syllables would have meaning, but he was not concerned—his main interest was in how associations *between* syllables were formed, not the relative meaningfulness of individual syllables. Individual syllables might have some meaning, but the chances were remote that two successive syllables would be *meaningfully related to each other*. That Ebbinghaus chose serial learning as his task is a further indication of his intent to analyze the buildup of associations between elements of a fixed sequence. Serial learning, in which correct recall includes accurately reproducing a set of stimuli in the exact order of their presentation, is well suited for examining associations in a meaningless sequence of nonsense syllables.

How Ebbinghaus actually hit upon the idea to use nonsense syllables is not clear, but Hilgard's (1964) analysis makes the most sense. Familiar with the mechanistic and atomistic assumptions of British empiricism/associationism, Ebbinghaus would have looked for the simplest possible unit that would still yield a large number of stimuli. Individual letters or numbers were too few, words too meaningful. Syllables of words comprise the simplest pronounceable unit in the language, so they would be a logical choice. The fact that Ebbinghaus called his stimuli nonsense "syllables" suggests that he was deliberately thinking of this reduction to a small functional unit. Once he had created the materials, Ebbinghaus turned to other control problems and set up a standardized set of procedures.

The following rules were made for the process of memorizing.

1. The separate series were always read through completely from beginning to end; they were not learned in separate parts which were then joined together; neither were especially difficult parts detached and repeated more frequently. There was a perfectly free interchange between the reading and the occasionally necessary tests of the capacity to reproduce by heart. For the latter there was an important rule to the effect that upon hesitation the rest of the series was to be read through to the end before beginning it again.
2. The reading and the recitation of the series took place at a constant rate. . . . A clockwork metronome placed at some distance was at first used to

regulate the rate; but very soon the ticking of a watch was substituted, that being much simpler and less disturbing to the attention. . . .

3. Since it is practically impossible to speak continuously without variation of accent, the following method was adopted to avoid irregular variations: either three or four syllables were united into a measure, and thus either the 1st, 4th, 7th, or the 1st, 5th, 9th . . . syllables were pronounced with a slight accent. Stressing of the voice was otherwise, as far as possible, avoided.

4. After the learning of each separate series a pause of 15 seconds was made, and used for the tabulation of results. Then the following series of the same test was immediately taken up.

5. During the process of learning, the purpose of reaching the desired goal as soon as possible was kept in mind as much as was feasible. Thus, to the limited degree to which conscious resolve is of influence here, the attempt was made to keep the attention concentrated on the tiresome task and its purpose. It goes without saying that care was taken to keep away all outer disturbances in order to make possible the attainment of this aim. The smaller distractions caused by carrying on the test in various surroundings were also avoided as far as that could be done.

6. There was no attempt to connect the nonsense syllables by the invention of special associations of the mnemotechnik type; learning was carried on solely by the influence of the mere repetitions upon the natural memory. As I do not possess the least practical knowledge of the mnemotechnical devices, the fulfillment of this condition offered no difficulty to me.

7. Finally and chiefly, care was taken that the objective conditions of life during the period of the tests were so controlled as to eliminate too great changes or irregularities. . . . In particular the activity immediately preceding the test was kept as constant in character as was possible. Since the mental as well as the physical condition of man is subject to an evident periodicity of 24 hours, it was taken for granted that like experimental conditions are obtainable only at like times of day. However, in order to carry out more than one test in a given day, different experiments were occasionally carried on together at different times of day. (pp. 24–26)

These last two points reveal an important feature of the study—Ebbinghaus was the *only* research participant. He completed the research during two year-long periods: 1879–1880 and 1883–1884, with the second set of experiments serving primarily to replicate those of the first. Also, in order to become proficient at the task, he spent an unspecified "long time" (p. 33) practicing before he began the 1879–1880 studies. Thus, for more than two years, he devoted a significant portion of his time to memorizing lists of nonsense syllables (about an hour or two per day). On just one set of experiments, the ones that produced his famous forgetting curve (below), Ebbinghaus memorized just over 1,300 different lists! One attribute said to characterize famous scientists is a total immersion in their research. Ebbinghaus was certainly a case in point.

Ebbinghaus described the results of his research in several different chapters. First, he examined how quickly a series of syllables could be learned as a function of the number of syllables per list.

> The question can be asked: What number of syllables can be correctly recited after only one reading? For me the number is usually seven. Indeed I have often succeeded in reproducing eight syllables, but this has happened only at the beginning of the tests and in a decided minority of cases. In the case of six syllables on the other hand, a mistake almost never occurs. (p. 47)

Beyond seven syllables, more repetitions were needed to reach the criterion of learning. Ebbinghaus reported the overall results in a table:

Number of syllables in a series	Number of repetitions necessary for first errorless reproduction (exclusive of it)	Probable Error
7	1	
12	16.6	+/− 1.1
16	30.0	+/− 0.4
24	44.0	+/− 1.7
36	55.0	+/− 2.8

(p. 47)

This result has recurred frequently in experimental psychology's history, and George Miller's (1956) systematic investigation of this "magic number seven" became a landmark paper in the rise of cognitive psychology in the late 1950s and early 1960s. You probably recall learning about the number "7 plus or minus 2" in the memory chapter of your general psychology course under the heading "capacity of short-term memory."

After showing that it takes more repetitions to learn longer lists, Ebbinghaus wondered whether increasing the number of *original* repetitions would strengthen memory. Thus, he repeated lists of 16 syllables 8, 16, 24, 32, 42, 53, or 64 times, and discovered that the ease of relearning the list 24 hours later was directly proportional to the number of original repetitions. He apparently considered extending the number of repetitions beyond 64, but thought better of it. Some aspects of the research were too exhausting even for the redoubtable Ebbinghaus.

> An increase of the readings used for the first learning beyond 64 repetitions proved impracticable.... For with this number each test requires about 3/4 of an hour, and toward the end of this time exhaustion, headache, and other symptoms were often felt which would have complicated the conditions of the test if the number of repetitions had been increased. (p. 55)

The most famous of the studies completed by Ebbinghaus concerned the rate of forgetting, over time, for information that had already been learned. Here,

Ebbinghaus relied on an ingenious measure of recall that he called the *savings method*, which enabled him to measure memory after the passage of time, even if nothing could be recalled immediately after the interval. He described the logic of it early in the book.

> A poem is learned by heart and then not again repeated. We will suppose that after a half year it has been forgotten: no effort at recollection is able to call it back into consciousness. At best only isolated fragments return. Suppose that the poem is again learned by heart. It then becomes evident that, although to all appearances totally forgotten, it still in a certain sense exists and in a way to be effective. The second learning requires noticeably less time or a noticeably smaller number of repetitions than the first. It also requires less time or repetitions than would now be necessary to learn a similar poem of the same length. In this difference in time and number of repetitions we have evidently obtained a certain measure for that inner energy which a half year after the first learning still dwells in that orderly complex of ideas which make up the poem. (pp. 8–9)

To examine the effects of time on memory, Ebbinghaus memorized lists of syllables, tried to relearn them after the passage of a fixed amount of time, and applied his savings method to assess the outcome.

> If syllable series of a definite kind are learned by heart and then left to themselves, how will the process of forgetting go on when left merely to the influence of time or the daily events of life which fill it? The determination of the losses suffered was made in the way described: after certain intervals of time, the series memorized were relearned, and the times necessary in both cases were compared.
>
> The investigations in question fell in the year 1879–1880 and comprised 163 double tests. Each double test consisted in learning eight series of 13 syllables each ... and then in relearning them after a definite time. The learning was continued until two errorless recitations of the series in question were possible. The relearning was carried to the same point; it occurred at one of the following seven times—namely, after about one third of an hour, after one hour, after 9 hours, one day, two days, six days, or 31 days. (pp. 65–66)

Ebbinghaus recorded the total time for the original learning of the eight 13-syllable lists, which was typically about 20 minutes, and the time for relearning. Original learning minus relearning yielded a measure of savings, which was converted to a percentage by dividing by the time of original learning. Thus, if original learning took 20 minutes and relearning took 5 minutes, 15 minutes or 75% (15/20 × 100) of the original learning time was saved.

Ebbinghaus reported the results for each of the 163 separate experiments (i.e., "double tests") that he completed over the different retention intervals. The results of this study have made their way into almost every introductory psychology textbook of the twentieth century. They are normally shown in a graph like this.

Retention (percent)

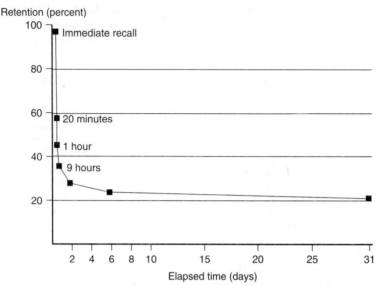

Source: Hermann Ebbinghaus, *Memory: A Contribution to Experimental Psychology,*
1885/1913

Ebbinghaus did not include this graph in his book (he presented the results as a table), but the results are clear—forgetting was very rapid at first, then slowed in its rate. Thus, after just 20 minutes, Ebbinghaus's memory held only about 60% of the learned material; 40% had been lost. After an hour, 55% was lost, and after just a day, about two-thirds was lost.

The forgetting curve is Ebbinghaus's best-known result, but he also studied other memory phenomena. For example, he provided an early example of the advantages of distributed over massed practice by showing that

> For the relearning of a 12-syllable series at a definite time, accordingly, 38 repetitions, distributed in a certain way over the three preceding days, had just as favorable an effect as 68 repetitions made on the day just previous. . . . It makes the assumption probable that *with any considerable number of repetitions* a suitable distribution of them over a space of time is decidedly more advantageous than the massing of them at a single time. (p. 89, italics in the original)

A final example of the Ebbinghaus research program is his investigation of remote associations. When the sequence of syllables A, B, and C, is to be learned in order, direct associations are formed between A and B and between B and C, but are they also formed (remotely) between A and C? If so, then the association concept extends beyond the idea of two immediately contiguous events. Ebbinghaus devised a clever procedure to test for these potential remote associations. He first learned a list of 16 syllables in the usual serial order (the numbers represent nonsense syllable #1, nonsense syllable #2, etc.).

LIST A. 1 2 3 4 5 6 7 8 9 10 11 12 13 14 15 16

Next he would relearn the list in an order that skipped a syllable.

LIST B. 1 3 5 7 9 11 13 15 2 4 6 8 10 12 14 16

Similarly, for other lists he would relearn a list that skipped two syllables.

LIST C. 1 4 7 10 13 16 2 5 8 11 14 3 6 9 12 15

If remote associations had been forming during the original learning of syllables 1 through 16 (list A), then the relearning of lists B and C would be faster than learning a new list of 16 syllables, and this is exactly what Ebbinghaus found. Furthermore, there was a direct relationship between the ease of relearning and the degree of remoteness of the associations. As Ebbinghaus put it,

> the associative threads, which hold together a remembered series, are spun not merely between each member and its immediate successor, but beyond intervening members to every member which stands to it in any close temporal relation. The strength of the threads varies with the distance of the members, but even the weaker of them must be considered as relatively of considerable significance. (p. 94)

The importance of the Ebbinghaus memory research cannot be overstated. At a time when scientific thinking was just starting to be applied to psychological questions, the work shows the extent to which precision and scientific rigor could be applied. In a retrospective review of the Ebbinghaus book, the prominent memory researcher Henry Roediger (1985) wrote

> In sum, the corpus of Ebbinghaus's experimental results is large. Considering that he only began his research in the same year that Wundt founded his psychology lab and that he performed all experiments on himself and still produced such regular and compelling results, his achievement is nearly incredible. (Roediger, 1985, p. 522)

The memory research was Ebbinghaus's greatest accomplishment, but not his only one. In 1890, he started the *Zeitschrift für Psychologie und Physiologie der Sunnesorgane* (*Journal of Psychology and Physiology of the Sense Organs*). The journal's catholicity of interests and the prestige of its contributing authors (e.g., Hermann Helmholtz) led one historian to describe it as "the most important psychological organ in Germany" (Shakow, 1930, p. 509). Ebbinghaus also wrote two popular introductory psychology texts, including a brief version just before his sudden death from pneumonia in 1909.

CONCEPT REVIEW QUESTIONS

1. What was Ebbinghaus's goal in creating nonsense syllables and using a serial learning procedure?

2. Describe the procedures used by Ebbinghaus to exercise some degree of methodological control.

3. Describe any two of the outcomes of the Ebbinghaus memory research.

DISCUSSION QUESTION

1. What was the method of savings, why was it a very creative way to study memory, and what does it imply about the nature of human memories?

CHAPTER 7

WILLARD S. SMALL (1870–1943): INVENTING MAZE LEARNING

Mazes are among psychology's most famous methodological tools. Although the British naturalist John Lubbock used a Y-shaped maze to study scent trails in ants and Edward Thorndike (next chapter) created simple mazes for baby chicks by standing books on their ends, credit for inventing the "labyrinth" method usually goes to Willard Small, who was a graduate student at Clark University in the late 1890s. The article excerpted here is the second in a set of articles that Small published on the "mental processes" of rats. In the first, he (Small, 1900) investigated rat behavior in a simple puzzle box—rats had to discover how to get into the box to obtain food and the solution depended on either digging or chewing. This second study originated from discussions among Small, his friend and fellow graduate student Linus Kline, and Edmund Sanford, Clark's laboratory director. They were interested in the rat's "home-finding" behavior, and the idea to use a maze developed from this recollection by Kline.

> I ... described to [Sanford] runways which I had observed several years ago made by large feral rats to their nests under the porch of an old cabin on my father's farm in Virginia. These runways were from three to six inches below the surface of the ground and when exposed during excavation presented a veritable maze. Sanford at once suggested the possibility of using the pattern of the Hampton Court maze for purposes of constructing a "home-finding" apparatus. (Miles, 1930, p. 331)

Other work prevented Kline from acting on Sanford's suggestion right away, and he apparently suggested that his friend Small take up the idea. Small did, and here is an excerpt of his account of psychology's first maze learning study with rats.

> The present paper ... presents in detail the results of some further experimental studies upon the mental life of the rat.... The paper describes the apparatus used and the conditions of the experiment, gives a detailed account of a typical series of experiments, compares the intelligence of wild rats with tame white rats ..., and makes some suggestions in regard to the mental facts involved in solving the problems set in the tests....

Excerpts from: Small, W. S. (1901). Experimental study of the mental processes of the rat. II. *American Journal of Psychology, 12*, 206–239.

The aim in these experiments ... was to make observations upon the free expression of the animal's mental processes, under as definitely controlled conditions as possible; and, at the same time, to minimize the inhibitive influence of restraint and unfamiliar or unnatural circumstances.... Conforming with such considerations, appeal was made to the rat's propensity for winding passages.

The Hampton Court Maze served as a model for the apparatus. The diagram given in the Encyclopedia Britannica was corrected to a rectangular form, as being easier of construction. Three mazes were made. The first was as follows. The dimensions were 6 by 8 feet. The bottom was of wood, the boards being fastened together so as to make a portable whole of the apparatus. All the rest: top, sides, and partitions between galleries [i.e., runways] were of wire netting, 1/4 in. mesh. The height of the sides was 4 inches; the width of the galleries, the same. In the center was a large open space. The accompanying diagram [below] gives the ground plan of the maze. The entrance is marked by the figure *O*. Figures *1* to *7* indicate seven blind alleys—seven possibilities of error. It will be observed that *4* does not lead necessarily into *cul-de-sac 5*, but does inevitably furnish a chance for error. The letter *x* marks a dividing of the ways either of which, however, may be followed without completely losing the trail. Certain other points are indicated by letters *a*, *b*, *c*, etc., for convenience in description. *C* stands for center. A glance at the maze will be sufficient to convince one of the difficulty of the problem. (pp. 206–208, italics in the original)

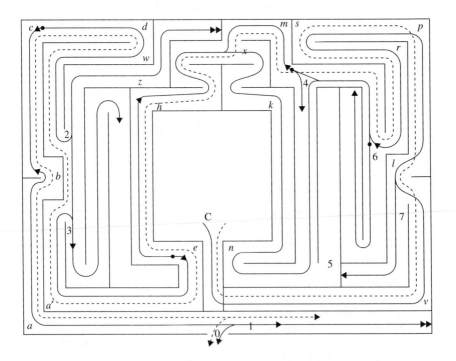

The other two mazes built by Small were identical in design, except that the floor of the mazes were also made of wire mesh, so that the mazes could be turned upside down, "and a mirror reproduction of the original form could be obtained" (p. 209).

> The rats were kept in an ordinary observation cage, a well-ventilated and commodious apartment, standing flush with the maze at *O*. Back of the cage, upon the same table, was a screen completely concealing the observer during experimentation, but permitting him to look down upon the maze and mark every movement of the rats. When ready for experimenting, the sliding glass door which closed the passage into the maze was lifted by means of a pulley connection. . . . Food was placed in the central enclosure. To obtain this, the rats had to find their way through the tangled maze. They were kept hungry enough so that they would set about the task vigorously. Experimenting was done in the evening to minimize the influence of distracting noises. . . .
>
> The original purpose was to use the wild rats exclusively; but the difficulties were considerable, and the white rats were found to serve the purposes of experiment quite as well in every way.
>
> [T]he rats were let into the maze at the time of experiment and were left until the following morning. The entire night was theirs for investigating the maze. (pp. 209–210, italics in the original)

Despite the difficulty with the wild rats, well known to those who have tried to experiment with them (hint—wear heavy-duty gloves when handling them), Small was able to make some interesting comparisons between wild and tame rats. In the following description, Small describes five trials with each of the two types of rat. However, the wild rats had great difficulty adapting to the maze environment at first (e.g., they showed more fear) and performed very poorly on their first two trials in the maze. Therefore, in comparing the two sets of five trials, Small was actually comparing trials 3–7 for the wild rats and 1–5 for the tame rats.

> Comparison of the time and error tables of the two series discloses no considerable superiority on either side, although in this comparison I disregarded entirely the first two experiments of Series I [i.e., with the wild rats], comparing the 5 trials recorded of Series I with the first 5 of Series II [i.e., with the tame rats]. The average of times required and errors made gives the white rats the advantage in regard to time; the brown rats, in regards to errors. In view of the handicap of two experiments, it will be seen that the advantage lies with the white rats throughout. The brown rats had gained comparatively little from the first two experiments, imperfectly conditioned to be sure, but in which they had the usual freedom of the maze during the entire night. I am of the opinion that even if the conditions of experiment had been identical, the balance still would have tipped in favor of the white rats, so potent is the inhibitive influence of fear with the wild rats. (p. 220)

Small seemed surprised by these results, believing that wild rats ought to perform well because they were more vigorous than the white rats, "and consequently this excess of activity increases his chances of accidentally hitting upon the right path" (p. 220). Also, he thought that domestication might have an adverse effect on a rat's intelligence. Given his results, however, Small argued that white rats were entirely adequate for laboratory work and that results with white rats would apply to all rats.

The conclusion [that white rats outperform wild ones] does not tally very well with the general opinion that animals suffer mental deterioration under domestication. However that may be with other animals, it evidently is doubtful in this instance. The white rat in comparison with his wild congener is somewhat less vigorous and hardy (especially does not endure cold or hunger so well), and has sloughed off some of the timidity and suspiciousness of the wild rat; on the other hand, his senses with the exception of sight are as keen, his characteristic rat traits are as persistent, and his mental adaptability is as considerable. The *modus operandi* of the two kinds in the maze shows little variation. Likewise there is no difference in the curiosity manifested, either in kind or degree. In view of the many generations of luxurious idleness of the white rat, this profound and enduring nature of specific psychic traits is striking. (p. 221, italics in the original)

The bulk of Small's descriptions, then, were of the behavior of his white rats. In great detail, covering five pages, he described their performances trial by trial, and the following gives the flavor of his descriptions. Note that on each trial, pairs of rats were in the maze at the same time. The example to follow also makes it clear why Thorndike (1900) criticized Small's work for being excessively anthropomorphic (i.e., attributing human characteristics to non-humans). Thorndike's comments were directed at Small's prior publication on rats and the puzzle boxes, but they could have applied equally well to the maze study. The following description is of two rats (A and B) on their fourth and eighth trials in the maze.

Exp. 4. *A*, 1 ¾ m. *B*, a few seconds longer. A's course: End of *1*—forward quickly and into *2*—stopped at last turn and back, seeming to recognize his error here—paused at 3, then to the end of the *cul-de-sac*—turned instantly, and ran swiftly and continuously to *4*—entered *4*, going slowly around the circuit *n*, *k*, *x*—paused meditatively at *x*—then suddenly started on a quick gallop, accelerating at *m* and *4*, and not pausing until he reached *C*. *B* followed about the same course, but went less quickly. He showed less the appearance of "trailing." In the case of both rats, something very like disgust was manifest when they found themselves at the end of a blind alley. The instant recoil, the swift retracing of their steps, and the decisiveness with which they turned from the blind alley into the right path, seldom going *back* now beyond the entrance of the *cul-de-sac*, seemed to indicate something more of mental content than the mere recognition of the impossibility of getting further that way. Another noticeable fact was the increased security and confidence of all their movements. The slow, blundering *modus operandi* of the first experiment had given place to rapid, definite, purposeful movements. . . .

Exp. 8. *B* 30 sec. . . . *A* was a few seconds later. . . . In making another trip to *C* a few seconds later, *A* went right away to *4*; here hesitated as if "scratching his head," then entered this gallery slowly and doubtfully—only a few steps however; then with a sudden turn and a triumphant flick of his tail he returned to the correct path. . . .

After the edge of the appetite is worn off a bit, the rats tend to let loose the play instinct in the fullest degree. In all their journeys they "play by the way," strolling nonchalantly into the blind alleys, now sniffing listlessly, now with half-eager curiosity in all the corners, and angles. That they *know* their way pretty well, however, is evident from the manner in which they take a sudden start from any place in the maze and "flash" to the end—either end. (pp. 215–218, italics in the original)

Small completed ten trials with the white rats A and B, with trial ten occurring twenty-two days after trial nine—the rats made more errors on trial ten than on nine, but they clearly remembered the maze. Small then summarized his results, essentially explaining the process in trial and error terms not very different from that of Thorndike (Chapter 8), and included a comparison of trials 1 and 8 that explains the solid and dotted lines in Figure 1 (note: the record for trial 1 was for rat A and that for trial 8 was for rat B; Small didn't portray the results for the same rat for both trials because he thought the differences between the two "inconsequential").

> In appreciating the results of this series of experiments, about the same facts come into view, only more distinctly, as in the case of the wild . . . rats; the initial indefiniteness of movements and the fortuitiveness of success; the just observable profit from the first experiences; the gradually increasing certainty of knowledge indicated by increase of speed and definiteness, and the recognition of critical points indicated by hesitation and indecision; the lack of imitation and the improbability of following by scent; the outbreak of the instincts of play and curiosity after the edge of appetite is dulled. In addition are to be noted the further observations upon the contrast between the slow and cautious entrance into, and the rapid exit from the blind alleys, after the first few trials; the appearance of disgust on reaching the end of a blind alley; the clear indication of centrally excited sensation (images) of some kind; memory . . . ; the persistence of certain errors; and the almost automatic character of the movements in the later experiments. Viewed objectively, these observations all converge towards one central consideration; the continuous and rapid improvement of the rats in threading the maze, amounting to almost perfect accuracy in the last experiments. No qualification of this view was found necessary in the light of many later experiments. Rather they all confirm it. . . . [For rats A and B t]he contrast between the first slow, blundering, accidental success and the definitely foreseen success of experiment 8 (taken as the best) is striking. This is brought out even more saliently by the graphic representation [in Figure 1]. . . . The solid line indicates the course followed in Exp. 1; the dotted line that followed in Exp. 8. The arrows mark the point where the rat stopped and turned about, and are pointed in the direction he was headed when he stopped. The dots . . . indicate points where considerable pauses were made. The arrow and dot between *4* and *m* indicate that the rat, when returning from an abortive essay into *4*, went as far as that arrow, then paused and went forward. (pp. 218–220, italics in the original)

In addition to his general description of maze learning as involving a trial and error process, Small also examined the relative influence of the various senses in maze learning. He thought that taste played a role because of the "pleasure-toned experience at the end" of finding food, but he did not believe that scent affected the learning process at all. Because the rats explored virtually the entire maze on trial one and then spent the following night in the maze, he didn't think there would be any useful scent trails for the rats to follow. And he found that when rats were very close to the food (i.e., the smell would be salient), even though quite far from solution (e.g., at *e*), they continued on without hesitating in any predictable manner. To test for the effects of vision, he changed the position of a light in the room and noticed no effect on learning. Then he considered a plan "to blindfold the rat" (p. 234), but quickly rejected it as implausible. Then he got lucky.

> Fortunately, nature stepped in and performed a conclusive experiment for me. A number of my rats came to me with diseased eyes. Before I discovered this, two of them an adult male, *X*, and a young female (about 10 weeks old), *Y*, had become blind. I had already started them learning the maze, with two others, when I noticed their blindness. After the fifth experiment they were totally blind.... At this time the general health, vigor and temperament of these rats were unaffected by their malady....
>
> The blind rats learned the original task as well as the normals—all the normals experimented with. Rat *X* in this case learned the path before either of his normal companions. In Exps. 5 and 6 he was the first to *C*, and made fewest errors. In Exp. 7 he made the round in 50 seconds, without error, and with slight hesitation at two points only. In the succeeding 15 experiments he showed practically perfect acquaintance, though occasionally making errors. His conduct in the maze did not differ materially from that of normal rats. He ran in the middle of the galleries, rounded the corners quickly and precisely, and carried on the usual investigations. At critical points there were the same hesitation and indecision manifested as with the normals, by alternately turning each way as if stayed in the grasp of conflicting images. Occasionally, he would nose along the several sides before starting on again. This probably was not a direct means of ascertaining the way, for, later, I cut off his feelers, also those of some normals, without any effect upon their ability to find their way. (p. 235, italics in the original)

A few years after Small's study, John Watson (Chapter 18) and Harvey Carr of the University of Chicago examined the question of how the various senses affected maze learning in a more systematic fashion (e.g., surgically blinding rats or severing connections necessary for smell to function properly), verifying Small's conclusion about the negligible effects of smell and vision on maze learning (Carr & Watson, 1908; Watson, 1907).

One final set of experiments conducted by Small indicated that his rats were learning the overall configuration of the maze, not just "memorizing" a series of correct turns. This is a finding that would not surprise Edward Tolman (Chapter 19), who believed on the basis of his studies some twenty-five years later that rats learned "cognitive maps" of the mazes they encountered. Small was intrigued by the fact that his rats learned to take the shorter of two paths to the goal when faced with the decision point at position *x* of the maze—they seemed to know the "shorter circuit." He decided to test directly the notion that rats could quickly sense if a shorter route to the goal was made available. Although his results appear dramatic, keep in mind that between trials 1 and 2 for all of his rats, the animal would spend the entire night in the maze.

The fact of the invariable adoption of the "shorter circuit" was brought out more clearly and forcibly by a special test. A normal [rat] and the blind rat X were used. Both had been familiar with both mazes (direct and reversed) for weeks. Their knowledge was as nearly automatic as possible. A path was opened, then, between d and h, by cutting the walls at w and z. A large part of the first (left) half of the journey thus was cut out.

In the first trial (normal rat) the rat went automatically *via* the old route—paid no attention to the new one. . . . In the next trial, however, he took the new path unhesitatingly through w and z, and turned correctly—i.e., to the right—at h. In the third trial he took the new path. . . . In the next two trials the right association became pretty well fixed; the new route was learned perfectly and the old abandoned.

The conduct of the blind rat was really striking. In the first trial he did not notice the new path. In the second, however, he selected it after a brief hesitation. The experience of the previous night was thus strikingly effective. Singularly enough, he perfectly acquired the new association more quickly than the normals. After the second trial he rarely went astray. . . . This preference for the shorter path is difficult to explain except upon the supposition that the path is known to be shorter. (pp. 237–238, italics in the original)

Small concluded his paper by acknowledging the aid of Sanford ("for the initial suggestion"—p. 239) and his fellow graduate student Kline, and for the "salutary and stimulating criticism" (p. 239) of G. Stanley Hall's legendary Monday evening seminars. The project earned Small a doctorate, but it was his final publication in psychology. Little is known of Small's career after he finished at Clark, but it is known that he taught for a while at two "normal" schools (i.e., colleges designed specifically for the training of teachers) and then moved into administration. He became Dean of the College of Education at the University of Maryland in 1923 (Dewsbury, 1984). Small died in 1943.

CONCEPT REVIEW QUESTIONS

1. What roles did Kline and Sanford play in the creation of the maze as a laboratory apparatus?
2. Describe the comparisons that Small made between the performance of wild rats and that of white rats.
3. What did Small have to say about the manner in which rats learned the maze? What was the role played by vision?

DISCUSSION QUESTION

1. Small's study has been criticized on the grounds that his descriptions are excessively anthropomorphic. Is this a fair criticism? Find examples in the excerpt to support your argument.

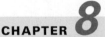

EDWARD L. THORNDIKE (1874–1949): CATS IN PUZZLE BOXES

Most of Edward Thorndike's professional life was spent in the area of educational psychology, but early in his career, he made his reputation as a scientist with a series of studies on animal behavior. He began the work as a graduate student at Harvard, studying the behavior of baby chicks as they tried to find their way out of crude mazes (constructed by turning books on their ends). His best-known research, however, was completed for his doctoral dissertation at Columbia, when he investigated the behavior of cats escaping from "puzzle boxes." The puzzle box studies were published first in 1898 (Thorndike, 1898), and then combined with other animal studies in book form in 1911 as *Animal Intelligence: Experimental Studies*. The excerpts that follow are from a reprinting of this latter source.

Thorndike began his book by stating the purpose of his research. He noted that a great deal was known about instinct in animals and about their sensory capacities ("sense-power"), but little was known about the effects of experience on their behavior—"this part of the field has received faulty and unsuccessful treatment" (p. 20). Yet the study of association (and therefore, learning) was essential in the quest for understanding the evolution of human mental activity. And understanding how human mental activity had evolved was a central function of the rapidly developing field of comparative psychology.

> The main purpose of the study of the animal mind is to learn the development of mental life down through the phylum, to trace in particular the origin of human faculty. In relation to this chief purpose of comparative psychology the associative processes assume a role predominant over that of sense-powers or instinct, for in the study of the associative processes lies the solution of the problem. Sense-powers have changed by addition and supersedence, but the cognitive side of consciousness has changed not only in quantity but also in quality. Somehow out of these associative processes have arisen human consciousnesses with their sciences and arts and religions. The association of ideas proper, imagination, memory, abstraction, generalization, judgment, inference, have here their source.... For the

Excerpts from: Thorndike, E. L. (2000). *Animal intelligence: Experimental studies*. New Brunswick, NJ: Transaction Publishers. (Original work published 1911) origin and development of human faculty we must look to these processes of association in lower animals. (p. 22)

Thorndike was a strong critic of most comparative psychologists, especially when they relied on nonrepresentative anecdotal data to support claims of higher mental powers for a variety of animals. He thought he could do better, and the most important aspect of the puzzle box studies was the methodological rigor that Thorndike brought to the project (Galef, 1998). Thorndike made it clear from the start that he was not impressed with the state of comparative psychology in his day. He was sometimes accused of displaying the arrogance of youthful exuberance, and you will see some justification for the charge here:

> Although no work done in [comparative psychology] is enough like the present investigation to require an account of its results, the *method* hitherto in use invites comparisons by its contrast and, as I believe, by its faults. In the first place, most of the books do not give us a psychology, but rather a *eulogy*, of animals. They have all been about animal *intelligence*, never about animal *stupidity*. Though a writer derides the notion that animals have reason, he hastens to add that they have marvelous capacity of forming associations, and is likely to refer to the fact that human beings only rarely reason anything out, that their trains of ideas are ruled mostly by association, as if, in this matter, animals were on a par with humans. The history of books on animals' minds thus furnishes an illustration of the well-nigh universal tendency in humans to find the marvelous wherever it can. . . .
>
> In the second place, the facts have generally been derived from anecdotes. Now quite apart from such pedantry as insists that a man's word about a scientific fact is worthless unless he is a trained scientist, there are really in this field special objections to the acceptance of the testimony about animals' intelligent acts which one gets from anecdotes. Such testimony is by no means on a par with testimony about the size of a fish or the migration of birds, etc. For here [with anecdotes] one has to deal not merely with ignorant or inaccurate testimony, but also with prejudiced testimony. Human folk are as a matter of fact eager to find intelligence in animals. And when the animal observed is a pet . . . , or when the story is one that has been told as a story to entertain, further complications are introduced. Besides commonly misstating what facts [these anecdotes] report, they report only such facts as show the animal at his best. Dogs get lost hundreds of times and no one ever notices it or sends an account of it to scientific magazines. But let one find his way from Brooklyn to Yonkers and the fact immediately becomes a circulating anecdote. Thousands of cats on thousands of occasions sit helplessly yowling, and no one takes thought of it or writes to his friend, the professor; but let one cat claw at the knob of a door supposedly as a signal to be let out, and straightway this cat becomes the representative of the cat-mind in all the books. . . .
>
> Finally, in all cases, whether of direct observation or reports by good observers or bad, there have been three other defects. Only a single case is studied, so the results are not necessarily true of the type; the observation is not repeated, nor are the conditions perfectly regulated; the previous history of the animal in question is not known. Such observations may tell us, if the observer is perfectly reliable, that a certain thing takes place; but they cannot assure us that it will take place universally among the animals of

that species, or universally with the same animal. Nor can the influence of previous experience be estimated. (pp. 22–25, italics in the original)

Disdaining the anecdotal strategy and the tendency to report only the "marvelous," Thorndike instead developed more systematic procedures to test claims for animal intelligence, deliberately aiming to correct the three defects just mentioned—he would study more than a single case, he would repeat the experiments, and he would control the learning history of the animals he studied.

> To remedy these defects, experiment must be substituted for observation and the collection of anecdotes.... You can repeat the conditions at will, so as to see whether or not the animal's behavior is due to mere coincidence. A number of animals can be subjected to the same test, so as to attain typical results. The animal may be put in situations where its conduct is especially instructive. After considerable preliminary observation of animals' behavior under various conditions, I chose for my general method one which, simple as it is, possesses several other marked advantages besides those accompanying experiment of any sort. It was merely to put animals when hungry in inclosures from which they could escape by some simple act, such as pulling at a loop of cord, pressing a lever, or stepping on a platform.... The animal was put in the inclosure, food was left outside in sight, and his actions observed. Besides recording his general behavior, special notice was taken of how he succeeded in doing the necessary act (in case he did succeed), and a record was kept of the time that he was in the box before performing the successful pull, clawing, or bite. This was repeated until the animal had formed a perfect association between the sense-impression of the interior of that box and the impulse leading to the successful movement. When the association was thus perfect, the time taken to escape was, of course, practically constant and very short. (p. 26)

Thorndike built 15 different boxes, fashioning them crudely out of crates, wire, string, and latches. He included this sketch of one of the more complicated of his puzzle boxes which required three different responses for a successful escape, and described it as follows:

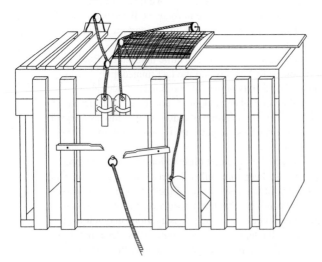

K was a box arranged so that three separate acts were required to open the door, which was held by two bolts at the top and two bars outside. One of the bolts was connected with a platform in the back center so that depressing the platform raised the bolt. The other was raised by a string which ran up over a pulley in the front, across the box 1 inch above the bars, over a pulley near the corner of the box, and down to the floor, where it was fastened. Pulling on this string . . . would raise the bolt. If both bolts were raised and *either* bar was pushed up or down far enough to be out of the way, the cat could escape. (p. 34, italics in the original)

Thorndike used thirteen different cats in his puzzle box research. It is not clear from his description exactly how many cats were tested in each of the boxes, but it appears that each cat was tested in at least several of the boxes. How did they behave?

When put into the box the cat would show evident signs of discomfort and of an impulse to escape from confinement. It tries to squeeze through any opening; it claws and bites at the bars or wire; it thrusts its paws out through any opening and claws at everything it reaches; it continues its efforts when it strikes something loose and shaky; it may claw at things within the box. It does not pay very much attention to the food outside, but seems simply to strive to escape its confinement. The vigor with which it struggles is extraordinary. For eight or ten minutes it will claw and bite and squeeze incessantly. . . . The cat that is clawing all over the box in her impulsive struggle will probably claw the string or loop or button so as to open the door. And gradually all the other nonsuccessful impulses will be stamped out and the particular impulse leading to the successful act will be stamped in by the *resulting pleasure*, until, after many trials, the cat will, when put in the box, immediately claw the button or loop in a definite way. . . .

Starting, then, with its store of instinctive impulses, the cat hits upon the successful movement, and gradually associates it with the sense-impression. The formation of each association may be represented graphically by a time-curve. (pp. 35–38)

Thorndike's explanation for this behavior was what he referred to as trial and accidental success—what we would today call trial and error learning. Because he believed that the cat learned to make *connections* between stimuli in the boxes and successful escape responses during this trial and error learning, Thorndike's learning model is sometimes called *connectionism*. When first placed in the puzzle box, the cat exhibits behavior that is a random sequence of acts—clawing, biting, trying to squeeze its way out, and so on. Eventually, the animal hits upon the correct response (e.g., claws a loop), but its first solution is accidental. Nonetheless, that behavior has been successful, and such behaviors "stamped in" by their pleasurable consequences (escape), as Thorndike put it. On subsequent trials, the failed behaviors are gradually eliminated and the successful one occurs earlier and earlier in the sequence. Before long, the animal is in and out of the box in a few seconds. Thorndike produced numerous graphs showing a gradual (but erratic in most cases) decline in the amount of time taken to escape.

Based on these results, Thorndike rejected the idea that cats are capable of more complex reasoning when escaping from the boxes.

> The first ... question is whether or not animals are ever led to do any of their acts by reasoning. Do they ever conclude from inference that a certain act will produce a certain desired result, and so do it? ... The great support of those who claim for animals the ability to infer has been their wonderful performances which resemble our own. These could not, they claim, have happened by accident. No animal could learn to open a latched gate by accident. The whole substance of the argument vanishes if, as a matter of fact, animals do learn those things by accident. *They certainly do.* (pp. 67–68, italics in the original)

Furthermore, Thorndike used Box K (shown on page 50) to provide a direct demonstration of a failure to reason. Cats attempting Box K, which combined three responses that had been learned in earlier individual-response boxes, showed no evidence of intelligently combining what they had learned into a more complex sequence of behaviors. Thus, Thorndike rejected the idea that cats can reason intelligently in favor of his more parsimonious trial and error explanation.

Thorndike also rejected the idea that cats can learn by imitation. One of his boxes had two chambers separated by wire mesh.

> The larger of these [chambers] had a front of wooden bars with a door which fell open when a string stretched across the top was bitten or clawed down. The smaller was closed by boards on three sides and by the wire screen on the fourth. Through the screen the cat could see the one to be imitated pull the string, go out through the door thus opened and eat the fish outside. When put in this compartment ... a cat soon gave up efforts to claw through the screen, quieted down and watched more or less the proceedings going on in the other compartment. Thus this apparatus could be used to test the power of imitation. A cat who had no experience with the means of escape from the large compartment was put in the closed one; another cat, who would do it readily, was allowed to go through the performance of pulling the string, going out, and eating the fish.... After the 'imitatee' had done the thing a number of times, the other was put in the big compartment alone, and the time it took him before pulling the string was noted and his general behavior closely observed. (pp. 85–86)

Thorndike found no evidence of observational learning with this procedure—when put to the test, the observer cats behaved exactly like other, naïve cats (i.e., cats not given the opportunity to observe successful escapes).

> No one, I am sure, who had seen them, would have claimed that their conduct was at all influenced by what they had seen. When they did hit the string the act looked just like the accidental success of the ordinary association experiment. But, besides these personal observations, we have in the impersonal time-records sufficient proofs of the absence of imitation. If the animals pulled the string from having seen [another cat] do so, they ought to pull it in each individual case at an approximately regular length of

time after they were put in, and presumably pretty soon thereafter. That is, if an association between the sight of that string in that total situation and a certain impulse and consequent freedom and food had been formed in their minds by the observation of the acts of [the other cat], they ought to pull it *on seeing it*, and if any disturbing factor required that a certain time should elapse before the imitative faculty got in working order, that time ought to be somewhere near constant. The times were, in fact, long and irregular in the extreme. (p. 89)

In his 1898 dissertation, Thorndike did not propose general principles of learning, but he did so in the 1911 monograph that I have been using for this excerpt. He postulated two principles, a *Law of Effect* and a *Law of Exercise*. The Law of Effect might remind you of B. F. Skinner's concept of operant conditioning, and Skinner (Chapter 20) explicitly recognized his debt to Thorndike, referring to the Columbia psychologist's work as "[o]ne of the first serious attempts to study changes brought about by the consequences of behavior" (Skinner, 1953, p. 59). Here are the two laws in Thorndike's words.

The Law of Effect is that: *Of several responses made to the same situation, those which are accompanied or closely followed by satisfaction to the animal will, other things being equal, be more firmly connected with the situation, so that, when it recurs, they will be more likely to recur; those which are accompanied or closely followed by discomfort to the animal will, other things being equal, have their connections with that situation weakened, so that, when it recurs, they will be less likely to recur. The greater the satisfaction or discomfort, the greater the strengthening or weakening of the bond.*

The Law of Exercise is that: *Any response to a situation will, other things being equal, be more strongly connected with the situation in proportion to the number of times it has been connected with that situation and to the average vigor and duration of the connections.*

These two laws stand out clearly in every series of experiments on animal learning and in the entire history of the management of human affairs. They give an account of learning that is satisfactory over a wide range of experience, so long as all that is demanded is a rough and general means of prophecy. We can, as a rule, get an animal to learn a given accomplishment by getting him to accomplish it, rewarding him when he does, and punishing him when he does not; or, if reward or punishment are kept indifferent, by getting him to accomplish it much oftener than he does any other response to the situation in question. (pp. 244–245, italics in the original)

In 1911, Thorndike was confident that his two laws could account for most learning, but he subsequently modified both, especially after studying human learning in his later years. For the Law of Effect, he eventually decided that the first half was more strongly supported than the second half—rewards are more effective than punishments in producing learning. As for the Law of Exercise, Thorndike reached the conclusion that it had limited value. Practice might make perfect for some types of learning (e.g., motor skills), but simple repetition was often unnecessary for higher forms of learning (e.g., comprehending textbook material).

After completing his puzzle box research and earning his doctorate, Thorndike taught at Case Western Reserve in Cleveland for a year, then returned to Columbia's Teachers College, where he spent the rest of his career. He became one of psychology's pioneers in the field of educational psychology, with his three-volume *Educational Psychology*, published in 1913, making him "practically synonymous with the field of educational psychology for many years to come" (Goodenough, 1950, p. 295). Thorndike retired from Columbia in 1940 and died nine years later.

CONCEPT REVIEW QUESTIONS

1. Describe Thorndike's attitude toward the comparative psychology of his day.
2. Describe a typical puzzle box study; how did Thorndike explain the outcome?
3. On the basis of his research Thorndike produced two "laws." What were they and how did Thorndike modify them over the years?

DISCUSSION QUESTION

1. What led Thorndike to conclude that his cats failed to show evidence of reasoning and imitation? Do you agree, and could there be another way to study the problem?

CHAPTER 9

WILLIAM JAMES (1842–1910): ON CONSCIOUSNESS AND EMOTION

William James was one of psychology's preeminent pioneers. As just one indication of his status, when James McKeen Cattell (Chapter 29) asked psychologists to rank their peers in a 1903 survey, not only did James achieve the overall top ranking, he was listed as number one on *every* ballot that was submitted (Hothersall, 1995). James earned an M.D. from Harvard in 1869, but graduated with no desire to practice medicine. Instead, while touring Europe, he encountered the new laboratory psychology that was developing in Germany and became intrigued with it. On his return, he accepted an offer to teach physiology at Harvard and, in 1875, he offered a course on physiology and psychology that incorporated much of what he had learned in Germany. Three years later, he contracted with the Boston publisher Henry Holt to spend two years writing a textbook for this new psychology. It took twelve years, not two, but his two-volume *Principles of Psychology* (James, 1890/1950) has become psychology's most famous textbook (Evans, 1990). In 1892 he wrote a condensed version—*Psychology: The Briefer Course*. The excerpts you are about to read, on consciousness and on emotion, are from this brief edition.

ON CONSCIOUSNESS

James defined psychology as the science of mental life and his nineteenth century peers would have agreed. However, considerable disagreement occurred over the nature of mental life and especially over the nature of human conscious experience. E. B. Titchener (Chapter 11), for example, argued that the best approach to studying consciousness was to analyze it into its most basic components. James opposed this "structuralist" approach, arguing instead for an approach that would eventually come to be called "functionalist" (see Angell,

Excerpts from: James, W. J. (1961). *Psychology: The briefer course*. New York: Harper & Row. (Original work published 1892.)

Chapter 12). In his chapter on consciousness, James was at his eloquent best. He began by criticizing a structuralist approach to the study of consciousness.

> We are now prepared to begin the introspective study of the adult consciousness itself. Most books adopt the so-called synthetic method. Starting with 'simple ideas of sensation,' and regarding these as so many atoms, they proceed to build up the higher states of mind out of their 'association,' 'integration,' or 'fusion,' as houses are built by the agglutination of bricks. This . . . commits one beforehand to the very questionable theory that our higher states of consciousness are compounds of units; and instead of starting with what the reader directly knows, namely his total concrete states of mind, it starts with a set of supposed 'simple ideas' with which he has no immediate acquaintance at all, and concerning whose alleged interactions he is very much at the mercy of any plausible phrase. (p. 18)

Instead of this 'synthetic' approach, James proposed starting with the fundamental fact that *"consciousness of some sort goes on. 'States of mind' succeed each other"* (p. 20, italics in the original). He then proposed that there were four main characteristics of consciousness. First, every state of consciousness is personal.

> It seems as if the elementary psychic fact were not *thought* or *this thought* or *that thought*, but *my thought*, every thought being *owned*. Neither contemporaneity, nor proximity in space, nor similarity of quality and content are able to fuse thoughts together which are sundered by this barrier of belonging to different personal minds. . . . Everyone will recognize this to be true, so long as the existence of *something* corresponding to the term 'personal mind' is all that is insisted on, without any particular view of its nature being implied. On these terms the personal self rather than the thought might be treated as the immediate datum in psychology. The universal conscious fact is not 'feelings and thoughts exist,' but 'I think' and 'I feel.' No psychology, at any rate, can question the *existence* of personal selves. Thoughts connected as we feel them to be connected are *what we mean* by personal selves. (pp. 20–21, italics in the original)

The second general characteristic of consciousness, according to James, is that it is continually changing.

> What I wish to lay stress on is this, that *no state* [of consciousness] *once gone can recur and be identical with what it was before.* Now we are seeing, now hearing; now reasoning, now willing; now recollecting, now expecting; now loving, now hating; and in a hundred other ways we know our minds to be alternately engaged. (p. 21, italics in the original)

The third characteristic of the Jamesian consciousness is that it is "sensibly continuous" (p. 19). That is, it seems to flow through time. James expressed this in a brief paragraph that, much like the opening paragraph of John Watson's so-called 'behaviorist manifesto' (Chapter 18), is quoted in full in virtually every history of psychology text.

> Consciousness, then, does not appear to itself chopped up into bits. Such words as 'chain' or 'train' do not describe it fitly as it presents itself in the

first instance. It is nothing jointed; it flows. A 'river' or 'stream' are the metaphors by which it is most naturally described. *In talking of it hereafter, let us call it the stream of thought, of consciousness, or of subjective life.* (p. 26, italics in the original) [note: James included this identical paragraph in his longer book, *The Principles*]

The fourth attribute of consciousness is that it "is interested in some parts of its object to the exclusion of others" (p. 19). This was James's way of introducing the topic of selective attention. Note the importance of the self again in this passage. James emphasized how things that are especially meaningful to us will influence our attention.

> The phenomena of selective attention and of deliberate will are of course patent examples of this choosing activity. But few of us are aware how incessantly it is at work.... [W]e do far more than emphasize things, and unite some, and keep others apart. We actually *ignore* most of the things before us....
>
> We notice only those sensations which are signs to us of things, which happen practically or aesthetically to interest us, to which we therefore give substantive names, and which we exalt to this exclusive status of independence and dignity.... Let four men take a tour of Europe. One will bring home only picturesque impressions—costumes and colors, parks and views and works of architecture, pictures and statues. To another all this will be non-existent; and distances and prices, populations and drainage-arrangements, door- and window fastenings, and other useful statistics will take their place. A third will give a rich account of the theatres, restaurants, and public halls, and naught besides; whilst the fourth will perhaps have been so wrapped in his own subjective broodings as to be able to tell little more than a few names of places through which he passed. Each has selected, out of the same mass presented objects, those which suited his private interest and has made his experience thereby. (pp. 37–40)

The Jamesian consciousness, then, is not a static collection of basic ideas, held together by associations, but an active, continuous stream of experiences, intensely personal, ever changing, and selective.

ON EMOTION

If you look back at the emotion chapter in your general psychology text, it is highly likely there will be a section on theories of emotion and the first one listed will be the James-Lange theory. The theory is not by any means the sole contribution of William James to psychology, but it is one that continues to have relevance for modern research on emotion. It is called the James-Lange theory because a Dutch physiologist, Carl Lange, proposed a similar theory at about the same time.

James began his chapter by distinguishing emotions from instincts. The former he referred to as tendencies to feel, while the latter were tendencies to act. He recognized that emotions had bodily "expression," however, so the distinction was not absolutely clear-cut. He then distinguished between the "coarser" emotions (e.g., anger, fear, joy, grief) from the "subtler" ones (e.g., aesthetic appreciation of art), but he had a longstanding aversion to classification schemes, so he refused to go any further in categorizing the emotions, writing that he would prefer to "read verbal descriptions of the shapes of rocks on a New Hampshire farm" (James, 1892/1961, p. 242). Instead, James proposed to look for general principles about emotion, with a focus on the coarser ones.

> **The feeling, in the coarser emotions, results from the bodily expression**. Our natural way of thinking about these coarser emotions is that the mental perception of some fact excites the mental affection called the emotion, and that this latter state of mind gives rise to the bodily expression. My theory, on the contrary, is that *the bodily changes follow directly the perception of the exciting fact, and that our feeling of the same changes as they occur IS the emotion*. Common-sense says, we lose our fortune, are sorry and weep, we meet a bear, are frightened and run; we are insulted by a rival, are angry and strike. The hypothesis here to be defended says that this order of sequence is incorrect, that the one mental state is not immediately induced by the other, that the bodily manifestations must first be interposed between, and that the more rational statement is that we feel sorry because we cry, angry because we strike, afraid because we tremble, and not that we cry, strike, or tremble because we are sorry, angry, or fearful, as the case may be. Without the bodily states following on the perception, the latter would be purely cognitive in form, pale, colorless, destitute of emotional warmth. We might then see the bear and judge it best to run, receive the insult and deem it right to strike, but we should not actually feel afraid or angry. (pp. 242–243, boldface and italics in the original)

This paragraph might seem vaguely familiar—portions of it are often quoted in introductory textbooks. After beginning with such a bold assertion, he spent the remainder of the chapter defending it. He began with some anecdotal examples, including an autobiographical one, that supported his case.

> To begin with, *particular perceptions certainly do produce wide-spread bodily effects by a sort of immediate physical influence, antecedent to the arousal of an emotion or emotional idea*. In listening to poetry, drama, or heroic narrative we are often surprised at the cutaneous shiver which like a sudden wave flows over us, and at the heartswelling and the lachrymal effusion that unexpectedly catch us at intervals. In hearing music the same is even more strikingly true. If we abruptly see a dark moving form in the woods, our heart stops beating, and we catch our breath instantly and before any particular idea of danger can arise. If our friend goes near to the edge of a precipice, we get the well-known feeling of "all-overishness," and we shrink back, although we positively *know* him to be safe, and have no distinct imagination of his fall. The writer well remembers his astonishment, when a boy of seven or eight, at fainting when he saw a horse bled. The blood was in a bucket, with a stick in it, and, if memory does not deceive him, he stirred it round and saw it drip from the stick with no feeling save that of childish curiosity. Suddenly the world grew black before his eyes, his ears began to buzz, and he knew no more. He had never heard of the sight of blood producing faintness or sickness, and he had so little repugnance to it,

and so little apprehension of any other sort of danger from it, that even at that tender age, as he well remembers, he could not help wondering how the mere physical presence of a pailful of crimson fluid could occasion in him such formidable bodily effects. (pp. 243–244, italics in the original)

James's argument was that the bodily changes that are the emotions are felt immediately, prior to the awareness of a cognitively recognizable emotion: Our heart pounds before we feel fearful. He also argued that we recognize different emotions because each one is associated with a unique pattern of bodily action.

When worried by any slight trouble, one may find that the focus of one's bodily consciousness is the contraction, often quite inconsiderable, of the eyes and brows. When momentarily embarrassed, it is something in the pharynx that compels either a swallow, a clearing of the throat, or a slight cough; and so on for as many more instances as might be named. The various permutations of which these organic changes are susceptible make it abstractly possible that no shade of emotion should be without a bodily reverberation as unique, when taken in its totality, as is the mental mood itself. (p. 245)

Research on the physiology of the emotions was not sufficiently advanced for James to realize that the preceding idea was a fatal flaw for his theory. For James-Lange to work, each emotion must have its own unique pattern of bodily reaction, and be recognized as such by the person experiencing the emotion. We now know that this is simply not the case. Rather, although there are well-documented physiological differences among many of the emotions, most strong emotions are accompanied by similar patterns of physiological arousal in the autonomic nervous system. There is no question, however, that the emotions are closely tied to bodily arousal. James drove the point home by asking the reader to imagine the opposite.

I now proceed to urge the vital point of my whole theory, which is this: *If we fancy some strong emotion, and then try to abstract from our consciousness of it all the feeling of its bodily symptoms, we find we have nothing left behind*, no "mind-stuff" out of which the emotion can be constituted, and that a cold and neutral state of intellectual perception is all that remains. . . . What kind of an emotion of fear would be left if the feeling neither of quickened heartbeats nor of shallow breathing, neither of trembling lips nor of weakened limbs, neither of goose-flesh nor of visceral stirrings, were present, it is quite impossible for me to think. Can one fancy the state of rage and picture no ebullition in the chest, no flushing of the face, no dilation of the nostrils, no clenching of the teeth, no impulse to vigorous action, but in their stead limp muscles, calm breathing, and a placid face? The present writer, for one, certainly cannot. The rage is as completely evaporated as the sensation of its so-called manifestations, and the only thing that can possibly be supposed to take its place is some cold-blooded and dispassionate judicial sentence, confined entirely to the intellectual realm, to the effect that a certain person or persons merit chastisement for their sins. In like manner of grief: what would it be without its tears, its sobs, its suffocation of the heart, its pang in the breast-bone? A feelingless cognition that certain circumstances are deplorable, and nothing more. Every passion in turn tells the same story.

A disembodied human emotion is a sheer nonentity. The more closely I scrutinize my states, the more persuaded I become that whatever 'coarse' affections and passions I have are in very truth constituted by, and made up of, those bodily changes which we ordinarily call their expression or consequence; and the more it seems to me that, if I were to become corporeally anesthetic, I should be excluded from the life of the affections, harsh and tender alike, and drag out an existence of merely cognitive or intellectual form. (pp. 246–247, italics in the original)

One of James's consistent attributes was his tendency to think pragmatically. In the case of emotions, practical application was a natural consequence of another argument for his theory.

If our theory be true, a necessary corollary of it ought to be this: that any voluntary and cold-blooded arousal of the so-called manifestations of a special emotion should give us the emotion itself. Now within the limits in which it can be verified, experience corroborates rather than disproves this inference. Everyone knows how panic is increased by flight, and how the giving way to the symptoms of grief or anger increases those passions themselves. Each fit of sobbing makes the sorrow more acute, and calls forth another fit stronger still, until at last repose only ensues with lassitude and with the apparent exhaustion of the machinery. In rage, it is notorious how we "work ourselves up" to a climax by repeated outbreaks of expression. Refuse to express a passion, and it dies. Count ten before venting your anger, and its occasion seems ridiculous. Whistling to keep up courage is no mere figure of speech. On the other hand, sit all day in a moping posture, sigh, and reply to everything with a dismal voice, and your melancholy lingers. There is no more valuable precept in moral education than this, as all who have experience know: if we wish to conquer undesirable emotional tendencies in ourselves, we must assiduously, and in the first instance cold-bloodedly, go through the *outward movements* of those contrary dispositions which we prefer to cultivate. The reward of persistency will infallibly come, in the fading out of the sullenness or depression, and the advent of real cheerfulness and kindliness in the stead. Smooth the brow, brighten the eye, contract the dorsal rather than the ventral aspect of the frame, and speak in a major key, pass the genial compliment, and your heart must be frigid indeed if it do not gradually thaw! (pp. 249–250, italics in the original)

The idea of making emotions occur by deliberately producing specific bodily reactions has been supported by some twentieth-century research on emotions. People whose facial muscles have been arranged to match certain emotions often experience those very emotions, at least to a degree. For example, in one clever study, subjects held pens either between their teeth (similar muscles as those used for smiling) or with their lips (muscles for frowning), and were asked to rate cartoons. The cartoons were rated as funnier in the "teeth" condition (Strack, Martin, & Strepper, 1988).

After publishing his two famous texts, *The Principles* and *The Briefer Course*, William James began losing interest in psychology. In 1892, tired of being involved in the Harvard laboratory, he convinced Hugo Münsterberg (Chapter 28) to come from Germany and run it. Although he became one of only two people ever to be elected to the Presidency of the American Psychological Association twice (1894 and 1902; the other person was G. Stanley Hall) and, as mentioned earlier, he achieved great status among his psychologist peers, his interests shifted increasingly to philosophy and religion in his later years. James produced books as well known in those disciplines as his *Principles* was in psychology (e.g., *Varieties of Religious Experience* in 1902 and *Pragmatism* in 1907).

CONCEPT REVIEW QUESTIONS

1. According to James, what are the fundamental attributes of consciousness?
2. What were the arguments used by James to support his theory of emotion?
3. What was the fatal flaw in the James-Lange theory of emotion?

DISCUSSION QUESTION

1. Describe the Jamesian criticism of a structuralist approach to the study of consciousness. Show how his "stream" metaphor is a direct assault on a structuralist account. After you read the Titchener chapter (Chapter 11), consider how Titchener might respond to James.

CHAPTER 10

MARY WHITON CALKINS (1863–1930): EXPERIMENTS ON ASSOCIATION

In the late 1880s, the administration at Wellesley College, a women's college in Massachusetts that had been created in 1875, decided that the college should offer instruction in the "new" laboratory psychology that was making a stir in academic circles. Mary Whiton Calkins was a young instructor in Greek at the time, and she had expressed interest in expanding her teaching areas. Upon the recommendation of a colleague, she was given leave time to gain expertise and, in the fall of 1890, found herself in a seminar at Harvard with none other than William James (previous chapter), whose massive *Principles of Psychology* (James, 1890) had just been published (Furumoto, 1979). Gaining entrance was not easy. Despite vigorous support from James, the Harvard administration had a strict policy of not admitting women, and Calkins was only grudgingly allowed to attend as a "guest." This seminar with James, which originally included five students, was quickly reduced to one when the four males dropped out. Hence, Calkins' introduction to psychology was a one-on-one seminar with William James.

After completing the seminar, Calkins went back to Wellesley, and then returned to Harvard in 1892 (again as a guest), this time to study laboratory techniques firsthand in the laboratory, under the direction of Hugo Münsterberg (Chapter 28). Calkins worked with Münsterberg for three years, combining the work with her teaching at Wellesley for two years, and then taking a year leave from Wellesley (1894–1895) to finish the work, a series of studies on association. The work was notable for its use of what would become a common technique in memory research, the *paired associates* method (Furumoto, 1991). Her experiments amounted to a doctoral dissertation, which she defended as other doctoral students would have done. Despite high praise from both James and Münsterberg, however, Harvard refused to grant her a Ph.D.—after all, she was only a "guest."

Undeterred, Calkins published her work in two issues of *Psychological Review* (Calkins, 1894; Calkins, 1896), and in a *Psychological Review*

Excerpts from: Calkins, M. W. (1896). Association: An essay analytic and experimental. *Psychological Review Monograph Supplement, 1*, No. 2.

Monograph (Calkins, 1896) that summarized everything. The excerpt in this chapter is from the 1896 monograph. She opened it with a discussion of methodological considerations.

> Experimental investigation may best supplement the purely introspective study of the nature of association by describing in relatively concrete terms the probable direction of trains of associated images. To this end there is necessary such a consideration of the so-called suggestibility of objects of consciousness as shall answer the question: what one of the numberless images which might conceivably follow upon the present percept or image will actually be associated with it?
>
> Ordinary self-observation has long recognized that the readily associated objects are the 'interesting' ones, and has further enumerated frequency, recency, vividness or impressiveness, and primacy ... as the factors of interest, and therefore the conditions of association. A given object, then, is likely to be suggested by one with which it was frequently, recently or vividly connected, and by one with which it stood at the beginning of a series. ...
>
> The relative significance of frequency, recency, primacy and vividness, was studied in about 2,200 experiments. ... There were 17 subjects, no one of whom assisted in more than 275 nor in less than 40 experiments; and the average number was 130 for each subject. ... All the subjects were entirely or comparatively ignorant of the aims and the problems of the investigation, which was not discussed until the conclusion of the work. ... Constant notes were kept of subjective experiences, but have not been reported, for none of them tended to modify the conclusions drawn from the experiments themselves except where the occurrence of natural associations made it necessary to reject entirely the results of particular experiments. (pp. 36–37)

Today, we normally use the term "experiment" to refer to a study as a whole, but Calkins used the term as it was used in the 1890s, to refer to what we would call a "trial" today. Hence, the 2,200 "experiments" were actually that many separate trials, where a trial was an event in which subjects studied a set of materials one time, and then performed a recall task. Note also that, long before APA codes of ethics, Calkins thought to mention that her subjects were debriefed at the end of the study.

Calkins used both visual and auditory means of presenting the materials to be learned. With visual presentation, subjects were shown a color patch (referred to in paired associate learning as the stimulus term) and a number (the response term). In a written recall task, they would be shown the color patch and had to respond with the number. In different sets of experiments, the stimulus-response pairs were presented either successively or simultaneously, in order to examine an old philosophical distinction between two types of associations—temporal and spatial. For the British associationist philosophers (e.g., David Hartley), *temporal* associations developed when two events were experienced one immediately after another, while *spatial* associations were formed when two events were experienced at the same time. Here is Calkins' description of a series of trials ("experiments") that involved *successive* presentation.

The method of the visual experiments was as follows: the subjects, of whom two to eight were present at one time, sat before a white screen large enough to shield the conductor of the experiment. Through an opening, 10 cm. square, a color was shown for four seconds, followed immediately by a numeral, usually black on a white ground, for the same time. After a pause of about eight seconds, during which the subject looked steadily at the white background, another color was shown, succeeded at once by a second numeral, each exposed for four seconds. The pause of eight seconds followed, and the series of 7, 10 or 12 pairs of quickly succeeding color and numeral was continued in the same way. At the close a series was shown of the same colors in altered order, and the subject was asked, as each color appeared, to write down the suggested numerals if any such occurred. The pause between the combination-series, in which colors and numerals appeared together, and the test-series, in which the colors only were shown, was eight seconds in the case of the short series and four to six seconds in the case of the longer. Color and numeral were placed together in their position behind the opening of the screen, the numeral at first concealed by the color, which was then slipped out. There was thus a merely momentary pause between the appearance of color and of numeral. During the eight-second pauses the opening was filled by a white ground, 1/2 cm. behind the screen. The subject thus saw nothing in the opening except this white ground, or the color, which filled the whole square, or the printed numeral; the movements of the experimenter were entirely concealed. The time was at first kept by following the ticks of a watch suspended close to the experimenter's ear; but in the last 1,200 tests by listening to the beats of a metronome, which rung a bell every four seconds; the metronome was enclosed in a sound-proof box, so that the subjects were not disturbed by the beats, which reached the experimenter through a rubber tube. . . .

In the first group of experiments, some one color appeared several times in each series, once in an unimportant position with any chance numeral, but also once or more in some emphasized connection-either repeatedly with the same numeral (a 'frequent' combination), or at the very beginning or very end of a series (cases of 'primacy' and of 'recency'), or with a numeral of unusual size or color (an instance of 'vividness').

The following are representative series:

Visual series 89. Frequency (3: 12)

I. (Combination Series.) Green, 47; brown, 73; *violet*, 61 *(f)*; light grey, 58; *violet*, 61 *(f)*; orange, 84; blue, 12; *violet*, 61 *(f)*; medium grey, 39; *violet, 26 (n);* light green, 78; strawberry, 52.

II. (Test Series.) Blue, light grey, strawberry, green, *violet (f)*, orange, brown, medium grey, light green. (pp. 37–38, italics in the original)

When examining frequency, then, Calkins paired the color violet with the number 61 on three occasions in the series, and with the number 26 one time. If frequency was an important factor in the formation of associations, subjects would respond with "61" on the test series, when shown the violet color patch, and not "26." Calkins allowed subjects to respond with both numbers (61 and 26) and her results were reported that way. Here are typical series for assessing vividness, recency, and primacy.

Visual Series, 213. Vividness.

I. Brown, 34; peacock, 65; orange, 51; *green, 792 (v);* blue, 19;
   violet, 48; *green,* 27 *(n);* grey, 36; strawberry, 87; dark red, 54.

II. Blue, grey, dark red, brown, *green (v),* orange, strawberry, grey,
   peacock.

Visual Series, 127. Recency.

I. Peacock, 46; *blue, 38 (n);* brown, 51; grey, 74; yellow, 29;
   blue, 52 (r).

II. Grey, *blue (r),* peacock, yellow, strawberry, brown.

Visual Series, 69b. Primacy.

I. *Light red, 48 (p);* strawberry, 13; violet, 60; grey, 82; orange, 29;
   light red, 31 (n); yellow, 53; green, 94; light violet, 17; blue, 69.

II. Green, grey, *light red (p),* light violet, strawberry, orange,
   violet, yellow, blue. (pp. 38–39, italics in the original)

In a manner similar to the way she tested for frequency, Calkins examined vividness by comparing an unusual number (three digits—792) with a usual one (two digits—27). Recency compared pairs (blue—52) at the end of the list (i.e., most recent) with another pair in the list (blue—38); primacy compared pairs at the beginning of the series (light red—48) with another pair (light red—31).

And the results? First, Calkins provided a baseline measure of memory performance by reporting the percent correct of the pairs that were not the critical ones in a given series (e.g., the ones not involved in an assessment of frequency).

To gain a basis of comparison about 1,300 series of all types, and from the records of all the subjects, have been considered as a mere memory test, leaving out of account, for the time being, the emphasized combinations which they contain. About *one-fourth of the ordinary combinations in the longer series* (10 to 12 pairs), *and one-third in the shorter series* (7 pairs) *are remembered.* This is shown in

Table I. Correct Associations

Series	Number of Series	Possible Correct Associations	Actual Correct Associations Full	Half	%
Long	867	7672	1728	558	26.1
Short	444	2144	674	170	35.2

(p. 39, italics in the original)

Thus, not counting the pairs involved in the assessment of frequency, vividness, recency, and primacy, subjects, when given the color on the test series, responded with the correct number 26.1% of the time when the list had ten or twelve pairs, and 35.2% of the time with list of seven pairs. She did the calculation of the first one as follows: out of 7,672 possible correct responses, subjects recalled both numbers of a response correctly 1,728 times, and one of the two numbers of a response 558 times. For these half-correct responses, she gave half credit. Thus, the 26.1% (26.2% actually) comes from adding together 1,728 and half of 558 (i.e., 279), and then dividing the total by 7,672.

Having established a baseline, Calkins then compared the effects of frequency, vividness, recency, and primacy. Here are her data for the frequency factor, where a pair was repeated either two or three times in a list of twelve pairs.

The tabulated results of the experiments on frequency as a condition of association are as follows:

Table II. Frequency, Visual

	Number of	Both			Normal Only			Frequent Only		
	Series	Full	Half	%	Full	Half	%	Full	Half	%
Freq. 3:12	200	37	3	19.2	7	9	5.7	83	12	44.5
Freq. 2:12	143	16	7	13.6	8	16	11.2	29	3	21.3

(p. 39, italics in the original)

The table shows the number of those cases in which both numerals were recalled, then the number of cases in which the color suggested only the numeral with which it had been but once associated, and in the last group the number of times in which that numeral was recalled with which the color had been twice or three times combined. . . . The comparison of the 'frequent' with the unemphasized, that is the 'normal,' shows that, with repetitions amounting to one in four [i.e., 3 out of 12], the *repeated numeral is associated in 63.7% of the possible cases* (44.5 + 19.2%), *the normal in only 24.9%* (5.7 + 19.2%). . . .

The comparison of both these per cents. with that representing the likelihood of recall for such long series (Table I.) leads to the same conclusion. *The frequently combined numeral is associated more than twice as often* (63.7% instead of 26.1%), while *the unemphasized numeral is associated slightly less often, than the average* (24.9% instead of 26.1%). . . .

It is noticeable, also, that the influence of repetition is much lowered when the 'frequent' combination appears twice only instead of three times. The second line of Table II. gives the results; the 'frequent' numeral is recalled in 34.9% of the series (21.3 + 13.6%) which is only 8.8% more than the ordinary average of associations without repetition [i.e., 26.1], and 28.8% less than the proportion of three times repeated associations. (pp. 39–41, italics in the original)

After dealing with frequency, Calkins reported the results for vividness, recency, and primacy over four pages. She found that each factor enhanced memory, but not to the extent that frequency did. She then examined the results for those trials in which the stimulus term (color patch) and response term (number) were presented simultaneously rather than sequentially. The same basic results occurred—all factors enhanced memory, frequency most of all.

These general results have been amplified, and at the same time verified, by introducing series in which the connected color and numeral were simultaneously shown. This method might have been used more often, since the simultaneous combination of stimuli is perhaps more common in ordinary experience than the successive; but the experiments of the successive type, in which the combination of color and numeral is emphasized by the long pause between each pair, were employed as affording a close comparison between the visual and the auditory series. So far, however, as these subjects are concerned, the results of the simultaneous series are so closely parallel with those of the successive ones that no characteristic differences appear. (p. 46)

In her experiments with auditory presentation of stimuli, Calkins substituted nonsense syllables for colors as stimulus terms; numbers remained as the response terms. She obtained results similar to ones resulting from the visual presentation.

All the varieties of experiment which have so far been described, except those in primacy, were repeated with nonsense syllables and numerals, as the association-elements, both pronounced to the subjects. These series were arranged in pairs of a nonsense syllable and a numeral each, with four seconds allowed to the pronunciation of each pair, and four seconds interval both between the pairs and between the two parts of the series. One series will serve as illustration of all.

Series 335b. Vivid, Auditory.

I. Zet, 24; Kip, 62; Tox, 96; *Wez, 319 (v);* Vit, 38; Lup, 45; Nuk, 29; *Wez, 73 (n);* Vab, 57; Muv, 41.

II. Vit, Kip, Muv, Zet, *Wez*, Nuk, Lup, Vab, Tox.

The results of the *experiments are generally parallel with those of the visual tests*, with certain suggestive variations which will be noticed later. . . .

The records of the recency experiments show *the very striking effect of auditory recency*. There are no individual variations from the general type, and *the number of cases in which the normal* is *remembered does not rise above one-eighth*. In about half the records the 'recent' is wholly or partially remembered in every case.

Auditory experiments to determine the effectiveness of primacy were undertaken, but were soon discontinued because they showed from the beginning the insignificance of this factor in long series. In the short auditory series, however, as in the visual, the first position proved very important: the first numeral was associated in 38.4% of the possible cases, that is, in 14% more than the average number. . . .

The general relations of the auditory to the visual series appear in the next table in which only per cents. are given (pp. 47–50, italics in the original)

In her table, more easily summarized than portrayed in full, Calkins found comparable results for visual vs. auditory presentation, with two main exceptions. First, as she indicated, she was not able to produce much of a primacy effect with auditory presentation. Second, and very striking, she found a much larger recency effect for auditory presentation (82.5% recall) than for visual presentation (54%). This is essentially the first description of what memory researchers later in the century referred to as a "modality" effect (Madigan & O'Hara, 1992), greater recency for an auditory than a visual "modality."

In her final set of experiments, using the method of sequential presentation with colors and numbers, Calkins compared different factors within the same list.

In showing that frequency, vividness, primacy and recentness are conditions of association these experiments have so far, of course, merely substantiated ordinary observation. The real purpose of the investigation is attained only by a comparison of these factors. Already it has appeared that the per cent. of correct 'frequency' associations is slightly the largest, and that recency is the principle of the combination in the next greatest number of cases. In order, however, to carry out the comparison under like conditions, these principles of combination were compared within the same series. To this end, long 'successive' series were arranged in which the significance of frequency was contrasted with that of vividness by showing a color three times with the same two-digit numeral (f) and once with a three-digit numeral (v); others, in which the color three times shown with a numeral (f) appeared also at the first of the series with another numeral (p). Short 'successive' series were formed in which the last color (r) had appeared once before with a three-digit numeral (v), or at the very beginning of the series (p), or twice before with a repeated numeral (f). (pp. 51–52)

Calkins then presented her results in great detail over the next four pages. In general, and not too surprising given the initial set of experiments, frequency emerged as the most potent factor determining the strength of associations. Calkins summed up, ending with a hint at a practical application of her results.

From this mass of figures a few conclusions emerge into prominence. Some of these have been already formulated, but the more important ones may be briefly stated again.

Frequency has been the most constant condition of suggestibility. The proportion of the frequent as compared with the normal associations is one-tenth greater than that of the vivid or of the recent. When directly compared with the vivid and the recent the proportion is still greater, though the number of associations with the contrasted numeral is larger than that of the associations with an ordinary one, because of the tendency of the repetition to accentuate the compared factor.

This significance of frequency is rather surprising. For though everybody recognizes the importance of repetition in forming associations, we are yet more accustomed to 'account for' these by referring to recent or to impressive combinations. The possibility that the prominence of frequency in our results is not fairly representative of ordinary trains of association is strengthened by the fact that it is contrasted with forms of vividness which are only two or three of many, and which do not approach the impressiveness, for instance, of richly emotional experiences. But this does not affect the importance of frequency as a corrective influence. Granted a sufficient number of repetitions, it seems possible to supplement, if not actually to supplant, associations which have been formed through impressive or through recent experiences. Moreover, the trustworthiness of the ordinary observation, which relegates frequency to a comparatively unimportant place among the factors of suggestibility, may be seriously questioned: I have found many cases, during experiments in free association in which the subject, asked to explain the association, does not always mention repetition, even when it has obviously occurred, but seems, as it were, to take it for granted. The prominence of frequency is of course of grave importance, for it means the possibility of exercising some control over the life of the imagination and of definitely combating harmful or troublesome associations. (pp. 55–56, italics in the original)

After completing her research on association, Calkins returned to Wellesley, where she remained for the rest of her prominent career. In 1905, she became the first woman elected to the presidency of the American Psychological Association (fourteenth president overall). Like her mentor, William James, she turned more to philosophy in her later years, and became the first woman elected president of *both* APAs (psychological and philosophical). She retired in 1929 (with no Ph.D. but several honorary doctorates) and died of cancer a year later.

CONCEPT REVIEW QUESTIONS

1. What were the factors that led Calkins to undertake her study of association?
2. Describe exactly how Calkins used the paired associates method to investigate association.
3. What were four factors she investigated? Pick any one and show how her method would have assessed that factor.

DISCUSSION QUESTION

1. What did Calkins conclude was the most critical factor affecting the formation of associations and what were the implications of her conclusion for everyday life? Is her conclusion in any way still valid?

CHAPTER 11

E. B. TITCHENER (1867–1927): A STRUCTURAL PSYCHOLOGY

Edward Bradford Titchener was a towering figure in the early history of experimental psychology. He was British by birth, but spent all of his postdoctoral life in the United States, lording over the psychology program at Cornell University. He was an undergraduate at Oxford University, and then traveled to Germany to earn a Ph.D. from Wundt (Chapter 5) at Leipzig in 1892. He came to Cornell in that same year. There he developed a world-class laboratory of experimental psychology and contributed much to our understanding of basic cognitive processes, especially those concerning sensation and perception.

For Titchener, at least in his early, more productive years, the primary goal for psychology was to analyze human conscious experience into its basic elements or structural components. Thus, Titchener's psychology was the science of the structure of the human mind, and the purpose of research was to determine the basic structural elements. A central method was that of systematic introspection, a close analysis of mental content occurring during the course of experiments on cognition. In contrast to Titchener's structuralist view, the majority of psychologists in the United States were more amenable to a position called functionism—in the next chapter you will read an excerpt from one of this school's best-known papers, an APA presidential address by James R. Angell.

Titchener's *Text-Book of Psychology*, which first appeared in 1909 and was dedicated to his first physiology teacher, Burdon-Sanderson of Oxford, provides insight into the world of psychology according to Titchener. Boring (1927/1961) considered it "the only thorough account of Titchener's psychology that we have in single covers" (p. 259). The following excerpts are from the first chapter of a 1916 reprinting of the book. Titchener's opening chapter outlined his views on the nature of the discipline of psychology. He started with some general observations about science, then began describing psychology by comparing the viewpoints of psychologists and physicists, opening with a sentence that reveals

Excerpts from: Titchener, E. B. (1909). *A text-book of psychology*. New York: Macmillan.

his debt to British empiricist philosophers, who believed the mind to be a blank slate at birth, with experience generating our knowledge of the world.

All human knowledge is derived from human experience; there is no other source of knowledge. But human experience ... may be considered from different points of view. Suppose that we take two points of view, as far as possible apart, and discover for ourselves what experience looks like in the two cases. First, we will regard experience as altogether independent of any particular person; we will assume that it goes on whether or not anyone is there to have it. Secondly, we will regard experience as altogether dependent upon the particular person; we will assume that it goes on only when someone is there to have it. We shall hardly find standpoints more diverse. What are the differences in experience, as viewed from them?

Take, to begin with, the three things that you first learn about in physics: space, time and mass. Physical space, which is the space of geometry and astronomy and geology, is constant, always and everywhere the same. Its unit is 1 cm., and the cm. has precisely the same value wherever and whenever it is applied. Physical time is similarly constant; and its constant unit is the 1 sec. Physical mass is constant; its unit, the 1 gr., is always and everywhere the same. Here we have experience of space, time and mass considered as independent of the person who experiences them. Change, then, to the point of view which brings the experiencing person into account. The two vertical lines [below] are physically equal; they measure alike in units of 1 cm. To you, who see them, they are not equal. The hour that you spend in the waiting-room of a village station and the hour that you spend in watching an amusing play are physically equal; they measure alike in units of 1 sec. To you, the one hour goes slowly, the other quickly; they are not equal. Take two circular cardboard boxes of different diameter (say, 2 cm. and 8 cm.), and pour sand into them until they both weigh, say, 50 gr. The two masses are physically equal; placed on the pans of a balance, they will hold the beam level. To you, as you lift them in your two hands, or raise them in turn by the same hand, the box of the smaller diameter is considerably the heavier. Here we have the experience of space, time and mass considered as dependent upon the experiencing person. It is the same experience that we were discussing just now. But our first point of view gives us facts and laws of physics; our second gives us facts and laws of psychology. . . .

We find, then, a great difference in the aspect of experience, according as it is viewed from the one or the other of our different standpoints. It is the same experience all through; physics and psychology deal with the same stuff, the same material; the sciences are separated simply—and sufficiently—by their point of view. (pp. 6–8)

After making this distinction between experience as independent of (physics) or dependent upon (psychology) the individual, Titchener addressed the question of the relationship between mental and physical events—the ancient mind-body problem. First, he rejected the "common sense" view of the mind as a separate entity somehow residing within us and directing our lives by interacting with the body. He traced that idea to the French philosopher Descartes (Chapter 1). Instead, Titchener argued, the mind should be understood as "the sum-total of human experience considered as dependent upon the experiencing person" (p. 9), and its relationship to the body, he argued, is best conceived of as a "psychophysical parallelism." Notice how Titchener tied the parallelism to his dependent/independent distinction.

Common sense says that we cry because we are sorry, laugh because we are amused, run because we are frightened; . . . Mind influences body and body influences mind. Our own position has been that mind and body, the subject-matter of psychology and the subject-matter of physiology, are simply two aspects of the same world of experience. They cannot influence each other, because they are not separate and independent things. . . . This doctrine of the relation of mind to body is known as the doctrine of psychophysical parallelism: the common sense doctrine is that of interaction.

From the point of view of psychophysical parallelism, then, it is not strictly true to say that we cry because we are sorry. If we look at the whole experience under its independent aspect, we find that certain physical events, certain stimuli, affect the body; they set up in the body, and especially in the nervous system, certain physical changes; these changes cause the secretion of tears. This is an exhaustive account of the experience, considered as independent of the experiencing person. If we look at the experience under its dependent aspect, we find that our consciousness has been invaded by grief or remorse or some kindred emotion. The two sets of events, physical and mental, are parallel, but they do not interfere with each other. (pp. 13–14)

Titchener next considered the distinction between mind and consciousness. Then, without mentioning William James by name, he directly addressed James's famous stream of consciousness metaphor (Chapter 9), pointing out that a precise science of consciousness is possible even if no two conscious moments are exactly the same.

We shall therefore take mind and consciousness to mean the same thing. But as we have the two different words, and it is convenient to make some distinction between them, we shall speak of mind when we mean the sum-total of mental processes occurring in the life-time of an individual, and we shall speak of consciousness when we mean the sum-total of mental processes occurring *now*, at any given 'present' time. Consciousness will thus be a section, a division, of the mind-stream. . . .

While, therefore, the subject-matter of psychology is mind, the direct object of psychological study is always a consciousness. In strictness, we can never observe the same consciousness twice over; the stream of mind flows on, never to return. Practically, we can observe a particular consciousness as often as we wish, since mental processes group themselves in the same way, show the same pattern of arrangement, whenever the organism is placed under the same circumstances. Yesterday's high tide will never recur, and yesterday's consciousness will never recur; but we have a science of psychology, as we have a science of oceanography. (pp. 18–19, italics in the original)

This last paragraph, especially the point about observing a particular consciousness "as often as we wish," led directly into a discussion of method. First, Titchener outlined the essence of any experimental procedure.

Scientific method may be summed up in the single word 'observation'; the only way to work in science is to observe those phenomena which form the subject-matter of science. And observation implies two things: attention to the phenomena, and record of the phenomena; that is, clear and vivid experience, and an account of the experience in words or formulas.

In order to secure clear experience and accurate report, science has recourse to experiment. An experiment is an observation that can be repeated, isolated and varied. The more frequently you can *repeat* an observation, the more likely you are to see clearly what is there and to describe accurately what you have seen. The more strictly you can *isolate* an observation, the easier does your task of observation become, and the less danger is there of your being led astray by irrelevant circumstances, or of placing emphasis on the wrong point. The more widely you can *vary* an observation, the more clearly will the uniformity of experience stand out, and the better is your chance of discovering laws. All experimental appliances, all laboratories and instruments, are provided and devised with this one end in view: that the student shall be able to repeat, isolate, and vary his observations. (pp. 19–20, italics in the original)

Next, Titchener outlined the essence of the method of introspection, which he believed was at the heart of experimental psychology. In essence, the procedure involved giving detailed reports of the conscious events occurring while completing some task (e.g., comparing the weights of two objects). Titchener began by describing simple reports, and then moved to more complicated situations, showing that they nonetheless fit into the "repeat, isolate, vary" framework.

Now let us take some cases in which the material of introspection is more complex. (1) Suppose that a word is called out to you, and that you are asked to observe the effect which this stimulus produces upon consciousness: how the word affects you, what ideas it calls up, and so forth. The observation may be repeated; it may be isolated—you may be seated in a dark and silent room, free from disturbances; and it may be varied—different words may be called out, the word may be flashed upon a screen instead of spoken, etc. Here, however, there seems to be a difference between introspection and inspection. The observer who is watching the course of a chemical reaction, or the movement of some microscopic creature, can jot down from moment to moment the different phases of the observed phenomenon. But if you try to report the changes in consciousness, while these changes are in progress, you interfere with consciousness; your translation of the mental experience into words introduces new factors into that experience itself. (2) Suppose, again, that you are observing a feeling or an emotion; a feeling of disappointment or annoyance, an emotion of anger or chagrin. Experimental control is still possible; situations may be arranged, in the psychological laboratory, such that these feelings may be repeated, isolated, and varied. But your observation of them interferes, even more seriously than before, with the course of consciousness. Cool consideration of an emotion is fatal to its very existence; your anger disappears, your disappointment evaporates, as you examine it. (pp. 21–22)

Thus, Titchener was aware of the fundamental problem of introspection— it is impossible to have a conscious experience and reflect on it at the same time. To deal with the problem, he suggested three solutions. First, rely on memory.

To overcome this difficulty of the introspective method, students of psychology are usually recommended to delay their observation until the process to be described has run its course, and then to call it back and describe it from memory. Introspection thus becomes retrospection; introspective examination becomes post mortem examination. (p. 22)

Titchener recognized that memory could be faulty, of course, so he argued that experiments could be repeated many times, with each repetition concentrating on a different piece of the experience.

There is, then, no reason why the observer to whom the word is called out, or in whom the emotion is set up, should not report at once upon the first stage of his experience: upon the immediate effect of the word, upon the beginnings of the emotive process. It is true that this report interrupts the observation. But, after the first stage has been accurately described, further observations may be taken, and the second, third and following stages similarly described; so that presently a complete report upon the whole experience is obtained. There is, in theory, some danger that the stages become artificially separated; consciousness is a flow, a process, and if we divide it up we run the risk of missing certain intermediate links. In practice, however, this danger has proved to be very small; and we may always have recourse to retrospection, and compare our partial results with our memory of the unbroken experience. Moreover, ... the practiced observer gets into an introspective habit, has the introspective attitude ingrained in his system; so that it is possible for him, not only to take mental notes while the observation is in progress, without interfering with consciousness, but even to jot down written notes, as the histologist does while his eye is still held to the ocular of the microscope. (pp. 22–23)

This last point is an important one, for it is part of the reason why Titchener insisted that introspective observers had to be highly trained. In effect, they were to become introspective machines, behaving so automatically that problems of memory and any biasing influences would presumably disappear. Training was also important to avoid what Titchener referred to as the *stimulus error*. This was a tendency to report events by describing the stimuli presented rather than the conscious experiences resulting from those stimuli. For instance, when observing a tree, a proper Titchenerian introspective description would include statements about the sensory elements present: shapes, colors, textures, and movements, along with the affective dimensions of pleasantness/unpleasantness and any accompanying images that came to mind when looking at the tree. Titchener believed that sensations, images, and affects were the fundamental structural elements of all human conscious experience, so an introspective account needed to include all three. To commit the stimulus error would be to report simply that you were observing a large "tree."

Titchener concluded the opening chapter of his *Text-Book* by discussing psychology's goals.

> Science seeks always to answer three questions in regards to its subject matter, the questions what, how, and why. What precisely, stripped of all complications and reduced to its lowest terms, is this subject-matter? How, then, does it come to appear as it does; how are its elements combined and arranged? And, finally, why does it appear now in just this particular combination or arrangements? All three questions are to be answered, if we are to have a science. . . .
>
> To answer the question 'what' is the task of analysis . . . The psychologist seeks, first of all, to analyse mental experience into its simplest components. He takes a particular consciousness and works over it again and again, phase by phase and process by process, until his analysis can go no further. He is left with certain mental processes which resist analysis, which are absolutely simple in nature, which cannot be reduced, even in part, to other processes. This work is continued, with other consciousnesses, until he is able to pronounce with some confidence upon the nature and number of elementary mental processes. Then he proceeds to the task of synthesis. He puts the elements together, under experimental conditions: first, perhaps, two elements of the same kind, then more of that kind, then elementary processes of diverse kinds: and he presently discerns that regularity and uniformity of occurrence which we have seen to be characteristic of all human experience. He thus learns to formulate the laws of connection of the elementary mental processes. If sensations of tone occur together, they blend or fuse; if sensations of colour occur side by side, they enhance one another: and all this takes place in a perfectly regular way, so that we can write out laws of tonal fusion and laws of colour contrast. (pp. 36–38)

To the goals of analysis (what) and synthesis (how), Titchener added the goal of explanation, which would be accomplished ultimately by understanding the operation of the nervous system. He then summed up.

> In fine, just as the method of psychology is, on all essential points, the method of the natural sciences, so is the problem of psychology essentially of the same sort as the problem of physics. The psychologist answers the question 'what' by analyzing mental experience into its elements. He answers the question 'how' by formulating the laws of connection of these elements. And he answers the question 'why' by explaining mental processes in terms of their parallel processes in the nervous system. His programme need not be carried out in this order: he may get the hint of a law before his analysis

is completed, and the discovery of a sense-organ may suggest the occurrence of certain elementary processes before he has found these processes by introspection. The three questions are intimately related, and an answer to any one helps towards the answers to the other two. The measure of our progress in scientific psychology is our ability to return satisfactory answers to all three. (p. 41)

Titchener spent a career attempting to realize his vision of psychology and, in so doing, made his major contribution—as much as anyone in psychology's history, Titchener was a champion of the importance of basic laboratory research as a way toward understanding human mental processes. As for his specific system of structuralism, it was not widely popular in the United States and it did not outlive him. By the time of Titchener's death in 1927, the ideal of basic research remained alive among American experimental psychologists, but introspection as a method had been shown to be fundamentally subjective (and therefore of questionable value for scientists), and researchers had moved on to a variety of topics beyond the structural analysis of human mental processes.

CONCEPT REVIEW QUESTIONS

1. Use the perceptual illusion reproduced by Titchener to illustrate his distinction between experience that was dependent on a person or independent of a person.

2. Describe the essence of all experimental procedure, according to Titchener.

3. What is introspection, and how did Titchener deal with the issues of introspection's subjectivity.

DISCUSSION QUESTION

1. Consider your current understanding of how psychology defines itself and how research in psychology occurs. How is it (a) similar to, and (b) different from Titchener's notion of the field?

CHAPTER 12

JAMES ROWLAND ANGELL (1869–1949): A FUNCTIONAL PSYCHOLOGY

In the traditional history and systems of psychology course, students learn that in psychology's early years, different "schools" of psychology emerged, each competing for the prize of being considered *the* school of thought that should guide the field. This notion vastly oversimplifies psychology's earliest years, but it is indeed the case that psychologists were aware of differences between those advocating, for example, a structural psychology, and those advocating, say, a functional psychology. The excerpt that follows deliberately contrasts structuralist and functionalist views, and advocates the latter. It is from an APA presidential address delivered by James Rowland Angell of the University of Chicago in December of 1906 and published the following year.

At the time of his election to the presidency of APA, Angell had been directing the psychology program at Chicago for two years, after having taught there since 1894, under the departmental leadership of John Dewey. Under Angell's guidance, Chicago became a center of the movement that came to be called *functionalism*, and his 1906 address was the first clear statement of functionalist ideals. Because it included a direct response to a paper published eight years earlier by E. B. Titchener (Chapter 11) (Titchener, 1898), the best-known advocate for a structuralist psychology, Angell's paper serves to contrast the two positions.

Angell began his address by arguing that it was inappropriate to consider functionalism a formal "school of thought." Rather, it was best thought of as a frame of mind, an attitude. Furthermore, it was not necessarily a new idea, but one with deep roots.

> Functional psychology is at the present moment little more than a point
> of view, a program, an ambition. It gains its vitality primarily perhaps as a
> protest against the exclusive excellence of another starting point for the study
> of the mind, and it enjoys for the time being at least the peculiar vigor which

Excerpts from: Angell, J. R. (1907). The province of functional psychology. *Psychological Review*, *14*, 61–91.

commonly attaches to Protestantism of any sort in its early stages before it has become respectable and orthodox. The time seems ripe to attempt a somewhat more precise characterization of the field of functional psychology than has as yet been offered. . . .

Whatever else it may be, functional psychology is nothing wholly new. In certain of its phases it is plainly discernible in the psychology of Aristotle and in its more modern garb it has been increasingly in evidence since Spencer wrote his *Psychology* and Darwin his *Origin of Species*. Indeed, as we shall soon see, its crucial problems are inevitably incidental to any serious attempt at understanding mental life. All that is peculiar to its present circumstances is a higher degree of self-consciousness than it possessed before, a more articulate and persistent purpose to organize its vague intentions into tangible methods and principles. (pp. 61–62)

Following this brief introduction, Angell drew a sharp contrast with structuralist thinking. One common theme of functionalist thinking was that it tried to understand the operation of mental processes as they occurred in everyday life, as opposed to an abstract analysis of the contents of consciousness, which functionalists considered highly artificial. That theme is evident in Angell's remarks here.

There is to be mentioned first the notion which derives most immediately from contrast with the ideals and purposes of structural psychology so-called. This involves the identification of functional psychology with the effort to discern and portray the typical *operations* of consciousness under actual life conditions, as over against the attempt to analyze and describe its elementary and complex *contents*. The structural psychology of sensation, *e.g.*, undertakes to determine the number and character of the various unanalyzable sensory materials, such as the varieties of color, tone, taste, etc. The functional psychology of sensation would on the other hand find its appropriate sphere of interest in the determination of the character of the various sense activities as differing in their *modus operandi* from one another and from other mental processes such as judging, conceiving, willing and the like. . . .

The more extreme and ingenuous conceptions of structural psychology seem to have grown out of an unchastened indulgence in what we may call the 'states of consciousness' doctrine. . . . If you adopt as your material for psychological analysis the isolated 'moment of consciousness,' it is very easy to become so absorbed in determining its constitution as to be rendered somewhat oblivious to its artificial character. The most essential quarrel which the functionalist has with structuralism in its thoroughgoing and consistent form arises from this fact and touches the feasibility and worth of the effort to get at mental process as it *is* under the conditions of actual experience rather than as it *appears* to a merely postmortem analysis. It is of course true that for introspective purposes we must in a sense always work with vicarious representatives of the particular mental processes which we set out to observe. But it makes a great difference even on such terms whether one is directing attention primarily to the discovery of the way in which such a mental process operates, and what the conditions are under which it appears, or whether one is engaged simply in teasing apart the fibres of its tissues. (pp. 63–65, italics in the original)

After drawing this initial contrast between structuralism and functionalism, Angell explicitly dismissed an analogy that Titchener had used in his 1898 paper to make the case for structuralism. Comparing psychology to biology, Titchener stated that structuralism in psychology was analogous to anatomy in biology, while functionalism was analogous to physiology. For the biologist, knowing physiology presupposes an understanding of anatomy, he contended; in like manner, it was essential for the psychologist to understand the *structure* of consciousness before attempting to understand its *function*. Angell disagreed with the idea that there was anything in our mental life that was analogous to the physical structures that comprise the anatomy of the body.

> It should be added that when the distinction is made between psychic structure and psychic function, the anomalous position of structure as a category of mind is often quite forgotten. In mental life the sole appropriateness of the term structure hinges on the fact that any moment of consciousness can be regarded as a complex capable of analysis, and the terms into which our analyses resolve such complexes are the analogues—and obviously very meager and defective ones at that—of the structures of anatomy and morphology.
>
> The fact that mental contents are evanescent and fleeting marks them off in an important way from the relatively permanent elements of anatomy. No matter how much we may talk of the preservation of psychical dispositions, nor how many metaphors we may summon to characterize the storage of ideas in some hypothetical deposit chamber of memory, the obstinate fact remains that when we are not experiencing a sensation or an idea it is, strictly speaking, non-existent. Moreover, when we manage by one or another device to secure that which we designate that same sensation or the same idea, we not only have no guarantee that our second edition is really a replica of the first, we have a good bit of presumptive evidence that from the content point of view the original never is and never can be literally duplicated.
>
> Functions, on the other hand, persist as well in mental as in physical life. We may never have twice exactly the same idea viewed from the side of sensuous structure and composition. But there seems nothing whatever to prevent our having as often as we will contents of consciousness which *mean* the same thing. They function in one and the same practical way, however discrepant their momentary texture. . . . Not only then are general functions like memory persistent, but special functions such as the memory of particular events are persistent and largely independent of the specific conscious contents called upon from time to time to subserve the functions. (pp. 65–68, italics in the original)

Having disposed of structuralism to his satisfaction, Angell then showed how functionalist thinking resonated with Darwinism—asking about the functions of human conscious experience, for instance, means asking about the manner in which consciousness enables the individual to successfully adapt to (Angell used the term "accommodate") the environment, thereby succeeding in the struggle for existence.

> A broader outlook and one more frequently characteristic of contemporary writers meets us in the next conception of the task of functional psychology. This conception is in part a reflex of the prevailing interest in the larger

formulae of biology and particularly the evolutionary hypotheses within
whose majestic sweep is nowadays included the history of the whole stellar
universe; in part it echoes the same philosophical call to new life which has
been heard as pragmatism, as humanism, even as functionalism itself. . . .

The functional psychologist then in his modern attire is interested not
alone in the operations of mental process considered merely of and by
and for itself, but also and more vigorously in mental activity as part of
a larger stream of biological forces which are daily and hourly at work
before our eyes and which are constitutive of the most important and most
absorbing part of our world. The psychologist of this stripe is wont to
take his cue from the basal conception of the evolutionary movement,
i.e., that for the most part organic structures and functions possess their
present characteristics by virtue of the efficiency with which they fit into
the extent conditions of life broadly designated the environment. With
this conception in mind he proceeds to attempt some understanding of the
manner in which the psychical contributes to the furtherance of the sum
total of organic activities, not alone the psychical in its entirety, but especially the psychical in its particularities—mind as judging, mind as feeling,
etc. . . .

This older . . . attitude toward the matter is, however, being rapidly displaced by a conviction of the need for light on the exact character of the
accommodatory service represented by the various great modes of conscious
expression. Such an effort if successful would not only broaden the founda-
tions for biological appreciation of the intimate nature of accommodatory
process, it would also immensely enhance the psychologist's interest in the
exact portrayal of conscious life. It is of course the latter consideration which
lends importance to the matter from our point of view. Moreover, not a few
practical consequences of value may be expected to flow from this attempt,
if it achieves even a measurable degree of success. Pedagogy and mental
hygiene both await the quickening and guiding counsel which can only
come from a psychology of this stripe. For their purposes a strictly structural
psychology is as sterile in theory as teachers and psychiatrists have found it
in practice. (pp. 68–69)

Thus, while arguing that functionalism can contribute to our understanding
of exactly how human mental processes contribute to our ability to "accommodate" to the environment, Angell sounded another theme of functionalism that
contrasts it with structuralism—its ability to deliver practical applications.

For Titchener, introspection was a prime method for studying human
conscious experience. Because he believed that introspection could only be
accomplished by highly trained psychological researchers, he rejected as "not
psychology" the study of animal behavior, child development, abnormal psychology, and other topics that were of great interest to most non-Titchenerians.
Angell made the point by showing how the study of such topics as animal psychology can enhance our understanding of the functions of consciousness in
adapting the organism to the environment.

As a concrete example of the transfer of attention from the more general
phases of consciousness as accommodatory activity to the particularistic
features of the case may be mentioned the rejuvenation of interest in the

quasi-biological field which we designate animal psychology. This movement is surely among the most pregnant with which we meet in our own generation. Its problems are in no sense of the merely theoretical and speculative kind, although, like all scientific endeavor, it possesses an intellectual and methodological background on which such problems loom large. But the frontier upon which it is pushing forward its explorations is a region of definite, concrete fact, tangled and confused and often most difficult of access, but nevertheless a region of fact, accessible like all other facts to persistent and intelligent interrogation. . . .

It seems hardly too much to say that the empirical conceptions of the consciousness of the lower animals have undergone a radical alteration in the past few years by virtue of the studies in comparative psychology. The splendid investigations of the mechanism of instinct, of the facts and methods of animal orientation, of the scope and character of the several sense processes, of the capabilities of education and the range of selective accommodatory capacities in the animal kingdom, these and dozens of other similar problems have received for the first time drastic scientific examination, experimental in character wherever possible, observational elsewhere, but observational in the spirit of conservative non-anthropomorphism as earlier observations almost never were. In most cases they have to be sure but shown the way to further and more precise knowledge, yet there can be but little question that the trail which they have blazed has success at its farther end. (pp. 69–70)

In a third major section of his address, Angell took up the ageless mind-body problem, pointing out that from a functionalist standpoint, it is essential to investigate both mental activity and bodily actions (i.e., behavior), without necessarily coming to a firm conclusion about the relationship between mental and physical events. He then summed up his three main points and tied them together.

If we now bring together the several conceptions of which mention has been made it will be easy to show them converging upon a common point. We have to consider (1) functionalism conceived as the psychology of mental operations in contrast to the psychology of mental elements; or, expressed otherwise, the psychology of the how and why of consciousness as distinguished from the psychology of the what of consciousness. We have (2) the functionalism which deals with the problem of mind conceived as primarily engaged in mediating between the environment and the needs of the organism. This is the psychology of the fundamental utilities of consciousness; (3) and lastly we have functionalism described as psychophysical psychology, that is the psychology which constantly recognizes and insists upon the essential significance of the mind-body relationship for any just and comprehensive appreciation of mental life itself.

The second and third delineations of functional psychology are rather obviously correlated with each other. No description of the actual circumstances attending the participation of mind in the accommodatory activities of the organism could be other than a mere empty schematism without making reference to the manner in which mental processes eventuate in motor phenomena of the physiological organism. The overt accommodatory act is, I take it, always sooner or later a muscular movement. . . .

It remains then to point out in what manner the conception of functionalism as concerned with the basal operations of mind is to be correlated with the other two conceptions just under discussion. The simplest view to take of the relations involved would apparently be such as would regard the first as an essential propaedeutic to the other two. Certainly if we are intent upon discerning the exact manner in which mental process contributes to accommodatory efficiency, it is natural to begin our undertaking by determining what are the primordial forms of expression peculiar to mind. However plausible in theory this conception of the intrinsic logical relations of these several forms of functional psychology, in practice it is extremely difficult wholly to sever them from one another. . . .

In view of the considerations of the last few paragraphs it does not seem fanciful nor forced to urge that these various theories of the problem of functional psychology really converge upon one another, however divergent may be the introductory investigations peculiar to each of the several ideals. Possibly the conception that the fundamental problem of the functionalist is one of determining just how mind participates in accommodatory reactions, is more nearly inclusive than either of the others, and so may be chosen to stand for the group. But if this vicarious duty is assigned to it, it must be on clear terms of remembrance that the other phases of the problem are equally real and equally necessary. Indeed the three things hang together as integral parts of a common program. . . .

A sketch of the kind we have offered is unhappily likely to leave on the mind an impression of functional psychology as a name for a group of genial but vaguer ambitions and good intentions. This, however, is a fault which must be charged to the artist and to the limitations of time and space under which he is here working. There is nothing vaguer in the program of the functionalist when he goes to his work than there is in the purposes of the psychologist wearing any other livery. He goes to his laboratory, for example, with just the same resolute interest to discover new facts and new relationships, with just the same determination to verify and confirm his previous observations, as does his colleague who calls himself perhaps a structuralist. But he looks out upon the surroundings of his science with a possibly greater sensitiveness to its continuity with other ranges of human interest and with certainly a more articulate purpose to see the mind which he analyzes as it actually is when engaged in the discharge of its vital functions. If his method tempts him now and then to sacrifice something of petty exactitude, he is under no obligation to yield, and in any case he has for his compensation the power which comes from breadth and sweep of outlook. (pp. 85–90)

In his closing sentence, Angell finished where he started—with a reminder that functionalism is a way of thinking about things, not a dogmatic school of thought.

> [Functionalism] seems at present a convenient term, but there is nothing sacrosanct about it, and the moment it takes unto itself the pretense of scientific finality its doom will be sealed. It means today a broad and flexible and organic point of view in psychology. The moment it becomes dogmatic and narrow its spirit will have passed and undoubtedly some worthier successor will fill its place. (p. 91)

Not long after delivering this APA presidential address, Angell moved further into administration, becoming Dean of the Faculty at Chicago in 1911. His career culminated in a highly successful tenure (e.g., his ability to quadruple the endowment landed him on the cover of *Time* magazine in 1936) as President of Yale University from 1921 until his retirement in 1937. Angell died in 1949.

DISCUSSION QUESTIONS

1. According to Angell, what is the essential difference between a structural and a functional psychology?

2. In his 1898 paper, Titchener drew an analogy between psychology and biology—he compared structuralism with anatomy and functionalism with physiology. What did Angell have to say about this analogy?

3. Sum up the three main points made by Angell in his APA presidential address.

DISCUSSION QUESTION

1. Assuming that you have read the Titchener excerpt in the previous chapter, how do you think he would respond to Angell's paper? What do you think are the strengths and weaknesses of Angell's argument(s)?

CHAPTER 13

KURT KOFFKA (1886–1941): GESTALT PSYCHOLOGY AND PERCEPTION

Gestalt psychology made its presence felt in experimental psychology after the publication of a paper by the German psychologist Max Wertheimer in 1912. Considered to be the "founder" of the gestalt movement, Wertheimer investigated a perceptual phenomenon called *apparent motion*—if two adjacent lights flash on and off in a particular sequence, they will be perceived as a single light that appears to be moving from one position to another. Wertheimer argued that such an experience cannot be meaningfully analyzed into its component sensory elements. As he famously wrote later, "[t]here are wholes, the behaviour of which is not determined by that of their individual elements, but where the part-processes are themselves determined by the intrinsic nature of the whole" (Wertheimer, 1924/1967, p. 2). Throughout the years of their influence, the gestaltists vigorously opposed those psychological systems that sought to understand human experience or behavior by analyzing it into its basic structural components. Thus, they opposed both the structuralism of E. B. Titchener (Chapter 11) and the behaviorism of John B. Watson (Chapter 18).

In his apparent motion studies, Wertheimer used two other young psychologists as participants, Kurt Koffka and Wolfgang Köhler. You will learn about how Köhler applied gestalt principles to problem solving in the next chapter. In this chapter, you will learn how Koffka introduced some gestalt principles, especially figure-ground perception, to an American audience.

Kurt Koffka began his studies of perception at the University of Berlin, earning a Ph.D. under Carl Stumpf in 1908. He then studied physiology briefly, spent some time in the lab of another well-known German psychologist (Oswald Külpe), and then landed in Frankfurt for the apparent motion experiments, where he became a convert to gestalt ideas. He left Frankfurt in 1911 and then spent a dozen productive years at the University of Geissen. There he wrote a developmental psychology book from the gestalt standpoint in 1921. And then in

Excerpts from: Koffka, K. (1922). Perception: An introduction to the *Gestalt-theorie*. *Psychological Bulletin*, *19*, 531–585.

1922 he wrote an article on gestalt theory that appeared in the American journal *Psychological Bulletin*. Most American psychologists had some awareness of gestalt psychology, but this article, excerpted here, was the one known for introducing the movement to the United States.

> When it was suggested to me that I should write a general critical review of the work recently carried on in the field of perception, I saw an opportunity of introducing to American readers a movement in psychological thought which has developed in Germany during the last ten years. In 1912 Wertheimer stated for the first time the principles of a *Gestalt-Theorie* which has served as the starting point of a small number of German psychologists. Wherever this new method of thinking and working has come in touch with concrete problems, it has not only showed its efficiency, but has also brought to light startling and important facts, which, without the guidance of this theory, could not so easily have been discovered.
>
> The *Gestalt-Theorie* is more than a theory of perception; it is even more than a mere psychological theory. Yet it originated in a study of perception, and the investigation of this topic has furnished the better part of the experimental work which has been done. Consequently, an introduction to this new theory can best be gained, perhaps, by a consideration of the facts of perception. (p. 531, italics in the original)

The second paragraph is important because the gestaltists always thought of their theory as a general theory of human behavior and mental processes, yet for many psychologists, the movement was only associated with perception. To this day, descriptions of gestalt psychology in introductory psychology texts typically appear in the perception chapter. Many historians believe that Koffka's 1922 article (consider the title alone) was the main reason that gestalt psychology became identified with perception and not with a more general psychology.

Koffka made it clear from the start that his notion of perception would be a common sense definition (he used the term "everyday perception") that emphasized direct experience, in contrast with structuralist theory, which considered perception as a complex process involving sensation, association, and attention.

> When I speak of perception in the following essay, I do not mean a specific psychical function; all I wish to denote by this term is the realm of experiences which are not merely "imagined," "represented," or "thought of." Thus, I would call the desk at which I am now writing a perception, likewise the flavor of the tobacco I am now inhaling from my pipe, or the noise of the traffic in the street below my window. That is to say, I wish to use the term perception in a way that will exclude all theoretical prejudice; for it is my aim to propose a theory of these everyday perceptions which has been developed in Germany during the last ten years, and to contrast this theory with the traditional views of psychology. With this purpose in mind, I need a term that is quite neutral. In the current textbooks of psychology the term perception is used in a more specific sense, being opposed to sensation, as a more complex process. Here, indeed, is the clue to all the existing theories of perception which I shall consider in this introductory section, together with a glance at the fundamental principles of traditional psychology. Thus

I find three concepts, involving three principles of psychological theory, in every current psychological system. In some systems these are the only fundamental concepts, while in others they are supplemented by additional conceptions; but for a long time the adequacy of these three has been beyond dispute. The three concepts to which I refer are those of *sensation, association*, and *attention*. I shall formulate the theoretical principles based upon these concepts and indicate their import in a radical manner so as to lay bare the methods of thinking which have been employed in their use. . . . (pp. 532–533, italics in the original)

Koffka then proceeded to give a detailed account of the traditional structuralist account of perception. In brief, this included the ideas that (a) environmental stimuli automatically produce sensations, which are the basic elements of perception and that "it is the first task of psychology to find out their number and their properties" (p. 533); (b) the basic elements originally experienced as sensation, "may also be experienced in the form of images" (p. 533); (c) these images, in effect, are memories, and are organized by the principles of association; and (d) some images and/or sensations are brought into closer focus due to attention. When we "perceive" a tree, we are attending to a particular set of stimuli that produce sensations; at the same time we are comparing those sensations with stored images from our past experiences with trees that are associated with each other. If the incoming sensations match the images stored as memory, the result is the perception "that's a tree." For Koffka, however, despite the intricacy of such a model, it missed a basic point of perception. He argued that the same stimulus could result in different experiences, depending on the relationships of the stimulus objects and their backgrounds.

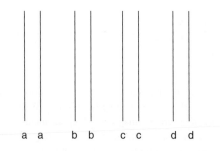

In [this figure] the intervals ab, bc, and cd are different from the intervals aa, bb, cc and dd, though both belong to the "fence-phenomenon." In trying to describe this difference we find one very striking feature which we shall here single out. The white spaces in the intervals ab, bc, cd, form part of the total white space, whereas the white spaces in the other intervals are limited to the regions between their respective black lines; they do not extend beyond these regions, nor do they form a part of the white space round about. Practiced observers can even describe the curves that mark off these white stripes, which are slightly convex toward the interior. We see, then, that the white surface of our pattern, though objectively the same throughout, gives rise to two different phenomena, one being limited to the "stripes," while the other comprises all the rest of the experience. We have two expressive terms to indicate this difference: we call the one phenomenon a "figure" and the other its "ground"; on recognizing at once that no visual figure can occur without a ground upon which it appears. . . . (p. 554)

Thus, even though the stimuli are just a series of vertical lines, the perception of them is influenced by how they are organized as "wholes," each whole (e.g., a fence post) being a figure against a ground. Koffka made the same point with auditory phenomena, and then returned to the perception of the "fence."

Let us revert to our fence-phenomenon. We found that the white intervals belonging to the figure were bounded, while those belonging to the ground were not, though objectively there was no border line in either case. Here we have a very general characteristic, namely, that the ground is always less "formed," less outlined, than the figure. Rubin was the first to investigate these facts systematically. . . . His method was peculiarly well-adapted to bring out the differences of figure and ground, in employing geometrical patterns which are phenomenally equivocal as to their figure-ground structure [note: the most famous example is a drawing that can be perceived either as a vase or goblet on the one hand or, alternatively, as two faces in profile, depending on which is perceived as figure and which is perceived as ground]. A simple example of such a pattern has already been discussed by Schumann. If we make the distances in our fence aa, bb, [etc.] equal to ab, bc, [etc.] we have a striking instance. For now bb may be a stripe [i.e., fence post], bc a piece of the ground, or inversely, bc may be a stripe, and bb a piece of the ground. In either case we find our old difference, that the stripes are always bounded, whether they are formed by bb or bc, while the intervals are not. . . .

Hand in hand with higher degrees of structure there goes a greater "liveliness" or vividness of the figure. As Schumann observed, the white space inside a figure is "whiter" than that outside, which can also be seen in the equidistant fence-design. A striking example of this is afforded by a certain kind of drawing, used frequently for advertising posters, where the contour is not fully drawn, but where, nonetheless, no gap appears in the figure. . . . [note: the gestaltists later referred to this as closure]

These . . . examples show . . . that phenomenal figures have boundary lines even when the corresponding objective figures have none. A good figure is always a "closed" figure, which the boundary line has the function of closing. So this line, separating the fields of figure and ground, has a very different relation to each of these, for though it bounds the figure, it does not bound the ground. The ground is unaffected by the contour and is partly hidden by the figure, yet it lies without interruption behind the figure. The cross of the accompanying figure [below] will make this description clear. Look at the fields with the arcs for [figure]. When forming a cross, these become true arcs, i.e., cut-off pieces of circles, but when forming the ground they look quite differently, for they are no longer cut off, becoming now the visible parts of a phenomenal series of complete circles.

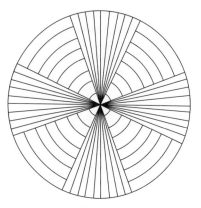

This property of the ground, that the figure's contour does not affect
it, is closely related to the first characteristic we mentioned, namely, its
lesser degree of structure. In our last instance this fact is revealed by the
observation that the whole circles when they constitute a ground are simpler
structures than the arcs which are necessary to the formation of the cross;
for in place of each single circle there appear four arcs. The lesser degree of
structure leads also to another indication noted by Rubin of the difference
between ground and figure: the ground has more of a substance- and the
figure more of a thing-character.

Let us return to the boundary line [separating figure and ground]. From
its variable relation to figure and ground there follows the inference that it
must have two different sides, an inside and an outside; the one includes, the
other excludes, or to use terms in this more general sense which have been
suggested by v. Hornbostel, the one is concave, and the other is convex.
Though these words are not psychological terms they are meant to indicate
true psychological descriptions. Look at the left line-b in our fence-figure
and you will understand what is meant by this description, for its left side
is hard and repelling, whereas its right side is soft and yielding. Very full
descriptions of these properties are given by v. Hornbostel who reduces the
illusions of reversible perspective to a change in these properties: to reverse
a figure is to make concave what was convex, and convex what was concave.
(pp. 556–559)

It is one thing to provide a description of figure-ground relationships.
Yet it is also important to show that these phenomena have behavioral consequences. That is, it is necessary to show that certain predictions about behavior can be made from what is hypothesized about figure-ground perception.
Another way to make this point is to refer, as Koffka does here, to "functional"
facts.

All good psychological descriptions must find their justification in functional
facts. Phenomena that are different in description must also prove to be
different in function, if the description is tenable. So we turn to the functional
facts which underlie the figure-ground distinction.

Two sets of experiments have been performed by Rubin, both employing patterns of the type of [the above figure]. These patterns are ambiguous, either the enclosed white space or the enclosing black space may appear as the figure. Let us call the first the positive, the second the negative reaction. According to the instructions given, it is possible for the O.'s to assume either a positive or a negative attitude before the exposure of the pattern. After some practice the attitude assumed will in most cases be effective, *i.e.*, a positive reaction will ensue from a positive attitude, and *vice versa*. In his first series of experiments, Rubin presented a number of such patterns with either positive or negative instructions. After a certain interval the experiment was repeated with instructions prescribing an indifferent attitude, neither positive nor negative. The result was that in the majority of cases a pattern once reacted to in a certain manner was reacted to the next time in the same manner. Rubin calls this a "figural after-effect". . . . It proves that the structure by which we react to a given stimulus-complex remains in the memory of the individual, a fact of paramount importance for the theory of learning, as I have elsewhere shown. The problem of the second series was to find out if a pattern seen the first time under one attitude, positive or negative, will be recognized when it is seen the second time under the reversed attitude. The procedure was similar to that of the previous experiment, except that the instruction of the test-series was either positive or negative. The result was in full accordance with the descriptive distinction, for when the reverse instruction was effective no recognition took place. . . .

Phenomenally, the figure is always a stronger and more resistant structure than the ground, and in extreme cases the ground may be almost formless, a mere background. For this distinction we have also found a functional counterpart. Kenkel has discovered that figures, when briefly exposed, appear with specific movements which expand with their appearance and contract with their disappearance. I have advanced the hypothesis that this movement, called by Kenkel the *gamma movement*, is the expression of a structural process. This hypothesis has been tested and proved by an investigation of Lindemann which will be more explicitly discussed in a later article. However, one experiment of this investigation belongs in the present context. Lindemann worked also with patterns that were ambiguous in their figure-ground structure. His figures were of the type of [the figure just] described above. If [this figure] is positively apprehended the O. sees violent outward movements of the white teeth, whereas, if observed negatively, the black indentures, particularly the lower claw-like one, move vigorously inwards. The goblet pattern [Rubin's famous figure-ground ambiguity] behaves similarly. If the goblet is seen, it performs extensive expansions and contractions, whereas, if the profiles appear they tend toward one another, the direction of the movement being reversed, but, on account of the close proximity of these two structures movement is in this case notably checked. These experiments show that the gamma movement takes place in the figure and not in the ground, and since they reveal a constructing process, they prove that functionally the figure is better formed than the ground. . . .

I believe that the functional facts I have adduced are sufficient to prove the essential difference between the figure and ground phenomena. This difference is fundamental and the figure-ground structure must therefore be considered one of the most primitive of all structures. (pp. 562–566, italics in the original)

Koffka continued his article by pointing out that while most of the discussion to that point had emphasized the "superiority of the figure-phenomenon over the ground phenomenon, [this fact] "must not lead us to disregard the latter, for the ground has a very important function of its own" (p. 566). He then launched into an extended discussion of how different backgrounds can have a significant effect on the perception of figures. For example, the perceived color of figures can be dramatically altered by placing these figures on different colored grounds.

As mentioned earlier, this 1922 article by Koffka is generally credited with introducing gestalt ideas to American psychologists. Koffka, considered the most vigorous propagandist for gestalt psychology (Boring, 1950), also spread the word in person in a thirty-campus lecture tour of the United States that started in 1924, in an invited address at the annual 1925 meeting of the American Psychological Association, and in two visiting professor appointments (Cornell and Wisconsin) (Sokal, 1984). He came to the United States permanently in 1927, accepting a position at Smith College in Massachusetts, where he remained until his death in 1941.

CONCEPT REVIEW QUESTIONS

1. Describe the approach to perception that Koffka was criticizing. How is the gestalt approach different?

2. Using the fence post example as portrayed in Koffka's first figure (page 86), describe the attributes of figure and ground. What happens to figure and ground when the distance between the lines becomes equal?

3. Use Koffka's second figure (page 88) to show what happens to "arcs" and "circles" when they are either figure or ground.

DISCUSSION QUESTION

1. After completing the next chapter on Köhler's research with primates, describe the similarities that you see in the chapters.

CHAPTER 14

WOLFGANG KÖHLER (1887–1967): PROBLEM SOLVING IN APES

Along with Max Wertheimer and Kurt Koffka (previous chapter), Wolfgang Köhler is considered one of the founders of the gestalt psychology movement that emerged from Germany in the early years of the twentieth century. Much of the gestalt work concerned perception, but the gestaltists considered their system to be a general psychology, and they also contributed much to our understanding of thinking and problem solving. In particular, Köhler's most famous research concerned the nature of problem solving in apes, culminating in *The Mentality of Apes*, a book summarizing his work. The book first appeared in German in 1917, then was translated into English and elaborated slightly in 1924. The following excerpt is from a 1926 reprinting.

While a young professor at Frankfurt's university in 1913, Köhler was invited to direct some primate research being sponsored by the Prussian Academy of Sciences on the island of Tenerife (part of the Canary Islands, off the northwest coast of Africa). He accepted, and he and his family lived on the island from 1913 to 1920. He completed most of the research reported in *The Mentality of Apes* in his first full year on Tenerife.

Early in the book, Köhler took dead aim at Thorndike's puzzle box experiments. As you recall from the reading in Chapter 8, Thorndike concluded that learning and problem solving was a process of trial and "accidental success," with unsuccessful behaviors gradually being eliminated in favor of behaviors that worked to produce an escape from the box. Köhler, however, strongly disagreed that problem solving was such a mechanical, gradual, step-by-step process.

> Thorndike's experiments ... were designed as *intelligence tests* of the same type as our own ... and ought, therefore, to have conformed to the same general conditions, and, above all, to have been arranged so as to be completely *visible* to the animals. For if essential portions of the experimental apparatus cannot be seen by the animals, how can they use their intelligence faculties in tackling the situation? It is somewhat astonishing to find out that (in Thorndike's experiments) cats ... were frequently placed in cages containing the *extreme end* of one or the other mechanism, or allowing a view

Excerpts from: Köhler, W. (1926). *The mentality of apes* (E. Winter, Trans.). New York: Harcourt Brace. (Original work published 1917) of ropes or other parts of the mechanism, but from which a survey over the *whole* arrangement was not possible. The task for the animal was to let itself out of the cage by pulling or pressing the accessible part of the mechanism; then—the cage door would open of itself. . . . The result of these experiments tends to show that prolonged 'learning' is necessary before the right action develops. (pp. 23–24, italics in the original)

Köhler was determined not to make the same "mistake" in his research. His animals would have the whole of the problem in front of them, with all of the elements needed to solve the problems in full view. This idea was in keeping with Köhler's gestalt orientation—he believed that intelligent solutions to problems would occur only when individuals could view the entire problem field and rearrange the elements of the problem into a new configuration that would lead to a successful solution. Köhler used the term *insight* to label this process of reorganizing the elements of the problem situation so as to bring about a solution.

In addition to allowing his apes to see all the elements of the problem situation, Köhler also designed his problems to take advantage of the animals' natural hand-eye coordination. That is, Köhler was keenly aware of what we would today refer to as the biological constraints on behavior.

[T]he response of the chimpanzee . . . will always be limited and determined by his own very pronounced natural proclivities. For I must most emphatically state, after a full acquaintance with chimpanzees, that it may perhaps be possible . . . by beating or such means, to compel them to an action, to a habit, an omission, or a method of procedure which is not spontaneous and the natural anthropoidal response to the particular conditions; but so to *weld* an alien nature into his own that the chimpanzee will continue to exhibit it when not under pressure, appears to me difficult in the extreme, and probably impossible. I should have the highest admiration for a pedagogic talent which could achieve such a result. It is a continuous source of wonder, and often enough of vexation, to observe how every attempt to re-mould his biological heritage "runs off" an otherwise clever and ductile animal of this species "like water from a duck's back." (p. 70, italics in the original)

The Mentality of Apes includes descriptions of dozens of experiments on problem solving. One of the most famous occurs in a chapter called "The Making of Implements" and concerned a problem in which bananas lying outside an enclosure were to be retrieved. Two hollow bamboo sticks with different diameters were available, each just a bit too short to reach the food. An ape named Sultan was tested.

Are two sticks ever combined so as to become technically useful? This time Sultan is the subject of the experiment. . . . His sticks are two hollow, but firm, bamboo rods, such as the animals often use for pulling along fruit. The one is so much smaller than the other, that it can be pushed in at either end quite easily. Beyond the bars lies the objective, just so far away that the animal cannot reach it with either rod. They are about the same length. Nevertheless, he takes great pains to try to reach it with one stick or the other, even pushing his right shoulder through the bars. When everything proves

futile, Sultan commits a 'bad error,' or, more clearly, a great stupidity, such
as he made sometimes on other occasions. He pulls a box from the back
of the room toward the bars; true, he pushes it away again at once as it is
useless, or rather, actually in the way. (pp. 130–131)

Sultan's bad error apparently resulted from an earlier problem, in which
a box had to be placed under a banana suspended from the ceiling in order to
retrieve it. The bad error was followed by some "good" errors.

Immediately afterwards, he does something which, although practically useless, must be counted among the "good errors": he pushes one of the sticks
out as far as it will go, then takes the second, and with it pokes the first one
cautiously towards the objective, pushing it carefully from the nearer end
and thus slowly urging it towards the fruit. This does not always succeed,
but if he has got pretty close in this way, he takes even greater precaution; he
pushes very gently, watches the movements of the stick that is lying on the
ground, and actually touches the objective with its tip. Thus, all of a sudden,
for the first time, the contact "animal-objective" has been established, and
Sultan visibly feels (we humans can sympathize) a certain satisfaction in having even so much power over the fruit that he can touch and slightly move it
by pushing the stick. The proceeding is repeated; when the animal has pushed
the stick on the ground so far out that he cannot possibly get it back by himself, it is given back to him. But although, in trying to steer it cautiously, he
puts the stick in his hand exactly to the cut (i.e. the opening) of the stick on
the ground, and although one might think that doing so would suggest the
possibility of pushing one stick into the other, there is no indication whatever
of such a practically valuable solution. Finally, the observer gives the animal some help by putting one finger into the opening of one stick under the
animal's nose (without pointing to the other stick at all). This has no effect;
Sultan, as before, pushes one stick with the other towards the objective,
and as this pseudo-solution does not satisfy him any longer, he abandons
his efforts altogether, and does not even pick up the sticks when they are
both again thrown through the bars to him. The experiment has lasted over
an hour, and is stopped for the present, as it seems hopeless, carried out like
this. As we intend to take it up again after a while, Sultan is left in possession
of his sticks; the keeper is left there to watch him. (pp. 131–132)

It is not hard to imagine Köhler being a bit frustrated here by Sultan's
inability to solve this two-stick problem, and perseverance with the ineffective
solution. Ironically, when Sultan did solve it, Köhler was not present. Instead,
the aforementioned keeper was the sole witness, producing one of psychology's
most quoted passages.

Keeper's report: 'Sultan first of all squats indifferently on the box, which has
been left standing a little back from the railings; then he gets up, picks up
the two sticks, sits down again on the box and plays carelessly with them.
While doing this, it happens that he finds himself holding one rod in either
hand in such a way that they lie in a straight line; he pushes the thinner one
a little way into the opening of the thicker, jumps up and is already on the
run towards the railings, to which he has up to now half turned his back, and
begins to draw a banana towards him with the double stick.' (p. 132)

In a footnote, Köhler considered and dismissed the possibility that the keeper might have cheated.

> The keeper's tale seems acceptable to me, especially as, upon inquiries, he emphasized the fact that Sultan had first of all connected the sticks in play and without considering the objective (his task). The animals are constantly poking about with straws and small sticks in holes and cracks in their play, so that it would be more astonishing if Sultan had never done this, while playing about with the two sticks. There need be no suspicion that the keeper quickly 'trained the animal'; the man would never dare it. If anyone continues to doubt, even that does not matter, for Sultan continually not only performs this act but shows that he realizes its meaning. (p. 132)

Having missed Sultan's initial solution to the two-stick problem, Köhler quickly returned to see its repetition. Sultan's solution was eventually, but not immediately, successful (the sticks kept falling apart at first).

> The keeper's report covers a period of scarcely five minutes, which had elapsed since stopping the experiment. Called by the man, I continued observation myself: Sultan is squatting at the bars, holding out one stick, and, at its end, a second bigger one, which is on the point of falling off. It does fall. Sultan pulls it to him and forthwith, with the greatest assurance, pushes the thinner one in again, so that it is firmly wedged, and fetches a fruit with the lengthened implement. But the bigger tube selected is a little too big, and so it slips from the end of the thinner one several times; each time Sultan rejoins the tubes immediately by holding the bigger one towards himself in the left and the thinner one in his right hand and a little backwards, and then sliding one into the other. The proceeding seems to please him immensely; he is very lively, pulls all the fruit, one after the other, towards the railings, without taking time to eat it, and when I disconnect the double-stick he puts it together again at once, and draws any distant objects whatever to the bars.
> The next day the test is repeated; Sultan begins with the proceeding which is in practice useless, but after he has pushed one of the tubes forward with the other for a few seconds, he again takes up both, quickly puts one into the other, and attains his objective with the double stick. (pp. 132–133)

Köhler's concept of insight in the two-stick problem is clearly perceptual in nature—when the two sticks were arranged so that they were in a line, the solution presented itself to Sultan and he seized upon it. That Sultan's solution to the problem depended on this perceptual aspect is clear from the following. Even after solving the problem many times, Sultan hesitated when he saw the sticks in certain configurations.

> Sometimes, however, he experiences a difficulty, where one would least expect it. Holding both tubes in his hand and wanting to proceed as usual to connect them, he hesitates for a few minutes and seems strangely uncertain; this is when the tubes lie in his hand in certain positions, namely almost parallel, or else across each other in the shape of a very narrow "X." This difficulty has now almost disappeared, but at first it occurred frequently. (pp. 135–136)

In addition to the double-stick problem and the problem of using a box to reach a banana, Köhler's chimps also retrieved suspended fruit when put in a situation where two or three boxes had to be stacked in order to reach their objective. They learned the task gradually, box by box, as Köhler raised the fruit higher and higher. They first learned to use a single box, then two, then three. In one experiment, Sultan was once again on stage, along with Grande, a female who was among the best at this box task.

> The objective hangs still higher up; Sultan has fasted all the forenoon and, therefore, goes at his task with great zeal. He lays the heavy box flat underneath the objective, puts the second one upright upon it, and, standing on the top, tries to seize the objective. As he does not reach it, he looks down and round about, and his glance is caught by the third box, which may have seemed useless to him at first, because of its smallness. He climbs down very carefully, seizes the box, climbs up with it, and completes the construction.
>
> Grande in particular progressed with time. Of the smaller animals she was the strongest and by far the most patient. She would not allow herself to be diverted by any number of mishaps, the collapse of the erection, or any other difficulties . . . , and soon was able to put three boxes on top of each other, like Sultan. She even managed once a beautiful construction of four boxes, when she found a fairly big cage near by, whose flat surface allowed of the addition of the three remaining parts with safety. (pp. 142–143)

Köhler was at pains to point out that his primate's abilities to solve problems did not reflect automatic instinctive behavior, but was of a higher level of mental ability. The box constructions might not be anywhere near the elegance of a spider's web, but the constructions represented genuine thought, he argued, not blind instinct.

> Without doubt, constructions such as those achieved by Grande . . . are considerable feats, especially when one considers that the constructions of insects (ants, bees, spiders) and other vertebrates (birds, beavers), though they may, when finished, be more perfect, yet are built by a very different and much more primitive process, from an evolutionary point of view. The . . . difference between the clever but clumsy constructions of a gifted chimpanzee, and the firm and objectively elegantly-spun web of a spider, for instance, is one of *genus*, which, of course, should be obvious from what has already been said. But, unfortunately, I have experienced that otherwise intelligent spectators will ask, in the matter of these constructions, 'whether this be not instinct'? Therefore I feel obligated to emphasize the following particularly: the spider and similar artists achieve true wonders, but the main *special* faculties *for this particular work alone* are within them, long before the incentive to use them occurs. The chimpanzee is not simply provided for life with any special disposition which will help him to attain objects placed high up, by heaping up any building material, and yet he can accomplish this much by his own efforts, when circumstances require it and when the material is available. (pp. 143–144, italics in the original)

Köhler declined to develop a new theory of intelligence to explain his findings ("In this book, no theory of intelligent behaviour is to be developed."—p. 194), but he spent the bulk of a chapter near the end of the book refuting the "theory of chance," his phrase for the approach taken by Thorndike and other American psychologists who were, he believed, wedded to a strategy based on associationist principles. In so doing, he described several attributes of what he considered to be insightful behavior. For example, in the early stages, the problem solver systematically surveys the field.

> We can ... distinguish sharply between the kind of conduct which from the very beginning arises out of a consideration of the characteristics of a situation, and one that does not. Only in the former case do we speak of insight, and only that behaviour of animals definitely appears to us intelligent which takes account from the beginning of the lie of the land, and proceeds to deal with it in a smooth, continuous course. Hence follows this characteristic: *to set up as a criterion of insight, the appearance of a complete solution with reference to the whole lay-out of the field.* (p. 198, italics in the original)

Another feature of insightful problem solving is that it is goal-directed. Contrary to Thorndike's "chance" theory, which had the animal behaving randomly at first, Köhler believed that animals behaved quite differently, unless placed in a situation (e.g., Thorndike's puzzle boxes) in which the inability to survey the field made it impossible for the animal to see the objective clearly.

> It is certainly not a characteristic of the chimpanzee, when he is brought into an experimental situation, to make any chance movements. . . . He is very seldom seen to attempt anything which would have been considered accidental in relation to the situation ... As long as his efforts are directed to the objective, all distinguishable stages of his behaviour (as with human beings in similar situations), tend to appear as complete attempts at solutions, *none* of which appears as the product of accidentally arrayed parts. This is true, most of all, of the solution which is finally successful. Certainly, it often follows upon a period of perplexity or quiet (often a period of survey), but in real and convincing cases, the solution never appears in a disorder of blind impulses. It is one continuous, smooth action, which can be resolved into its parts *only by the imagination* of the onlooker. . . . (pp. 199–200, italics in the original)

According to Köhler, then, when placed in a problem situation, the animal first surveys the whole field with reference to some clear objective. Eventually, the animal will insightfully reorganize the problem elements in the field into a new configuration which quickly solves the problem. The necessary condition for insight is that all aspects of the problem must be within the animal's field of view.

Köhler's explanation did not go unchallenged by American psychologists, who questioned the methodological sophistication of Köhler's demonstrations and pointed out that a careful reading of the descriptions found ample evidence of trial-and-error learning. Some attempts to replicate the research produced ambiguous results and suggested that the more prior experience the animal had with similar problems, the more likely a "quick" (i.e. insightful) solution would appear (Windholz & Lamal, 1985). On the other hand, Köhler's research introduced a new way of thinking into the debate about learning and problem solving and extended animal research methodology beyond puzzle boxes and mazes.

Following his experience on Tenerife, Köhler returned to Germany and, by 1922, he was named director of the prestigious Psychological Institute at the University of Berlin. Under the cloud of advancing Nazism, he left Germany for the United States in 1935, remained at Swarthmore College for the rest of his career, and retired in 1958 (he was also elected president of the American Psychological Association that year).

CONCEPT REVIEW QUESTIONS

1. Describe the "two-stick" experiment and how Sultan committed both "bad errors" and "good errors" on the way to solving it.

2. How did Köhler interpret Sultan's behavior in solving the two-stick problem; show how his notion of insightful problem solving has a perceptual tone to it.

3. In addition to the two-stick problem, what other problems did Köhler's apes confront and how did they fare?

DISCUSSION QUESTION

1. What did Köhler think of Thorndike's puzzle box studies? If you were Thorndike (see Chapter 8), what would you think of Köhler's evidence for "insight" in his apes?

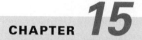

FRANCIS GALTON (1822–1911): THE INHERITANCE OF MENTAL ABILITY

Francis Galton was a nineteenth-century intellectual whose financial security and individual talent enabled him to devote his life to science. He made important contributions to geographical exploration, meteorology, statistics, and criminology (Forrest, 1974). In psychology, he completed important research on the nature of association and mental imagery and, with his attempts to measure human intellect, he was a pioneer in the study of human individual differences in ability. In one of his books, *English Men of Science: Their Nature and Nurture* (Galton, 1874), Galton popularized the two words that have become the labels for one of psychology's recurring issues. The excerpt here is from a 1950 reprinting of *Hereditary Genius* (Galton, 1869/1950) Galton's best-known book. As he made abundantly clear in the book's opening sentence, Galton was firmly on the nature side of the nature-nurture issue when it came to intellect.

> I propose to show in this book that a man's natural abilities are derived by inheritance, under exactly the same limitations as are the form and physical features of the whole organic world. Consequently, as it is easy, not withstanding those limitations, to obtain by careful selection a permanent breed of dogs or horses gifted with peculiar powers of running, or of doing anything else, so it would be quite practicable to produce a highly-gifted race of men by judicious marriages during several consecutive generations.... I conclude that each generation has enormous power over the natural gifts of those that follow, and maintain that it is a duty we owe to humanity to investigate the range of that power, and to exercise it in a way that, without being unwise towards ourselves, shall be most advantageous to future inhabitants of the earth....
>
> The general plan of my argument is to show that high reputation is a pretty accurate test of high ability; next to discuss the relationships of a large body of fairly eminent men—namely, the Judges of England from 1660 to 1868, the Statesmen of the time of George III, the Premiers during the

Excerpts from: Galton, F. (1950). *Hereditary Genius: An Inquiry into its Laws and Consequences.* London: Watts & Co. (Original work published 1869) last 100 years—and to obtain from these a general survey of the laws of heredity in respect to genius. (pp. 1–2)

In addition to judges and the others just mentioned, Galton examined the family relationships of other eminent men (no women) (e.g., those in the arts and sciences, the clergy, and even athletes). He then indicated that he would restrict his study to the English. Galton's strategy was to assume that a high degree of eminence was associated with a high level of ability, and then to see if people who were eminent also tended to have prominent close relatives ("relations"). At the close of his introductory chapter, Galton aggressively challenged readers to extend his research to other populations if they doubted his conclusions or thought him overly biased.

> There is one advantage to a candid critic in my having left so large a field untouched; it enables me to propose a test that any well-informed reader may easily adopt who doubts the fairness of my examples. He may most reasonably suspect that I have been unconsciously influenced by my theories to select men whose kindred were most favorable to their support. If so, I beg he will test my impartiality as follows:—Let him take a dozen names of his own selection, as the most eminent in whatever profession and in whatever country he knows most about, and let him trace out for himself their relations. . . . If he does what I propose, I am confident he will be astonished at the completeness with which the results will confirm my theory. I venture to speak with assurance, because it has often occurred to me to propose this very test to incredulous friends, and invariably, so far as my memory serves me, [a] large . . . proportion of the men who were named were discovered to have eminent relations, as the nature of my views on heredity would have led me to expect. (p. 4)

Galton's first task was to determine a baseline level of eminence. That is, for the English population as a whole, what proportion could be considered "eminent"? He started by looking at a biographical handbook called *Men of the Time*, which included "none but those whom the world honours for their ability" (p. 6). After eliminating the non-English entries, Galton also decided to limit his list to those over the age of fifty.

> On looking over the book, I am surprised to find how large a proportion of the "Men of the Time" are past middle age. It appears that in cases of high . . . merit, a man must outlive the age of fifty to be sure of being widely appreciated. It takes time for an able man, born in the humbler ranks of life, to emerge from them and to take his natural position. It would not, therefore, be just to compare the numbers of Englishmen in the book with that of the whole adult male population of the British Isles; but it is necessary to confine our examination to those of the celebrities who are past fifty years of age, and to compare their number with that of the whole male population who are also above fifty years. I estimate, from examining a large part of the book, that there are about 850 of these men, and that 500 of them are decidedly well known to persons with literary and scientific society. Now, there are about two millions of adult males in the British isles above fifty years of age; consequently, the total number of the "Men of the Times" are as 425 to a million, and the more select part of them as 250 to a million.

The qualifications for belonging to what I call the more select part are, in my mind, that a man should have distinguished himself pretty frequently either by purely original work, or as a leader of opinion. I wholly exclude notoriety obtained by a single act. (p. 7)

So on the basis of his examination of "Men of the Times," Galton concluded that out of every million Britishers, about 250 met his definition of eminence. Concerned that the estimate might be a unique function of the one source he used, he examined two other sources, the list of obituaries in the London *Times* for 1868, and a set of obituaries for earlier years. Assuming that an obituary in the *Times* was a reflection of eminence, Galton compared the number of obituaries with the number of male deaths overall, and was satisfied that it gave the same results as his initial estimate.

These considerations define the sense in which I propose to employ the word "eminent." When I speak of an eminent man, I mean one who has achieved a position that is attained by only 250 persons in each million of men, or by one person in each 4000. (p. 9)

Having established a baseline, but before getting to his primary genealogical data, the eminence of the blood relatives of his sample, Galton addressed the issue of whether an eminent man might be the result of environmental circumstances, rather than heredity. While recognizing that "education and social influence" can affect one's fate, he believed such influences had severe limits, and he strongly rejected the nurture argument. Everyone eventually finds their place, their relative ranking in ability among their peers.

I have no patience with the hypothesis occasionally expressed, and often implied, especially in tales written to teach children to be good, that babies are born pretty much alike, and that the sole agencies in creating differences between boy and boy, and man and man, are steady application and moral effort. It is in the most unqualified manner that I object to pretensions of natural equality. The experiences of the nursery, the school, the University, and of professional careers, are a chain of proofs to the contrary. I acknowledge freely the great power of education and social influences in developing the active powers of the mind, just as I acknowledge the effect of use in developing the muscles of a blacksmith's arms, [but] no further....

Everybody who has trained himself to physical exercise discovers the extent of his muscular powers.... So long as he is a novice, he perhaps flatters himself there is hardly an assignable limit to the education of his muscles; but the daily gain is soon discovered to diminish, and at last it vanishes altogether. His maximum performance becomes a rigidly determinate quantity.... So it is in running, in rowing, in walking, and in every other form of physical exertion. There is a definite limit to the muscular powers of every man, which he cannot by any education or exertion overpass.

This is precisely analogous to the experience that every student has had of the working of his mental powers. The eager boy, when he first goes to school and confronts intellectual difficulties, is astonished at his progress. He glories in his newly-developed mental grip and growing capacity for application, and, it may be, fondly believes it to be within his reach to become one of the heroes who have left their mark upon the history of the world. The years go by; he competes in the examinations of school and college, over and over again with his fellows, and soon finds his place among them. He knows he can beat such and such of his competitors; that there are some with whom he runs on equal terms, and others whose intellectual feats he cannot even approach.... In a few years more, unless he is incurably blinded by self-conceit, he learns precisely of what performances he is capable, and what other enterprises lie beyond his compass. (pp. 12–14)

Later in *Hereditary Genius*, Galton bolstered his argument that nurture could explain little about eminence in three ways. First, he argued that someone of natural genius would succeed even if raised in impoverished circumstances—nothing could suppress native ability. Second, he compared England with America. The greater opportunity for advancement for those of lower and middle classes in America ought to lead to higher rates of eminence in America, if eminence resulted from opportunity, he contended. His third argument was that someone with low or average natural ability, given great advantage, would be unlikely to achieve eminence. With this third argument, which involved Popes, Galton proposed the essence of the *adoption method*, a technique that eventually became standard in the study of behavioral genetics.

First, it is a fact, that numbers of men rise, before they are middle-aged, from the humbler ranks of life to that worldly position, in which it is of no importance to their future career, how their youth has been passed. They have overcome their hindrances.... If a man is gifted with vast intellectual ability, eagerness to work, and power of working, I cannot comprehend how such a man should be repressed.

Another argument to prove, that the hindrances of English social life, are not effectual in repressing high ability is, that the number of eminent men in England is as great as in other countries where fewer hindrances exist. Culture is more widely spread in America, than with us, and the education of their middle and lower classes far more advanced; but, for all that, America most certainly does not beat us in first-class works of literature, philosophy, or art....

[M]y third argument.... I shall now maintain that social advantages are incompetent to give [eminence] to a man of moderate ability....

It is difficult to specify two large classes of men, with equal social advantages, in one of which they have high hereditary gifts, while in the other they have not. I must not compare the sons of eminent men with those of non-eminent, because much which I should ascribe to breed, others might ascribe to parental encouragement and example. Therefore, I will compare the sons of eminent men with the adopted sons of Popes and other dignitaries of the Roman Catholic Church. The practice of nepotism among ecclesiastics is universal. It consists in their giving those social helps to a nephew, or other more distant relative, that ordinary people give to their children. Now, I shall show abundantly in the course of this book, that the nephew of an eminent man has far less chance of becoming eminent than a son, and that a more remote kinsman has far less chance than a nephew. We may therefore make a very fair comparison, for the purposes of my argument, between the successes of the sons of eminent men and that of the nephews or more distant relatives, who stand in the place of sons to the highly unmarried ecclesiastics of the Romish Church. If social help is really of the highest importance, the nephews of the Popes will attain eminence as frequently, or nearly so, as the sons of other eminent men; otherwise, they will not.

Are, then, the nephews, &c., of the Popes, on the whole, as highly distinguished as are the sons of other equally eminent men? I answer, decidedly not.... I do not profess to have worked up the kinships of Italians with any especial care, but I have seen amply enough of them, to justify me in saying that the individuals whose advancement has been due to nepotism, are curiously undistinguished. The very common combination of an able son and an eminent parent, is not matched, in the case of high Romish ecclesiastics, by an eminent nephew and an eminent uncle. The social helps are the same, but hereditary gifts are wanting in the latter case (pp. 34–38)

A cornerstone of Darwin's theory of natural selection was that individual variation existed within a species. One of Galton's main interests was in examining these individual differences and trying to determine if these differences followed any general principle. They did, he believed. In *Hereditary Genius*, he pointed out that large individual differences in ability occurred; furthermore, they could be regularized with reference to what was then called the "law of deviation from an average"—today we call it the normal curve, bell curve, or normal distribution.

[T]he range of mental power between ... the greatest and the least of English intellects, is enormous. There is a continuity of natural ability reaching from one knows not what height, and descending to one can hardly say what depth. I propose ... to range men according to their natural abilities, putting them into classes separated by equal degrees of merit, and to show the relative number of individuals included in the several classes. Perhaps some person might be inclined to make an offhand guess that the number of men included in the several classes would be pretty equal. If he thinks so, I can assure him he is most egregiously mistaken.

The method I shall employ for discovering all this is an application of the very curious law of "deviation from an average." First, I will explain the law, and then I will show that the production of natural intellectual gifts comes justly within its scope. (pp. 22–23)

Galton then described the work of the Belgian astronomer and statistician Adolph Quetelet, who had shown that certain physical measurements (e.g., the height of French army conscripts and the chest measurements of Scottish soldiers) were, as we would say today, normally distributed. Galton saw no reason why mental abilities would not also be distributed in like fashion (note that Galton assumes that physical measures of the brain correlate with mental ability, a common nineteenth century idea).

I argue from the results obtained from Frenchmen and from Scotchmen, that, if we had measurements of the adult males of the British Isles, we should find those measurements to range in close accordance with the law of deviation from an average.... Now, if this be the case with stature, then it will be true as regards every other physical feature—as circumference of head, size of brain, weight of grey matter, number of brain fibers, &c.; and thence, by a step on which no physiologist will hesitate, as regards mental capacity.

This is what I am driving at—that analogy clearly shows there must be a fairly constant average mental capacity in the inhabitants of the British Isles, and that the deviations from that average—upwards toward genius, and downward towards stupidity—must follow the law that governs deviations from true averages. (pp. 27–28)

Galton then proposed that men could be ranked from the highest to the lowest level of ability, and then arranged into categories separated by equal amounts of ability, with the number of men per category estimated with reference to the normal curve. He decided (arbitrarily) on eight categories of ability above the average, and another eight below. Then he examined some real data related to ability, examination scores in 1868 for admission to the military college of Sandhurst, and concluded that they fit the normal distribution reasonably well.

Having disposed (to his satisfaction) of the nurture argument, and having shown that natural ability was normally distributed, Galton turned to the main body of genealogical data that he accumulated. As mentioned earlier, he examined family relationships among judges and a variety of other categories of eminence. Why judges?

The Judges of England, since the restoration of the monarchy in 1660, form a group peculiarly well adapted to afford a general outline of the extent and limitations of heredity in respect to genius. A judgeship is a guarantee of its possessor being gifted with exceptional ability; the Judges are sufficiently numerous and prolific to form a base for statistical inductions, and they are the subjects of several excellent biographical treatises. We shall quickly arrive at definite results, which subsequent chapters, treating of more illustrious men, and in other careers, will check and amplify.

It is necessary that I should first say something in support of my assertion, that the office of a judge is really a sufficient guarantee that its possessor is exceptionally gifted. In other countries it may be different to what it is with us, but we all know that in England, the Bench is never spoken of without reverence for the intellectual power of its occupiers. A seat on the Bench is a great prize, to be won by the best men. (p. 49)

Remember that Galton had decided that by chance, and on the basis of normal curve expectations, that only one man in 4000 (250 per million) should be "eminent" (and therefore intellectually gifted, according to Galton's definition). If he could show that among men of eminence (i.e., judges), however, that the proportions were different, then it would support his case that eminence ran in families.

What I profess to prove is this: that if two children are taken, of whom one has a parent exceptionally gifted in a high degree—say as one in 4000 ...
—and the other has not, the former child has an enormously greater chance

of turning out to be gifted in a high degree, than the other. Also, I argue that, as a new race can be obtained in animals and plants, and can be raised to so great a degree of purity that it will maintain itself, with moderate care in preventing the more faulty members of the flock from breeding, so a race of gifted men might be obtained, under exactly similar conditions. (pp. 57–58)

So what did Galton discover upon examining his list of judges (and others)? In brief, he found support for his hypothesis—eminence seemed to run in families. Specifically, judges were much more likely than expected to have eminent sons. Approximately 1 judge in 10 had an eminent relative, much greater than the 1 in 4000 that would be expected by chance (Fancher, 1985). Also, the chances of eminence were directly proportional to the degree of hereditary relationship—an eminent judge was more likely to have an eminent son or father than an eminent grandson or grandfather.

A detailed analysis of Galton's data is beyond the scope of this chapter—his analysis of judges ran to 49 pages, and his analysis of the other categories that he studied (e.g., there are chapters on "Statesmen," "English Peerages," "Commanders," "Literary Men," "Men of Science," "Poets," "Musicians," "Painters," "Divines" (clergy), "Oarsmen," and "Wrestlers") occupied another 209 pages. He believed that the clear consensus from all of his data was that genius ran in families, and that it was therefore inherited.

Although Galton dismissed the nurture argument, others were not so convinced. The American author H. G. Wells, for example, pointed out the obvious alternative explanation—the opportunities available to those who have "social advantage."

[Galton ignores] the consideration of social advantage, of what Americans call the "pull" that follows any striking success. The fact that the sons and nephews of a distinguished judge or great scientific man are themselves eminent judges or successful scientific men, may after all be far more due to a special knowledge of the channels of professional advancement than to any distinctive gift. (Wells, quoted in Gillham, 2001, p. 329)

One final point. You might have noticed that on two occasions in the above excerpt (including the book's opening paragraph), Galton made reference to the fact that if genius is inherited, that it is possible to take deliberate steps to improve the level of genius in society. Later in his life, Galton acted directly on this potential strategy, creating the term *eugenics* and vigorously promoting the concept in his remaining years. Galton became Sir Francis after being knighted in 1909, and he died two years later.

CONCEPT REVIEW QUESTIONS

1. What was the essential logic of Galton's research on English judges and their relatives?
2. How did Galton dismiss the "nurture" argument?

3. Galton is said to have created what later came to be called the adoption method. What did he do and what did he conclude from it?

DISCUSSION QUESTION

1. Why does Galton's idea of ability lead naturally to eugenics and what were the two points in the article where he addressed the issue? Why do you think Galton's ideas about eugenics became popular, and why do you think they are viewed skeptically today?

CHAPTER 16

HENRY H. GODDARD (1866–1957): THE KALLIKAK STUDY

Henry Goddard earned a doctorate from G. Stanley Hall at Clark University in 1899. Instead of pursuing an academic career, he took a position at the Vineland Training School for the Feebleminded and began to develop a research program there. After discovering the Binet tests (Chapter 30) while on a tour of Europe, Goddard brought them to America, translated them, and began using them to test the children under his care. He soon became a strong advocate for the Binet tests and for the value of places like Vineland. In 1912, he wrote a short (117 pages) book about the family history of one of his residents, given the pseudonym of Deborah Kallikak. Kallikak was not the true name of the family described in the book, of course, but a name created by Goddard, taken from the Greek terms *kallos* (for beauty or good) and *kakos* (for bad). You will soon learn why the name was perfectly chosen. Goddard used the Kallikak story to support his strong belief that feeblemindedness was inherited, not a product of environmental conditions. The excerpt here is from that book: *The Kallikak Family: A Study in the Heredity of Feeblemindedness* (Goddard, 1912).

That Goddard was writing primarily for the general public, rather than for a scientific audience, is clear from the tone of the opening paragraphs of chapter 1, where he tells the story of Deborah, the central character.

> One bright October day, fourteen years ago, there came to the Training School at Vineland, a little eight-year-old girl. She had been born in an almshouse. Her mother had afterwards married, not the father of this child, but the prospective father of another child, and later had divorced him and married another man, who was also the father of some of her children. She had been led to do this through the efforts of well-meaning people who felt that it was a great misfortune for a child to be born into the world illegitimately. From their standpoint the argument was good, because the mother with four or five younger children was unable to provide adequately for this little girl, whom both husbands refused to support.
>
> On the plea that the child did not get along well at school and might possibly be feeble-minded, she gained admission to the Training School, there

Excerpts from: Goddard, H. H. (1912). *The Kallikak family: A study in the heredity of feeblemindedness*. New York: Macmillan.

to begin a career which has been interesting and valuable to the Institution, and which has led to an investigation that cannot fail to prove of great social import. (pp. 1–2)

Goddard then proceeded, in the next five pages, to quote from notes taken about Deborah during her years at Vineland. The notes are unsystematic and often contradictory; in general she seemed to be poor academically, occasionally disobedient, but talented in several non-academic areas (gardening, sewing, and woodworking). Goddard summed up as follows.

> The reader will see that Deborah's teachers have worked with her faithfully and carefully, hoping for progress, even seeing it where at a later date it became evident that no real advance had been made. Note the oft-repeated "She could if she would," or "If she would only pay attention," and similar expressions, which show the unwillingness of the teachers to admit even to themselves that she is really feeble-minded. In the earliest records it was noted that Deborah was not fond of music, while in later reports it is shown to be her one great accomplishment. Today she is a woman of twenty-two. The consensus of opinion of those who have known her for the last fourteen years in the Institution is as follows: "She is cheerful, inclined to be quarrelsome, very active and restless, very affectionate, willing, and tries; is quick and excitable, fairly good-tempered. Learns a new occupation quickly, but requires a half hour or twenty-four repetitions to learn four lines. Retains well what she has once learned. Needs close supervision. Is bold towards strangers, kind towards animals. Can run an electric sewing machine, cook, and do practically everything about the house. Has no noticeable defect. She is quick and observing, has a good memory, writes fairly, does excellent work in wood-carving and kindergarten, is excellent in imitation. Is a poor reader and poor at numbers. Does fine basketry and gardening. Spelling is poor; music is excellent; sewing excellent; excellent in entertainment work. Very fond of children and good in helping care for them. Has a good sense of order and cleanliness. Is sometimes very stubborn and obstinate. Is not always truthful and has been known to steal, although does not have a reputation for this. Is proud of her clothes. Likes pretty dresses and likes to help in other cottages, even to temporarily taking charge of a group." (pp. 7–8)

Goddard then reported details of the results of several Binet tests with Deborah, pronounced her feebleminded (using the term *moron*, which he invented and defined as an adult with a mental age of 8–12), and made a strong assertion about the hereditary basis of her problem. Note also the presence of a theme that became an important one for Goddard. Like many of his peers, he believed that feeblemindedness was the root cause of many of society's ills (e.g., prostitution, delinquency). One way to improve social conditions, then, was to identify the feebleminded, and then isolate them from normal society. Identification was difficult, because the physical features of "morons" were quite normal. Correct diagnosis therefore required a sophisticated scientific instrument, and for Goddard, this meant the Binet tests. Thus, in Goddard's view, the Binet tests were indispensable, and places like Vineland were essential for the greater good (Zenderland, 1998).

By the Binet Scale this girl showed, in April, 1910, the mentality of a nine-year-old child with two points over; January, 1911, 9 years, 1 point; September, 1911, 9 years, 2 points; October, 1911, 9 years, 3 points. . . .

This is a typical illustration of the mentality of a high-grade feeble-minded person, the moron, the delinquent, the kind of girl or woman that fills our reformatories. They are wayward, they get into all sorts of trouble and difficulties, sexually and otherwise, and yet we have been accustomed to account for their defects on the basis of viciousness, environment, or ignorance.

It is also the history of the same type of girl in the public school. Rather good-looking, bright in appearance, with many attractive ways, the teacher clings to the hope, indeed insists, that such a girl will come out all right. Our work with Deborah convinces us that such hopes are delusions.

Here is a child who has been most carefully guarded. She has been per-sistently trained since she was eight years old, and yet nothing has been accomplished in the direction of higher intelligence or general education. Today if this young woman were to leave the Institution, she would at once become a prey to the designs of evil men or evil women and would lead a life that would be vicious, immoral, and criminal, though because of her men-tality she herself would not be responsible. There is nothing that she might not be led into, because she has no power of control, and all her instincts and appetites are in the direction that would lead to vice.

We may now repeat the ever insistent question, and this time we indeed have good hope of answering it. The question is, "How do we account for this kind of individual?" The answer is in a word "Heredity,"—bad stock. We must recognize that the human family shows varying stocks or strains that are as marked and that breed as true as anything in plant or animal life.

Formerly such a statement would have been a guess, a hypothesis. We submit in the following pages what seems to us conclusive evidence of its truth. (pp. 10–12)

In the following pages, Goddard described his basic method—he con-structed a genealogy of Deborah's family, looking for evidence of feeblemind-edness in her relatives. The procedure involved using "field workers," women whose normal responsibilities at Vineland involved interviewing families of the children in residence there. One goal was to determine if feeblemindedness occurred among relatives, and when Deborah's family was interviewed, it quickly became apparent that anomalies occurred—many were indeed feeble-minded, but some seemed to be among the leading citizens of the region!

Thorough and carefully conducted investigations in the small town and among the farmers of this region showed that [Deborah's extended] family had always been notorious for the number of defectives and delinquents it had produced; and this notoriety made it possible to trace them back for no less than six generations.

It was determined to make a survey of the entire family and to discover the condition, as far as possible, of every person in each generation.

The surprise and horror of it all was that no matter where we traced them, whether in the prosperous rural district, in the city slums to which some had drifted, or in the more remote mountain regions, or whether it was a question of the second or the sixth generation, an appalling amount of defectiveness was everywhere found.

In the course of the work of tracing various members of the family, our field worker occasionally found herself in the midst of a good family of the same name, which apparently was in no way related to the girl whose ancestry we were investigating. In such cases, there was nothing to be done but to beat a retreat and start again in another direction. However, these cases became so frequent that there gradually grew the conviction that ours must be a degenerate offshoot from an older family of better stock. Definite work was undertaken in order to locate the point at which the separation took place. . . .

When Martin Sr., of the good family, was a boy of fifteen, his father died, leaving him without parental care or oversight. Just before attaining his majority, the young man joined one of the numerous military companies that were formed to protect the country at the beginning of the Revolution. At one of the taverns frequented by the militia he met a feeble-minded girl by whom he became the father of a feeble-minded son. This child was given, by its mother, the name of the father in full, and thus has been handed down to posterity the father's name and the mother's mental capacity. This illegitimate boy was Martin Kallikak Jr., the great-great-grandfather of our Deborah, and from him have come four hundred and eighty descendants. One hundred and forty-three of these, we have conclusive proof, were or are feeble-minded, while only forty-six have been found normal. The rest are unknown or doubtful. (pp. 16–18)

Thus, Deborah descended from a line that could be traced to a sexual encounter between a young soldier and a feebleminded young woman he met in a tavern. Now you might be asking yourself at this point just how Goddard knew that the young woman was feebleminded. Although Goddard claimed to have some independent evidence, careful archival research by his biographer, Leila Zenderland, has shown that he had no such evidence (Zenderland, 1998). It appears that she was considered feebleminded because her behavior was considered typical of someone who may have been feebleminded (note: no blame placed on the male).

This "bad side" (*kakos*) of the Kallikak family was then described in detail. The next eleven pages contain a litany of woe—"[t]his is the ghastly story of the descendants of Martin Kallikak Sr., from the nameless feeble-minded girl" (p. 29). But what of the relatives who had become the "good" (*kallos*) side of the family? As it happened, the frisky soldier, Martin, abandoned the "nameless feebleminded girl" and married a "respectable" young woman, thus beginning a family line very different from the one that eventually produced Deborah.

Martin Sr., on leaving the Revolutionary Army, straightened up and married a respectable girl of good family, and through that union has come another line of descendants of radically different character. These now number four hundred and ninety-six in direct descent. All of them are normal people. Three men only have been found among them who were somewhat degenerate, but they were not defective. Two of these were alcoholic, and the other sexually loose.

All of the legitimate children of Martin Sr. married into the best families in their state, the descendants of colonial governors, signers of the Declaration of Independence, soldiers and even the founders of a great university. Indeed, in this family and its collateral branches, we find nothing but good representative citizenship. There are doctors, lawyers, judges, educators, traders, landholders, in short, respectable citizens, men and women prominent in every phase of social life. They have scattered over the United States and are prominent in their communities wherever they have gone. Half a dozen towns in New Jersey are named from the families into which Martin's descendants have married. There have been no feeble-minded among them; no illegitimate children; no immoral women; only one man was sexually loose. There has been no epilepsy, no criminals, no keepers of houses of prostitution. Only fifteen children have died in infancy. There has been one "insane," a case of religious mania, perhaps inherited, but not from the Kallikak side. The appetite for strong drink has been present here and there in this family from the beginning. It was in Martin Sr., and was cultivated at a time when such practices were common everywhere. But while the other branch of the family has had twenty-four victims of habitual drunkenness, this side scores only two. (pp. 29–30)

After giving this general description of the two sides of the case, Goddard presented a series of genealogical charts, included the following one, which is a basic summary.

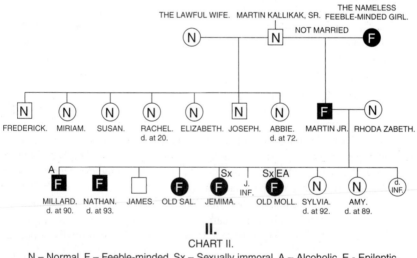

II.

CHART II.

N – Normal. F – Feeble-minded. Sx – Sexually immoral. A – Alcoholic. E - Epileptic. d. INF. – died in infancy.

Although Goddard gave highly detailed descriptions of the "bad" side of the family, he omitted descriptions of the "good" side because he worried that readers would easily recognize these family members. He apparently thought that members of the "bad" side would be unlikely to read his book.

There was no question in Goddard's mind that the two sides of the Kallikak family went their separate ways because of heredity.

The foregoing charts and text tell a story as instructive as it is amazing. We have here a family of good English blood of the middle class, settling upon the original land purchased from the proprietors of the state in Colonial times, and throughout four generations maintaining a reputation for honor and respectability of which they are justly proud. Then a scion of this family, in an unguarded moment, steps aside from the paths of rectitude and with the help of a feeble-minded girl, starts a line of mental defectives that is truly appalling. After this mistake, he returns to the traditions of his family, marries a woman of his own quality, and through her carries on a line of respectability equal to that of his ancestors.

We thus have two series from two different mothers but the same father. These extend for six generations. Both lines live out their lives in practically the same region and in the same environment, except in so far as they themselves, because of their different characters, changed that environment. . . .

Fortunately for the cause of science, the Kallikak family, in the persons of Martin Kallikak Jr. and his descendants, are not open to [an argument concerning environmental influence]. They were feeble-minded, and no amount of education or good environment can change a feeble-minded individual into a normal one, any more than it can change a red-haired stock into a black-haired stock. The striking fact of the enormous proportion of feeble-minded individuals in the descendants of Martin Kallikak Jr. and the total absence of such in the descendants of his half brothers and sisters is conclusive on this point. Clearly it was not environment that has made that good family. They made their environment; and their own good blood, with the good blood in the families into which they married, told. (pp. 50–53)

From the vantage point of the early twenty-first century, it is hard to see how Goddard failed to recognize what seems obvious—whatever might be true about their gene pools, these two family lines clearly illustrate the effects of privilege and grinding poverty. Yet the Kallikak story is a good example of the dangers of what historians call "presentist" thinking—imposing current knowledge and values on the past. Goddard was very much a product of his time, a time when IQ testing was in its infancy and seemed to be an exciting new technology, and a time when Darwinian evolutionary ideas had just been strengthened by the discovery of Mendelian genetics. At that time in his life (Goddard later had second thoughts), Goddard genuinely believed that his work would improve society.

Goddard concluded his book by asking and answering the question "what is to be done?" Although he recognized that people like Martin ought to be more careful whom they meet in bars, he placed most of the blame on the "nameless feeble-minded girl." He argued that if she had not become pregnant after meeting Martin, it probably would have been someone else making her pregnant. Hence, although Goddard considered the possibility of using sterilization to prevent the feebleminded from procreating, his primary solution was to identify the feebleminded and place them in such places as Vineland, where they could learn some simple skills, contribute to society by taking on simple jobs under close supervision, and reduce the need for new prisons (because, for Goddard, most criminals were feebleminded). As he summed up:

> The Kallikak family presents a natural experiment in heredity. A young man of good family becomes through two different women the ancestor of two lines of descendants,—the one characterized by thoroughly good, respectable, normal citizenship, with almost no exceptions; the other being equally characterized by mental defect in every generation. This defect was transmitted through the father in the first generation. In later generations, more defect was brought in from other families through marriage. In the last generation it was transmitted through the mother, so that we have here all combinations of transmission, which again proves the truly hereditary character of the defect.
>
> We find on the good side of the family prominent people in all walks of life and nearly all of the ... descendants owners of land or proprietors. On the bad side we find paupers, criminals, prostitutes, drunkards, and examples of all forms of social pest with which modern society is burdened ... .
>
> Feeble-mindedness is hereditary and transmitted as surely as any other character. We cannot successfully cope with these conditions until we recognize feeble-mindedness and its hereditary nature, recognize it early, and take care of it.
>
> In considering the question of care, segregation through colonization seems in the present state of our knowledge to be the ideal and perfectly satisfactory method. (pp. 116–117)

Goddard remained at Vineland only until 1918, when he moved to Ohio and became director of the state's Bureau of Juvenile Research. He joined the faculty at Ohio State four years later, and retired from there in 1938. Interestingly enough, while at Ohio State he became interested in children at the other end of the continuum—gifted children. As for the Kallikak study, it eventually was dismissed as bad science, with criticism about preconceived biases influencing data interpretation and overlooked environmental factors coming as early as the 1920s (Fancher, 1987). The book remained influential in Germany during the 1930s, however. While the Nazis were burning the books of Freud and others, they reprinted *Die Familie Kallikak*, a translated version of Goddard's work in 1933 (Zenderland, 1998). When the Nazis began killing people as part of their eugenics program, their first victims were the mentally infirm and the "feebleminded."

CONCEPT REVIEW QUESTIONS

1. Why did Goddard consider people like Deborah Kallikak such a threat to society, and why did Goddard consider Vineland the best possible place for Deborah?

2. What was the method used in Goddard's Kallikak study that accounted for the fact that there seemed to be two entirely different groups of Kallikaks living in the same region?

3. Explain Goddard's ideas about the best way to identify and cope with the problem of feeblemindedness.

DISCUSSION QUESTION

1. From today's standpoint, it seems obvious that differences between the two groups of Kallikaks resulted more from the different effects of privilege and poverty. Goddard, a brilliant scientist, failed to see this. Why do you think this was the case?

CHAPTER 17

IVAN PAVLOV (1849–1936): CONDITIONED REFLEXES

All psychology students know the work of the Russian scientist Ivan Petrovich Pavlov, even if they have taken no more than an introductory course. Ask students about Pavlov and the response invariably includes descriptions of bells and drooling dogs. What students seldom appreciate is the extent of the research that Pavlov completed on conditioning—it occupied more than thirty-five years of his life. Students also normally do not know that Pavlov never thought of himself as a research psychologist; in fact, he was sometimes derogatory in his comments about psychology and always insisted that he was a physiologist first and foremost. His interest in conditioning was merely a means to the end of understanding the physiology of the brain.

For his work on the physiology of digestion, Pavlov won a Nobel Prize in 1904, and it was in the process of conducting this research that he decided to investigate more thoroughly what he referred to as "psychic reflexes"—regular and predictable salivation in response to stimuli other than food (e.g., the sight of the lab worker bringing food). In his Nobel Prize address, Pavlov talked little of his digestion research, focusing his comments on his new work on conditioning. Scholars in other countries first learned of his research in the Nobel Prize address, in an invited address he gave in England in 1906 (Pavlov, 1906), and in an article by Robert Yerkes (American psychologist) and Sergius Morgulis (Russian student) in 1909 (Yerkes & Morgulis, 1909). Yet Pavlov's work did not become widely known in English-speaking countries until the translation, in 1927, of a series of lectures that he gave in 1924, summarizing his work to that time. The series included twenty-three lectures, and filled more than 400 pages in the 1960 reprinting that is used here. The excerpt comes from Lectures 1 (historical), 2 (methodology and basic conditioning), 4 (extinction), 17 (experimental neurosis) and 23 (conclusions). In his opening lecture, Pavlov outlined some of the history of research on the reflex, and then explained why physiologists ought to be studying reflexes, not psychologists.

> The activities of the hemispheres have been talked about as some kind of special psychical activity, whose workings we feel and apprehend in ourselves, and by analogy suppose to exist in animals. This is an anomaly which has

Excerpts from: Pavlov, I. (1960). *Conditioned Reflexes: An Investigation of the Physiological Activity of the Cerebral Cortex*. (G. V. Anrep, Trans.). New York: Dover. (Original work published 1927) placed the physiologist in an extremely difficult position. On the one hand it would seem that the study of the activities of the cerebral hemispheres, as of the activities of any other part of the organism, should be within the compass of physiology, but on the other hand it happens to have been annexed to the special field of another science—psychology.

What attitude then should the physiologist adopt? Perhaps he should first of all study the methods of this science of psychology, and only afterwards hope to study the physiological mechanism of the hemispheres? This involves a serious difficulty. It is logical that in its analysis of the various activities of living matter physiology should base itself on the more advanced and more exact sciences—physics and chemistry. But if we attempt an approach from this science of psychology to the problem confronting us we shall be building our superstructure on a science which has no claim to exactness as compared even with physiology. In fact it is still open to discussion whether psychology is a natural science, or whether it can be regarded as a science at all. . . .

If this be the case there is no need for the physiologist to have recourse to psychology. It would be more natural that experimental investigation of the physiological activities of the hemispheres should lay the foundation for a future true science of psychology. (pp. 3–4)

Despite the criticism, however, Pavlov did give some credit to the American psychologist Edward Thorndike (Chapter 8) for pioneering the research on conditioning. He preceded his description of Thorndike by describing the increasing tendency for research on animal behavior to become more objective.

Under the influence of these new tendencies in biology, which appealed to the practical bent of the American mind, the American School of Psychologists—already interested in the comparative study of psychology—evinced a disposition to subject the highest nervous activities of animals to experimental analysis under various specially devised conditions. We may fairly regard the treatise by Thorndyke [sic], *The Animal Intelligence* (1898), as the starting point for systematic investigations of this kind. In these investigations the animal was kept in a box, and food was placed outside the box so that it was visible to the animal. In order to get the food the animal had to open a door, which was fastened by various suitable contrivances in the different experiments. . . . The whole process was understood as being the formation of an association between the visual and tactile stimuli on the one hand and the locomotor apparatus on the other. . . .

At about the same time as Thorndyke was engaged on this work, I myself (being then quite ignorant of his researches) was also led to the objective study of the hemispheres, by the following circumstance: In the course of a detailed investigation into the activities of the digestive glands I had to inquire into the so-called psychic secretion of some of the glands, a task which I attempted in conjunction with a collaborator. As a result of this investigation an unqualified conviction of the futility of subjective methods of inquiry was firmly stamped upon my mind. It became clear that the only satisfactory solution of the problem lay in an experimental investigation by strictly objective methods. For this purpose I started to record all the external stimuli falling on the animal at the time its reflex reaction was manifested (in this particular case the secretion of saliva), at the same time recording all changes in the reaction of the animal.

This was the beginning of these investigations, which have gone on now for twenty-five years—years in which numerous fellow workers on whom I now look back with tender affection have united with mine in this work their hearts and hands. . . . Work on the lines of purely objective investigation into the higher nervous activities has been conducted in the main in the laboratories under my control, and over a hundred collaborators have taken part. (pp. 5–7)

Following a long description of the concept of a reflex, and an analysis of the difference between reflexes and instincts, Pavlov ended his first lecture with a brief narrative of "the simplest reflex from which our investigations started" (p. 13).

If food or some rejectable substance finds its way into the mouth, a secretion of saliva is produced. The purpose of this secretion is in the case of food to alter it chemically, in the case of a rejectable substance to dilute and wash it out of the mouth. . . . But, in addition to this, a similar reflex secretion is evoked when these substances are placed at a distance from the dog and the receptor organs affected are only those of smell and sight. Even the vessel from which the food has been given is sufficient to evoke an alimentary reflex complete in all its details; and, further, the secretion may be provoked even by the sight of the person who brought the vessel, or by the sound of his footsteps. . . . The great advantage to the organism of a capacity to react to [these] stimuli is evident, for it is in virtue of their action that food finding its way into the mouth immediately encounters plenty of moistening saliva, and rejectable substances, often [noxious] to the mucous membrane, find a layer of protective saliva already in the mouth. (pp. 13–14)

In his second lecture, Pavlov described in detail the methodology he developed to examine these "psychic" reflexes systematically. He then defined what he meant by "conditioned" reflexes and "unconditioned" reflexes and described the basic process of acquiring a conditioned reflex.

The path of an inborn reflex is already completed at birth; but the path of the signalizing reflex has still to be completed in the higher nervous centres. We are thus brought to consider the mode of formation of new reflex mechanisms. A new reflex is formed inevitably under a given set of physiological conditions, and with the greatest ease, so that there is no need to take the subjective states of the dog into consideration. With a complete understanding of all the factors involved, the new signaling reflexes are under the absolute control of the experimenter; they proceed according to rigid laws as do any other physiological processes, and must be regarded as being in every sense a part of the physiological activity of living beings. I have termed this new group or reflexes **conditioned reflexes** to distinguish them from the inborn or **unconditioned reflexes**. The term "conditioned" is becoming more and more generally employed, and I think its use is fully justified in that, compared with the inborn reflexes, these new reflexes actually do depend on many conditions, both in their formation and in the maintenance of their physiological activity. . . .

We now come to the precise conditions under which new conditioned reflexes or new connections of nervous paths are established. The fundamental requisite is that any external stimulus which is to become the signal in a conditioned reflex must overlap in point of time with the action of an unconditioned stimulus. In the experiment which I chose as my example the unconditioned stimulus was food. Now if the intake of food by the animal takes places simultaneously with the action of a neutral stimulus which has been hitherto in no way related to food, the neutral stimulus readily acquires the property of eliciting the same reaction in the animal as would food itself. This was the case with the dog employed in our experiment with the metronome. On several occasions the animal had been stimulated by the sound of the metronome and immediately presented with food—i.e. a stimulus which was neutral of itself had been superimposed upon the action of the inborn alimentary reflex. We observed that, after several repetitions of the combined stimulation, the sounds from the metronome had acquired the property of stimulating salivary secretion and of evoking the motor reactions characteristic of the alimentary reflex. . . . Precisely the same occurs with the mild defense reflex to rejectable substances. Introduction into the dog's mouth of a little of an acid solution brings about a quite definite responsive reaction. The animal sets about getting rid of the acid, shaking its head violently, opening its mouth and making movements with its tongue. At the same time it produces copious salivary secretion. The same reaction will infallibly be obtained from any stimulus which has previously been applied a sufficient number of times while acid was being introduced into the dog's mouth. Hence a first and most essential requisite for the formation of a new conditioned reflex lies in a coincidence in time of the action of any previously neutral stimulus with some definite unconditioned stimulus. Further, it is not enough that there should be overlapping between the two stimuli; it is also and equally necessary that the conditioned stimulus should begin to operate before the unconditioned stimulus comes into action.

If this order is reversed, the unconditioned stimulus being applied first and the neutral stimulus second, the conditioned reflex cannot be established at all. (p. 25–27, boldface in the original)

Once a conditioned reflex has been acquired, it can also be eliminated, a process involving cortical inhibition and referred to as *extinction* by Pavlov. He described an example in lecture 4.

We are taking for this experiment the same dog that was used in the second lecture for the conditioned reflex to the sound of the metronome. In testing the reflex the metronome is sounded for 30 seconds during which the secretion of saliva is measured in drops, and at the same time the interval between the beginning of the stimulus and the beginning of the salivary secretion is recorded. This interval is customarily called the latent period. . . . Stimulation by the metronome is not followed in this particular experiment by feeding, i.e. contrary to our usual routine the conditioned reflex is not reinforced.

The stimulus of the metronome is repeated during periods of 30 seconds at intervals of two minutes. The following results are obtained:

Latent Period In Seconds	Secretion of Saliva in Drops During 30 seconds
3	10
7	7
5	8
4	5
5	7
9	4
13	3

One detail ... stands out quite clearly, namely that repeated application of a conditioned stimulus which is not followed up by reinforcement leads to a weakening of the conditioned reflex. If the experiment had been pushed further there would have come a stage when the reflex would entirely disappear. This phenomenon of a rapid and more or less smoothly progressive weakening of the reflex to a conditioned stimulus which is repeated a number of times without reinforcement may appropriately be termed **experimental extinction of conditioned reflexes**. (pp. 48–49, boldface in the original)

For the rest of lecture 4, Pavlov detailed the factors that influenced the rate of extinction. For example, the amount of time between successive trials was important—the shorter the time, the more quickly extinction occurred. Near the end of the lecture, Pavlov described his discovery of what has become known as *spontaneous recovery*.

We shall consider what happens to the conditioned reflexes after they have been subjected to experimental extinction and inquire whether they ever regain their original strength. Left to themselves extinguished conditioned reflexes spontaneously recover their full strength after a longer or shorter interval of time, but this of course does not apply to conditioned reflexes which are only just in process of formation. Such reflexes, being weak and irregular, may require for their recovery after extinction a fresh reinforcement by the underlying unconditioned reflex. However, all those conditioned reflexes which have been fully established invariably and spontaneously return sooner of later to their full strength. This provides one way of determining the depth of extinction; it is measured, other conditions being equal, by the time taken for spontaneous restoration of the extinguished reflex to its original strength. Such time interval may vary for the different reflexes from a few minutes to a number of hours. I shall give a few experiments in illustration. The first is an experiment by Dr. Babkin:
    Presentation of meat powder a short distance away at intervals of three minutes; the reflex is not reinforced.

Time	Secretion of Saliva in c.cs.
11.33 a.m.	1.0
11.36 a.m.	0.6
11.39 a.m.	0.3
11.42 a.m.	0.1
11.45 a.m.	0.0
11.48 a.m.	0.0
Interval of 2 hours	
1.50 p.m.	0.15

(pp. 57–58)

The Babkin results made the point about spontaneous recovery and Pavlov replicated the result with two additional examples. Incidentally, Boris Babkin was an assistant in Pavlov's lab in the years immediately following the 1904 Nobel Prize. He became a prominent Russian physiologist until the early 1920s, when he made the mistake of criticizing the new Communist regime. Told by the authorities to leave Russia, he spent a brief time in London and then moved to Canada, where he became a distinguished professor at Dalhousie University in Nova Scotia and then McGill University in Montreal. He is perhaps best known for writing the first full-length biography of Pavlov (Babkin, 1949). It was published in 1949 to commemorate the 100th anniversary of Pavlov's birth.

In his remaining lectures, Pavlov considered such conditioning phenomena as generalization, discrimination (he called it differentiation), and higher order conditioning. In lecture 17, he explained what he called "pathological disturbances." The dogs occasionally became disturbed, and Pavlov described two types of situations likely to bring about these problems—a breakdown in discrimination ability and a situation of "extreme stimulation." The latter occurred accidentally during a flood when the dogs had to be moved a half-mile from their ground level kennels into the lab.

> During the terrific storm, amid the breaking of the waves of the increasing water against the walls of the building and the noise of breaking and falling trees, the animals had to be quickly transferred by making them swim in little groups from the kennels into the laboratory, where they were kept on the first floor, all huddled up indiscriminately. All this produced a very strong and obvious inhibition in all the animals, since there was no fighting or quarreling among them whatever, otherwise a usual occurrence when the dogs are kept together. (p. 313)

After this trauma, Pavlov found that the carefully conditioned reflexes had been completely disrupted in many of his dogs, especially those of an "inhibitable type" (p. 313). In some cases, it took weeks to reestablish the reflexes. A second type of pathological disturbance occurred as the result of a specific laboratory procedure, referred to in texts today as a procedure resulting in *experimental neurosis*.

A projection of a luminous circle on to a screen in front of the animal was repeatedly accompanied by feeding. After the reflex had become well established a differentiation between the circle and an ellipse with a ratio of the semi-axes 2:1, of the same luminosity and the same surface area, was obtained by the usual method. ... A complete and constant differentiation was obtained fairly quickly. The shape of the ellipse was now approximated by stages to that of the circle (ratios of the semi-axes were 3:2, 4:3, and so on) and the development of differentiation continued through the successive ellipses. The differentiation proceeded with some fluctuations ... until an ellipse with a ratio of semi-axes 9:8 was reached. In this case, although a considerable degree of discrimination did develop, it was far from being complete. After three weeks of work upon this discrimination not only did the discrimination fail to improve, but it became considerably worse, and finally disappeared altogether. At the same time the whole behaviour of the animal underwent an abrupt change. The hitherto quiet dog began to squeal in its stand, kept wriggling about, tore off with its teeth the apparatus for mechanical stimulation of the skin, and bit through the tubes connecting the animal's room with the observer, a behaviour which never happened before. On being taken into the experimental room the dog now barked violently, which was also contrary to its usual custom; in short it presented all the symptoms of a condition of acute neurosis. On testing the cruder differentiations they also were found to be destroyed, even the one with the ratio of the semi-axes 2:1. (pp. 290–291)

In his closing lecture, Pavlov made some observations about human behavior based on his research, being suitably cautious—it would be "the height of presumption to regard these first steps in elucidating the physiology of the cortex as solving the intricate problems of the higher psychic activities in man" (p. 395). He was especially intrigued by the "pathological disturbances" research with his dogs, and thought he saw parallels to human behavior. He closed his lectures by indicating that much work remained.

In concluding this series of lectures I want to repeat that all the experiments, those of other workers as well as our own, which have set as their object a purely physiological interpretation of the activity of the higher nervous system, I regard as being in the nature only of a preliminary inquiry. Which has however, I fully believe, entirely justified its inception. We have indisputably the right to claim that our investigation of this extraordinarily complex field has followed the right direction, and that, although not a near, nevertheless a complete, success awaits it. So far as we ourselves are concerned we can only say that at present we are confronted with many more problems than ever before. At first, not to lose sight of the main issue, we were compelled to simplify, and, so to speak, schematize the subject. At present, after having acquired some knowledge of its general principles, we feel surrounded, nay crushed, by the mass of details, all calling for elucidation. (pp. 410–411)

Pavlov remained active for more than a decade after delivering these lectures. Meanwhile, their publication in English in 1927 helped bring about an era of "neobehaviorism" in American psychology in the 1930s. In his 1948 summary of the various neobehavioristic theories of learning, Ernest Hilgard had this to say about Pavlov's impact on American behaviorism.

> The study of conditioned salivary responses in dogs was carried out systematically by Pavlov over many years, and he discovered most of the relationships which later studies have more fully explored. The translations of his terms have become common in the literature of learning. (Hilgard, 1948, p. 55)

CONCEPT REVIEW QUESTIONS

1. Describe the origins of Pavlov's conditioning research.
2. Describe the method for establishing a conditioned reflex.
3. How did Pavlov demonstrate (a) extinction and (b) spontaneous recovery?

DISCUSSION QUESTION

1. What is experimental neurosis and how did Pavlov demonstrate it? Do you see any connections between Pavlov's concept of neurosis and modern ideas about mental illness?

CHAPTER 18

JOHN BROADUS WATSON (1878–1958): A BEHAVIORIST MANIFESTO

John B. Watson, usually considered the founder of the school of psychological thought called Behaviorism, was one of psychology's most colorful and controversial figures, never one to understate an argument when a rhetorical overstatement would do, and not shy about self-promotion. He was a product of the Chicago school of functionalist thinking, taught there by James Angell (Chapter 12), Henry Donaldson, and John Dewey. Trained in the new laboratory psychology that emphasized the study of human mental processes, Watson quickly discovered that he enjoyed working with animals as subjects and disliked the experimental study of human conscious experience (in part because he failed to become competent at or interested in introspection). This preference reflected his upbringing as a farm boy from rural South Carolina and was strong enough for his son to reflect in later years that his father "preferred the company of animals to people most of the time" (Hannush, 1987, p. 150). After completing a doctorate (with a dissertation on developmental changes in the brain and behavior of infant rats) in 1903, Watson was appointed to the faculty at Chicago, where he continued his studies on animal behavior.

Watson left Chicago for Johns Hopkins in 1908 and within a year became head of the psychology program there. Over the next few years he solidified his reputation as a rising star and began to hint in several of his writings that it was time for a change in psychology. In early 1913 he delivered a series of eight lectures on his ideas and research at Columbia University. The opening talk, which has come to be called the "behaviorist manifesto," was entitled "Psychology as the Behaviorist Views It." Within a month of delivering the talk, Watson published it in *Psychological Review* (Watson, 1913). Right from the opening paragraph of this famous paper, it is clear that Watson wanted to attract the attention of his peers.

> Psychology as the behaviorist views it is a purely objective experimental branch of natural science. Its theoretical goal is the prediction and control of behavior. Introspection forms no essential part of its methods, nor is the scientific value of its data dependent upon the readiness with which they

Excerpts from: Watson, J. B. (1913). Psychology as the behaviorist views it. *Psychological Review, 20*, 158–177.

lend themselves to interpretation in terms of consciousness. The behaviorist, in his efforts to get a unitary scheme of animal response, recognizes
no dividing line between man and brute. The behavior of man, with all of
its refinement and complexity, forms only a part of the behaviorist's total
scheme of investigation. (p. 158)

This is a passage quoted in virtually every history of psychology text-
book. In five sentences, Watson (a) firmly assigned psychology to the natural
sciences, (b) articulated a clear set of goals for a scientific psychology, (c) completely rejected the introspection-based research of the majority of his peers, and
(d) fully accepted an evolutionary model of behavior. The remainder of the paper
elaborated on these points. He began by attacking the introspective method
that was in vogue at the time, describing in several paragraphs the difficulties
inherent in defining psychology as the study of consciousness. He then focused
specifically on the problem of the subjectivity of the introspective method as
championed by Titchener's structuralist strategy (Chapter 11), again not failing
to mince words.

I do not wish unduly to criticize psychology. It has failed signally, I believe,
during the fifty-odd years of its existence as an experimental discipline to
make its place in the world as an undisputed natural science. Psychology,
as it is generally thought of, has something esoteric in its methods. If you
fail to reproduce my findings, it is not due to some fault in your apparatus
or in the control of your stimulus, but it is due to the fact that your introspection is untrained. The attack is made upon the observer and not upon
the experimental setting. In physics and in chemistry the attack is made
upon the experimental conditions. The apparatus was not sensitive enough,
impure chemicals were used, etc. In these sciences a better technique will
give reproducible results. Psychology is otherwise. If you can't observe 3–9
states of clearness in attention, your introspection is poor. If, on the other
hand, a feeling seems reasonably clear to you, your introspection is again
faulty. You are seeing too much. Feelings are never clear.

The time seems to have come when psychology must discard all reference to consciousness; when it need no longer delude itself into thinking
that it is making mental states the object of observation. We have become
so enmeshed in speculative questions concerning the elements of mind, the
nature of conscious content ... that I, as an experimental student, feel that
something is wrong with our premises and the types of problems which
develop from them. There is no longer any guarantee that we all mean the
same thing when we use the terms now current in psychology. Take the case
of sensation. A sensation is defined in terms of its attributes. One psychologist will state with readiness that the attributes of a visual sensation are
quality, extension, duration, and intensity. Another will add clearness. Still
another that of order. I doubt if any one psychologist can draw up a set of
statements describing what he means by sensation which will be agreed to
by three other psychologists of different training.... Titchener, who has
fought the most valiant fight in this country for a psychology based upon
introspection, feels that these differences of opinion ... are perfectly natural
in the present undeveloped state of psychology. While it is admitted that
every growing science is full of unanswered questions, surely only those

who are wedded to the system as we now have it, who have fought and suffered for it, can confidently believe that there will ever be any greater uniformity than there is now in the answers we have to such questions. I firmly believe that two hundred years from now, unless the introspective method is discarded, psychology will still be divided on the question as to whether auditory sensations have the quality of 'extension', whether intensity is an attribute which can be applied to color, whether there is a difference in 'texture' between image and sensation and upon many hundreds of others of like character. (pp. 163–164)

Because they also were unwilling to reject introspection as method and because they also investigated consciousness (from the standpoint of its adaptive value rather than to identify its structural contents, however), functionalist psychologists were also targets for Watson's criticism. One might think that Watson might have been more sympathetic to an approach that was so deeply rooted in evolutionary thinking, and perhaps would have been more respectful of his own intellectual roots, but not so.

My psychological quarrel is not with the systematic and structural psychologist alone. The last fifteen years have seen the growth of what is called functional psychology. This type of psychology decries the use of elements in the static sense of the structuralists. It throws emphasis upon the biological significance of conscious processes instead of upon the analysis of conscious states into introspectively isolable elements. I have done my best to understand the difference between functional psychology and structural psychology. Instead of clarity, confusion grows upon me. The terms sensation, perception, affection, emotion, volition are used as much by the functionalist as by the structuralist. The addition of the word 'process' . . . after each serves in some way to remove the corpse of 'content' and to leave 'function' in its stead. Surely if these concepts are elusive when looked at from a content standpoint, they are still more deceptive when viewed from the angle of function, and especially so when function is obtained by the introspection method. It is rather interesting that no functional psychologist has carefully distinguished between 'perception' . . . as employed by the systematist, and 'perceptual process' as used in functional psychology. It seems illogical and hardly fair to criticize the psychology which the systematist gives us, and then to utilize his terms without carefully showing the changes in meaning which are to be attached to them. I was greatly surprised some time ago when I opened Pillsbury's [a student of Titchener] book and saw psychology defined as the 'science of behavior'. A still more recent text states that psychology is the 'science of mental behavior'. When I saw these promising statements I thought, now surely we will have texts based upon different lines. After a few pages the science of behavior is dropped and one finds the conventional treatment of sensation, perception, imagery, etc., along with certain shifts in emphasis and additional facts which serve to give the author's personal imprint. (pp. 165–166)

Having rejected structuralist and functional approaches to psychology, Watson shifted his argument to his behaviorist alternative. A key statement is his admittedly simplistic assertion ("crass and raw," in Watson's terms) that the fundamental goal of his behaviorism is to be able to specify stimulus-response connections.

> This leads me to the point where I should like to make the argument constructive. I believe we can write a psychology, define it as Pillsbury, and never go back upon our definition: never use the terms consciousness, mental states, mind, content, introspectively verifiable, imagery, and the like.... It can be done in terms of stimulus and response, in terms of habit formation, habit integrations and the like. Furthermore, I believe that it is really worthwhile to make this attempt now.
>
> The psychology which I should attempt to build up would take as a starting point, first, the observable fact that organisms, man and animal alike, do adjust themselves to their environment by means of hereditary and habit equipments. These adjustments may be very adequate or they may be so inadequate that the organism barely maintains its existence; secondly, that certain stimuli lead the organisms to make the responses. In a system of psychology completely worked out, given the response the stimuli can be predicted; given the stimuli the response can be predicted. Such a set of statements is crass and raw in the extreme, as all such generalizations must be. Yet they are hardly more raw and less realizable than the ones which appear in the psychology texts of the day. (pp. 166–167)

To illustrate the research strategy he had in mind, Watson referred to some research he had completed on migrating birds in the Dry Tortugas, an island in the Gulf of Mexico. Note how he makes it clear that behavioral strategies for investigating animals can also be applied to humans.

> Some time ago I was called upon to make a study of certain species of birds. Until I went to Tortugas I had never seen these birds alive. When I reached there I found the animals doing certain things: some of the acts seemed to work peculiarly well in such an environment, while others seemed to be unsuited to their type of life. I first studied the responses of the group as a whole and later those of individuals. In order to understand more thoroughly the relation between what was habit and what was hereditary in these responses, I took the young birds and reared them. In this way I was able to study the order of appearance of hereditary adjustments and their complexity, and later the beginnings of habit formation. My efforts in determining the stimuli which called forth such adjustments were crude indeed. Consequently my attempts to control behavior and to produce responses at will did not meet with much success. Their food and water, sex and other social relations, light and temperature conditions were all beyond control in a field study. I did find it possible to control their reactions in a measure by using the nest and egg (or young) as stimuli. It is not necessary in this paper to develop further how such a study should be carried out and how work of this kind must be supplemented by carefully controlled laboratory experiments. Had I been called upon to examine the natives of some of the Australian tribes, I should have gone about my task in the same way. I should have found the problem more difficult: the types of responses called forth by physical stimuli would have been more varied, and the number of effective stimuli larger. I should have had to determine the social setting of their lives in a far more careful way. These savages would be more influenced by the responses

of each other than was the case with the birds. Furthermore, habits would have been more complex and the influences of past habits upon the present responses would have appeared more clearly. Finally, if I had been called upon to work out the psychology of the educated European, my problem would have required several lifetimes. But in the one I have at my disposal I should have followed the same general line of attack. In the main, my desire in all such work is to gain an accurate knowledge of adjustments and the stimuli calling them forth. My final reason for this is to learn general and particular methods by which I may control behavior. My goal is not 'the description and explanation of states of consciousness as such', nor that of obtaining such proficiency in mental gymnastics that I can immediately lay hold of a state of consciousness and say, 'this, as a whole, consists of gray sensation number 350, of such and such extent, occurring in conjunction with the sensation of cold of a certain intensity; one of pressure of a certain intensity and extent,' and so on *ad infinitum*. (pp. 167–168, italics in the original)

In the final portion of Watson's paper, he argued that, unlike introspective psychology, behaviorism had the potential to deliver direct applications that would positively affect people's lives. The potential to apply psychology to better people's lives ultimately made behaviorism attractive to psychologists and to the American public at large.

If psychology would follow the plan I suggest, the educator, the physician, the jurist and the business man could utilize our data in a practical way, as soon as we are able, experimentally, to obtain them. Those who have occasion to apply psychological principles practically would find no need to complain as they do at the present time. Ask any physician or jurist today whether scientific psychology plays a practical part in his daily routine and you will hear him deny that the psychology of the laboratories finds a place in his scheme of work. I think the criticism is extremely just. One of the earliest conditions which made me dissatisfied with psychology was the feeling that there was no realm of application for the principles which were being worked out in content terms.

What gives me hope that the behaviorist's position is a defensible one is the fact that those branches of psychology which have already partially withdrawn from the parent, experimental psychology, and which are consequently less dependent upon introspection are today in a most flourishing condition. Experimental pedagogy, the psychology of drugs, the psychology of advertising, legal psychology, the psychology of tests, and psychopathology are all vigorous growths. These are sometimes wrongly called 'practical' or 'applied' psychology. Surely there was never a worse misnomer. In the future there may grow up vocational bureaus which really apply psychology. At present these fields are truly scientific and are in search of broad generalizations which will lead to the control of human behavior. For example, we find out by experimentation whether a series of stanzas may be acquired more readily if the whole is learned at once, or whether it is more advantageous to learn each stanza separately and then pass to the succeeding. We do not attempt to apply our findings. The application of this principle is purely voluntary on the part of the teacher. In the psychology of drugs we may show the effect upon behavior of certain doses of caffeine. We may reach the conclusion that caffeine has a good effect upon the speed and accuracy of work. But these are general principles. We leave it to the individual as to whether the results of our tests shall be applied or not. Again, in legal testimony, we test the effects of recency upon the reliability of a witness's report. We test the accuracy of the report with respect to moving objects, stationary objects, color, etc. It depends upon the judicial machinery of the country to decide whether these facts are ever to be applied. . . .

In concluding, I suppose I must confess to a deep bias on these questions. I have devoted nearly twelve years to experimentation on animals. It is natural that such a one should drift into a theoretical position which is in harmony with his experimental work. Possibly I have put up a straw man and have been fighting that. There may be no absolute lack of harmony between the position outlined here and that of functional psychology. I am inclined to think, however, that the two positions cannot be easily harmonized. Certainly the position I advocate is weak enough at present and can be attacked from many standpoints. Yet when all this is admitted I still feel that the considerations which I have urged should have a wide influence upon the type of psychology which is to be developed in the future. What we need to do is to start work upon psychology, making behavior, not consciousness, the objective point of our attack. Certainly there are enough problems in the control of behavior to keep us all working many lifetimes without ever allowing us time to think of consciousness. . . . Once launched in the undertaking, we will find ourselves in a short time as far divorced from an introspective psychology as the psychology of the present time is divorced from faculty psychology. (pp. 168–175)

From the force of Watson's argument, you might think that Behaviorism quickly prevailed over its foes. Yet as Samelson (1981; 1985) has shown convincingly, there was little initial reaction to the paper. Titchener (1914) predictably criticized it, but most psychologists saw it as just one of a number of assaults on the increasingly beleaguered method of introspection. And the paper hardly started a stampede of psychologists to the behaviorist camp—six years later Watson wrote to a colleague that his brand of psychology wasn't very popular among psychologists (Samelson, 1981). Behaviorism did become popular, of course, but it did not have a firm hold in American psychology until the late 1920s. Watson certainly played a key role—he could always point to the 1913 paper as a clear articulation of behaviorism, and he continued to promote his ideas both within and outside of the academic world.

The behaviorist manifesto certainly did Watson no harm—within two years he was elected president of the American Psychological Association, and he maintained his status as a leader in the field over the next few years. In part to show that behaviorism could be applied to human affairs, and in part due to an opportunity afforded to him to have access to a virtually unlimited supply of infants from the nearby obstetrical ward of Johns Hopkins Medical School, Watson plunged into a program of research on newborns and infants, investigating and categorizing basic reflexes, for instance, and studying their emotional lives. His initial goal, consistent with the "given the stimulus, predict the response" strategy proposed in the manifesto, was to identify fundamental emotions and the stimuli that produced them. The outcome was a paper by Watson and Morgan (1917) entitled "Emotional Reactions and Psychological Experimentation." They identified three basic human emotions, each produced by a small range of stimuli. The response of fear, for example, was called out by just two stimuli—loud noises and loss of support (e.g., being dropped). Finding that just two stimuli instinctively caused fear, Watson then set out to demonstrate that conditioning produced the longer list of fears typically shown by older children. The result was the famous "Little Albert" experiment (Watson & Rayner, 1920), in which Watson and a graduate student, Rosalie Rayner, attempted to condition fear in an infant. Despite being seriously flawed methodologically (Harris, 1979), it continues to be a regular feature of the learning chapter in every introductory psychology text to this day.

As for the remainder of Watson's career, the events surrounding the Little Albert study changed his life dramatically (Buckley, 1989). He fell in love with his graduate student co-author, but he happened to be married at the time, and the ensuing divorce scandal resulted in his forced resignation from Johns Hopkins. He never returned to academia, but turned to the world of business and became successful as an advertising executive. Throughout the 1920s, he continued to advocate for behaviorism in the popular press and in several books, including one on child rearing (Watson, 1928). He and Rosalie married and had two sons, but she died suddenly from pneumonia in 1935. Watson died in 1958, a year after being honored for his work by the American Psychological Association.

CONCEPT REVIEW QUESTIONS

1. The opening paragraph of Watson's "manifesto" is one of psychology's most quoted passages. What is it about this paragraph that should have shaken up the psychology "establishment" of the time?

2. How did Watson's work with birds on Dry Tortugas illustrate his new approach to psychology?

3. What was the basis for Watson's criticism of introspective structural psychology? And why did he include functionalism in his criticism?

DISCUSSION QUESTION

1. Behaviorism became popular in American psychology, in part because it promised to be useful in improving lives. What did Watson have to say about how behaviorism could deliver useful applications?

CHAPTER 19

EDWARD C. TOLMAN (1886–1959): COGNITIVE MAPS

In the section about the origins of behaviorism, you learned about the work of Pavlov and Watson. In the 1920s, behaviorism began gathering momentum as a movement and, by the 1930s, this school of thought began to be the dominant one in American experimental psychology. Several researchers became prominent during this era of what came to be called Neobehaviorism. They included Edwin Guthrie, Clark Hull, B. F. Skinner (next chapter), and the author of this chapter's excerpt, Edward Tolman. Tolman was educated in electrochemistry at M.I.T. in Boston, earned a Ph.D. in psychology from Harvard in 1915, and then, after a brief stay at Northwestern University, spent the majority of his career at the University of California at Berkeley. There he developed an extensive research program, mostly involving rats in mazes.

Neobehaviorists agreed on two important points—that light could be shed on human behavior by studying simpler animals (e.g., white rats), and that the most important phenomenon to understand about behavior was learning or conditioning (Goodwin, 2008). Understanding what an individual was like meant, in essence, understanding that individual's conditioning history. Where the neobehaviorists disagreed was in the manner in which conditioning occurred. Thus, each of the neobehaviorists developed a unique "theory of learning." The major expression of Tolman's views appeared in his 1932 book, *Purposive Behavior in Animals and Men* (Tolman, 1932). This chapter's excerpt comes from a well-known paper he wrote fourteen years later, a paper often cited when Tolman is referred to as the creator of the term "cognitive map."

Tolman started the paper by outlining his goals (notice the assumption that human behavior can be understood by generalizing from animal behavior). He then gave a general description of a typical maze learning experiment with rats, and pointed out that the explanations for these experiments varied considerably among different learning theorists.

> I shall devote the body of this paper to a description of experiments with rats. But I shall also attempt in a few words at the close to indicate the significance of these findings on rats for the clinical behavior of men. . . .

Excerpts from: Tolman, E. C. (1948). Cognitive maps in rats and men. *Psychological Review, 55*, 189–208.

In the typical [maze learning] experiment a hungry rat is put at the entrance of the maze (alley or elevated), and wanders about through the various true path segments and blind alleys until he finally comes to the food box and eats. This is repeated (again in the typical experiment) one trial every 24 hours and the animal tends to make fewer and fewer errors (that is, blind-alley entrances) and to take less and less time between start and goal-box until finally he is entering no blinds at all and running in a very few seconds from start to goal. The results are usually presented in the form of average curves of blind-entrances, or of seconds from start to finish, for groups of rats.

All students agree as to the facts. They disagree, however, on theory and explanation.

(1) First, there is a school of animal psychologists which believes that the maze behavior of rats is a matter of mere simple stimulus-response connections. Learning, according to them, consists in the strengthening of some of these connections and in the weakening of others. According to the "stimulus-response" school the rat in progressing down the maze is helplessly responding to a succession of external stimuli—sights, sounds, smells, pressures, etc. impinging upon his external sense organs—plus internal stimuli coming from the viscera and from the skeletal muscles. These external and internal stimuli call out the walkings, runnings, turnings, retracings, smellings, rearings, and the like which appear. The rat's central nervous system, according to this view, may be likened to a complicated telephone switchboard. There are the incoming calls from sense-organs and there are the outgoing messages to muscles. . . .

It must be noted in addition, however, that this stimulus-response school divides further into two subgroups.

(a) There is a subgroup which holds that the mere mechanics involved in the running of a maze is such that the crucial stimuli from the maze get presented simultaneously with the correct responses more frequently than they do with any of the incorrect responses. Hence, just on the basis of this greater frequency, the neural connections between the crucial stimuli and the correct responses will tend, it is said, to get strengthened at the expense of the incorrect ones.

(b) There is a second subgroup in this stimulus-response school which holds that the reason the appropriate connections get strengthened relative to the inappropriate ones is, rather, the fact that the responses resulting from the correct connections are followed more closely in time by need-reductions. Thus a hungry rat in a maze tends to get to food and have his hunger reduced *sooner* as a result of the true path responses than as a result of the blind alley responses. And such immediately following need-reductions or, to use another term, such "positive reinforcement" tend somehow, it is said, to strengthen the connections which have most closely preceded them. This is as if . . . the satisfaction-receiving part of the rat telephoned back to Central and said . . . : "Hold that connection; it was good; and see to it that you blankety-blank well use it again the next time these same stimuli come in." These theorists also assume (at least some of them do some of the time) that if bad results—"annoyances," "negative reinforcements"—follow, then this same satisfaction-and-annoyance-receiving part of the rat will telephone back and say, "Break that connection and don't you dare use it next time either." (pp. 189–192, italics in the original)

It is clear from Tolman's tone that he was not very impressed with stimulus-response explanations of maze learning, whether they emphasize pure repetition and frequency (John Watson, for example) or reinforcement and drive reduction (Clark Hull, for example). As an alternative, Tolman proposed an approach that reflected the influence of gestalt psychology on his thinking. Rather than learning a series of mechanical S-R connections, the rat develops a *cognitive map*, Tolman believed, an overall knowledge of the general configuration of the maze. Rather than a telephone switchboard as a metaphor for the brain, Tolman likened the brain to a "map control room" (p. 192).

So much for a brief summary of the two subvarieties of the "stimulus-response," or telephone switchboard school.

(2) Let us turn now to the second school. This group (and I belong to them) may be called the field theorists. We believe that in the course of learning something like a field map of the environment gets established in the rat's brain. We agree with the other school that the rat in running a maze is exposed to stimuli and is finally led as a result of these stimuli to the responses which actually occur. We feel, however, that the intervening brain processes are more complicated, more patterned and often, pragmatically speaking, more autonomous than do the stimulus-response psychologists. Although we admit that the rat is bombarded by stimuli, we hold that his nervous system is surprisingly selective as to which of these stimuli it will let in at any given time.

Secondly, we assert that the central office itself is more like an old-fashioned telephone exchange. The stimuli, which are allowed in, are not connected by just simple one-to-one switches to the outgoing responses. Rather, the incoming impulses are usually worked over and elaborated in the central control room into a tentative, cognitive-like map of the environment. And it is this tentative map, indicating routes and paths and environmental relationships, which finally determines what responses, if any, the animal will finally release.

Finally, I personally, would hold further that it is also important to discover in how far these maps are relatively narrow and strip-like or relatively broad and comprehensive. Both strip-maps and comprehensive-maps may be either correct or incorrect in the sense that they may (or may not), when acted upon, lead successfully to the animal's goal. The differences between such strip maps and such comprehensive maps will appear only when the rat is later presented with some change within the given environment. Then, the narrower and more strip-like the original map, the less it will carry over successfully to the new problem; whereas, the wider and more comprehensive it was, the more adequately it will serve in the new setup. In a strip-map the given position of the animal is connected by only a relatively simple and single path to the position of the goal. In a comprehensive-map a wider arc of the environment is represented, so that, if the starting position of the animal be changed or variations in the specific routes be introduced, this wider map will allow the animal still to behave relatively correctly and to choose the appropriate new route. (pp. 192–193)

Having introduced his map concept, and emphasized the greater value of broad "comprehensive" cognitive maps, as opposed to narrower "strip" maps, Tolman then turned to a detailed description of five different sets of experiments to support his theory. The first involved what Tolman called "latent" learning, and he began with a study completed by one of his graduate students (Blodgett, 1929). Blodgett used a relatively simple maze called a 6-unit T-maze—rats had to make six different decisions about whether to make a left or a right turn at the point where the lines of a "T" join.

> [Blodgett] ran three groups of rats through a six-unit alley maze.... He had a control group and two experimental groups. The error curves for these groups appear [below]. The solid line shows the error curve for Group I, the control group. These animals were run in orthodox fashion. That is, they were run one trial a day and found food in the goal-box at the end of each trial. Groups II and III were the experimental groups. The animals of Group II, the dash line, were not fed in the maze for the first six days but only in their home cages some two hours later. On the seventh day (indicated by the small cross) the rats found food at the end of the maze for the first time and continued to find it on subsequent days. The animals of Group III were treated similarly except that they first found food at the end of the maze on the third day and continued to find it there on subsequent days. It will be observed that the experimental groups as long as they were not finding food did not appear to learn much. (Their error curves did not drop.) But on the days immediately succeeding their first finding of the food their error curves did drop astoundingly. It appeared, in short, that during the non-rewarded trials these animals had been learning much more than they had exhibited. This learning, which did not manifest itself until after the food had been introduced, Blodgett called "latent learning." Interpreting these results anthropomorphically, we would say that as long as the animals were not getting any food at the end of the maze they continued to take their time in going through it—they continued to enter many blinds. Once, however, they knew they were to get food, they demonstrated that during these preceding non-rewarded trials they had learned where many of the blinds were. They had been building up a "map," and could utilize the latter as soon as they were motivated to do so. (pp. 194–195)

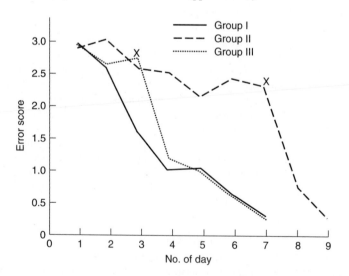

Tolman followed up on the Blodgett experiment with a similar study that he completed with another graduate student (Tolman & Honzik, 1930). It used a larger maze (a 14-unit T-maze), a larger number of animal subjects, and found the same result—rats learned the maze even if they were not immediately reinforced for doing so.

After the latent learning studies, Tolman described other research that questioned the stimulus-response model. He tried to show that rats did some decision-making at choice points in a maze; that the rats actively processed information while they were learning a maze, rather than having S-R connections produced mechanically and automatically; and that they tested various hypotheses about the layout of the maze. In a final set of studies, he returned to the "cognitive map" concept. Tolman labeled the studies "spatial orientation" experiments and began with an anecdotal reference to an observation made by fellow experimentalist Karl Lashley about rats in mazes. Note that in a typical experiment with an alley maze (i.e., a maze with side walls), experimenters kept rats from getting out of the maze by putting a glass cover on top of the maze.

> As early as 1929, Lashley reported incidentally the case of a couple of rats who, after having learned an alley maze, pushed back the cover near the starting box, climbed out and ran directly across the top to the goal-box where they climbed down in again and ate. Other investigators have reported related findings. All such observations suggest that rats really develop wider spatial maps which include more than trained-upon specific paths. In the experiments now to be reported this possibility has been subjected to further examination.
>
> In the first experiment, Tolman, Ritchie, and Kalish ... used the set-up shown in [the diagram below].

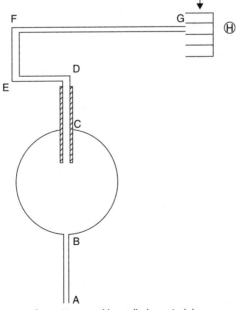

Apparatus used in preliminary training

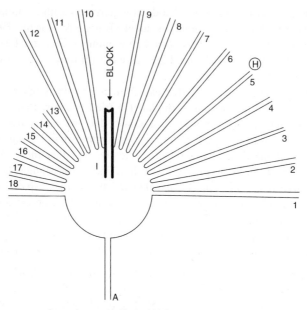

Apparatus used in the test trial

This was an elevated maze. The animals ran from A across the open circular table through CD (which had alley walls) and finally to G, the food box. H was a light which shown directly down the path from G to F. After four nights, three trials per night, in which the rats learned to run directly and without hesitation from A to G, the apparatus was changed to the sun-burst shown in [the diagram above]. The starting path and the table remained the same but a series of radiating paths was added.

The animals were again started at A and ran across the circular table into the alley and found themselves blocked. They then returned onto the table and began exploring practically all the radiating paths. After going out a few inches only on any one path, each rat finally chose to run all the way out on one. (pp. 203–204)

Tolman then displayed a bar graph that showed the rats' choices. The most frequently chosen path was #6, chosen by 34% of the rats. Path #1 was chosen by 17%, and no other path was chosen by more than 9% (Tolman, Ritchie, & Kalish, 1946).

It appears there was a preponderant tendency to choose path No. 6 which ran to a point some four inches in front of where the entrance to the food-box had been. The only other path chosen with any appreciable frequency was No. 1—that is, the path which pointed perpendicularly to the food-side of the room.

The results seem to indicate that the rats in this experiment had learned not only to run rapidly down the original roundabout route but also, when this was blocked and radiating paths presented, to select one pointing rather directly towards the point where the food had been or else at least to select a path running perpendicularly to the food-side of the room.

> As a result of their original training, the rats had, it would seem, acquired not merely a strip-map to the effect that the original specifically trained-on path led to food but, rather, a wider comprehensive map to the effect that food was located in such and such a direction in the room. (p. 204)

Tolman next described a second experiment with a similar design and outcome, and then spent the final portion of his paper drawing broad conclusions and trying to extend the lessons of his maze studies into the wider world of human behavior.

> And now, at last, I come to the humanly significant and exciting problem: namely, what are the conditions which favor narrow strip-maps and what are those which tend to favor broad comprehensive maps not only in rats but also in men?
>
> There is considerable evidence scattered throughout the literature bearing on this question both for rats and for men. . . . I have not time to present it in any great detail. I can merely summarize it by saying that narrow strip-maps rather than broad comprehensive maps seem to be induced: (1) by a damaged brain, (2) by an inadequate array of environmentally presented cues, (3) by an overdose of repetitions on the original trained-on path and (4) by the presence of too strongly motivational or of too strongly frustrating conditions. (pp. 205–207)

Tolman indicated that he wished to focus on the fourth of these points, and then launched into a long and rambling account of the dangers of too much motivation and/or too much frustration on people's lives, addressing such clinical topics as regression, fixation, and displaced aggression. He then concluded, without providing any indication of how this could occur, that a solution to many of the world's problems was to train people for broad rather than narrow maps. He then finished with this paragraph.

> We must, in short, subject our children and ourselves (as the kindly experimenter would his rats) to the optimal conditions of moderate motivation and of an absence of unnecessary frustrations, whenever we put them and ourselves before the great God-given maze which is our human world. I cannot predict whether or not we will be able, or be allowed, to do this; but I *can* say that, only insofar as we *are* able and *are* allowed, have we cause for hope. (p. 208, italics in the original)

Although Tolman was a vigorous advocate for his theory, and was known in particular for his disagreements with Clark Hull, he also had a healthy perspective on his work, recognizing that it was not all that critical in the general scheme of things. Near the end of his life, when he was asked for a final description of his theory, he produced an elaborate 66-page chapter, but concluded with this paragraph:

> I started out, as I indicated in the introduction, with considerable uneasiness. I felt that my so-called system was outdated and that it was a waste of time for me to try to rehash it. . . . I have to confess, however, that as I have gone along I have become again more and more involved in it, though I still realize its many weak points. The system may well not stand

up to any final canons of scientific procedure. But I do not much care. I have liked to think about psychology in ways that have proved congenial to me. Since ... psychology [is] still immersed in such tremendous realms of the uncertain and the unknown, the best that any individual scientist ... can do seems to be to follow his own gleam and his own bent, however inadequate they may be. In fact, I suppose that actually this is what we all do. In the end, the only sure criterion is to have fun. And I have had fun. (Tolman, 1959, p. 152)

This closing paragraph of Tolman's final description of his theory appeared in 1959, the year he died.

CONCEPT REVIEW QUESTIONS

1. Tolman clearly disagreed with what he called the "stimulus-response" school. What were the two varieties of this so-called school? What did Tolman propose as an alternative to the "stimulus-response" school?
2. What did Tolman mean by "latent learning," and how did he demonstrate it?
3. What did Tolman mean by a "cognitive map," and how did he demonstrate it?

DISCUSSION QUESTION

1. Maze learning studies with rats were and continue to be common. What arguments could you make about the relevance for such research, in terms of what can be learned about human behavior?

CHAPTER 20

B. F. SKINNER (1904–1990): AN EXPERIMENTAL ANALYSIS OF BEHAVIOR

During the mid to late twentieth century, no psychologist was more prominent than B. F. Skinner, heir to John Watson (Chapter 18) as the voice of behaviorism. Like Watson, Skinner was an enthusiastic public advocate for his behaviorist beliefs. Unlike Watson, whose professional life was shortened by scandal, Skinner had a long and productive research career. In addition, Skinner was more effective than Watson in showing how behaviorism could be applied for human benefit.

An English major in college, Skinner tried but failed as a writer, and then discovered behaviorism in the 1920s when he came upon the writings of Watson and Pavlov (Chapter 17). He completed a doctorate at Harvard in 1931, remained there for several more years as a prestigious Harvard Fellow, and then taught at the University of Minnesota and Indiana University before returning to Harvard in 1948. There he remained until his retirement in 1974 (Bjork, 1993).

Skinner (like Watson) believed that psychology should have two main goals—the prediction and control of behavior. This could be accomplished through an "experimental analysis of behavior," that is, a full description of behaviors (e.g., key pecking by a pigeon); the environments in which these behaviors occurred (e.g., a small lighted chamber with a key to be pecked, and a retractable food tray—an apparatus that has come to be called the Skinner box); and the immediate consequences of the behaviors (e.g., food reinforcement for key pecking). The analysis applied equally well to humans, he believed (e.g., a child's tantrum behavior occurring in a toy store environment resulting in the consequence of getting a toy). While recognizing that behaviors are influenced by an individual's innate behavioral tendencies and capabilities, Skinner focused on how behaviors were shaped by the environment. In that sense, then, he made contact with the environmentalism of Watson and illustrated neobehaviorism's emphasis on the importance of learning.

An excellent summary of operant conditioning in Skinner's words can be found in *Science and Human Behavior*, a book he wrote in 1953. The following excerpt, from a 1969 paperback reprinting, includes material from Chapters 5 (Operant Behavior), 6 (Shaping and Maintaining Operant Behavior),

Excerpts from: Skinner, B. F. (1953). *Science and human behavior*. New York: Macmillan.

and 7 (Operant Discrimination). In Chapter 4, Skinner described Pavlovian conditioning, the conditioning of reflexes. In Chapter 5, he opened by distinguishing these conditioned reflexes from "operant behavior."

> Reflexes, conditioned or otherwise, are mainly concerned with the internal physiology of the organism. We are most often interested, however, in behavior which has some effect upon the surrounding world. Such behavior raises most of the practical problems in human affairs and is also of particular theoretical interest because of its special characteristics. The consequences of behavior may 'feed back' into the organism. When they do so, they may change the probability that the behavior which produced them will occur again. The English language contains many words, such as 'reward' and 'punishment,' which refer to this effect, but we can get a clear picture of it only through experimental analysis. (p. 59)

Skinner then credited Thorndike (Chapter 8) with being among the first "to study changes brought about by the consequences of behavior" (p. 59), and went on to describe a simple operant conditioning situation for a pigeon isolated in an experimental chamber.

> To study the process which Thorndike called stamping in, we must have a 'consequence.' Giving food to a hungry organism will do. We can feed our subject conveniently with a small food tray which is operated electrically. When the tray is first opened, the organism will probably react to it in ways which interfere with the process we plan to observe. Eventually, after being fed from the tray repeatedly, it eats readily, and we are then ready to make this consequence contingent upon behavior and to observe the results.
>
> We select a relatively simple bit of behavior which may be freely and rapidly repeated, and which is easily observed and recorded. If our experimental subject is a pigeon, for example, the behavior of raising the head above a given height is convenient. This may be observed by sighting across the pigeon's head at a scale pinned on the far wall of the box. We first study the height at which the head is normally held and select some line on the scale which is reached only infrequently. Keeping our eye on the scale we then begin to open the food tray very quickly whenever the head rises above the line. If the experiment is conducted according to specifications, the result is inevitable: we observe an immediate change in the frequency with which the head crosses the line. . . . We may advance almost immediately to a higher line in determining when food is to be presented. In a minute or two, the bird's posture has changed so that the top of the head seldom falls below the line which we first chose. . . .
>
> A response which has already occurred cannot, of course, be predicted or controlled. We can only predict that *similar* responses will occur in the future. The unit of a predictive science is, therefore, not a response but a class of responses. The word 'operant' will be used to describe this class. The term emphasizes the fact that the behavior operates upon the environment to generate consequences. . . . The term will be used both as an adjective (operant behavior) and as a noun to designate the behavior defined by a given consequence.
>
> A single instance in which a pigeon raises its head is a *response*. It is a bit of history which may be reported in any frame of reference we wish to use.

The behavior called 'raising the head,' regardless of when specific instances occur, is an *operant*. (pp. 63–65, italics in the original)

In this simple case, then, an animal is observed and when it raises its head above a certain height, it receives food immediately. As a result, head-raising behavior increases in frequency. Skinner chose the term *operant* to describe this head-raising activity because the behavior "operates" on the environment—when the head raises, it produces a predictable outcome for the pigeon (i.e., food arrives). The behavior has been changed by the reinforcing consequences. The head-raising behavior can also be made to disappear through the process of *extinction*, and the rapidity of extinction can be predicted by the pigeon's prior reinforcement history.

> When reinforcement is no longer forthcoming, a response becomes less and less frequent in what is called 'operant extinction.' If food is withheld, the pigeon will eventually stop lifting its head. In general when we engage in behavior which no longer 'pays off,' we find ourselves less inclined to behave in that way again. If we lose a fountain pen, we reach less and less often into the pocket which formerly held it.
>
> Behavior during extinction is the result of the conditioning which has preceded it, and in this sense the extinction curve gives an additional measure of the effect of reinforcement. If only a few responses have been reinforced, extinction occurs quickly. A long history of reinforcement is followed by protracted responding. The resistance to extinction cannot be predicted from the probability of response observed at any given moment. We must know the history of reinforcement. For example, though we have been reinforced with an excellent meal in a new restaurant, a bad meal may reduce our patronage to zero; but if we have excellent food in a restaurant for many years, several poor meals must be eaten there, other things being equal, before we lose the inclination to patronize it again. (pp. 69–70)

So a behavior can be conditioned to occur more frequently if it is reinforced, and its frequency will decline if reinforcement is withheld. But what defines a *reinforcer*? Answer—it depends, and it is also necessary to distinguish between *positive* reinforcers and *negative* reinforcers.

> The only way to tell whether or not a given event is reinforcing to a given organism is to make a direct test. We observe the frequency of a selected response, then make an event contingent upon it and observe any change in frequency. If there is a change, we classify the event as reinforcing to the organism under the existing conditions. . . .
>
> Events which are found to be reinforcing are of two sorts. Some reinforcements consist in *presenting* stimuli, of adding something—for example, food, water, or sexual contact—to the situation. These we call *positive* reinforcers. Others consist of removing something—for example, a loud noise, a very bright light, extreme cold or heat, or electric shock—from the situation. These we call *negative* reinforcers. In both cases the effect is the same—the probability of response is increased. (p. 73, italics in the original)

In the example of a pigeon being conditioned to raise its head more frequently, the operant behavior (head raising) was a fairly typical behavior for pigeons. All that the researcher had to do was wait for a head raise and reinforce it. But what about the creation of a new behavior, one that seldom occurs naturally? In this case, the researcher would have a long wait before the desired operant would occur. The answer is *shaping*, described by Skinner in Chapter 6.

> Operant conditioning shapes behavior as a sculptor shapes a lump of clay. Although at some point the sculptor seems to have produced an entirely novel object, we can always follow the process back to the original undifferentiated lump, and we can make the successive stages by which we return to this condition as small as we wish. At no point does anything emerge which is very different from what preceded it. The final product seems to have a special unity or integrity of design, but we cannot find a point at which this suddenly appears. In the same sense, an operant is not something which appears full grown in the behavior of the organism. It is the result of a continuous shaping process.
>   ... In the pigeon, the response of pecking at a spot on the wall of the experimental box seems to differ from stretching the neck because no other behavior of the pigeon resembles it.... To get the pigeon to peck the spot as quickly as possible we proceed as follows: We first give the bird food when it turns slightly in the direction of the spot from any part of the cage. This increases the frequency of such behavior. We then withhold reinforcement until a slight movement is made toward the spot. This again alters the general distribution of behavior without producing a new unit. We continue by reinforcing positions closer to the spot, then by reinforcing only when the head is moved slightly forward, and finally only when the beak actually makes contact with the spot.... The original probability of the response in its final form is very low; in some cases it may even be zero. In this way we can build complicated operants which would never appear in the repertoire of the organism otherwise. By reinforcing a series of successive approximations, we bring a rare response to a very high probability in a short time. This is an effective procedure because it recognizes and utilizes the continuous nature of a complex act. The total act of turning toward the spot from any point in the box, walking toward it, raising the head, and striking the spot may seem to be a functionally coherent unit of behavior; but it is constructed by a continual process of differential reinforcement from undifferentiated behavior, just as the sculptor shapes his figure from a lump of clay. (pp. 91–93)

Skinner called his Chapter 6 "Shaping and Maintaining Operant Behavior." After a behavior has been shaped through operant conditioning procedures, is it necessary to keep reinforcing the behavior all the time in order to maintain it? For Skinner, the answer was no, and his work on what he called *schedules of reinforcement* was perhaps his greatest research contribution, culminating in the massive 739-page *Schedules of Reinforcement* (Ferster & Skinner, 1957). The book is essentially an atlas of dozens of different kinds of reinforcement schedules, each accompanied by graphs ("cumulative records") portraying behavior—921 of them in all! In *Science and Human Behavior*, Skinner introduced the topic of schedules and described two basic ones.

> It is important to distinguish between schedules which are arranged by
> a system outside the organism and those which are controlled by the

behavior itself. An example of the first is a schedule of reinforcement which is determined by a clock—as when we reinforce a pigeon every five minutes, allowing all intervening responses to go unreinforced. An example of the second is a schedule in which a response is reinforced after a certain number of responses have been emitted—as when we reinforce every fiftieth response the pigeon makes. The cases are similar in the sense that we reinforce intermittently in both, but subtle differences in the contingencies lead to very different results, often of great practical significance. (p. 100)

These two varieties of reinforcement schedules are known as interval and ratio schedules, respectively, and both types can be "fixed" or "variable." This produces four varieties of reinforcement schedule—fixed interval, variable interval, fixed ratio, and variable ratio—and each variety produces a different pattern of behavior. As you might recall from general psychology, in the chapter on learning:

Fixed Interval:	• behavior reinforced after fixed periods of time
	• produces high rate of behavior just prior to the end of the interval and a low rate at the start of an interval
Variable Interval:	• behavior reinforced after periods of time that vary from trial to trial
	• produces a relatively slow but steady rate of behavior
Fixed Ratio:	• behavior reinforced after a fixed number of responses
	• produces a generally high rate of behavior
Variable Ratio:	• behavior reinforced after a number of responses that varies from trial to trial
	• produces a very high rate of behavior

Ratio schedules, because they rely directly on the individual responding, produce higher rates of responding than interval schedules. High fixed ratio schedules, however, can produce pauses after reinforcement, a problem solved by variable ratio schedules. Variable ratios, however, can produce some pathological behavior (e.g., excessive gambling).

Under ratios of reinforcement which can be sustained, the behavior eventually shows a very low probability just after reinforcement.... The effect is marked under high fixed ratios because the organism has "a long way to go" before the next reinforcement. Wherever a piecework schedule is used—in industry, education, salesmanship, or the professions—low morale or low interest is most often observed just after a unit of work has been completed....

We get rid of the pauses after reinforcement on a fixed-ratio schedule by adopting essentially the same practice as in variable-interval reinforcement: we simply vary the ratios over a considerable range around some mean value. Successive responses may be reinforced or many hundreds of unreinforced responses may intervene.... This 'variable-ratio reinforcement' is much more powerful than a fixed-ratio schedule.... A pigeon may respond as rapidly as five times per second and maintain this rate for many hours.

The efficacy of such schedules in generating high rates has long been known to the proprietors of gambling establishments. Slot machines, roulette wheels, dice cages, horse races, and so on pay off on a schedule of variable-ratio reinforcement. Each device has it own auxiliary reinforcements, but the schedule is the important characteristic. Winning depends upon placing a bet and in the long run upon the number of bets placed, but no particular payoff can be predicted. The ratio is varied by any one of several 'random' systems. The pathological gambler exemplifies the result. Like the pigeon with its five responses per second for many hours, [the gambler] is the victim of an unpredictable contingency of reinforcement. The long-term net gain or loss is almost irrelevant in accounting for the effectiveness of this schedule. (pp. 103–104)

Operant behavior is shaped and maintained through the reinforcement, often administered intermittently on a schedule, but behavior also comes under the control of the environment. *Stimulus control* is a key operant concept, elaborated in Chapter 6 of *Science and Human Behavior*. Skinner started with an important distinction between elicited and emitted behavior, referring back to the original head-raising experiment with pigeons.

Operant conditioning may be described without mentioning any stimulus which acts before the response is made. In reinforcing neck-stretching in the pigeon it was necessary to wait for the stretching to occur; we did not elicit it. When a baby puts his hand to his mouth, the movement may be reinforced by the contact of hand and mouth, but we cannot find any stimulus which elicits the movement and which is present each time it occurs. Stimuli are always acting on an organism, but their functional connection with operant behavior is not like that in a reflex. Operant behavior, in short, is *emitted*, rather than *elicited*. . . .

   Most operant behavior, however, acquires important connections with the surrounding world. We may show how it does so in our pigeon experiment by reinforcing neck-stretching when a signal light is on and allowing it to be extinguished when the light is off. Eventually stretching occurs only when the light is on. We can then demonstrate a stimulus-response connection which is roughly comparable to a conditioned or unconditioned reflex: the appearance of the light will be quickly followed by an upward movement of the head. But the relation is fundamentally different. It has a different history and different current properties. We describe the contingency by saying that a *stimulus* (the light) is the occasion upon which a *response* (stretching the neck) is followed by *reinforcement* (with food). We must specify all three terms. The effect upon the pigeon is that eventually the response is more likely to occur when the light is on. The process through which this comes about is called *discrimination*. Its importance in a theoretical analysis, as well as in the practical control of behavior, is obvious: when discrimination has been established, we may alter the probability of a response instantly by presenting or removing the discriminative stimulus. (pp. 107–108, italics in the original)

At the beginning of this excerpt, I mentioned that Skinner believed that psychology should have just two goals—the prediction and control of behavior. From his own words, you can get a sense of what he meant. If we can understand the contingencies of behavior—the environment in which a behavior has resulted in predictable consequences, then we are in a position to predict and control. For example, if a pigeon has been reinforced for head raising whenever the light is on, we can (a) predict head raising with the light and no movement without the light, and (b) control the behavior by turning the light on or off. Ultimately, he believed, virtually all non-instinctive and non-reflexive behavior could be understood in this way.

This is but a small sample of Skinner's writing from a fairly large book (449 pages). I have chosen to excerpt passages describing some of Skinner's fundamental ideas, but the book also ranges far and wide, as is evident from some of the other chapter titles: "Aversion, Avoidance, Anxiety," "The Self," "Religion," and "Designing a Culture." This last example is part of a three chapter closing section collectively labeled "The Control of Human Behavior" by Skinner, and it shows that fairly early in his career, he was thinking far beyond the Skinner box into the realm of how his ideas applied to life.

Skinner was active up to the day of his death. He gave his final public address on August 18, 1990, to a packed house at the opening session of that year's American Psychological Association meeting in Boston. Although he needed assistance getting to the podium, once there he delivered a typical and forceful attack on what he believed to be the misguided efforts of cognitive psychologists. Skinner died eight days later, still working on the article based on his talk; it appeared in *American Psychologist* later that year (Skinner, 1990).

CONCEPT REVIEW QUESTIONS

1. Describe how you could use operant technology to train a pigeon to reliably raise its head above a certain point. How might you then accomplish extinction?

2. What is a schedule of reinforcement? Give two examples and explain their importance.

3. What did Skinner mean by stimulus control, how is it accomplished, and how is it connected to the concept of discrimination?

DISCUSSION QUESTION

1. What is meant by the operant concept of shaping, why is it necessary for most learning to occur, and why did Skinner liken an operant conditioning researcher to a sculptor? Can you think of ways in which your actions "shape" the behavior of your friends?

CHAPTER 21

SIGMUND FREUD (1887–1967): THE CLARK LECTURES ON PSYCHOANALYSIS

In 1909, Clark University in Worcester, Massachusetts, had reached its twentieth birthday. Its President, G. Stanley Hall, decided to mark the event with a series of lectures by those most prominent in the fields of study present at Clark. The well-known photo of the group of psychologists at the event includes such luminaries as William James (Chapter 9), E. B. Titchener (Chapter 11), and James McKeen Cattell (Chapter 29). Hall was determined to add an international flavor to the event, and to that end he invited Wundt (Chapter 5), who declined, and Ebbinghaus (Chapter 6), who died that year. But the main attraction was an up-and-coming Viennese physician whose theories about human nature were starting to be widely known, and had captured Hall's imagination (Ross, 1972). This, of course, was Sigmund Freud, who accepted Hall's invitation and made his first and only trip to America. Hall also invited Freud's colleague Carl Jung, who lectured on his new word association technique.

From Tuesday, September 7, 1909 through Saturday, the 11th, Freud gave five improvised lectures, in German, to the assembled audience of educators, scientists, and press. They were soon published in Hall's journal, the *American Journal of Psychology*. In the opening lecture, Freud paid homage to his Viennese colleague Joseph Breuer and described the origins of psychoanalysis in Breuer's Anna O. case, with its famous quote about hysterics suffering from their traumatic memories. Lecture two focused on the related processes of resistance and repression and described how Freud shifted from hypnosis to free association as a key method for delving into the unconscious. The following excerpt comes from lectures three and four, and is taken from a 1957 translation of the talks by James Strachey.

Lecture three continued the discussion of psychoanalytic methodology, discussing how the unconscious can be probed by analyzing dreams and seemingly meaningless everyday behaviors (e.g., "Freudian slips"). After opening his talk with some further discussion of free association and Jung's related word

Excerpts from: Freud, S. (1957). *Five lectures on psycho-analysis* (J. Strachey, Trans.). London: Hogarth. (Original work published 1909)

association procedure, Freud began to discuss dreams, starting with an attempt to disarm those who might be initially skeptical about "dream interpreters." Dreams, Freud believed, were a "royal road" to the unconscious.

> Working over the ideas that occur to patients when they submit to the main rule of psycho-analysis is not our only technical method of discovering the unconscious. The same purpose is served by two other procedures: the interpretation of patients' dreams and the exploitation of their faulty and haphazard actions.
>
> I must admit, Ladies and Gentlemen, that I hesitated for a long time whether, instead of giving you this condensed general survey of the whole field of psycho-analysis, it might not be better to present you with a detailed account of dream-interpretation. I was held back by a purely subjective and seemingly secondary motive. It seemed to me almost indecent in a country which is devoted to practical aims to make my appearance as a "dream interpreter," before you could possibly know the importance that can attach to that antiquated and derided art. The interpretation of dreams is in fact the royal road to a knowledge of the unconscious; it is the securest foundation of psycho-analysis and the field in which every worker must acquire his convictions and seek his training. If I am asked how one can become a psycho-analyst, I reply, "By studying one's own dreams." Every opponent of psycho-analysis hitherto has, with a nice discrimination, either evaded any consideration of *The Interpretation of Dreams*, or has sought to skirt over it with the most superficial objections. If, on the contrary, you can accept the solutions of the problems of dream-life, the novelties with which psycho-analysis confronts your minds will offer you no further difficulties. (p. 33)

Freud's comments about critics "evading any consideration" of the dream book or superficially dismissing it, combined with his complaints at other times that nobody would read the book, were a bit disingenuous. Sales were indeed slow at first—it took six years to sell the first printing of 600 copies—but Freud's *Interpretation of Dreams* (Freud, 1900/1938) was neither ignored nor condemned. In fact, it was widely reviewed and generally praised as "epoch-making" (Decker, 1975).

Dreams hold great significance for us, Freud argued, even though we tend to dismiss them, our low opinion based on "the strange character even of those dreams that are not confused and meaningless, and on the obvious absurdity and nonsensicalness of other dreams" (p. 34). Their significance, he believed, lies in their central purpose, which for Freud was the fulfillment of our deepest wishes. Wish fulfillment is easy to see in children's dreams, but disguised in adult dreams.

> In the first place, not all dreams are alien to the dreamer, incomprehensible and confused. If you inspect the dreams of very young children, from eighteen months upwards, you will find them perfectly simple and easy to explain. Small children always dream of the fulfillment of wishes that were aroused in them the day before but not satisfied. You will need no interpretative art in order to find this simple solution; all you need do is to enquire into the child's experiences on the previous day (the "dream day").

Certainly the most satisfactory solution of the riddle of dreams would be to find that adults' dreams too were like those of children—fulfillments of wishful impulses that had come to them on the dream-day. And such in fact is the case. The difficulties in the way of this solution can be overcome step by step if dreams are analyzed more closely.

The first and most serious objection is that the content of adults' dreams is as a rule unintelligible and could not look more unlike the fulfillment of a wish. And here is the answer. Such dreams have been subjected to distortion; the psychical process underlying them might originally have been expressed in words quite differently. You must distinguish the *manifest content of the dream*, as you vaguely recollect it in the morning and laboriously (and, as it seems, arbitrarily) clothe it in words, and the *latent dream-thoughts*, which you must suppose were present in the unconscious. This distortion in dreams is the same process that you have already come to know in investigating the formation of hysterical symptoms. It indicates, too, that the same interplay of mental forces is at work in the formation of dreams as in that of symptoms. The manifest content of the dream is the distorted substitute for the unconscious dream-thoughts and this distortion is the work of the ego's forces of defense—of resistances. In waking life these resistances altogether prevent the repressed wishes of the unconscious from entering consciousness; and during the lowered state of sleep they are at least strong enough to oblige them to adopt a veil of disguise. Thereafter, the dreamer can no more understand the meaning of his dreams than the hysteric can understand the connection and significance of his symptoms. (pp. 34–35, italics in the original)

In therapy, Freud developed the method free association to enable the "hysteric" to achieve some insight into origins of the hysteric symptoms. In like manner, in order to achieve a better understanding of dreams, it was necessary to incorporate the free association method into the effort.

You can convince yourself that there are such things as latent dream-thoughts and that the relation between them and the manifest content of the dream is really as I have described it, if you carry out an analysis of dreams, the technique of which is the same as that of psycho-analysis. You entirely disregard the apparent connections between the elements in the manifest dream and collect the ideas that occur to you in connection with each separate element of the dream by free association according to the psycho-analytic rule of procedure. From this material you arrive at the latent dream-thoughts, just as you arrived at the patient's hidden complexes from his associations to his symptoms and memories . . . The true meaning of the dream, which has now taken the place of its manifest content, is always clearly intelligible; it has its starting-point in experiences of the previous day, and proves to be a fulfillment of unsatisfied wishes. The manifest dream, which you know from your memory when you wake up, can therefore only be described as a *disguised* fulfillment of *repressed* wishes. (pp. 35–36, italics in the original)

If the manifest content of dreams represents a distortion, by the unconscious, of the true meaning, the question of exactly how this occurs remains. Freud's answer was in the concept of "dream work," involving such processes as "condensation" and "displacement." Note also the importance of symbolism to Freud's theory.

You can also obtain a view, by a kind of synthetic work, of the process which
has brought about the distortion of the unconscious dream-thoughts into the
manifest content of the dream. We call this process the "dream-work." It
deserves our closest theoretical interest, since we are able to study in it,
as nowhere else, what unsuspected psychical processes can occur in the
unconscious, or rather, to put it more accurately, *between* two separate psychical systems like the conscious and the unconscious. Among these freshly
discovered psychical processes those of *condensation* and *displacement*
are especially noticeable. The dream-work is a special case of the effects
produced by two different mental groupings on each other—that is, of the
consequences of mental splitting; and it seems identical in all essentials with
the process of distortion which transforms the repressed complexes into
symptoms where there is unsuccessful repression. . . .

I should like you to notice, too, that the analysis of dreams has shown us
that the unconscious makes use of a particular symbolism, especially for representing sexual complexes. This symbolism varies partly from individual
to individual; but partly it is laid down in a typical form and seems to coin-
cide with the symbolism which, as we suspect, underlies our myths and fairy
tales. It seems not impossible that these creations of the popular mind might
find an explanation through the help of dreams. (p. 36, italics in the original)

Hence, the manifest content of the dream includes images that serve as
symbols for the deeper, more meaningful latent content. For Freud, as you
might guess, many of the symbols had sexual content. Elongated objects symbolized male sexuality, while anything symbolizing containers represented females.
Both condensation and displacement involve symbolism. In *condensation*, two
or more latent or unconscious thoughts combine to form a single thought that is
symbolized in an image reported in the manifest dream. For example, a dream
in which a person hesitates about going into a church with a large (i.e., elongated) steeple might symbolize the conflict between the unconscious thoughts
associated with sexuality and morality. In *displacement*, a minor part of the
manifest content might be the major part of the latent content, and vice versa.
Thus, a long dream about a golf match might include a single moment of inde-
cision about which club to choose. That small part of the manifest content, for a
Freudian, might in fact symbolize a deeper problem about the lack of direction
in one's life (and because a "club" is involved, sex would surely find a way into
the interpretation).

In the second portion of his third lecture, Freud discussed events that
appear to be trivial, yet provide another glimpse of the unconscious mind. He
also made his determinist beliefs clear—even the simplest of accidents points
to some predictable unconscious motive.

The phenomena in question are the small faulty actions performed by both
normal and neurotic people, to which as a rule no importance is attached:
forgetting things that might be known and sometimes in fact *are* known
(e.g., the occasional difficulty in recalling proper names), slips of the tongue
in talking, by which we ourselves are so often affected, analogous slips of
the pen and misreadings, bungling the performance of actions, losing objects
or breaking them. All of these are things for which as a rule no psychological

determinants are sought and which are allowed to pass without criticism as consequences of distraction or inattention or similar causes. Besides these there are the actions and gestures which people carry out without noticing them at all, to say nothing of attributing any psychological importance to them; playing about and fiddling with things, humming tunes, fingering parts of one's own body or one's clothing and so on. These small things, faulty actions and symptomatic or haphazard actions alike, are not so insignificant as people, by sort of conspiracy of silence, are ready to suppose. They always have a meaning, which can usually be interpreted with ease and certainty from the situation in which they occur. And it turns out that once again they give expression to impulses and intentions which have to be kept back and hidden from one's own consciousness, or that they are actually derived from the same repressed wishful impulses and complexes which we have already come to know as the creators of symptoms and the constructors of dreams. They therefore deserve to be rated as symptoms, and if they are examined they may lead, just as dreams do, to the uncovering of the hidden part of the mind. . . .

As you already see, psycho-analysts are marked by a particularly strict belief in the determination of mental life. For them there is nothing trivial, nothing arbitrary or haphazard. They expect in every case to find suffi-cient motives where, as a rule, no such expectation is raised. Indeed, they are prepared to find *several* motives for one and the same mental occur-rence, whereas what seems to be our innate craving for causality declares itself satisfied with a *single* psychical cause. (pp. 37–38, italics in the original)

Freud did not give any specific examples of these Freudian slips in the Clark lecture, but *The Psychopathology of Everyday Life* (Freud, 1901/1938) is full of them. For instance, when a lecturer referred to the "Freuer-Breudian" theory of hysteria instead of "Breuer-Freudian," when referring to their jointly authored hysteria book, Freud suggested that a hostile motive was behind the mistake. In another case, a female patient who couldn't recall (i.e., had repressed) where a man had touched her, quickly changed the subject to her summer home. When asked where it was located, she said "near the mountain loin" instead of "mountain lane."

Freud's fourth Clark lecture was a summary of his *Three Contributions on the Theory of Sex* (Freud, 1905/1938), and it included a discussion of childhood sexuality and the famous Oedipal complex. He began with a bold assertion.

First and foremost we have found out one thing. Psycho-analytic research traces back the symptoms of patient's illnesses with really surprising regu-larity to impressions from their *erotic life*. It shows us that the pathogenic wishful impulses are in the nature of erotic instinctual components; and it forces us to suppose that among the influences leading to the illness the pre-dominant significance must be assigned to erotic disturbances, and that this is the case in both sexes. (p. 40, italics in the original)

Freud next tried to convince his audience that understanding what happens during childhood is essential for an understanding of the development of hysteric symptoms, even if these symptoms appeared long after childhood.

> In another set of cases psycho-analytic investigation traces the symptoms back, it is true, not to sexual experiences but to commonplace traumatic ones. But this distinction loses its significance owing to another circumstance. For the work of analysis required for the thorough explanation and complete recovery of a case never comes to a stop at events that occurred at the time of the onset of the illness, but invariably goes back to the patient's puberty and early childhood; and it is only there that it comes upon the impressions and events which determined the later onset of the illness. It is only experiences in childhood that explain susceptibility to later traumas and it is only by uncovering these almost invariably forgotten memory-traces and by making them conscious that we acquire the power to get rid of symptoms. (p. 41)

And what are these childhood experiences that are so critical? For Freud, they were sexual in nature. He tried to convince his audience of the reality of childhood sexuality by defining sexuality broadly as virtually any type of pleasurable bodily activity.

> Put away your doubts, then, and join me in a consideration of infantile sexuality from the earliest age. A child's sexual instinct turns out to be put together out of a number of factors; it is capable of being divided up into numerous components which originate from various sources. Above all, it is still independent of the reproductive function, into the service of which it will be later brought. It serves for the acquisition of different kinds of pleasurable feeling, which, basing ourselves on analogies and connections, we bring together under the idea of sexual pleasure. The chief source of infantile sexual pleasure is the appropriate excitation of certain parts of the body that are especially susceptible to stimulus: apart from the genitals, these are the oral, anal and urethral orifices, as well as the skin and other sensory surfaces. Since at this first phase of infantile sexual life satisfaction is obtained from the subject's own body and extraneous objects are disregarded, we term this phase (from a word coined by Havelock Ellis) that of *auto-erotism*. We call the parts of the body that are important in the acquisition of sexual pleasure "erotogenic zones." (p. 43–44, italics in the original)

As examples of autoerotic behaviors, Freud mentioned such things as thumb-sucking and innocent genital manipulation. He then turned to the question of object-choice, which led him to the Oedipal complex, one of his best known and most controversial ideas.

> Children's relations to their parents, as we learn alike from direct observations of children and from later analytic examination of adults, are by no means free from elements of accompanying sexual excitation. The child takes both of its parents, and more particularly one of them, as the object of its erotic wishes. In so doing, it usually follows some indication from its parents, whose affection bears the clearest characteristics of a sexual activity, even though of one that is inhibited in its aims. As a rule a father prefers his daughter and a mother her son; the child reacts to this by wishing, if he is a son, to take his father's place, and, if she is a daughter, her mother's. The feelings which are aroused in these relations between parents and children and in the resulting ones between brothers and sisters are not only of a positive or affectionate kind but also of a negative or hostile one. The complex which is thus formed is doomed to early repression; but it continues to

exercise a great and lasting influence from the unconscious. It is to be suspected that, together with its extensions, it constitutes the *nuclear complex* of
every neurosis, and we may expect to find it no less actively at work in other
regions of mental life. The myth of King Oedipus, who killed his father and
took his mother to wife, reveals, with little modification, the infantile wish,
which is later opposed and repudiated by the *barrier against incest*. Shake-
speare's *Hamlet* is equally rooted in the soil of the incest-complex, but under
a better disguise. . . .

It is inevitable and perfectly normal that a child should take his parents as
the first objects of his love. But his libido should not remain fixated to these
first objects; later on, it should merely take them as a model, and should
make a gradual transition from them on to extraneous people when the time
for the final choice of an object arrives. (pp. 47–48, italics in the original)

Freud's fifth and final lecture described the importance of transference
for the successful outcome of psychoanalysis and held out the hope that the
individual's libido, the psychic energy associated with the sex drive, could be
directed toward socially useful activities, a process he referred to as sublimation.

Freud always had fond memories of being invited to Clark, believing that
it enhanced the status of psychoanalysis and gave it some international standing (Gay, 1988). Among academic psychologists in the United States, Freud's
ideas received mixed reviews, however. Although generally impressed with the
breadth of Freud's theory, William James (Chapter 9), for instance, thought that
Freud was "obsessed with fixed ideas" and, concerning the dream theory, "I
can make nothing in my own case with [it], and obviously 'symbolism' is a
most dangerous method" (quotes from Rosenzweig, 1992, p. 174). Yet psychoanalysis became quite popular in the United States, especially in the 1920s, and
especially in the medical community as a basis for treatment (Hornstein, 1992).
As for Freud, he continued to develop and refine his theory over his remaining
years. In the 1920s, for example, he introduced his three-part theory of personality (id, ego, superego) that can be found in the personality chapters of every
introductory psychology text (Freud, 1923/1959).

CONCEPT REVIEW QUESTIONS

1. Freud described dreams as the "royal road" to the unconscious. Explain.
2. Freud discussed what later came to be called "Freudian slips." Why did he
   consider the analysis of these errors to be relevant to understanding a patient?
3. Why did Freud consider the study of childhood to be so important?

DISCUSSION QUESTION

1. Imagine that it is 1909 and you are learning about Freud's ideas for the first
   time by listening to these lectures. Why do you think psychoanalysis was
   controversial?

CHAPTER 22

KAREN HORNEY (1885–1952): CONFLICT, ANXIETY, AND NEUROSIS

By the time of the Clark lectures (previous chapter) in 1909, Freud had attracted a number of followers to psychoanalysis. A few remained loyal to him throughout their lives; Ernest Jones, for example, spread the Freudian gospel faithfully and eventually became Freud's handpicked biographer. Others were initially part of Freud's inner circle, but parted ways with him for various reasons; Carl Jung and Alfred Adler are the best-known examples. A third and much larger group of psychoanalysts were not directly associated with Freud, but strongly influenced by him. This third group includes Karen Horney (pronounced HORN-eye), a German psychiatrist who was initially an enthusiastic supporter of Freud, but eventually struck out on her own. As you will see in this chapter, while she accepted the Freudian emphasis on the unconscious and the potentially disastrous effects of a dysfunctional childhood, she rejected Freud's core belief that the conflict between biological instincts and societal restrictions fueled neurosis, and she was scornful of Freud's ideas about women. For Horney, neurosis developed out of interpersonal conflict and was strongly influenced by culture, and gender differences reflected society more than biology.

Horney earned her medical degree, with a specialty in psychiatry, in 1915. Her own experiences as a psychoanalytic patient of Karl Abraham, a well-known member of Freud's inner circle, first inclined her toward the practice of psychoanalysis. She helped found the Berlin Psychoanalytic Institute in 1920, but over the next decade, her increasing criticism of Freud led to strained relations with colleagues, and she sought greener pastures in the United States (Cloninger, 2004). In 1932, she accepted an invitation to be an associate director of a psychoanalytic institute in Chicago; two years later, she moved to New York and became an important member of the New York Psychoanalytic Institute. Throughout the decade of the 1930s and into the 1940s, she developed her theoretical position, which she explained in a series of books—*The Neurotic Personality of Our Time* (Horney, 1937), *New Ways in Psychoanalysis* (Horney, 1939), and *Our Inner Conflicts: A Constructive Theory of Neurosis*

Excerpts from: Horney, K. D. (1945). *Our inner conflicts: A constructive theory of neurosis*. New York: Norton.

(Horney, 1945). This chapter's excerpt comes from the 1945 book. Horney opened the book by outlining her differences with Freud.

Freud's postulations in regard to feminine psychology set me thinking about the role of cultural factors. Their influence on our ideas of what constitutes masculinity or femininity was obvious, and it became just as obvious to me that Freud had arrived at erroneous conclusions because he failed to take [cultural influences] into account. My interest in this subject grew over the course of fifteen years.... And my impressions were confirmed when I came to the United States in 1932. I saw then that the attitudes and the neuroses of persons in this country differed in many ways from those I had observed in European countries, and that only the difference in civilizations could account for this. My conclusions finally found their expression in *The Neurotic Personality of Our Time*. The main contention here was that neuroses are brought about by cultural factors—which more specifically meant that neuroses were generated by disturbances in human relations.

In the years before I wrote *The Neurotic Personality* I pursued another line of research that followed logically from the earlier hypothesis. It revolved around the question as to what the driving forces are in neurosis. Freud had been the first to point out that these were compulsive drives. He regarded these drives as instinctual in nature, aimed at satisfaction and intolerant of frustration. Consequently he believed that they were not confined to neuroses *per se* but operated in all human beings. If, however, neuroses were an outgrowth of disturbed human relationships, this postulation could not possibly be valid. The concepts I arrived at on this score were, briefly, these. Compulsive drives are specifically neurotic; they are born of feelings of isolation, helplessness, fear and hostility, and represent ways of coping with the world despite these feelings; they aim primarily not at satisfaction but at safety; their compulsive character is due to the anxiety lurking behind them. Two of these drives—neurotic cravings for affection and for power—stood out at first in clear relief and were presented in detail in *The Neurotic Personality*.

Though retaining what I considered the fundamentals of Freud's teachings, I realized by that time that my search for a better understanding had led me in directions that were at variance with Freud. If so many factors that Freud regarded as instinctual were culturally determined, if so much that Freud considered libidinal was a neurotic need for affection, provoked by anxiety and aimed at feeling safe with others, then the libido theory was no longer tenable. Childhood experiences remained important, but the influence they exerted on our lives appeared in a new light. Other theoretical differences inevitably followed. Hence it became necessary to formulate in my own mind where I stood in reference to Freud. The result of this clarification was *New Ways in Psychoanalysis*....

My questionings have since proved justified. In the years following, my focus of interest shifted to the role of conflicts in neurosis.... Freud had been increasingly aware of the significance of inner conflicts; he saw them, however, as a battle between repressed forces. The conflicts I began to see were of a different kind. They operated between contradictory sets of neurotic trends, and although they originally concerned contradictory attitudes toward others, in time they encompassed contradictory attitudes toward the self, contradictory qualities and contradictory sets of values....

Freud's pessimism as regards neuroses and their treatment arose from the depths of his disbelief in human goodness and human growth. Man, he postulated, is doomed to suffer or destroy. The instincts which drive him can only be controlled, or at best "sublimated." My own belief is that man has the capacity as well as the desire to develop his potentialities and become a decent human being, and that these deteriorate if his relationship to others and hence to himself is, and continues to be, disturbed. I believe that man can change and go on changing as long as he lives. And this belief has grown with deeper understanding. (pp. 11–19, italics in the original)

For Horney, then, neurosis resulted from interpersonal conflict, and was influenced more by the environment (culture) than by biological instincts. Like Freud, she believed that the events of childhood had an important influence on a person, but she emphasized problems in relationships (e.g., with uncaring parents), rather than the biological forces surrounding such Freudian concepts as the Oedipal complex. Out of dysfunctional relationships, especially with parents, came an important concept for Horney—*basic anxiety*.

Proceeding now to evolve my own position, I see the basic conflict of the neurotic in the fundamentally contradictory attitudes he has acquired toward other persons. . . .

To approach the problem genetically, we must go back to what I have called basic anxiety, meaning by this the feeling a child has of being isolated and helpless in a potentially hostile world. A wide range of adverse factors in the environment can produce this insecurity in the child: direct or indirect domination, indifference, erratic behavior, lack of respect for the child's individual needs, lack of real guidance, disparaging attitudes, too much admiration or the lack of it, lack of reliable warmth, having to take sides in parental disagreements, too much or too little responsibility, overprotection, isolation from other children, injustice, discrimination, unkept promises, hostile atmosphere, and so on and so on.

The only factor to which I should like to draw special attention in this context is the child's sense of lurking hypocrisy in the environment: his feeling that the parents' love, their Christian charity, honesty, generosity, and so on may only be pretense. Part of what the child feels on this score is really hypocrisy; but some of it may be just his reaction to all the contradictions he senses in the parents' behavior. Usually, however, there is a combination of cramping factors. They may be out in the open or quite hidden, so that in analysis one can only gradually recognize these influences on the child's development.

Harassed by these disturbing conditions, the child gropes for ways to keep going, ways to cope with this menacing world. Despite his own weakness and fears he unconsciously shapes his tactics to meet the particular forces operating in his environment. In doing so, he develops not only *ad hoc* strategies but lasting character trends which become a part of his personality. I have called these "neurotic trends." (pp. 40–42, italics in the original)

In an attempt to deal with basic anxiety, Horney argued, the individual can become obsessed with a need for safety and can become neurotic. This can take many forms ("neurotic trends"), but Horney emphasized three—moving toward people, moving against them, and moving away from them.

When moving *toward* people he accepts his own helplessness, and in spite of his estrangement and fears tries to win the affection of others and to lean on them. If there are dissenting parties in the family, he will attach himself to the most powerful person or group. By complying with them, he gains a feeling of belonging and support which makes him feel less weak and less isolated.

When he moves *against* people he accepts and takes for granted the hostility around him, and determines, consciously or unconsciously, to fight. He implicitly distrusts the feelings and intentions of others toward himself. He rebels in whatever ways are open to him. He wants to be the stronger and defeat them, partly for his own protection, partly for revenge.

When he moves *away from* people he wants neither to belong nor to fight, but keeps apart. He feels he has not much in common with them, they do not understand him anyhow. He builds up a world of his own—with nature, with his dolls, his books, his dreams.

In each of these three attitudes, one of the elements in basic anxiety is overemphasized: helplessness in the first, hostility in the second, and isolation in the third. But the fact is that the child cannot make any of these moves wholeheartedly, because under the conditions in which the attitudes develop, all are bound to be present. What we have seen from our panoramic view is only the predominant move.

That this is so will become evident if we jump ahead now to the fully developed neurosis. We all know adults in whom one of the attitudes we have sketched stands out. But we can see, too, that his other tendencies have not ceased to operate. In a predominantly leaning and complying type we can observe aggressive propensities and some need for detachment. A predominantly hostile person has a compliant strain and needs detachment too. And a detached personality is not without hostility or a desire for affection.

The predominant attitude, however, is the one that most strongly determines actual conduct. It represents those ways and means of coping with others in which the particular person feels most at home. (pp. 42–44, italics in the original)

As for the importance of early childhood, Horney argued that it depended on the significance of specific early events, but she was not optimistic that it would be easy for someone to change their basic pattern of relating to others. Furthermore, what starts as a problem relating to others can come to affect how neurotics think of themselves and of the world around them.

[These considerations], it should be added, throw some light on the frequent question whether later experience counts for nothing, whether we are definitely channeled, conditioned once and for all, by our childhood situation. Looking at neurotic development from the point of view of conflicts enables us to give a more adequate answer than is usually offered. These are the possibilities: if the early situation is not too prohibitive of spontaneous growth, later experiences, particularly in adolescence, can have a molding influence. If, however, impact of early experiences has been powerful enough to have molded the child to a rigid pattern, no new experience will be able to break through. In part this is because his rigidity does not leave him open to any new experience: his detachment, for instance, may be too great to permit of anyone's coming close to him, or his dependence is so deep-rooted that he is forced always to play a subordinate role and invite exploitation. In part it is because he will interpret any new experience in the language of his established pattern: the aggressive type, for instance, meeting with friendliness, will view it either as a manifestation of stupidity or an attempt to exploit him; the new experience will tend only to reinforce the old pattern. . . .

Another factor, and one that considerably widens the scope of the conflict, is that the attitudes do not remain restricted to the area of human relationships but gradually pervade the entire personality, as a malignant tumor pervades the whole organic tissue. They end by encompassing not only the person's relation to others but also his relation to himself and to life in general. . . .

It is not accidental that a conflict that starts with our relation to others in time affects the whole personality. Human relationships are so crucial that they are bound to mold the qualities we develop, the goals we set for ourselves, the values we believe in. All these in turn react upon our relations with others and so are inextricably interwoven. (pp. 44–47)

While neurotics are displaying a characteristic way of behaving, either moving toward, against, or away from people, they are also developing a highly distorted self-image that Horney called the *idealized image*. For example, the "moving toward" neurotic might come to believe that he is a perfect person and that everyone would love and admire him. The "moving against" person might believe she is always right and others are necessarily inferior to her and should be scorned. Finally, "moving away" might include the idealized image that the person is so capable that nothing will ever be needed from someone else.

[T]he image is always in large degree removed from reality, though the influence it exerts on the person's life is very real indeed. What is more, it is always flattering in character, as illustrated by a cartoon in the *New Yorker* in which a middle-aged woman sees herself in the mirror as a young girl. The particular features of the image vary and are determined by the structure of the personality: beauty may be held to be outstanding, or power, intelligence, genius, saintliness, honesty, or what you will. Precisely to the extent that the image is unrealistic, it tends to make the person arrogant, in the original meaning of the word; for arrogance, though used synonymously with superciliousness, means to arrogate to oneself qualities that one does not have, or that one has potentially but not factually. And the more unrealistic the image, the more it makes the person vulnerable and avid for outside affirmation and recognition. We do not need confirmation for qualities of which we are certain, but we will be extremely touchy when false claims are questioned. . . .

In all its essentials the idealized image is an unconscious phenomenon. Although his self-inflation may be most obvious even to an untrained observer, the neurotic is not aware that he is idealizing himself. Nor does he know what a bizarre conglomeration of characters is assembled here. He may have a vague sense that he is making high demands upon himself, but mistaking such perfectionist demands for genuine ideals he in no way questions their validity and is indeed rather proud of them. . . .

In contrast to authentic ideals, the idealized image has a static quality. It is not a goal toward whose attainment he strives but a fixed idea which he worships. [Authentic] [i]deals have a dynamic quality; they arouse an incentive to approximate them; they are an indispensable and invaluable force for growth and development. The idealized image is a decided hindrance to growth because it either denies shortcomings or merely condemns them. Genuine ideals make for humility, the idealized image for arrogance. (pp. 96–99)

Because the idealized image is at odds with reality, Horney argued, the neurotic is continually faced with conflicts between this unrealistic self-image and reality. The "moving toward" person who thinks that anyone would love him encounters many who don't. The "moving against" person who believes she is superior to everyone occasionally encounters a truly superior person. And the "moving away" neurotic will, in fact, need others in certain circumstances. To deal with these conflicts, the person develops elaborate defense mechanisms. A major one that Horney referred to was *externalization*, which was similar to the Freudian concept of projection, but went further.

We have seen how all the pretenses to which a neurotic resorts in order to bridge the gap between his real self and his idealized image serve in the end only to widen it. But because the image is of such tremendous subjective value he must continue unremittingly to try to come to terms with it. The ways in which he goes about this are manifold.... Here we shall confine ourselves to examining one ... whose influence on the structure of neurosis is incisive.

When I call this attempt *externalization* I am defining the tendency to experience internal processes as if they occurred outside oneself and, as a rule, to hold these external factors responsible for one's difficulties. It has in common with idealization the purpose of getting away from the real self. But while the process of retouching and recreating the actual personality remains, as it were, within the precincts of self, externalization means abandoning the territory of self altogether. To put it simply, a person can take refuge from his basic conflict in his idealized image; but when discrepancies between the actual self and the idealized one reach a point where tensions become unbearable, he can no longer resort to anything within himself. The one thing left then is to run away from himself entirely and see everything as if it lay outside.

Some of the phenomena that occur here are covered by the term projection, meaning the objectifying of personal difficulties. As commonly applied, projection means the shifting of blame and responsibility to someone else for subjectively rejected trends or qualities such as suspecting others of one's own tendencies toward betrayal, ambition, domination, self-righteousness, meekness, and so on.... Externalization, however, is a more comprehensive phenomenon; the shifting of responsibility is only a part of it. Not only one's faults are experienced in others but to a greater or less degree all feelings.... What is particularly important in this connection, he is unaware of his own attitudes toward himself; he will, for example, feel that someone else is angry with him when he is actually angry with himself. Or he will become conscious of anger at others that in reality he directs at himself. Further, he will ascribe not only his disturbances but also his good moods or achievements to external factors. While his failures will be seen as the decree of fate, his successes will be laid to fortuitous circumstances, his high spirits to the weather, and so on. (pp. 115–116, italics in the original)

The solution for all of these problems is psychoanalysis, of course, and Horney devoted the final chapter of *Our Inner Conflicts* to a description of the process of analysis, the Horney version. Similar to traditional Freudian psychoanalysis, the strategy involved getting patients to achieve insight. In the Horney approach, for example, it is essential that the person come to realize that the idealized image and the tendency to externalize are errors and must be replaced with more realistic ways of thinking. Also, one must recognize one's major tendencies to move toward, against, or away from people, and develop healthier strategies when relating to others.

As mentioned earlier, Horney moved to New York in 1934, after spending two years in Chicago, and became actively involved in the New York Psychoanalytic Institute. As her views diverged more significantly from Freud's, however, conflicts with more traditional analysts at the Institute became acute (similar to the problem she faced earlier in Berlin). Because the Institute was a training center, her colleagues began to believe that her views were detrimental to the program. Consequently, she was essentially ousted from the Institute in 1941—her colleagues voted to remove her as a clinical instructor (Quinn, 1988). Her response was to create her own training institute in New York (The American Institute for Psychoanalysis), an organization (Association for the Advancement of Psychoanalysis), and a journal (the *American Journal of Psychoanalysis*). She produced a final book in 1950 (*Neurosis and Human Growth: The Struggle Toward Self-Realization*), two years before cancer claimed her in 1952.

CONCEPT REVIEW QUESTIONS

1. According to Horney, what causes neurosis?
2. Describe the three strategies that neurotics develop in their relationships with others.
3. What is the idealized self and why is it a problem, according to Horney?

DISCUSSION QUESTION

1. Think back to the previous chapter, on Freud, and the early portion of this excerpt by Horney, and compare Freud's and Horney's ideas about the human condition.

LIGHTNER WITMER (1867–1956): THE PSYCHOLOGICAL CLINIC

Much like Hugo Münsterberg (Chapter 28) and Walter Dill Scott (Chapter 27), Lightner Witmer was trained in experimental psychology at Leipzig, but eventually turned to applied psychology. Witmer earned his doctorate with Wundt in 1892, and then returned to his home state of Pennsylvania and became the director of the psychology laboratory at the University of Pennsylvania. Throughout most of the 1890s he was a vigorous advocate for laboratory psychology, but his interests began to shift in 1896 when a young schoolteacher, who had taken a summer course with Witmer, arrived in the lab with a story about a student of hers who was having serious academic difficulties. The fourteen-year-old seemed to be generally competent, but had problems with spelling. She wondered if Witmer could help.

The boy with poor spelling would be just the first of a number of school children who began appearing in Witmer's lab and, before long, Witmer began to think of his lab as serving the function of a "clinic." From this derives the term "clinical psychology," the title of an article that he wrote in 1907. It was the lead article in a journal that he created, *Psychological Clinic*, and this chapter's excerpt comes from a reprinting of this article in a 1931 book that commemorated Witmer's work (Brotemarkle, 1931, pp. 341–352). Witmer began the article by describing the general operation of the clinic, which was a decade old in 1907, and a recent and typical case. In the first paragraph, note that Witmer dealt not just with cognitive problems, but with behavioral ones as well.

> During the last ten years the laboratory of psychology at the University of Pennsylvania has conducted, under my direction, what I have called "a psychological clinic". Children from the public schools of Philadelphia and adjacent cities have been brought to the laboratory by parents or teachers; these children had made themselves conspicuous because of an inability to progress in school work as rapidly as other children, or because of moral defects which rendered them difficult to manage under ordinary discipline.
>
> When brought to the psychological clinic, such children are given a physical and mental examination; if the result of this examination shows it to be desirable, they are then sent to specialists for the eye or ear, for the nose

Excerpts from: Witmer, L. (1907). Clinical psychology. *Psychological Clinic*, *1*, 1–9.

and throat, and for nervous diseases, one or all, as each case may require. The result of this conjoint medical and psychological examination is a diagnosis of the child's mental and physical condition and the recommendation of appropriate medical and pedagogical treatment. The progress of some of these children has been followed for a term of years.

To illustrate the operation of the psychological clinic, take a recent case sent to the laboratory. . . . The child was brought by his parents, on the recommendation of the Superintendent of Schools. Examination revealed a boy ten years of age, without apparent physical defect, who had spent four years at school, but had made so little progress that his ignorance of the printed symbols of the alphabet made it necessary to use the illiterate card to test his vision. Nothing in the child's heredity or early history revealed any ground for the suspicion of degeneracy, nor did the child's physical appearance warrant this diagnosis. The boy appeared to be of normal intelligence, except for the retardation in school work. The examination of the neurologist . . . confirmed the absence of conspicuous mental degeneracy and of physical defect. The oculist . . . found nothing more serious than a slight far-sighted astigmatism, and the examination . . . for adenoids, gave the child a clean bill of health, so far as the nose and pharynx were concerned. On the conclusion of this examination he was, necessarily, returned to the school from which he came, with the recommendation to the teacher of a course of treatment to develop the child's intelligence. It will require at least three months' observation to determine whether his present pedagogical retardation is based upon an arrest of cerebral development or is merely the result of inadequate methods of education. This case is unequivocally one for the psychologist. (pp. 341–342)

Although 1896 is the traditional starting date for Witmer's clinic, it is clear that Witmer had been interested in the problem of poor performance in school for some time. This passage also makes clear Witmer's passionate belief that remediation was possible.

My attention was first drawn to the phenomena of retardation in the year 1889. At that time, while a student of psychology at the University of Pennsylvania, I had charge of the English branches in a college preparatory school of Philadelphia. In my classes at this academy I was called upon to give instruction in English to a boy preparing for entrance to college, who showed a remarkable deficiency in the English language. His compositions seldom contained a single sentence that had been correctly formed. For example, there was little or no distinction between the present and the past tenses of verbs; the endings of many words were clipped off, and this was especially noticeable in those words in which a final ending distinguished the plural from the singular, or an adverb from an adjective. As it seemed doubtful whether he would ever be able to enter college without special instruction in English, I was engaged to tutor him in the English branches.

I had no sooner undertaken this work than I saw the necessity of beginning with the elements of language and teaching him as one would teach a boy, say, in the third grade. Before long I discovered that I must start still further back. I had found it impossible, through oral and written exercises, to fix in his mind the elementary forms of words as parts of speech in a sentence. This seemed to be owing to the fact that he had verbal deafness.

He was quite able to hear even a faint sound, like the ticking of a watch, but he could not hear the difference in the sound of such words as *grasp* and *grasped*. This verbal deafness was associated with, and I now believe was probably caused by, a defect of articulation. Thus the boy's written language was a fairly exact replica of his spoken language; and he probably heard the words that others spoke as he himself spoke them. I therefore undertook to give him an elementary training in articulation to remedy the defects which are ordinarily corrected, through imitation, by the time a child is three or four years old. I gave practically no attention to the subjects required in English for college entrance, spending all my time on the drill in articulation and in perfecting his verbal audition and teaching him the simplest elements of written language. The result was a great improvement in all his written work, and he succeeded in entering the college department of the University of Pennsylvania in the following year....

I felt very keenly how much this boy was losing through his speech defect. His school work, his college course, and doubtless his professional career were all seriously hampered. I was confident at the time, and this confidence has been justified by subsequent experience with similar cases, that if he had been given adequate instruction in articulation in the early years of childhood, he could have overcome his defect. With the improvement in articulation there would have come an improved power of apprehending spoken and written language. That nothing was done for him in the early years, nor indeed at any time, excepting for the brief period of private instruction in English and some lessons in elocution, is remarkable, for the speech defect was primarily owing to an injury to the head in the second year of life, and his father was a physician who might have been expected to appreciate the necessity of special training in a case of retardation caused by a brain injury. (pp. 342–344, italics in the original)

After describing this early case, Witmer described the event that launched the clinic in 1896. In the second paragraph, you will see his argument for why psychology ought to be able to help with such school-related problems as poor spelling. Also note that Witmer directly addressed the issue of the relationship between basic and applied science.

The second case to attract my interest was a boy fourteen years of age, who was brought to the laboratory of psychology by his grade teacher. He was one of those children of great interest to the teacher, known to the profession as a chronic bad speller. His teacher ... was at that time a student of psychology at the University of Pennsylvania; she was imbued with the idea that a psychologist should be able, through examination, to ascertain the causes of a deficiency in spelling and to recommend the appropriate pedagogical treatment for its amelioration or cure.

With this case, in March, 1896, the work of the psychological clinic was begun. At that time I could not find that the science of psychology had ever addressed itself to the ascertainment of the causes and treatment of a deficiency in spelling. Yet here was a simple developmental defect of memory; and memory is a mental process of which the science of psychology is supposed to furnish the only authoritative knowledge. It appeared to me that if psychology was worth anything to me or to others it should be able to assist the efforts of a teacher in a retarded case of this kind. . . .

> I believe that there is no valid distinction between a pure science and an applied science. The practical needs of the astronomer to eliminate the personal equation from his observations led to the invention of the chronograph and the chronoscope. Without these two instruments, modern psychology and physiology could not possibly have achieved the results of the last fifty years. If Helmholtz had not made the chronograph an instrument of precision in physiology and psychology; if Fechner had not lifted a weight to determine the threshold of sensory discrimination, the field of scientific work represented to-day by clinical psychology could never have been developed. The pure and the applied sciences advance in a single front. What retards the progress of one, retards the progress of the other; what fosters one, fosters the other. But in the final analysis the progress of psychology, as of every other science, will be determined by the value and amount of its contributions to the advancement of the human race. (pp. 344–345)

Witmer didn't describe the outcome of his clinic's first client in this 1907 article, but his case notes were quite detailed. Part of the boy's problem was a visual deficiency, and he improved somewhat following surgery, but he also exhibited symptoms of what would today be called dyslexia, or what Witmer labeled *verbal visual amnesia*, a deficiency "in the ability to call up visual images of words" (McReynolds, 1997, p. 85). With Witmer's help the boy showed some improvement in reading and spelling. Other cases soon came Witmer's way and, as he makes clear here, he proceeded by trial and error to develop his training methods. Also during that first year, in December of 1896, he delivered a talk to the annual meeting of APA, outlining an ambitious program for his new clinic.

> The absence of any principles to guide me made it necessary to apply myself directly to the study of these children, working out my methods as I went along. In the spring of 1896 I saw several other cases of children suffering from the retardation of some special function, like that of spelling, or from general retardation, and I undertook the training of these children for a certain number of hours each week. Since that time the psychological clinic has been regularly conducted in connection with the laboratory of psychology at the University of Pennsylvania. The study of these cases has also formed a regular part of the instruction offered to students in child psychology.
>
> In December, 1896, I outlined in an address delivered before the American Psychological Association a scheme of practical work in psychology. The proposed plan of organization comprised:
>
> 1. The investigation of the phenomena of mental development in school children, as manifested more particularly in mental and moral retardation, by means of the statistical and clinical methods.
> 2. A psychological clinic, supplemented by a training school in the nature of a hospital school, for the treatment of all classes of children suffering from retardation or physical defects interfering with school progress.
> 3. The offering of practical work to those engaged in the professions of teaching and medicine, and to those interested in social work, in the observation and training of normal and retarded children.
> 4. The training of students for a new profession—that of the psychological expert, who should find his career in connection with the school

system, through the examination and treatment of mentally and morally retarded children, or in connection with the practice of medicine.

In the summer of 1897 the department of psychology in the University of Pennsylvania was able to put the larger part of this plan into operation. A four weeks' course was given under the auspices of the American Society for the Extension of University Teaching. In addition to lecture and laboratory courses in experimental and physiological psychology, a course in child psychology was given to demonstrate the various methods of child psychology, but especially the clinical method. The psychological clinic was conducted daily, and a training school was in operation.... At the clinic, cases were presented of children suffering from defects of the eye, the ear, deficiency in motor ability, or in memory and attention; and in the training school, children were taught throughout the session of the Summer School, receiving pedagogical treatment for the cure of stammering and other speech defects, for defects of written language (such as bad spelling), and for motor defects.

From that time until the present I have continued the examination and treatment of children in the psychological clinic. The number of cases seen each week has been limited, because the means were not at hand for satisfactorily treating a large number of cases. I felt, also, that before offering to treat these children on a large scale I needed some years of experience and extensive study, which could only be obtained through the prolonged observation of a few cases. Above all, I appreciated the great necessity of training a group of students upon whose assistance I could rely. The time has now come for a wider development of this work. To further this object and to provide for the adequate publication of the results that are being obtained in this new field of psychological investigation, it was determined to found this journal, *The Psychological Clinic*. (pp. 345–347)

After outlining the rationale for his new journal, Witmer described his interpretation of the relationship between clinical psychology and medicine, psychiatry in particular. He referred to the history of medical treatment of psychopathology (e.g., Pinel), and argued that those trained in psychiatry needed to be aware of the recent work in psychology. One positive example he cited was Emil Kraepelin, a physician who studied briefly with Wundt and developed a theory about schizophrenia (Kraepelin first identified the disorder and called it *dementia praecox*) that was based on what he had learned at Leipzig about attention. As Witmer put it, "perhaps the most prominent name connected with psychiatry today is that of Kraepelin, who was among the first to seek the training in experimental psychology afforded by the newly established laboratory at Leipzig" (p. 348).

In addition to medicine, however, clinical psychology has had close ties to other disciplines. And in the future, Witmer argued, clinical psychology will require a new, interdisciplinary form of training.

Although clinical psychology is closely related to medicine, it is quite as closely related to sociology and to pedagogy. The school room, the juvenile court, and the streets are a larger laboratory of psychology. An abundance of material for scientific study fails to be utilized, because the interest of psychologists is elsewhere engaged, and those in constant touch with the actual phenomena do not possess the training necessary to make their experience and observation of scientific value.

While the field of clinical psychology is to some extent occupied by the physician, especially by the psychiatrist, and while I expect to rely in a great measure upon the educator and social worker for the more important contributions to this branch of psychology, it is nevertheless true that none of these has quite the training necessary for this kind of work. For that matter, neither has the psychologist, unless he has acquired this training from other sources than the usual course of instruction in psychology. In fact, we must look forward to the training of men to a new profession which will be exercised more particularly in connection with educational problems, but for which the training of the psychologist will be a prerequisite. . . .

The phraseology of "clinical psychology" and "psychological clinic" will doubtless strike many as an odd juxtaposition of terms relating to quite disparate subjects. While the term "clinical" has been borrowed from medicine, clinical psychology is not a medical psychology. I have borrowed the word "clinical" from medicine, because it is the best term I can find to indicate the character of the method which I deem necessary for this work. Words seldom retain their original significance, and clinical medicine, is not what the word implies—the work of a practicing physician at the bedside of a patient. The term "clinical" implies a method, and not a locality. . . .

The clinical psychologist is interested primarily in the individual child. As the physician examines his patient and proposes treatment with a definite purpose in view, namely the patient's cure, so the clinical psychologist examines a child with a single definite object in view,—the next step in the child's mental and physical development. It is here that the relation between science and practice becomes worthy of discrimination. The physician *may* have solely in mind the cure of his patient, but if he is to be more than a mere practitioner and to contribute to the advance of medicine, he will look upon his efforts as an experiment, every feature of which must indeed have a definite purpose,—the cure of the patient,—but he will study every favorable or unfavorable reaction of the patient with reference to the patient's previous condition and the remedial agents he has employed. In the same way the purpose of the clinical psychologist, as a contributor to science, is to discover the relation between cause and effect in applying the various pedagogical remedies to a child who is suffering from general or special retardation. (pp 348–351)

In his final paragraph, Witmer envisioned a clinical psychology that encompassed a range of situations far beyond the problem school child.

I would not have it thought that the method of clinical psychology is limited necessarily to mentally and morally retarded children. These children are not, properly speaking, abnormal, nor is the condition of many of them to be designated as in any way pathological. They deviate from the average of children only in being at a lower stage of individual development. Clinical psychology, therefore, does not exclude from consideration other types of children that deviate from the average—for example, the precocious child and the genius. Indeed, the clinical method is applicable even to the so-called normal child. For the methods of clinical psychology are necessarily invoked wherever the status of an individual mind is determined by observation and experiment, and pedagogical treatment applied to effect a change, i.e., the development of such individual mind. Whether the subject be a child or an adult, the examination and treatment may be conducted and their results expressed in the terms of the clinical method. (pp. 351–352)

Witmer's clinic prospered, and was eventually expanded into a series of more specialized clinics—one for "speech defects," another for "vocational and industrial guidance," and a third for the school problems of college-aged students (Fernberger, 1931). In 1922, Witmer made good on his final paragraph above by expanding the clinic to work with gifted children.

Although Witmer's clinic is always mentioned in descriptions of the history of clinical psychology, his work was closer to what would today be called school psychology. The modern clinician is primarily concerned with the diagnosis and treatment of psychopathology among clients of all ages, while the modern school psychologist focuses on school-related problems, as did Witmer (at least initially). Indeed, Division 16 of the APA, the division for school psychology, gives an annual Lightner Witmer (Early Career) Award to a promising school psychologist.

CONCEPT REVIEW QUESTIONS

1. Describe how Witmer first became interested in the type of school problems that eventually led to the creation of his clinic.
2. Describe Witmer's plan for applied psychology, as outlined in his APA talk.
3. Witmer's vision for clinical psychology was an interdisciplinary one. Explain.

DISCUSSION QUESTION

1. Explain why it might be more appropriate to consider Witmer the founder of modern school psychology than modern clinical psychology.

MARY COVER JONES (1896–1987): BEHAVIOR THERAPY

Behavior therapy, the use of conditioning principles to bring about therapeutic change, is normally thought to have begun in the 1950s, with the work of Joseph Wolpe, a South African psychologist who developed a procedure eventually called systematic desensitization (Wolpe, 1958). Wolpe, however, readily acknowledged that his therapy had important historical roots in the work of Mary Cover Jones (1896–1987), who he once described as the "mother of behavior therapy" (Rutherford, 2006, p. 189). Wolpe was referring to research on removing fears that Jones completed in the 1920s, and the excerpt in this chapter is from one of the articles that she wrote describing this work.

At the time of her research on the elimination of fear, Mary Cover Jones was a graduate student at Columbia University. In 1924, the university created an institute for child study and John B. Watson (Chapter 18) was hired as a consultant to oversee the research work of the institute (at the time, Watson was working in advertising in New York) (Buckley, 1989). Watson, usually considered the founder of behaviorism, was famous for having conducted the "Little Albert" study, in which an 11-month-old boy had been conditioned to fear a white rat (Watson & Rayner, 1920). Jones was a good friend and former college classmate (Vassar) of Rosalie Rayner, who co-authored the fear conditioning study and was Watson's second wife. Jones became interested in studying children's fears, but was more interested in how to remove them than how to create them. Under Watson's supervision, Jones completed a series of studies and published two articles at about the same time in 1924.

The first article, to be considered here, was published in the *Journal of Experimental Psychology* and was called "The Elimination of Children's Fears." Jones started with a reference to the Watson and Rayner study, a statement of the purpose of her research, and a description of her subjects.

> The investigation of children's fears leads directly to a number of important problems in the genetic study of emotion. At the Johns Hopkins laboratory Dr. John B. Watson has analyzed the process by which fears are acquired in infancy and has shown that the conditioned reflex formula may apply to

Excerpts from: Jones, M. C. (1924a). The elimination of children's fears. *Journal of Experimental Psychology, 7*, 382–390.

the transfer of emotional reactions from original stimuli (pain, loud noises, or loss of bodily support) to various substitute fear objects in the child's environment.... A study of how children's fears may be reduced or eradicated would seem to be the next point for an experimental attack. Such a study should include an attempt to evaluate, objectively, the various possible methods which laboratory experience has suggested....

The subjects, 70 children from 3 months to 7 years of age, were maintained in an institution for the temporary care of children. Admission to this institution depended as a rule upon conditions which made it difficult or impossible to keep the children at home: a case of illness in the family, the separation of father and mother, or an occupation which kept the mother away from home for a part of the day. As there was a charge for weekly care, those homes which were in actual poverty were not represented; the economic and social status of the parents, as well as the results of our intelligence tests (Kuhlmann and Terman) would indicate that this group of children was normal, and superior to the average for orphan asylums and similar institutions....

In our selection of children from this group, we attempted to find those who would show a marked degree of fear under conditions normally evoking positive (pleasant) or mildly negative (unpleasant) responses. A wide range of situations were presented in a fairly standardized way to all of the children: such as being left alone, being in a dark room, being with other children who showed fear, the sudden presentation of a snake, a white rat, a rabbit, a frog, false faces, loud sounds, etc. This procedure served to expose fear trends if they were already present; it was not designed as a conditioning process, but merely as a method of revealing prior conditionings. (pp. 382–383)

Having identified a group of children with specific fears, Jones tried a number of strategies to eliminate these fears, with her narrative including descriptions taken from case notes. As you will see, she tried seven different strategies, five of which failed. Here are the first two.

The Method of Elimination Through Disuse

A common assumption with regard to children's fears is that they will die out if left alone, *i.e.*, if the child is carefully shielded from stimuli which would tend to re-arouse the fear ... The following case from our records provides suggestive material:

Case 33. Eleanor J. Age 21 months.

Jan.17. While playing in the pen, a frog was introduced from behind her. She watched, came nearer, and finally touched it. The frog jumped. She withdrew and later presented with the frog, shook her head and pushed the experimenter's hand away ...

March 26. After two months of no further experience with animals, Eleanor was taken to the laboratory and offered the frog. When the frog hopped she drew back, ran from the pen and cried.

[This] and similar cases show that an interval of "disuse" extending over a period of weeks or months, may not result in eliminating a fear response, and that when other conditions are approximately constant there may be no diminution in the degree of fear manifested. From our experience, it would appear to be an unsafe method to attempt the cure of a fear trend by ignoring it.

The Method of Verbal Appeal

As most of our subjects were under four years of age, the possibilities of verbal analysis and control were very limited. We attempted to find out how much we could accomplish toward breaking down a negative reaction by merely talking about the fear-object, endeavoring to keep it in the child's attention, and connecting it verbally with pleasant experiences. This method showed no applicability except in the case of one subject, Jean E., a girl in her fifth year. At the initial presentation of the rabbit a marked fear response was registered. This was followed by ten minutes daily conversation about the rabbit; to hold her interest the experimenter introduced such devices as the picture book of "Peter Rabbit," toy rabbits, and rabbits drawn or modeled from plastocene. . . . However, when the rabbit was actually presented again, at the end of a week, her reaction was practically the same as at the first encounter . . . She had learned to speak freely of rabbits, but this altered verbalization apparently was not accompanied by any change in her response to the rabbit itself. . . . (pp. 384–385)

Methods three and four were likewise unsuccessful. The third method was called "the method of negative adaptation" (p. 386). Although Jones did not use the term, it was based on the conditioning principle of extinction. If the feared object can be considered a conditioned stimulus (CS), and extinction involved the repeated presentation of a CS by itself, then the fear response should diminish over time. Although the case described by Jones seemed to produce something of an extinction effect, Jones did not consider the strategy effective. She thought it might make the child a bit less fearful, but would not bring about the desired goal—"an acceptance reaction" (p. 386).

The fourth strategy Jones called the "method of repression" (p. 387), which involved having a child ridiculed by peers for being afraid. Jones did not deliberately instruct some children to make fun of others, but she observed it on occasion in the lab, concluding that the result of social ridicule is that the fear is "re-suggested and entrenched, rather than stamped out" (p. 387).

In the home, as well as in the school and playground, social repression is perhaps the simplest and most common method of dealing with fear symptoms. . . . In our laboratory we used no repressive punishment, but within a group of children the familiar situations of ridicule, social teasing and scolding frequently appeared. Because of shame, a child might try to contain his fears without overt expression, but after a certain point had been reached, the reaction appeared notwithstanding.

Case 41. Arthur G. Age 4 years.

Arthur was shown the frogs in an aquarium, no other children being present. He cried, said "they bite," and ran out of the play-pen. Later, however, he was brought into the room with four other boys; he swaggered up to the aquarium, pressing ahead of the others who were with him. When one of his companions picked up a frog and turned to him with it, he screamed and fled; at this he was chased and made fun of, but with naturally no lessening of the fear on this particular occasion. (p. 387)

Method five, the "method of distraction," involved getting the child to think about something other than the feared object. As Jones suspected, however, it had no effect on the fear. With methods six and seven, however, Jones experienced her first clear indications that fears could be unlearned. Method six was the one that Wolpe rediscovered thirty years later.

The Method of Direct Conditioning

Under this heading ... we include all specific attempts to associate with the fear-object a definite stimulus, capable of arousing a positive (pleasant) reaction. The hunger motive appears to be the most effective to use in this connection. During a period of craving for food, the child is placed in a high chair and given something to eat. The fear-object is brought in, starting a negative response. It is then moved gradually away until it is at a sufficient distance not to interfere with the child's eating. ... While the child is eating, the object is slowly brought nearer to the table, then placed upon the table, and finally as the tolerance increases it is brought close enough to be touched. ... The effectiveness of this method increases greatly as the hunger grows, at least up to a certain point. The case of Peter (reported in detail elsewhere) illustrates our procedure; one of the most serious problem cases, he was treated by the method daily or twice daily for a period of two months. The laboratory notes for the first and last days of the training period show an improvement which we were able to attribute specifically to the training measures used.

Case 30. Peter. Age 2 years, 10 months.

March 10, 10:15 A.M. Peter sitting in high chair, eating candy. Experimenter entered room with a rabbit in an open meshed wire cage. The rabbit was placed on the table 4 feet from Peter who immediately began to cry, insisting that the rabbit be taken away. Continued crying until the rabbit was put down 20 feet away. He then started again on the candy, but continued to fuss, "I want you to put Bunny outside." After three minutes he once more burst into tears; the rabbit was removed.

April 29, 9:55 A.M. Peter standing in high chair, looking out of the window. He inquired, "Where is the rabbit?" The rabbit was put down on the chair at Peter's feet. Peter patted him, tried to pick him up, but finding the rabbit too heavy asked the experimenter to help in lifting him to the window sill, where he played with him for several minutes.

This method obviously requires delicate handling. Two response systems are being dealt with: food leading to a positive reaction, and fear-object leading to a negative reaction. The desired conditioning should result in transforming the fear-object into a source of positive response. (pp. 388–389)

In the history of behavior therapy, Peter has become almost as famous as Watson's unfortunate Albert. As Jones mentioned parenthetically, the case was elaborated in a separate article, also published in 1924, and called "A Laboratory Study of Fear: The Case of Peter" (Jones, 1924b). In this more detailed article, Jones also showed that, in addition to direct conditioning, Peter's fears also were treated effectively with a method that later became another powerful weapon in the behavior therapist's arsenal—modeling. And modeling, labeled "social imitation" (p. 389) by Jones, was the final method described in the article being excerpted here. As you will see, modeling can both produce and reduce fears.

The Method of Social Imitation

We have used this method extensively, as it was one of the first signs of yielding results.

Case 8. Bobby G. Age 30 months.

Bobby was playing in the pen with Mary and Laurel. The rabbit was introduced in a basket. Bobby cried "No, no," and motioned for the experimenter to remove it. The two girls, however, ran up readily enough, looked in at the rabbit and talked excitedly. Bobby became promptly interested, said "What? Me see," and ran forward, his curiosity and assertiveness in the social situation overmastering other impulses.

Case 43. Vincent W. Age 21 months.

Jan. 19. Vincent showed no fear of the rabbit, even when it was pushed against his hands or face. His only response was to laugh and reach for the rabbit's fur. On the same day he was taken into the pen with Rosey, who cried at the sight of the rabbit. Vincent immediately developed a fear response; in the ordinary playroom situation he would pay no attention to her crying, but in connection with the rabbit, her distress had a marked suggestive value. The fear transferred in this way persisted for over two weeks.

Feb. 6. Eli and Herbert were in the play-pen with the rabbit. When Vincent was brought in, he remained cautiously standing at some distance. Eli led Vincent over to the rabbit, and induced him to touch the rabbit. Vincent laughed.

The second case illustrated a fear socially induced (this is perhaps the most common source of maladjustive fear trends) and the later removal of the fear by social suggestion. Many of the fears we studied pointed to an origin in a specific traumatic experience; it would probably have been a valuable aid in our procedure, had we been able to trace the developmental history of each of these fears. (pp. 389–390)

Jones earned her doctorate at Columbia in 1926 by completing an extensive normative study of the development of 365 infants (Jones, 1926). With her husband and psychologist colleague, Harold Jones, she continued doing research on children's fears for a few years. The couple then moved to California in 1927, where Harold joined the psychology department at Berkeley and Mary became a research associate at the just established Institute of Child Welfare (also part of Berkeley) and eventually joined her husband on the faculty at Berkeley. After a distinguished career as a research psychologist, investigating developmental changes across the lifespan, Mary Cover Jones died in 1987.

CONCEPT REVIEW QUESTIONS

1. How did Jones' research strategy differ from that of Watson, in his Little Albert case?

2. Describe the fear elimination techniques used by Jones that failed.

3. What is the effect that modeling can have on fear?

DISCUSSION QUESTION

1. Describe how Jones successfully removed Peter's fear of rabbits using what she called "direct conditioning." Think of something that you fear; how would you apply the Jones method to cure yourself?

LETA STETTER HOLLINGWORTH (1886–1939): SEX DIFFERENCES IN APTITUDE

Leta Stetter Hollingworth was a vigorous advocate for women's rights and, as a psychologist, known for her research on sex differences and for her work with gifted children. Concerning the latter, for example, she taught (in 1918) what appears to have been the first college course on the education of gifted children (Klein, 2002), and she wrote the first textbook on gifted education, *Gifted Children: Their Nature and Nurture* (L. Hollingworth, 1926). One of her strong beliefs was that gifted children should not be advanced in grade (they needed to be with their age peers), but should have their education enriched with experiences that extended beyond the normal curriculum.

Leta Stetter met Harry Hollingworth when they were students at the University of Nebraska. Harry became a well-known applied psychologist (Benjamin, 2003). Once married, the couple moved to New York, where Harry, and then Leta, completed doctorates at Columbia University. They spent their professional careers living in the New York area, Harry joining the faculty at Barnard College, and Leta teaching at Columbia's Teachers College. The excerpt you are about read is from a chapter on the "vocational aptitudes of women" that Leta contributed to a text in applied psychology that Harry wrote in 1916—*Vocational Psychology: Its Problems and Methods* (H. Hollingworth, 1916). As you read this, keep in mind that arguments over women's rights were becoming increasingly vocal at this time, and an important milestone for women was just on the horizon—in 1920, the Nineteenth Amendment to the Constitution gave women the vote.

Hollingworth's opening paragraphs make it clear that those believing in the inherent superiority of males would not enjoy the chapter.

Excerpts from: Hollingworth, L. S. (1916). The vocational aptitudes of women. Chapter 10 in:
H. L. Hollingworth, *Vocational psychology: Its problems and methods* (pp. 222–244). New York:
D. Appleton and Company.

It is customary for authors, in discussing vocational problems, to assume that the vocational future of girls is determined in advance by the fact of sex. Not infrequently the lack of provision for domestic training in our high schools and colleges is indicated at length, and suggestions for establishing the domestic arts and sciences on a firmer basis in the educational system are advanced. Some paragraphs may be devoted to a discussion of the statistics which show that thousands of girls go from school into industry, and to an inquiry as to what training is best fitted to assist them in earning a living for the period intervening between graduation and matrimony. With this the discussion of vocational problems ends, so far as girls are concerned, and the remaining space is given over to more adequate consideration of the vocational aptitudes and guidance of boys.

It is the purpose of this chapter to inquire whether there are any innate and essential sex differences in tastes and abilities, which would afford a scientific basis for the apparently arbitrary and traditional assumption that the vocational future of all girls must naturally fall in the domestic sphere, and consequently presents no problem, while the future of boys is entirely problematical, and may lie in any one of a score of different callings, according to personal fitness. We shall try to determine whether the present expectation that all women will follow the same vocation, i.e., housekeeping, is founded on any fact or facts of human intellect, or whether it arises merely from ideas of traditional expediency connected with the care of the young, and whether it leads to a waste of energy and of intellectual talents. (pp. 222–223)

Hollingworth was not mincing words here, and her interest in trying to determine if there was any reasonable or empirical basis for the fact that women seemed destined for the "domestic sphere" was undoubtedly influenced by her own history. Despite a brilliant career as a student at Nebraska, followed by two years of teaching experience in Nebraska, she was unable to find work in New York when she arrived in 1908. The plan was for Harry to finish his graduate program while Leta worked as a teacher in New York, and then it would be Leta's turn for graduate school. What the young couple had not counted on, however, was a Board of Education restriction that prohibited married women from teaching in the New York City school system. Such institutional barriers to women were not uncommon at the time.

Their initial plans thwarted, Leta began taking graduate courses part-time when the young couple could afford it. Meanwhile, Harry, who had planned a traditional academic career of teaching and research, had a life-changing experience when given the opportunity to conduct a study for the Coca-Cola company on the psychological effects of caffeine. Coca-Cola was under attack for including this "dangerous" additive in their drinks, and the company wished to demonstrate that the caffeine did not have deleterious effects. For more on this fascinating story, see Benjamin, Rogers, and Rosenbaum (1991). For here, it is enough to say that the money earned from this work made it possible for Leta to complete graduate studies, while it set Harry on a path toward a lucrative career in applied psychology.

As she continued the introductory portion of her chapter on sex differences, Hollingworth indicated that she would address five different questions, and examine whether the answers could be determined with solid scientific evidence. Here are the questions.

> (1) Are there innate sex differences in average intelligence? (2) Is either sex more variable than the other in mental traits? (3) Are there any special causes of intellectual inefficiency affecting one sex but not the other? (4) Are there any sex differences in affective or instinctive equipment which would naturally lead to vocational differentiation of the sexes? (5) What explanation is to be given of the traditional division of labor between the sexes? (pp. 223–224)

Concerning the first question, about the possibility of sex differences being innate, Hollingworth pointed out that serious research on the question had only occurred in recent years, after a long period in which male superiority was simply taken for granted by those in power (i.e., males). She then highlighted a study that had been published in 1906 by Helen Bradford Thompson; it was her doctoral dissertation completed under the direction of James Angell (Chapter 12) at the University of Chicago. It was the first study to uncover what is now a fairly standard finding in sex differences research—greater variability within the sexes than between them.

> The result of her tests in various mental traits is that the differences between the sexes were in no case as great as the individual differences within either sex. Men differed from each other in these experiments (as did women also, among themselves), as much as men differed from women. In only two of the traits was there a reliable difference found between the central tendencies of the sexes. In speed of voluntary movement (tapping) men were quicker than women, and in memory women were superior to men. . . . It will be enough for our present purposes to say that after about twenty years of collecting data by scientific experiment, the hypothesis that there is any innate sex difference in average intellectual ability has been abandoned by all psychologists who base their statements on scientific evidence. (pp. 226–227)

As for her second question, Hollingworth was able to point to some of her own research on what was known as the *variability hypothesis*, the idea that men varied considerably on a number of traits, while women tended to be more similar to each other. This hypothesis was important because of its vocational implications. The question is whether

> the members of one sex [are] very much alike in tastes, interests and abilities, while the members of the other sex differ over a wide range of tastes, interests and abilities[.] . . . The answer to this . . . question will be of decided significance for vocational guidance. For example, if it were shown by experimental data that human females are, by original nature, rather closely alike, whereas human males differ from one another by wide extremes, we should have scientific grounds for concluding that social justice and social economy are well served by the present policy of guiding all females into a single occupation, while males are encouraged to enter the greatest possible variety of callings. (pp. 228–229)

Hollingworth then pointed out (with a measure of sarcasm) that, prior to Darwin, women were considered more variable than men, and this variability was seen as a sign of weakness. When Darwin made variability a cornerstone of natural selection and therefore something of value, however, "the greater variability of the male began to be affirmed everywhere in the literature of opinion" (p. 230). But the data suggested otherwise, as in a study by Pearson, the famous British statistician (e.g., Pearson's r, the well known correlation coefficient).

> Karl Pearson alone took issue with this view, which was current in the nineteenth century and is still widely credited, and pointed out that there existed as yet no literature of fact regarding comparative variability (though men of science had not on this account restrained themselves from uttering the most positive statements concerning it). Pearson thereupon actually gathered and computed hundreds of measurements of human beings, and presented his results in 1897, in a comprehensive article entitled "Variation in Man and Woman." He clearly demonstrated that there is, in fact, no indication of greater male variability, when actual anatomical measurements of adult human beings are treated with mathematical insight. (p. 230)

Hollingworth pointed out that Pearson's results were criticized because he used adults as subjects, and the cumulative effects of environmental influence might have masked any inherent differences in variability. So in her study (Montague & Hollingworth, 1914), Hollingworth examined newborns; she also addressed another criticism—whether studying physical attributes would shed light on mental attributes.

> In 1914 Montague and Hollingworth published in the *American Journal of Sociology* an article setting forth in full the measurements of two thousand new-born infants, one thousand of each sex. The statistical result shows no differences whatever in variability between the sexes.
>
> It may seem irrelevant to dwell upon anatomical data, when the purpose of this chapter is to deal with mental aptitudes. The pertinence of the data cited, however, lies in the fact that if any sex differences in physical variability could be established, this would suggest (though it would not prove) the existence of a sex difference in mental variability also. . . . [A]ccording to those studies wherein presumably correct methods of measurement have been employed, there is no reason to suppose that there is any sex difference in variability. (pp. 231–232)

Having disposed of the variability hypothesis, Hollingworth considered her third question, whether there were any special circumstances that might affect the ability of one sex but not the other. The most obvious candidate—menstruation.

> We now come to the inquiry as to whether there are any special causes of intellectual inefficiency which affect one sex but not the other. Under this topic we may consider the periodic function, which characterizes girls and women, but which does not characterize boys and men. This periodic function has always been the object of superstition and taboo, and is such even among civilized peoples of today. . . .
>
> The literature of opinion abounds in different notions, inconsistencies, and contradictory instances in the matter of periodic function, and its alleged enormous influence on the intellectual and vocational life of women. Much of the opposition to the education of women was based on it, and it has even

been exploited as a good reason why political freedom should be denied
to women. It is positively stated that women are on this account unfitted
to pursue professional and commercial life; yet it is not proposed that
cooks, scrub women, mothers, nursemaids, housekeepers, or dancers
should be periodically relieved from their labors and responsibilities.
(pp. 233–235)

It is not hard to detect Hollingworth's attitude that the "periodic function"
was being used by the male establishment as a means of maintaining their power
and influence. But if menstruation should prevent women from professional
careers, Hollingworth argued, then why should women also not get a break
from the lower status occupations that were the primary ones available to them?
Note that when she uses the phrase "literature of opinion," she is referring
to all the non-scientific information available (e.g., in the popular press). This
she distinguished from the "literature of fact," by which she meant scientific
evidence. And as for the evidence in this case, she granted that it was minimal,
but was able to point to two studies—one in a physical education journal that
found no adverse effects of menstruation, and one of her own (Hollingworth,
1914).

The second study, which appeared in 1914, was by the present writer. She
made a prolonged and careful study of twenty-three women (using as a
control the records of men subjects), and failed to demonstrate any influence
of periodicity on those mental abilities which she tested. These included
speed and accuracy of perception, controlled association, steadiness, speed
of voluntary movement, fatigability, and rate of learning.

A great amount of scientific work remains to be done before any final
answer of any kind can be given to the question, Does functional periodicity exercise a fundamental and characteristic influence on the intellectual
abilities of women? We must answer our third question in this way: There is
very little experimental evidence on which to base a reply, but the few data
which we do possess show no influence, either detrimental or beneficial.
(pp. 236–237)

Hollingworth's fourth question concerned whether males and females differ in "affective or instinctive equipment" that could result in differences in
their suitability for various vocations. Here she acknowledged that while there
was a large "literature of opinion," there were no scientific data available.
Instead, she addressed matters of emotion and instinct with reference to the
nature-nurture issue, in so doing raising serious questions about the so-called
"maternal instinct," which she saw as yet another concept that served to sub-
jugate women. Notice how she used statistical information (the normal curve)
and an unusual analogy (motherhood and soldiering) to refute the idea that a
maternal instinct ought to limit vocational opportunities for women.

Men and women as we see them in the world do differ in affective behavior, but no one can say whether these differences in behavior are original
or acquired. There are different conventional standards of emotional behavior for men and women, but no one would be justified in saying that such
standards arose from inherent affective differences between the sexes. . . .

[There has been] one instinct which has repeatedly been stated to characterize women, and to constitute in itself a natural justification for differentiating the sexes vocationally. This is the "maternal instinct." . . . There has been a continuous social effort to establish as a norm the woman whose vocational proclivities are completed and "naturally" satisfied by child-bearing and child-rearing.

In the absence of all data, it would seem most reasonable to suppose that if it were possible to obtain a quantitative measurement of "maternal instinct," we should find this trait distributed among women just as we have found all other traits distributed, which have yielded to quantitative measurement. It is most reasonable to assume that we should obtain a curve of distribution, varying from an extreme where individuals have a zero or negative interest in the care of infants, through a mode where there is a moderate amount of impulse to tend infants, to a second extreme where the only vocational interest lies in such activity. The bearing and rearing of children is in many respects analogous to the work of soldiers. It is necessary to national existence, it means great sacrifice of personal advantage, and it involves suffering and danger, and, in a certain percentage of cases, the actual loss of life. Thus, as in the case of soldiers, every effort is and must be made to establish as a norm the extreme end of the distribution curve, where there is an all-consuming interest in patriotism, in the one case, and in motherhood in the other. In the absence of all scientific data, we should, therefore, guard against accepting as an established fact about human nature a doctrine that we might expect to find in use as a means of social control. (pp. 238–239)

Having argued that there exists no strong evidence for the separation of the sexes along vocational lines, Hollingworth turned to her final question—how does one explain the "traditional division of labor between the sexes" (p. 224). Her answer was partly biological (i.e., women are the ones giving birth to children) and partly societal (women are the ones expected to raise these children in the early years).

The fact that women have not in the past equaled men in "philosophy, science, art, invention and management" is frequently adduced as evidence of their innate unfitness for pursuits other than the domestic. From such evidence, however, we glean in reality no information whatever about the vocational aptitudes of women. We should not expect any notable achievement by women in the fields mentioned above, for the following reasons. Women must bear and nourish infants, and men cannot. The period of gestation and the period of infancy are very protracted in the human species, together covering, for each infant reared, about six years. Until very recently no scientific methods of controlling procreation have been generally known or utilized. Thus women have borne great numbers of infants, all their youth and maturity being consumed by bearing and rearing young. . . . [note: Leta and Harry Hollingworth did not have children]

In the irrational trial and error method by which our human institutions have been developed, the logical expectation would be that the great physiological sex difference in reproductive function would probably influence vocational activities just as it has done. We find in the traditional division of labor between the sexes exactly what we should expect to find, even though there were an identity of intellectual abilities and interests. It seems both psychologically and socially desirable that the one incontestable conditioning factor in the vocational differentiation of men and women be raised clearly to consciousness, rather than submerged, as in the past, by an elaborate system of defense mechanisms and traditional devices of social control. It would be going afield from the immediate purpose of this chapter to offer constructive suggestions for such changes in economic and domestic management as might be necessary to overcome this conditioning factor, and thus to give free vocational opportunity to both sexes alike. . . .

The essential thing at present is to know whether any basis for future action may now be found in the established facts of human nature. In the present state of scientific knowledge it would be as dogmatic (and therefore as undesirable) to state that significant sex differences in intellect do not exist, as to state that such differences do exist. All we can say is that up to the present time experimental psychology has disclosed no sex differences in mental traits which would imply a division of labor on psychological grounds. The social gain would be very great if the public could be brought to recognize intelligently that to many of the questions regarding the vocational aptitudes of women no definite answers can at present be given, because the necessary data for the formulation of answers have never been collected. So far as is at present known, women are as competent intellectually as men are, to undertake any and all human vocations. (pp. 241–244)

As mentioned earlier, Hollingworth had a distinguished career at Columbia's Teachers College, gradually developing a specialty in the education of gifted children. As an indication of her influence in this area, the National Association for Gifted Children gives an annual "Hollingworth Award" to a promising researcher (Klein, 2002). In addition, there is a Hollingworth Center for Highly Gifted Children in Maine. After a protracted battle with a stomach cancer that she refused for years to acknowledge or treat, Leta Hollingworth died in 1939.

CONCEPT REVIEW QUESTIONS

1. What was the variability hypothesis, how did Hollingworth address the issue, and what did she conclude?
2. What was the periodic function, how did Hollingworth address the issue, and what did she conclude?
3. How did Hollingworth counter the argument that a woman's "maternal instinct" would incline her naturally toward a lifetime as wife and mother?

DISCUSSION QUESTION

1. The final issue addressed by Hollingworth was the reason for the "traditional division of labor between the sexes." What did she argue? How does her argument compare with the arguments that might be used today?

KENNETH B. CLARK (1914–2005) AND MAMIE PHIPPS CLARK (1917–1983): THE DOLL STUDIES

One of the most important Supreme Court decisions in the twentieth century was delivered on May 17, 1954, when the seven justices decided, in a unanimous vote, that "in the field of education the doctrine of 'separate but equal' has no place. Separate educational facilities are inherently unequal" (quoted in Morison, 1965, p. 1086). Known as *Brown* v. *Board of Education*, the ruling meant that schools could no longer be segregated by race. What was especially interesting for psychologists was that social science research was included (in a famous footnote) in the decision; psychologists (and sociologists) had shown that forced segregation had adverse effects on the early development and identity of African-American children, and that research helped sway the court. One of the studies that influenced the decision has come to be known simply as the "doll study."

The research originated in and evolved from the master's thesis of Mamie Phipps Clark (Lal, 2002), who earned her master's degree in 1939 from Howard University. The year before, she had eloped with another Howard student, Kenneth Clark, the man who had first interested her in psychology. The following excerpt is from a chapter that the Clarks wrote for a book of readings in social psychology. In an opening note, the Clarks indicated that the chapter was "[c]ondensed by the authors from an unpublished study made possible by a fellowship grant from the Julius Rosenwald Fund, 1940–1941" (Clark & Clark, 1958, p. 602).

The Clarks opened their chapter with a general statement of purpose and some definitions.

> The specific problem of this study is an analysis of the genesis and
> development of racial identification as a function of ego development and
> self-awareness in Negro children.

Excerpts from: Clark, K. B., & Clark, M. P. (1958). Racial identification and preference in Negro children. In E. E. Maccoby, T. M. Newcomb, & E. L. Hartley (Eds.) *Readings in social psychology* (3rd ed.) (pp. 602–611). New York: Holt, Rinehart, Winston.

Race awareness, in a primary sense, is defined as a consciousness of the self as belonging to a specific group which is differentiated from other observable groups by obvious physical characteristics which are generally accepted as being racial characteristics.

Because the problem of racial identification is so definitely related to the problem of the genesis of racial attitudes in children, it was thought practicable to attempt to determine the racial attitudes or preferences of these Negro children—and to define more precisely, as far as possible, the developmental pattern of this relationship. (p. 602)

Preceding their description of procedure, the Clarks pointed out that the doll study was just one of several procedures designed to investigate racial identification. For example, in one test (Clark & Clark, 1939), children were given drawings of human figures that had skin tones ranging from light to dark, and asked to indicate which figure was "like them." African-American children tended to pick drawings with lighter skin than their own. The doll studies, as will be seen, and which became more famous, produced similar results.

The subjects were presented with four dolls, identical in every respect save skin color. Two of these dolls were brown with black hair and two were white with yellow hair. In the experimental situation these dolls were unclothed except for white diapers. The position of the head, hands, and legs on all the dolls was the same. For half of the subjects the dolls were presented in the order: white, colored, white, colored. For the other half the order of presentation was reversed. In the experimental situation the subjects were asked to respond to the following requests by choosing *one* of the dolls and giving it to the experimenter.

1. Give me the doll that you like to play with—(a) like best.
2. Give me the doll that is a nice doll.
3. Give me the doll that looks bad.
4. Give me the doll that is a nice color.
5. Give me the doll that looks like a white child.
6. Give me the doll that looks like a colored child.
7. Give me the doll that looks like a Negro child.
8. Give me the doll that looks like you.

Requests 1 through 4 were designed to reveal preferences; requests 5 through 7 to indicate a knowledge of "racial differences"; and request 8 to show self-identification.

It was found necessary to present the preference requests first in the experimental situation because in a preliminary investigation it was clear that the children who had already identified themselves with the colored doll had a marked tendency to indicate a preference for this doll and this was not necessarily a genuine expression of actual preference, but a reflection of ego involvement. This potential distortion of the data was controlled by merely asking the children to indicate their preferences first and then to make identifications with one of the dolls. (pp. 602–603, italics in the original)

The subjects in the study were 253 African-American children, ranging in age from three to seven. Of this total, 134 constituted a "southern group," and the remaining 119 formed a "northern group." The southern group included children from schools in Arkansas (including Hot Springs, Mamie Phipps Clark's home town) where segregation in schools was mandated by state law; these children therefore had "no experience in racially mixed school situations" (p. 603); northern group children were from western Massachusetts, where segregation was not legally mandated; they were from "racially mixed nursery and public schools" (p. 603). The Clarks also, apparently using their own judgment (no mention of interrater reliability), classified the children into three groups based on the skin color—light ("practically white," p. 603), medium ("light brown to dark brown," p. 603) and dark ("dark brown to black," p. 603). Most fell in the middle range and there were similar proportions of each in both the northern and southern groups.

In reporting the results, the Clarks began with questions 5, 6, and 7, those concerned with knowledge of racial terms, and then moved on to question 8.

> The results of the responses to requests 5, 6, and 7, which were asked to determine the subjects' knowledge of racial differences, may be seen [as follows]. Ninety-four percent of these children chose the white doll when asked to give the experimenter the white doll; 93 percent of them chose the brown doll when asked to give the colored doll; and, 72 percent chose the brown doll when asked to give the Negro doll. These results indicate a clearly established knowledge of a "racial difference" in these subjects—and some awareness of the relation between the physical characteristics of skin color and the racial concepts of "white" and "colored." Knowledge of the concept of "Negro" is not so well developed as the more concrete verbal concepts "white" and "colored" as applied to racial differences. . . .
>
> The responses to request 8, designed to determine racial self-identification follow the following pattern: 66 percent of the total group of children identified themselves with the colored doll, while 33 percent identified themselves with the white doll. . . .
>
> Comparing the results of request 8 (racial self-identification) with those of requests 5, 6, and 7 (knowledge of racial difference) it is seen that the awareness of racial differences does not necessarily determine a socially accurate self-identification—since approximately nine out of ten of these children are aware of racial differences as indicated by their correct choice of a "white" and "colored" doll on request, and only a little more than six out of ten make socially correct identifications with the colored doll. (pp. 603–604)

Perplexed with this initial finding, the Clarks looked to see if any patterns existed as a function of age, skin color, and geography. For age, no noticeable patterns occurred for questions 5, 6, and 7—knowledgeable responses occurred for all, even three-year olds (although again there was an indication that the children were more familiar with the term "colored" than "Negro"). On question 8, however, there was a tendency (with an odd deviation for the four-year olds) for older children to consider the "brown" doll "like me." Here are the data (note: the percentages don't all add to 100—some individuals failed to make a choice).

	3 yr.	4 yr.	5 yr.	6 yr.	7 yr.
% choosing brown doll	36	66	48	68	87
% choosing white doll	61	31	52	32	13

The Clarks next considered the responses as a function of the three categories of skin color. Again, there was no problem on the knowledge questions. On question 8, this occurred:

	light	medium	dark
% choosing brown doll	20	73	81
% choosing white doll	80	26	19

> These results suggest further that correct racial identification of these Negro children at these ages is to a large extent determined by the concrete fact of their own skin color, and further that this racial identification is not necessarily dependent upon the expressed knowledge of a racial difference as indicated by the correct use of the words "white," "colored," or "Negro" when responding to white and colored dolls. This conclusion seems warranted in the light of the fact that those children who differed in skin color from light through medium to dark were practically similar in the pattern of their responses which indicated awareness of racial differences but differed markedly in their racial identification. (p. 606)

The Clarks described the differences between the light-skinned subjects and the other two groups as statistically significant, while the difference between the medium- and dark-skinned groups was not significant. This was similar to results from another of their studies (Clark & Clark, 1940).

> Again, as in previous work, it is shown that the percentage of the medium groups' identifications with the white or the colored representation resembles more that of the dark group and differs from the light group. Upon the basis of these results, one may assume that some of the factors and dynamics involved in racial identification are substantially the same for the dark and medium children, in contrast to dynamics for the light children. (p. 607)

As for geography, the Clarks, found no significant differences between the northern and southern groups on questions 5 through 8. They then turned to the preference questions—1 through 4—and found some unsettling results. Here are the data they reported in Table 5.

choice	#1 (play with)	#2 (nice doll)	#3 (looks bad)	#4 (nice color)
brown doll (%)	32	38	59	38
white doll (%)	67	59	17	60
no response (%)	1	3	24	2

It is clear from Table 5 that the majority of these Negro children prefer the *white* doll and reject the colored doll.

Approximately two thirds of the subjects indicated by their responses to requests 1 and 2 that they like the white doll "best," or that they would like to play with the white doll in preference to the colored doll, and that the white doll is a "nice doll."

Their responses to request 3 show that this preference for the white doll implies a concomitant negative attitude toward the brown doll. Fifty-nine percent of these children indicated that the colored doll "looks bad," while only 17 percent stated that the white doll "looks bad." . . . That this preference and negation in some way involve skin color is indicated by the results for request 4. Only 38 percent of the children thought that the brown doll was a "nice color," while 60 percent of them thought that the white doll was a "nice color." . . .

The importance of these results for an understanding of the origin and development of racial concepts and attitudes in Negro children cannot be minimized. Of equal significance are their implications, in the light of the results of racial identification already presented, for racial mental hygiene. (p. 609)

As they did for questions 5 through 8, the Clarks further examined responses to questions 1 through 4 as a function of age, skin color, and geography. For all age groups, they found the same pattern as for the group as a whole—a preference for the white doll. The only slightly encouraging outcome was that the pattern of "preference for white doll" was not quite as clear for the 7-year-olds. As for skin color and geography,

Results . . . reveal that there is a tendency for the majority of these children, in spite of their own skin color, to prefer the white doll and to negate the brown doll. This tendency is most pronounced in the children of light skin and least so in the dark children. . . .

[I]t is clear that the southern children in segregated schools are less pronounced in their preference for the white doll, compared to the northern children's definite preference for this doll. Although still in a minority, a higher percentage of southern children, compared to northern, prefer to play with the colored doll [southern = 37%; northern = 28%] or think that it is a "nice" doll [southern = 46%; northern = 30%] . . .

A significantly higher percentage (71) of the northern children, compared to the southern children (49) think that the brown doll looks bad . . .

In general, it may be stated that northern and southern children in these age groups seem to be similar in the degree of their preference for the white doll—with the northern children tending to be somewhat more favorable to the white doll than are the southern children. (pp. 610–611)

The Clarks closed their article with some qualitative data—comments from specific children that illustrated their general conclusions. They also revealed that some of the children found the experience distressing.

Many of the children entered into the experimental situation with a freedom similar to that of play. They tended to verbalize freely and much of this unsolicited verbalization was relevant to the basic problems of the study.

On the whole, the rejection of the brown doll and the preference for the white doll, when explained at all, were explained in rather simple, concrete terms: for white-doll preference—" 'cause he's pretty" or " 'cause he's white"; for rejection of the brown doll—" 'cause he's ugly" or " 'cause it don't look pretty" or " 'cause him black" or "got black on him."

On the other hand, some of the children who were free and relaxed in the beginning of the experiment broke down and cried or became somewhat negativistic during the latter part when they were required to make self-identifications. Indeed, two children ran out of the room, inconsolable, convulsed in tears. This type of behavior, although not so extreme, was more prevalent in the North than in the South. The southern children who were disturbed by this aspect of the experiment generally indicated their disturbance by smiling or matter of factly attempting to escape their dilemma either by attempted humor or rationalization.

Rationalization of the rejection of the brown doll was found among both northern and southern children, however. A northern medium six-year-old justified his rejection of the brown doll by stating that he "looks bad 'cause he hasn't got a eyelash." A seven-year-old medium northern child justified his choice of the white doll as the doll with the "nice color" because "his feet, hands, ears, elbows, knees, and hair are clean."

A northern five-year-old dark child felt compelled to explain his identification with the brown doll by making the following unsolicited statement: "I burned my face and made it spoil." A seven-year-old northern light child went to great pains to explain that he is actually white but: "I look brown because I got a suntan in the summer." (p. 611)

The Clark doll studies have become famous over the years, but they have also been controversial, sometimes criticized on methodological grounds (e.g., failure to counterbalance, lack of clear evidence for differentiation of the groups based on skin color), and sometimes on the grounds that the conclusion (segregation harms children) is not really supported by the data. For example, shortly after the *Brown* decision, sociologist Ernest van den Haag argued that the difference between Northern and Southern children (Northern children slightly more likely to prefer the white doll) would lead one to think that integrating schools would actually make the problem worse. Clark responded that the overall pattern of the results made it clear that the self-identity of the children had been adversely affected by a pervasive racism in the schools. And historian John Jackson (2000) has argued that the Clark doll studies, despite being singled out as the "only" evidence supporting desegregation, were in fact just a portion of a large amount of social science information brought to bear on the case.

As for the Clarks, both went on to earn doctorates in psychology from Columbia (1940 for Kenneth and 1943 for Mamie Phipps). Both then fashioned distinguished careers, Mamie in the practice of psychology (e.g., founder and Executive Director of the Northside Center for Child Development in Harlem), and Kenneth as an academician (e.g., City College of New York). In 1971, Kenneth became the first (and so far the only) African-American elected president of the American Psychological Association.

CONCEPT REVIEW QUESTIONS

1. Explain how the Clarks determined that the children in their study showed "knowledge of racial differences" but a lack of "racial self-identification."

2. How were the results influenced by the Clarks' judgment about the skin color of the children?

3. Explain how this study might be used to argue that segregation had an adverse effect on African-American children.

DISCUSSION QUESTION

1. Were this study to be replicated today, what do you think would happen? (for one possibility, do a Google search for "A Girl Like Me")

CHAPTER 27

WALTER DILL SCOTT (1869–1955): PSYCHOLOGY AND ADVERTISING

Walter Dill Scott was one of a number of psychologists trained in the basic psychology of the laboratory who left the lab for the world of applied psychology. In Scott's case, his scientific training was at the German Mecca for experimental psychology, Leipzig. In 1900, he earned a Ph.D. from Wundt (Chapter 5) and was appointed instructor and laboratory director at Northwestern University in Chicago. Early in his career at Northwestern, he was contacted by a local executive and asked for his opinion about whether psychological principles could be applied to advertising. Scott was intrigued, and he soon became immersed in the subject, enough so that he is sometimes considered the original American applied psychologist (Strong, 1955).

Scott's interest in advertising yielded *The Psychology of Advertising in Theory and Practice* (Scott, 1903). Five years later, he wrote a shorter version simply called *The Psychology of Advertising* (Scott, 1908). The excerpt here is from a 1913 reprinting of the briefer book's fifth edition.

Scott opened his book by pointing out that business leaders had long recognized the importance of advertising, but that it was only recently that advertising had been influenced by systematic research. In particular, although advertising had improved over the years, the world of advertising was just beginning to recognize the importance of the new field of scientific psychology.

> These improvements have been as beneficial as the most sanguine could have hoped for, but in and of themselves they were not sufficient to place advertising upon a scientific basis. Advertising has as its one function the influencing of human minds. . . . As it is the human mind that advertising is dealing with, its only scientific basis is psychology, which is simply a systematic study of those same minds which the advertiser is seeking to influence. This fact was seen by wise advertisers and such conceptions began to appear in print and to be heard in conventions of advertising men some ten years ago. (pp. 1–2)

Scott went on to say that during the 1890s, advertisers found little of use in psychology, because "[a]s far as the advertiser could see all psychologies

Excerpts from: Scott, W. D. (1908). *The psychology of advertising*. Boston: Small and Maynard.

were written with a purely theoretical end in view" (p. 3). Things were changing, though, and some psychologists beginning to develop "laboratories ... fitted up to make various tests upon advertisements" (p. 3). The purpose of Scott's book would be to summarize this work. He began by describing what psychologists had learned about memory and how that knowledge could benefit advertising.

> What the practical business man wants to know about memory can be put in two questions.
>
> First, how can I improve my own memory?
>
> Second, how can I so present my advertisements that they will be remembered by the public?
>
> It is not possible for a person with a poor memory to develop a good one, but everyone can improve his memory by the observance of a few well-known and thoroughly established principles. The first principle is *repetition*. If you want to make sure that you will remember a name, say it over to yourself. Repeat it in all the ways possible—say it over aloud, write it, look at it after it is written, think how it sounded when you heard the name, recall it at frequent periods and until it has become thoroughly fixed in your mind.
>
> The second principle is *intensity*. If you want to remember a name, pay the strictest possible attention to it. If you apply the first principle and repeat the name, then you should pay the maximum amount of attention to every repetition. . . .
>
> The third principle is that of *association*. The things which we think over, classify and systematize, and thus get associated with our previous experience, are the things which we commit most easily and retain the longest. . . .
>
> The fourth principle is that of *ingenuity*. I remember the name of Miss Low, for she is a short woman. I remember a friend's telephone, which is 1391, by thinking how unfortunate it is to have such a number to remember—13 is supposed to be an unlucky number, and 91 is seven times 13. (pp. 8–10, italics in the original)

Having described four basic principles of memory (today, we would call the fourth one "use of mnemonic devices"), Scott turned to the question of how they could be applied to advertising. (Note: throughout his book, Scott illustrated his point by reprinting examples of real ads. The 248-page book includes 67 of them).

> When the question arises,—how to construct an advertisement so that the reader cannot forget it, we find that the question is answered by the proper application of the principles enunciated above. The advertisement that is repeated over and over again at frequent intervals gradually becomes fixed in the memory of the reader. It may be a crude and expensive method, but it seems to be effective.
>
> This method gains added effect by repeating one or more characteristic features, and by changing some of the features at each appearance of the advertisement. Thus the reproduced advertisement of Vitalized Phosphites ... is frequently repeated in identical form. We cannot forget this advertisement, but it has taken too many repetitions to secure the desired result.

The reproduced advertisement of Cream of Wheat . . . is but one of a
series of advertisements in all of which the colored chef appears promi-
nently. This characteristic feature causes us to associate all of the series, and
hence the effect of association is secured. At the same time, there is sufficient
diversity, because the colored chef is never represented in the same way in
any two of the advertisements as they appear from month to month. Similar statements could be made of a host of other excellent advertisements.
(pp. 11–13)

Thus, mere repetition of an identical ad is not a good strategy, according
to Scott. By presenting the same ad for "vitalized phosphates," it did indeed
make its way into memory, but it would have been fixed in memory sooner if
the ad had been slightly varied from time to time, while maintaining its central
theme, as was the case in the Cream of Wheat ad. Vitalized phosphates, by
the way, described in the ad as "brain and nerve food," was apparently some
combination of "ox brain and embryo of wheat." It was designed for "active
business men and women, from whom sustained, vigorous application of brain
and nervous power is required," and worked by "feeding the brain and nerves
with the exact food they require for their nutrition and normal action" (p. 12).
The Cream of Wheat ad included, with the drawing of the chef, this text: "You
will always relish Cream of Wheat, no matter how little you want to eat. A
dainty breakfast. A delightful luncheon. A delicious dessert" (p. 13).

Having considered repetition, Scott moved on to the second principle,
"intensity." Note that his second example uses what memory researchers today
would call the serial position effect.

The advertisement which makes an intense impression is one which the
[reader] does not easily forget. The methods for securing this intensity are
many, but a few examples will serve to make the method plain.

Bright colors impress us more than dull ones. The bright-colored inserts
and advertisements run in colors are remembered better than others, because
they make a greater impression on us.

In any experience it is the first and the past parts of it that impress us most
and get fixed most firmly in our memories. The first and last advertisement
in a magazine are the most effective. Likewise the first and last parts of
any particular advertisement (unless very short) are the parts we remember
best. . . .

Anything humorous or ridiculous—even a pun—is hard to forget. But
unless the attempt is successful, the result is ludicrous and futile. Furthermore, that which impresses one person as funny may seem silly to
another. . . . Advertising is a serious business, and unless the advertisement
is extremely clever, it is unwise to attempt to present the humorous side of
life, although it is highly valuable when well done. (pp. 13–17)

Scott's third principle was association, by which he meant that the advertiser should make the reader associate the product with something important in
the reader's life.

The writer of advertisements must consider the principle of association, and
ordinarily does so, even if he does it unconsciously. He should present his

argument in such a form that it will naturally and easily be associated by the reader with his former experience. This is best done by appealing to those interests and motives which are the prime ruling principles of the reader's thinking. Personally, I should forget a recipe for a cake before I had finished reading it, but to a cook it is full of interest, and does not stand out as an isolated fact, but as a modification or addition of something already in mind. The statement that the bond bears four per cent interest is not forgotten by the capitalist; for he immediately associates the bond of which this statement is made with the group of similar bonds, and so the statement is remembered, not as an isolated fact, but in connection with a whole series of facts which are constantly before his mind. (p. 18)

Scott then reproduced an ad for "Buster Brown boys socks," which violated his principle. The ad said that coupons for these socks were "as good as 5% gold bonds" (p. 19). Scott argued that the ad would be ineffective because "men do not buy the stockings" (p. 19)—presumably mothers buy the socks, and Moms, with little experience in business, would not make the association between a good deal in socks and a good deal in bonds. (Actually, Scott might have overlooked a clever play on words—the phrase "socks and bonds" is quite close to "stocks and bonds").

Scott then closed his chapter on memory with some examples illustrating his fourth principle. Note: Uneeda biscuits, which first appeared in 1898, were the first products manufactured by the National Biscuit Company, which later changed its name to Nabisco.

The principle of ingenuity can have but an occasional application, but there are instances when it has been employed with great effectiveness. Thus "Uneeda" is a name which cannot be forgotten. It pleases by its very ingenuity, although most of the attempts in this direction have been futile. Thus "Uwanta" is recognized as an imitation, and is neither impressive nor pleasing. . . .

A tailor in Chicago advertised himself and his shop in such an ingenious way that no one could read his advertisement and forget the essential features of it. His street number was 33. His telephone number was the same. There were 33 letters in his name and address. He sold a business suit for $33. The number 33 stood out prominently as the striking feature of his advertisement and impressed many as being unique, and at the same time fixed in their minds his name and address, and the cost of his suits.

The four principles enunciated above for impressing advertisements on the minds of possible customers are capable of unlimited application, and will not disappoint any; for they are the laws which have been found to govern the minds of all persons as far as their memories are concerned. (pp. 20–21)

Implied in Scott's examples of how to use the principles of memory to sell is the notion that buyers do not make their decisions by rationally thinking through the choices among products, and then buying the best one. This notion, that buyers are not especially rational, became a major theme in Scott's writings about advertising. He elaborated on this theme in a later chapter. For example, in a chapter on "human instincts," he showed how successful ads could be aimed at various instincts. To demonstrate, he argued that the "hoarding" instinct would be activated in an ad about starting a "nest egg" with a small deposit at the American Reserve Bond Company (p. 65); that the "hunting" instinct would attract men to an ad featuring the successful use of "Stevens rifles" in killing game (p. 66); and that the "parental" instinct, shown in a cereal ad with a mother feeding a child, would increase the sales of that cereal brand (p. 71).

Another illustration of Scott's argument that buyers are not especially rational in their purchasing decisions appears in a chapter on "suggestion." He began by defining the term; as he meant to use it, suggestion meant being influenced to act by some factor other than one's own reasoning abilities.

> *Suggestion must be brought about by a second person or an object.* In my musings and deliberations I should not say that one idea suggested another, but if the same idea were called forth at the instigation of a second person or upon the presentation of an object, I should then call it suggestion—if it met the second essential condition of suggestion. This second condition is that *the resulting conception, conclusion or action must follow with less than the normal amount of deliberation.* Suggestion is thus a relative term, and in many instances it might be difficult to say whether or not a particular act was suggestion. If the act followed a normal amount of consideration after a normal time for deliberation, it would not be suggestion, while if the same act followed too abruptly or with too little consideration it might be a true case of suggestion. . . .
>
> It was once supposed that suggestion was something abnormal and that reason was the common attribute of men. Today we are finding that suggestion is of universal application to all persons, while reason is a process which is exceptional, even among the wisest. We reason rarely, but act under suggestion constantly.
>
> There has been a great agitation of late among advertisers for "reason why" copy. This agitation has had some value, but it is easily over-emphasized. Occasionally customers are persuaded and convinced, but more frequently they make their purchases because the act is suggested at the psychological moment. Suggestion and persuasion are not antagonistic; both should be kept in mind. However, in advertising, suggestion should not be subordinated to persuasion but should be supplemented by it. The actual effect of modern advertising is not so much to convince as to suggest. The individual swallowed up by a crowd is not aware of the fact that he is not exercising a normal amount of deliberation. His actions appear to him to be the result of reason, although the idea, as presented, is not criticized at all and no contradictory or inhibiting idea has any possibility of arising in his mind. In the same way we think that we are performing a deliberate act when we purchase an advertised commodity, while in fact we may never have deliberated upon the subject at all. The idea is suggested by the advertisement, and the impulsiveness of human nature enforces the suggested idea, hence the desired result follows in a way unknown to the purchaser. (pp. 80–83, italics in the original)

Later in the book, Scott reported on an informal observational study he had completed of people reading magazines in libraries. He estimated that readers did not spend much time reading ads. That of course made it even more critical for advertisers to use the principles he was advocating.

> As a result of investigations upon magazine and newspaper advertising the conclusion was reached that on the average only ten per cent of the time devoted to newspapers and magazines was spent in looking at advertisements.... As a conclusion deduced from these results it was recommended that advertisements should be so constructed that the gist of each could be comprehended at a glance, for most advertisements in newspaper and magazines receive no more than a glance from the average reader. The ordinary reader of newspapers and magazines *glances* at all of the advertising pages and sees all the *larger and more striking* advertisements.... Magazines and newspapers have become so numerous and the daily duties so pressing that we cannot take time to read all the advertisements, and so we devote but a few minutes to them, and in those few minutes we see a great number. We cannot afford the time to do more. (pp. 218–219)

Scott also noted, however, that there existed a special opportunity for advertisers to take advantage of a captive audience, thereby increasing the likelihood of readers paying closer attention to ads and, in turn, the ads having a greater effect. The situation involved "street railways."

> The case is different with street railway advertising. Here there is no shortage of time. There is sufficient opportunity to see every person in the car and to devote as much time to the process as good breeding allows. Thereafter one is compelled to look at the floor or else above the heads of the passengers.... In defense of one's good breeding and to drive away the weariness of the ride many a passenger is compelled to turn his gaze on the placards which adorn the sides of the car. The passenger has for once an abundance of time. He reads the card then reads it again because he has nothing else to do....
>
> There is indeed no form of advertising which is presented to such a large number of possible purchasers for such a long period of time and so frequently as is the advertising in street railway cars. In most other forms of advertising we devote to any particular advertisement only as much time as we think it is worth. In street railway advertising we devote longer time than we think is due to the advertisements, and then we turn around and estimate the value of the good advertised by the amount of time that we have devoted to the advertisement. This is the psychological explanation of the amazing potency of the particular form of advertising. (pp. 224–225)

Scott concluded his book with a chapter on what would today be called marketing research, in this particular case the use of questionnaires about newspapers to help advertisers develop a campaign to increase readership.

During the remainder of his career at Northwestern, Scott became one of America's best-known applied psychologists. He published additional books on industrial psychology (e.g., *Increasing Human Efficiency in Business* in 1911), contributed expertise on mental testing to the war effort (World War I), and was elected president of the American Psychological Association in 1919. In the academic year 1916–1917, he spent a leave of absence as director of the Bureau of Salesmanship Research at Carnegie Institute of Technology in Pittsburgh (now Carnegie-Mellon University), where he became the first American psychologist to hold the title of Professor of Applied Psychology (Landy, 1993). In 1920, he was named President of Northwestern, a position he held until retirement in 1939.

CONCEPT REVIEW QUESTIONS

1. What did Scott have to say about improving memory?
2. Use examples to show how Scott applied his principles of memory to advertising.
3. Explain, using examples, Scott's views on the issue of the "rationality" of the typical consumer.

DISCUSSION QUESTION

1. How do Scott's ideas about advertising compare with what you see in the world of advertising today?

HUGO MÜNSTERBERG (1863–1916): APPLYING PSYCHOLOGY TO BUSINESS

Like Walter Dill Scott (Chapter 27), Hugo Münsterberg was trained as an experimental psychologist and earned his Ph.D. in Wundt's laboratory at Leipzig. At the invitation of William James (Chapter 9), Münsterberg came to the United States in 1892 to run the laboratory at Harvard and to continue his program of basic research. Although it might seem unlikely that such a background would produce a leader in applied psychology, such was the case. By the time of his death in 1916, Münsterberg had forsaken basic laboratory research and become a pioneer in the fledgling field of industrial psychology (he called it "economic" psychology). He also made a substantial contribution to the application of psychology to law with his 1908 book, *On the Witness Stand*, and he even dabbled in the treatment of mental illness, producing *Psychotherapy* in 1909. The excerpt you are about to read is from his writings on industrial psychology.

As he did with most of his books, Münsterberg compiled his industrial psychology text from a set of lectures. He published it in German in 1912, then in English a year later as *Psychology and Industrial Efficiency* (Münsterberg, 1913). After three introductory chapters, he divided his book into three main sections, with these headings:

The Best Possible Man → nine chapters on employee selection

The Best Possible Work → six chapters on how to optimize productivity and efficiency

The Best Possible Effect → six chapters on such topics as marketing and advertising

In his opening chapter, Münsterberg described the rationale for his book.

> Our aim is to sketch the outline of a new science which is intermediate
> between the modern laboratory psychology and the problems of economics:
> the psychological experiment is systematically to be placed at the service of

Excerpts from: Münsterberg, H. (1913). *Psychology and industrial efficiency*. Boston: Houghton Mifflin.

commerce and industry.... What is most needed today at the beginning of the new movement are clear, concrete illustrations which demonstrate the possibilities of the new method. In the following pages, accordingly, it will be my aim to analyze the results of experiments which have actually been carried out, experiments belonging to many different spheres of economic life. (pp. 3–4)

In Münsterberg's first main section of the book, his concern was how psychological methods could be used to select workers. He argued for the importance of efficient selection of human resources by drawing an interesting parallel to the threats then existing to natural resources (which would soon lead to the creation, by President Theodore Roosevelt, of National Parks such as Yellowstone and Yosemite). Just as the country was beginning to recognize "how the richness of the forests and the mines and the rivers had been recklessly squandered without any thought of the future" (p. 38), so too were economists coming to believe that "no waste of valuable possessions is so reckless as that which results from the distribution of living force by chance methods instead of examining carefully how work and workmen can fit one another" (p. 38).

To show how psychology could contribute to the process of fitting work and workers together, Münsterberg described three specific examples— "motormen," ship captains, and telephone operators. Motormen were the driver/ operators of the electric streetcars that provided the primary means of public transportation found in cities in those days, but now requires a trip to San Francisco to experience anything comparable. The job was not easy in the days before agreed-upon traffic signals, for the motorman had to stay on schedule while watching out for the carriages, motorcars, and pedestrians that filled the typically chaotic city street. Mishaps were not uncommon—Münsterberg wrote that railway companies reported "up to fifty thousand accident indemnity cases a year" (p. 64)! Some operators had better records than others, and Münsterberg was asked by the Boston Elevated Railway Company to identify the attributes of the competent ones. If he could, then the initial selection process would be improved. Münsterberg believed there were two different ways to proceed, either by simulating, as a whole, the essential processes involved in successful work, or breaking the work down into component processes and developing tests for each.

One way is to take the mental process which is demanded by the industrial work as an undivided whole. In this case we have to construct experimental conditions under which this total activity can be performed in a gradual, measurable way. The psychical part of the vocational work thus becomes schematized and is simply rendered experimentally on a reduced scale. The other way is to resolve the mental process into its components and to test every single elementary function in its isolated form. In this latter case the examination has the advantage of having at its disposal all the familiar methods of experimental psychology, while in the first case for every special vocational situation perfectly new experimental tests must be devised. (p. 59)

Of Münsterberg's three examples of employee selection, his work with motormen illustrates the simulation approach, while his telephone operator project used the more analytic approach. With regard to motormen, Münsterberg first considered using the analytic approach. Competent workers might be expected to have faster reaction times, for instance. He quickly discovered a ceiling effect, however: no differences in reaction time could be found between good and bad drivers. As Münsterberg put it, "the slow individuals do not remain in the service at all" (p. 65). Having rejected the piecemeal approach, Münsterberg turned to his first method—simulation. After observing several motormen, he identified what he thought to be the critical process in a rather complex job.

> I found this to be a particular complicated act of attention by which the mani-
> foldness of objects, the pedestrians, the carriages, and the automobiles, are
> continuously observed with reference to the rapidity and direction in the
> quickly changing panorama of the street. Moving figures come from the
> right and from the left toward and across the track, and are embedded in a
> stream of men and vehicles which moves parallel to the track. In the face of
> such manifoldness there are men whose impulses are almost inhibited and
> who instinctively desire to wait for the movement of the nearest objects; they
> would evidently be unfit for the service, as they would drive the electric car
> too slowly. There are others who, even with the car at high speed, can adjust
> themselves for a time to the complex moving situation, but whose attention
> soon lapses, and while they are fixating a rather distant carriage, may over-
> look a pedestrian who carelessly crosses the track immediately in front of
> the car. In short, we have a great variety of mental types of this characteristic
> unified activity, which may be understood as a particular combination of
> attention and imagination. (p. 66)

But how could this "combination of attention and imagination" be simu-
lated in the laboratory? Münsterberg ruled out using miniaturized versions of the streetcars, in which individuals would have to maneuver tiny models of electric cars on models of streets. Instead, he argued that a task should be created that catches the *essence* of the mental processes being evaluated.

> The essential point for the psychological experiment is not the external
> similarity of the apparatus, but exclusively the inner similarity of the mental
> attitude. The more the external mechanism with which or on which the action
> is carried out becomes schematized, the more the action itself will appear in
> its true character.
>   In the method of my experiments with the motormen, accordingly, I
> had to satisfy only two demands. The method of examination promised
> to be valuable if, first, it showed good results with reliable motormen and
> bad results with unreliable ones; and, secondly, if it vividly aroused in all
> the motormen the feeling that the mental function which they were going
> through during the experiment had the greatest possible similarity with their
> experience on the front platform of the electric car. These are the true tests of
> a desirable experimental method, while it is not necessary that the apparatus
> be similar to the electric car or that the external activities in the experiment
> be identical with their performance in the service. (pp. 68–69)

After several false starts, Münsterberg created a clever simulation, one that at least met his second demand—his participants indeed reported that the task was similar to what they encountered on the job. He created cards 4.5 inches wide and 13 inches long, divided into half-inch squares. Two parallel lines ran down the middle, representing tracks. In the squares on either side of the "tracks" was a random array of numbers representing people, horses, and automobiles, moving at different speeds, and moving either parallel to or perpendicular to the electric trolleys. Münsterberg rigged an apparatus so that the card was covered except for an area the width of the card and 2.5 inches long. By turning a crank, the motormen would successively expose various portions of the card and would be asked to identify objects that could end up being on the track, and therefore be dangerous. He recorded accuracy and how quickly they went through the cards. There were three groups of subjects.

> After developing this method in the psychological laboratory, I turned to the study of men actually in the service of a great electric railway company which supported my endeavors in the most cordial spirit. In accordance with my request, the company furnished me with a number of the best motormen in its service, men who for twenty years and more had performed their duties practically without accidents, and, on the other hand, with a large number of motormen who had only just escaped dismissal and whose record was characterized by many more or less important collisions or other accidents. Finally, we had men whose activity as motormen was neither especially good nor especially bad. (p. 74)

Münsterberg tested each individual motorman on 12 different cards, then combined time and errors into a weighted measure when describing the results. Unfortunately, his description of the outcome is incomplete. For example, the reader never learns exactly how many men were tested in each of the three groups, and he failed to report exactly how the groups differed in performance, noting only that there was a "far-reaching correspondence between efficiency in the experiment and efficiency in the actual service" (p. 75). Despite his claims for success, it appears that group differences might not have occurred, perhaps due to what researchers today would call a subject selection confound. That is, the reliable workers had also been with the company longer and were significantly older than the other workers. The fact that Münsterberg went out of his way to point out that older workers might be slower to pick up the simulation procedure suggests that these men did not do as well as he otherwise claimed.

> We must consider . . . that those men whom the company naturally selects as models are men who have had twenty to thirty years of service without accidents, but consequently they are rather old men, who no longer have the elasticity of youth and are naturally less able to think themselves into an artificial situation like that of such an experiment. It is therefore not surprising, but only to be expected, that such older, model men, while doing fair work in the test, are yet not seldom surpassed by bright, quick, young motormen who are twenty years younger, even though they are not yet ideal motormen. (p. 75)

Despite the ambiguity of these results, Münsterberg proclaimed the simulation a success and made a series of recommendations about what score should be obtained before a potential motorman could be considered competent. Although he recognized that the "experiments could be improved in many directions" (p. 81), he concluded that

> an experimental investigation of this kind which demands from each individual hardly 10 minutes would be sufficient to exclude perhaps one fourth of those who are nowadays accepted into the service as motormen. (p. 81)

Münsterberg had clearer results with his experiments on telephone operators. These underpaid and overworked women handled an average of about 225 calls per hour, which sometimes resulted in "fatigue and finally to a nervous breakdown of the employees and to confusion in the service" (pp. 98–99). The Bell Telephone Company was spending a lot of time and money on training, so they were looking for a way to screen those most likely to have difficulty and not last very long. Enter Münsterberg.

After observing operators for a time, Münsterberg was impressed with the complexity of their task.

> The user of the telephone is little inclined to consider how many actions have to be carried out . . . before the connection is made and finally broken again. From the moment when the speaker takes off the receiver to the cutting off of the connection, fourteen separate psychophysical processes are necessary in the typical case, and even then it is presupposed that the telephone girl understood the exchange and number correctly. (p. 97)

Instead of developing a simulation task, as he did with the motormen, Münsterberg chose to use his second strategy of breaking down a complex task into its elements and testing each component separately.

> After carefully observing the service in the central office for a while, I came to the conviction that it would not be appropriate here to reproduce the activity at the switchboard in the experiment, but that it would be more desirable to resolve that whole function into its elements and to undertake the experimental test of a whole series of elementary mental dispositions. Every one of these mental acts can then be examined according to well-known laboratory methods without giving to the experiments any direct relation to the characteristic telephone operation as such. I carried on the first series of experiments with about thirty young women who a short time before had entered into the telephone training school. . . . I examined them with reference to eight different psychophysical functions. (p. 100)

The young women who participated in the study were tested in a group setting for "memory, attention, intelligence, exactitude, and rapidity" (p. 101). To give you the flavor of these tests, consider the first two.

> The memory examination consisted of reading to the whole class at first two numbers of 4 digits, then two of 5 digits, then two of 6 digits, and so on up to figures of 12 digits, and demanding that they be written down as soon as a signal was given. The experiments on attention . . . made use of a method the principle of which has frequently been applied in the experimental psychology of individual differences and which I adjusted to our special needs.

The requirement is to cross out a particular letter in a connected text. Every one of the thirty women in the classroom received the same first page of a newspaper of that morning. . . . As soon as the signal was given, each one of the girls had to cross out with a pencil every 'a' in the text for six minutes. After a certain time, a bell signal was given and each of them then had to begin a new column. In this way we could find out, first, how many letters were correctly crossed out in those six minutes, secondly, how many letters were overlooked, and thirdly, how the recognition and the oversight were distributed in the various parts of the text. (pp. 101–102)

After the group tests, the women were tested individually on word association, card sorting, and accuracy in touching a pencil to crosses drawn on a page (i.e., similar to hitting the correct hole in the switchboard). Three months after the tests were completed, Münsterberg examined the work performance of the women he had tested. Once again, he failed to describe the results in any detail, but a sly move on the part of Bell Telephone, inserting some veterans into what Münsterberg had thought was a class of 30 novices, provided some unexpected validation.

These three months had been sufficient to secure at least a certain discrimination between the best, the average, and the unfit. The result of this comparison was on the whole satisfactory. First, the skeptical telephone company had mixed with the class a number of women who had been in the service for a long while and had even been selected as teachers in the telephone school. I did not know, in figuring out the results, which of the participants in the experiments these particularly gifted outsiders were. . . . The results showed . . . that these women who had proved most able in practical service stood at the top of our list. Correspondingly, those who stood the lowest in our psychological rank list had in the mean time been found unfit in practical service and had either left the company of their own accord or else had been eliminated. (pp. 108–109)

The "motorman" and telephone operator selection examples are the best known of the studies reported in Münsterberg's pioneering book, but there are dozens more, examining such topics as the effects of monotony on productivity, whether magazines should place ads together in one section or spread them throughout the magazine, and the effects of the size of ads on memory for products. Concerning the latter, Münsterberg did a study in his Harvard lab in which he found that four quarter-page ads, spread through an array, produced better recall of the product than a single full-page ad (pp. 263–267).

Münsterberg closed his book with a chapter called "The Future Development of Economic Psychology." In it, he recommended the creation of a "government bureau for applied psychology" (p. 306) and painted a rosy picture of the "splendid betterments" (p. 308) resulting from the study of economic psychology.

We must not forget that the increase of industrial efficiency by future psychological adaptation and by improvement of the psychophysical conditions is not only in the interest of the employers, but still more of the employees; their working time can be reduced, their wages increased, their level of life raised. And above all, still more important than the naked commercial profit on both sides, is the cultural gain which will come to the total economic life of the nation, as soon as every one can be brought to the place where his best energies may be unfolded and his greatest personal satisfaction secured. The economic experimental psychology offers no more inspiring idea than this adjustment of work and psyche by which mental dissatisfaction in the work . . . may be replaced in our social community by overflowing joy and perfect inner harmony. (pp. 308–309)

By the time of his sudden death in 1916 (in the middle of a lecture to a psychology class at Radcliffe College), Münsterberg was one of the most visible and best-known psychologists in America. His books sold well, and he was a regular contributor to several popular magazines. One of his efforts, however, quickly made him one of the most hated public figures in America. In the years leading up to World War I, he took it upon himself to extol the virtues of German culture to Americans (to his credit, he also tried to explain American culture to his native Germans). But this was not the time to be defending Germany in America and the response was vitriolic—in his collected papers, for example, are four folders of hate mail that include death threats (Benjamin, 2000). One consequence of his sullied reputation was that he was rather quickly forgotten after his death. His contributions to applied psychology have only recently been reexamined and found to have been substantial (Hale, 1980; Spillman & Spillman, 1993).

CONCEPT REVIEW QUESTIONS

1. Describe the contributions made by Münsterberg to applied psychology. Concerning his "economic psychology" book, what three general topics were considered?

2. Describe and critically analyze the employee selection research completed by Münsterberg for Boston Elevated Railway Company.

3. Describe and critically analyze the employee selection research completed by Münsterberg for the Bell Telephone Company.

DISCUSSION QUESTION

1. In general, describe the two different research strategies used by Münsterberg in his employee selection work. In light of modern conceptions of work, what would you see as strengths and weaknesses of each?

JAMES MCKEEN CATTELL (1860–1944): MENTAL TESTS

James McKeen Cattell (1860–1944) was prominent among the first generation of academic psychologists in the United States. During the 1880s, he studied for a time with G. Stanley Hall at Johns Hopkins, and he earned a doctorate in 1886 from Wundt (Chapter 5) at Leipzig, specializing in reaction time research. But Francis Galton (Chapter 15) had the most important formative influence on him, and Cattell is sometimes referred to as the "American Galton." Cattell met Galton soon after the young American finished his work at Leipzig, when Cattell studied briefly at Cambridge, and they later corresponded. Like Galton, Cattell believed in an inductive approach to science, one that valued accumulating as much data as possible, assuming that general principles would gradually emerge from the activity. Cattell was especially enamored of Galton's approach to measurement, as you will see shortly.

Cattell's first academic position was at the University of Pennsylvania in 1889, but he only stayed for two years before moving (and doubling his salary, to $2500) to Columbia in New York (Sokal, 1981). At Columbia, he developed one of the premier psychology programs in the country and, of importance for this chapter's excerpt, he continued a Galton-inspired program of "mental testing" that he had begun at Penn. That program produced an 1890 paper that will be excerpted here, and then a decade of collecting test data from college students. This 1890 paper first used the term "mental test." In it, Cattell outlined his rationale for using the tests he selected, and described ten tests in some detail. After arriving at Columbia, he continued his testing program, and eventually commissioned a graduate student, Clark Wissler, to determine whether the tests related to academic work at Columbia. Unfortunately for Cattell, Wissler's 1901 paper effectively destroyed the Galton-Cattell approach to mental testing, as will be seen below.

In his 1890 article, Cattell began by describing the reasons why he developed his testing program. In so doing, he clearly revealed his inductivist philosophy. Note also that he hints at practical applications for the tests.

> Psychology cannot attain the certainty and exactness of the physical sciences, unless it rests on a foundation of experiment and measurement. A

Excerpts from: Cattell, J. M. (1890). Mental tests and measurements. *Mind, 15,* 373–381.

step in this direction could be made by applying a series of mental tests and measurements to a large number of individuals. The results would be of considerable scientific value in discovering the constancy of mental processes, their interdependence, and their variation under different circumstances. Individuals, besides, would find their tests interesting, and, perhaps, useful in regard to training, mode of life or indication of disease. The scientific and practical value of such tests would be much increased should a uniform system be adopted, so that determinations made at different times and places could be compared and combined. With a view to obtaining agreement among those interested, I venture to suggest the following series of tests and measurements, together with methods of making them.

The first series of ten tests is made in the Psychological Laboratory, of the University of Pennsylvania on all who present themselves, and the complete series on students of Experimental Psychology. The results will be published when sufficient data have been collected. Meanwhile, I should be glad to have the tests, and the methods of making them, thoroughly discussed.

The following ten tests are proposed:

   I. Dynamometer Pressure.
  II. Rate of Movement.
 III. Sensation-areas.
  IV. Pressure causing Pain.
   V. Least Noticeable difference in Weight.
  VI. Reaction-time for Sound.
 VII. Time for naming Colours.
VIII. Bi-section of a 50 cm Line.
  IX. Judgment of 10 sec. Time.
   X. Number of Letters remembered on once Hearing.

It will be noticed that the series begins with determinations rather bodily than mental, and proceeds through psychophysical to more purely mental measurements.

The tests may be readily made on inexperienced persons, the time required for the series being about an hour. The laboratory should be conveniently arranged and quiet, and no spectators should be present while the experiments are being made. The amount of instruction the experimentee should receive, and the number of trials he should be given, are matters which ought to be settled in order to secure uniformity of result. The amount of instruction depends on the experimenter and experimentee, and cannot, unfortunately, be exactly defined. It can only be said that the experimentee must understand clearly what he has to do. A large and uniform number of trials would, of course, be the most satisfactory, the average, average variation, maximum and minimum being recorded. Time is, however, a matter of great importance if many persons are to be tested. The arrangement most economical of time would be to test thoroughly a small number of persons, and a large number in a more rough-and-ready fashion. The number of trials I allow in each test is given below, as also whether I consider the average or 'best' trial the most satisfactory for comparison. (pp. 373–374)

The measurement of mental ability and intelligence has evolved considerably, of course, and today the idea of using what Cattell called "bodily and psychophysical" measures might appear to be far removed from modern notions. As you read the following list of tests, however, it is important to regard them in the context of the time Cattell was writing, and not with reference to what we know about intelligence testing today. In 1890, the term IQ did not exist, for example, and the intelligence testing tradition that began with Alfred Binet in France (next chapter), which focused more on school-related mental abilities, was still more than a decade away. Rather, Cattell was following Galton's lead, and Galton, following British empiricist tradition (e.g., refer to Mill in Chapter 2) had argued that there was nothing in the mind that was not first in the senses. If a sharp mind meant finely tuned senses, then it appeared reasonable to measure sensory capacity. As Galton had put it, "[t]he only information that reaches us concerning outward events appears to pass through the avenue of our senses; and the more perceptible our senses are of difference, the larger is the field upon which our judgment and intelligence can act" (Galton, 1883/1965, p. 421). With this in mind, here are the ten tests proposed by Cattell. Note that in several places he justifies the particular test (in ways that Galton would approve) for those who might question whether it relates to "mental" ability.

> I. *Dynamometer Pressure.* The greatest possible squeeze of the hand may be thought by many to be a purely physiological quantity. It is, however, impossible to separate bodily from mental energy. The 'sense of effort' and the effects of volition on the body are among the questions most discussed in psychology and even in metaphysics. Interesting experiments may be made on the relation between volitional control or emotional excitement and dynamometer pressure. Other determinations of bodily power could be made (in the second series I have included the 'archer's pull' and pressure of the thumb and fore-finger), but the squeeze of the hand seems the most convenient. It may be readily made, cannot prove injurious, is dependent on mental conditions, and allows comparison of right-and left-handed power. The experimentee should be shown how to hold the dynamometer in order to obtain the maximum pressure. I allow two trials with each hand (the order being right, left, right, left), and record the maximum pressure of each hand.
>
> II. *Rate of Movement.* Such a determination seems to be of considerable interest, especially in connexion with the preceding. Indeed, its physiological importance is such as to make it surprising that careful measurements have not hitherto been made. The rate of movement has the same psychological bearings as the force of movement. Notice, in addition to the subjects already mentioned, the connexion between force and rate of movement on the one hand and the 'four temperaments' on the other. I am now making experiments to determine the rate of different movements. As a general test, I suggest the quickest possible movement of the right hand and arm from rest through 50 cm. . . . An electric current is closed by the first movement of the hand, and broken when the movement through 50 cm. has been completed. I measure the time the current has been closed with the Hipp chronoscope, but it may be done by any chronographic method. . . .
>
> III. *Sensation-areas.* The distance on the skin by which two points must be separated in order that they may be felt as two is a constant, interesting both to the physiologist and psychologist. Its variation in different parts of the body (from 1 to 68 mm.) was a most important discovery. What the

individual variation may be, and what inferences may be drawn from it, cannot be foreseen; but anything which may throw light on the development of the idea of space deserves careful study. Only one part of the body can be tested in a series such as the present. I suggest the back of the closed right hand, between the tendons of the first and second fingers, and in a longitudinal direction. Compasses with rounded wooden or rubber tips should be used, and I suggest that the curvature have a radius of 5 mm. This experiment requires some care and skill on the part of the experimenter. The points must be touched simultaneously, and not too hard. The experimentee must turn away his head. In order to obtain exact results, a large number of experiments would be necessary, and all the tact of the experimenter will be required to determine, without undue expenditure of time, the distance at which the touches may just be distinguished.

IV. *Pressure causing Pain*. This, like the rate of movement, is a determination not hitherto much considered, and if other more important tests can be devised they might be substituted for these. But the point at which pressure causes pain may be an important constant, and in any case it would be valuable in the diagnosis of nervous diseases and in studying abnormal states of consciousness. The determination of any fixed point or quantity in pleasure or pain is a matter of great interest in theoretical and practical ethics, and I should be glad to include some such test [in] the present series. To determine the pressure causing pain, I use an instrument . . . which measures the pressure applied by a tip of hard rubber 5 mm. in radius. I am now determining the pressure causing pain in different parts of the body; for the present series commend the centre of the forehead. The pressure should be gradually increased and the maximum read from the indicator after the experiment is complete. As a rule, the point at which the experimentee says the pressure is painful should be recorded, but in some cases it may be necessary to record the point at which signs of pain are shown. I make two trials, and record both.

V. *Least noticeable difference in Weight*. The just noticeable sensation and the least noticeable difference in sensation are psychological constants of great interest. Indeed, the measurement of mental intensity is probably the most important question with which experimental psychology has at present to deal. The just noticeable sensation can only be determined with great pains, if at all: the point usually found being in reality the least noticeable difference for faint stimuli. This latter point is itself so difficult to determine that I have postponed it to the second series. The least noticeable difference in sensation for stimuli of a given intensity can be more readily determined, but it requires some time, and consequently not more than one sense and intensity can be tested in a preliminary series. I follow Mr. Galton in selecting 'sense of effort' or weight. I use small wooden boxes, the standard one weighing 100 gms. and the others 101, 102, up to 110 gms. The standard weight and another (beginning with 105 gms.) being given to the experimentee, he is asked which is the heavier. I allow him about 10 secs for decision. I record the point at which he is usually right, being careful to note that he is always right with the next heavier weight.

VI. *Reaction-time for Sound*. The time elapsing before a stimulus calls forth a movement should certainly be included in a series of psychophysical tests: the question to be decided is what stimulus should be chosen. I prefer sound; on it the reaction-time seems to be the shortest and most regular, and the apparatus is most easily arranged. I measure the time with a Hipp chronoscope, but various chronographic methods have been used. There is need of a simpler, cheaper and more portable apparatus for measuring short times. Mr. Galton uses an ingenious instrument, in which the time is measured by the motion of a falling rod, and electricity is dispensed with, but this method will not measure times longer than about 1/3 sec. In measuring the reaction-time, I suggest that three valid reactions be taken, and the minimum recorded. Later, the average and mean variation may be calculated.

VII. *Time for naming Colours.* A reaction is essentially reflex, and, I think, in addition to it, the time of some process more purely mental should be measured. Several such processes are included in the second series; for the present series I suggest the time needed to see and name a colour. This time may be readily measured for a single colour by means of suitable apparatus . . . , but for general use sufficient accuracy may be attained by allowing the experimentee to name ten colours and taking the average. I paste coloured papers (red, yellow, green and blue) 2 cm. square, 1 cm. apart, vertically on a strip of black pasteboard. This I suddenly uncover and start a chronoscope, which I stop when the ten colours have been named. I allow two trials (the order of colours being different in each) and record the average time per colour in the quickest trial.

VIII. *Bisection of a 50 cm Line.* The accuracy with which space and time are judged may be readily tested, and with interesting results. I follow Mr. Galton in letting the experimentee divide an ebony rule (3 cm. wide) into two equal parts by means of a movable line, but I recommend 50 cm. in place of 1 ft., as with the latter the error is so small that it is difficult to measure, and the metric system seems preferable. The amount of error in mm. (the distance from the true middle) should be recorded, and whether it is to the right or left. One trial would seem to be sufficient.

IX. *Judgment of 10 sec. Time.* This determination is easily made. I strike on the table with the end of a pencil and again after 10 seconds, and let the experimentee in turn strike when he judges an equal interval to have elapsed. I allow only one trial and record the time, from which the amount and direction of error can be seen.

X. *Number of Letters repeated on once Hearing.* Memory and attention may be tested by determining how many letters can be repeated on hearing once. I name distinctly and at the rate of two per second six letters, and if the experimentee can repeat these after me I go on to seven, then eight, &c.; if the six are not correctly repeated after three trials (with different letters), I give five, four, &c. The maximum number of letters which can be grasped and remembered is thus determined. Consonants only should be used in order to avoid syllables. (pp. 374–377, italics in the original)

Cattell closed out his article by making specific reference to the potential of using these tests in an educational setting and by listing, without further explanation, a longer series of tests, the "second series" that he mentioned several times in his initial list above. He included 50 tests, most similar in concept to his basic ten (e.g., psychophysics tests for the various senses). As he concluded,

Experimental psychology is likely to take a place in the educational plan of our schools and universities. It teaches accurate observation and correct reasoning in the same way as the other natural sciences, and offers a supply of knowledge interesting and useful to everyone. I am at present preparing a laboratory manual which will include tests of the senses and measurements of mental time, intensity and extensity, but it seems worth while to give here a list of the tests which I look on as the more important in order that attention may be drawn to them, and co-operation secured in choosing the best series of tests and the most accurate and convenient methods. (pp. 377–378)

Cattell never completed the laboratory manual, but he spent the decade of the 1890s advocating for his brand of testing and administering tests to Columbia students. Similar testing programs were established at a few other universities (e.g., Wisconsin), and the APA established a "Committee on Mental and Physical Tests" to see if testing activities among universities could be coordinated (Sokal, 1981). Cattell's approach died almost overnight, however, after the results of a study by one of his own students was published in 1901.

Clark Wissler was a doctoral student of Cattell's, and for his dissertation he examined the related questions of whether the Cattell tests were interrelated and, more critically, whether the tests were related to academic performance at Columbia. Presumably, if the tests related to mental ability, good students should outperform poor students. Wissler's main innovation was using the newly developed correlation coefficient, invented by Galton and perfected by Karl Pearson, a close colleague of Galton's. The results were devastating—the tests did not correlate well with each other and failed to correlate with academic success. For instance, the correlation between reaction time and color naming was $+.15$, and that between reaction time and "college standing" was effectively zero ($r = -0.02$). On the other hand, correlations among school subjects were reasonably high (e.g., $+.58$ between Latin and math), and, perhaps most embarrassing of all to Cattell, gym class was a better predictor of academic status ($r = +.53$) than *any* of Cattell's tests. Wissler (1901/1965) concluded:

> In general it appears that correlations in any of the foregoing tests are not of a degree sufficient for practical purposes. We do not learn much of an individual by any one or any group of them. It appears that we are dealing here with special and quite independent abilities and that the importance attributed to such measurements of elementary processes by many investigators is not justified in this case. (p. 444)

After the Wissler debacle, Cattell's career shifted direction. He abandoned his mental testing work and focused his attention more on departmental administrative work, journal editing, and what could be called the professionalization of psychology. He remained at Columbia until 1917, when he was fired for his strong advocacy of pacifism during the World War I era, and for his strong support of academic freedom at the university. He successfully sued the university for libel and in his remaining years, he continued his editorial work and he remained visible and active in the APA.

While Cattell's approach to mental testing was failing, a different strategy was developing in France, led by Alfred Binet, the subject of the next reading.

CONCEPT REVIEW QUESTIONS

1. Cattell, like his mentor Galton, was said to be an inductivist. What does this mean and how did it affect Cattell's research?

2. Cattell wrote that his ten tests were arranged in a kind of "progression." Explain.

3. What happened in the Wissler study and why was it so devastating for Cattell?

DISCUSSION QUESTION

1. Describe and then critically evaluate the Galton-Cattell rationale for the types of tests they chose to measure mental ability. Is there some way in which this approach makes some sense?

ALFRED BINET (1857–1911): THE BINET-SIMON TESTS OF INTELLIGENCE

Mental tests preceded Alfred Binet, primarily in the work of Francis Galton (Chapter 15) and James McKeen Cattell (Chapter 29), who invented the term. As you recall from the Cattell chapter, the Galton-Cattell testing strategy collapsed with the Wissler study (1901/1965)—measuring basic sensory processes did not seem to be the best way to measure mental ability. An alternative approach appeared in France at about the same time as the Wissler study, in the work of Alfred Binet and his colleague Theodore Simon. It represents the start of the modern intelligence testing movement.

During the 1890s, Binet was director of the Laboratory of Physiological Psychology at the Sorbonne in Paris, where he had developed an approach to psychology that he called *individual psychology*—his emphasis was on studying how individuals differed from each other, rather than on discovering general laws that applied to everyone (Fancher, 1985). Thus, he was a natural appointee to a commission in 1904 that was asked to study the problem of individual differences in school-related abilities. The goal was to find a way to classify students into different ability levels, so those who were slow but nonetheless somewhat capable of schoolwork could be identified, organized into separate classes, and given special training. Out of this effort came Binet and Simon's attempt to measure school-related mental abilities and, eventually (after Binet's death), the well-known IQ test.

The excerpts in this chapter come from a book published in 1916 that was compiled from five different articles published by Binet and Simon, between 1905 and 1911, in the journal *L'Année Psychologique*. The prime mover behind the book was Henry Goddard (Chapter 16), the American psychologist who first brought the Binet scales to the United States. Goddard wrote a laudatory introduction, referring to Binet's work as "masterly" (p. 6). The articles were translated into English by Mary Kite, one of Goddard's assistants at the Vineland Institute in New Jersey (a key field worker in Goddard's Kallikak study). This

Excerpts from: Binet, A., & Simon, T. (1916). *The development of intelligence in children* (E. S. Kite, Trans.). Baltimore, MD: Williams and Wilkins.

excerpt will sample from the first two papers, both published in 1905. The first (called "Upon the necessity of establishing a scientific diagnosis of inferior states of attention") describes the Binet-Simon scale's origins and the nature of the basic problem to be solved, while the second provides a description of the original 1905 version of the Binet-Simon scale, (it was revised in 1908 and again in 1911). Binet and Simon began their opening article by describing the origins of the project.

> We here present the first rough sketch of a work which was directly inspired by the desire to serve the interesting cause of the education of subnormals.
>
> In October, 1904, the Minister of Public Education named a commission which was charged with the study of measures to be taken for insuring the benefits of instruction to defective children.... [The commission] decided that no child suspected of retardation should be eliminated from the ordinary school and admitted to a special class, without first being subjected to a pedagogical and medical examination from which it could be certified that because of the state of his intelligence, he was unable to profit, in an average measure, from the instruction given in the ordinary schools....
>
> The problem which we have to solve presents many difficulties both theoretical and practical. It is a hackneyed remark that the definitions, thus far proposed, for the different states of subnormal intelligence, lack precision. These inferior states are indefinite in number, being composed of a series of degrees which mount from the lowest depths of idiocy, to a condition easily confounded with normal intelligence.... [I]n spite of certain individual divergence of ideas to be found in all questions, there has been an agreement to accept *idiot* as applied to the lowest state, *imbecile* to the intermediate, and *moron* (débile) to the state nearest normality. (pp. 9–10, italics in the original)

Kite inserted a footnote at this point, indicating that Binet used the term *débile* ("weak") to describe this group, but that she would translate it as "moron," thus using the term created by Goddard, taken from the Greek term *moros*, for "foolish."

Although there was some consensus about the three broad categories of subnormality, Binet lamented the lack of agreement about the definitions for these three terms.

> The distinction between idiot, imbecile, and moron is not understood in the same way by all practitioners. We have abundant proof of this in the strikingly divergent medical diagnoses made only a few days apart by different alienists upon the same patient.
>
> Dr. Blin, physician of the Vaucluse Asylum, recently drew the attention of his fellow physicians to these regrettable contradictions. He states that the children who are sent to the colony come provided with several different certificates. "One child, called imbecile in the first certificate, is marked idiot in the second, feeble-minded (débile) in the third, and degenerate in the fourth." ...
>
> We cannot sufficiently deplore the consequence of this state of uncertainty recognized today by all alienists. The simple fact, that specialists do not

agree in the use of the technical terms of their science, throws suspicion upon their diagnoses, and prevents all work of comparison. . . .

What importance can be attached to public statistics of different countries concerning the percentage of backward children if the definition of backward children is not the same in all countries? How will it be possible to keep a record of the intelligence of pupils who are treated and instructed in a school, if the terms applied to them, feeble-minded, retarded, imbecile, idiot, vary in meaning according to the doctor who examines them? . . . But a still more serious fact is that, because of lack of methods, it is impossible to solve those essential questions concerning the afflicted, whose solution presents the greatest interest; for example, the real results gained by the treatment of inferior states of intelligence by doctor and educator; the educative value of one pedagogical method compared with another; the degree of curability of incomplete idiocy, etc. (pp. 10–11)

Having identified a serious problem, the lack of uniformity in the diagnosis of subnormality, Binet considered three reasons for it. He discarded the first, incompetence on the part of physicians, of minor importance. He then considered the remaining two.

Of these three kinds of error, which is the one that actually appears in the diagnosis of inferior states of intelligence? Let us set aside the first. There remain the fault of nomenclature, and the insufficiency of methods of examination.

The general belief seems to be that the confusion arises wholly from an absence of uniform nomenclature. There is some truth in this opinion. . . . Undoubtedly it would be a good work to bring about a unification of this nomenclature as has been done for the standard of measurements and for electric units. But this reform in itself is not sufficient and we are very sure that they deceive themselves who think that at the bottom this is only a question of terminology. It is very much more serious. We find physicians who, though using the same terminology, constantly disagree in their diagnosis of the same child. The example cited from Mr. Blin proves this. There the doctors had recourse to the terminology of Morel, who classified those of inferior intelligence as idiots, imbeciles, and *"débiles."* Notwithstanding this use of the same terms, they do not agree in the manner of applying them. Each one according to his own fancy, fixes the boundary line separating these states. It is in regard to the facts that the doctors disagree.

In looking closely one can see that the confusion comes principally from a fault in the method of examination. When an alienist finds himself in the presence of a child of inferior intelligence, he does not examine him by bringing out each one of the symptoms which the child manifests and by interpreting all symptoms and classifying them; he contents himself with taking a subjective impression, an impression as a whole, of his subject, and of making his diagnosis by instinct. We do not think that we are going too far in saying that at the present time very few physicians would be able to cite with absolute precision the objective and invariable sign, or signs, by which they distinguish the degrees of inferior mentality. (pp. 13–14, italics in the original)

Binet and Simon finished their first 1905 article by describing a number of historical attempts to define the categories of subnormality (e.g., by well-known French scientists including Pinel, Esquirol, and Sequin). They ended with another reference to the example Dr. Blin mentioned in one of their earlier passages. Blin had developed a test that involved asking subjects a series of questions, some of them similar to the kinds of questions eventually used by Binet and Simon in their 1905 scale. Binet praised Blin's work, but criticized the scoring method; Blin simply categorized children by the total number of correct responses. Binet's criticism hints at what would be a major innovation in the Binet Simon scale, the idea of *mental level*—scored by indicating the kinds of things known to typical children of a specific age.

> The child who has [taken Blin's test] comes before us with a certain total of marks, 36 for instance, or 70. We understand that 70 is nearer normal than 36 and that is all. We have no precise notion of the mental level of these candidates, no notion of what they can do or not do. Did the one who obtained 36 have any comprehension of abstract ideas? We do not know, and cannot divine. How much is he behind normal children of the same age? We know this no better.
>
> This brings us very naturally to an exposition of the plan of our work. It will be seen that our directing idea is different from that of Mr. Blin although our system of measurement, like his, is essentially psychological. (pp. 35–36)

This final paragraph of their first 1905 paper led naturally to a description of their strategy for identifying and classifying subnormal children. They took the issue up immediately in their second 1905 article in *L'Année Psychologique*, which was called "New methods for the diagnosis of the intellectual level of subnormals." After indicating that their purpose was to "measure the intellectual capacity of a child who is brought to us in order to know whether he is normal or retarded," (p. 37), they described three main methods—medical, pedagogical, and psychological—and elaborated on each. The focus here will be on the third of these methods.

> In order to recognize the inferior states of intelligence we believe that three different methods should be employed. We have arrived at this synthetic view only after many years of research, but we are now certain that each of these methods renders some service. These methods are:
>
> 1. *The medical method*, which aims to appreciate the anatomical, physiological, and pathological signs of inferior intelligence.
> 2. *The pedagogical method*, which aims to judge of the intelligence according to the sum of acquired knowledge.
> 3. *The psychological method*, which makes direct observations and measurements of the degree of intelligence.
>
> From what has gone before it is easy to see the value of each of these methods. The medical method is indirect because it conjectures the mental from the physical. The pedagogical method is more direct; but the psychological is the most direct of all because it aims to measure

the state of the intelligence as it is at the present moment. It does this by experiments which oblige the subject to make an effort which shows his capability in the way of comprehension, judgment, reasoning, and invention.

I. The Psychological Method

The fundamental idea of this method is the establishment of what we shall call a measuring scale of intelligence. This scale is composed of a series of tests of increasing difficulty, starting from the lowest intellectual level that can be observed, and ending with that of average normal intelligence. Each group in the series corresponds to a different mental level.

This scale properly speaking does not permit the measure of the intelligence, because intellectual qualities are not superposable, and therefore cannot be measured as linear surfaces are measured, but are on the contrary, a classification, a hierarchy among diverse intelligences; and for the necessities of practice this classification is equivalent to a measure. We shall therefore be able to know, after studying two individuals, if one rises above the other and to how many degrees, if one rises above the average level of other individuals considered as normal, or if he remains below. Understanding the normal progress of intellectual development among normals, we shall be able to determine how many years such an individual is advanced or retarded. In a word we shall be able to determine to what degrees of the scale idiocy, imbecility, and moronity correspond.

The scale that we shall describe is not a theoretical work; it is the result of long investigations, first at the Salpêtrière, and afterwards in the primary schools of Paris, with both normal and subnormal children.... All the tests which we propose have been repeatedly tried, and have been retained from among many, which after trial have been discarded. We can certify that those which are here presented have proved themselves valuable.

We have aimed to make all our tests simple, rapid, convenient, precise, heterogeneous, holding the subject in continued contact with the experimenter, and bearing principally upon the faculty of judgment. Rapidity is necessary for this sort of examination. It is impossible to prolong it beyond twenty minutes without fatiguing the subject. During this maximum of twenty minutes, it must be turned and turned about in every sense, and at least ten tests must be executed, so that not more than about two minutes can be given to each....

Another consideration. Our purpose is to evaluate a level of intelligence. It is understood that we here separate natural intelligence and instruction. It is the intelligence alone that we seek to measure, by disregarding in so far as possible, the degree of instruction which the subject possesses. He should, indeed, be considered by the examiner as a complete ignoramus knowing neither how to read nor write. This necessity forces us to forego a great many exercises having a verbal, literary or scholastic character. These belong to a pedagogical examination. We believe that we have succeeded in completely disregarding the acquired information of the subject. We give him nothing to read, nothing to write, and submit him to no test in which he might succeed by means of rote learning. In fact we do not even notice his inability to read if a case occurs. It is simply the level of his natural intelligence that is taken into account. (pp. 40–42, italics in the original)

As Binet and Simon turned to the question of how intelligence was to be defined, note two things. First, without mentioning Galton or Cattell by name, they argue the pointlessness of using sensory measures of intelligence. Second, they arrive at their own definition of intelligence, which centers on the concept of *judgment*, and has a distinctly functional tone to it ("adapting one's self to circumstances").

But here we must come to an understanding of what meaning to give to that word so vague and so comprehensive, "the intelligence." Nearly all the phenomena with which psychology concerns itself are phenomena of intelligence; sensation, perception, are intellectual manifestations as much as reasoning. Should we therefore bring into our examination the measure of sensation after the manner of the psycho-physicists? Should we put to the test all of his psychological processes? A slight reflection has shown us that this would indeed be wasted time.

It seems to us that in intelligence there is a fundamental faculty, the alteration or the lack of which, is of the utmost importance for practical life. This faculty is judgment, otherwise called good sense, practical sense, initiative, the faculty of adapting one's self to circumstances. To judge well, to comprehend well, to reason well, these are the essential activities of intelligence. A person may be a moron or an imbecile if he is lacking in judgment; but with good judgment he can never be either. Indeed the rest of the intellectual faculties seem of little importance in comparison with judgment. What does it matter, for example, whether the organs of sense function normally? Of what import that certain ones are hyperesthetic, or that others are anesthetic or are weakened? Laura Bridgman, Helen Keller and their fellow-unfortunates were blind as well as deaf, but this did not prevent them from being very intelligent. Certainly this is demonstrative proof that the total or even partial integrity of the senses does not form a mental factor equal to judgment. We may measure the acuteness of the sensibility of subjects; nothing could be easier. But we should do this, not so much to find out the state of their sensibility as to learn the exactitude of their judgment.

The same remark holds good for the study of the memory. At first glance, memory being a psychological phenomenon of capital importance, one would be tempted to give it a very conspicuous part in an examination of intelligence. But memory is distinct from and independent of judgment. One may have good sense and lack memory. The reverse is also common. Just at the present time we are observing a backward girl who is developing before our astonished eyes a memory very much greater than our own. We have measured that memory and we are not deceived regarding it. Nevertheless that girl presents a most beautifully classic type of imbecility.

As a result of all this investigation, in the scale which we present we accord the first place to judgment; that which is of importance to us is not certain errors which the subject commits, but absurd errors, which prove that he lacks judgment. We have even made special provision to encourage people to make absurd replies. In spite of the accuracy of this directing idea, it will be easily understood that it has been impossible to permit of its regulating exclusively our examinations. For example, one can not make tests of judgment on children of less than two years when one begins to watch their first gleams of intelligence. Much is gained when one can discern in them traces of coordination, the first delineation of attention and memory. We shall therefore bring out in our lists some tests of memory; but so far as we are able, we shall give these tests such a turn as to invite the subject to make absurd replies, and thus under cover of a test of memory, we shall have an appreciation of their judgment. (pp. 42–44)

The 1905 Binet-Simon scale contained thirty items, graded in difficulty by the age at which children were expected to pass each item. The more sophisticated 1908 scale increased the number of tests to fifty-eight, and could be scored for children from mental ages three to thirteen. From the 1908 scale, as listed in Binet and Simon's 1908 *L'Année Psychologique* paper (pp. 238–239 in the book excerpted here), the following is a brief sample of the tests used at different mental levels.

3 yrs → show eyes, nose, mouth; name objects in a picture

5 yrs → copy a square; repeat a sentence of 10 syllables

7 yrs → indicate omissions in drawings; describe a picture

9 yrs → name the days of the week; retain six memories after reading

11 yrs → criticize sentences containing absurdities; give abstract definitions

13 yrs → paper cutting; give differences of meaning

Binet died in 1911. Hence he did not live to see his approach to intelligence testing turn into the modern IQ test. Not long after Goddard brought the test to America, Lewis Terman of Stanford conducted an extensive standardization, producing the Stanford-Binet IQ test, which remains to this day an important measure of intelligence.

It is unlikely that Binet would have been pleased by developments subsequent to his work. He would have resisted the idea that mental ability can be reduced to a single number (an "intelligence quotient"), and he would have disagreed with the belief, held by most American psychologists doing IQ testing, that IQ represented one's basic, native ability. Rather, Binet always held to the belief that intelligence, once properly assessed, could then be improved through training (Fancher, 1985).

CONCEPT REVIEW QUESTIONS

1. One reason for the failure of uniformity in diagnosis was "faulty nomenclature." What does this mean and why did Binet and Simon consider it only of minor importance?

2. Describe Binet and Simon's "psychological method" for identifying and classifying subnormal children.

3. Why did Binet and Simon exclude sensory capacity and memory from their definition of intelligence?

DISCUSSION QUESTION

1. Critically evaluate Binet and Simon's definition of intelligence. How does it compare with modern versions?

GORDON ALLPORT (1897–1967): THE UNIQUENESS OF PERSONALITY

One important research tradition in psychology, represented by most of the chapters in this reader, emphasizes the search for general principles, laws of behavior that are assumed to apply to everyone, at least to a degree. In the Ebbinghaus chapter (6), for example, the principles of memory that he investigated apply to human memory in general. There is a second research tradition in psychology, though, one that focuses on the individual and examines ways in which one person differs from another. An example was the work done by Francis Galton (Chapter 15), who examined individual differences in intellect. This chapter provides another illustration of this second strategy, in the person of Gordon Allport, a Harvard University psychologist who was primarily responsible for establishing the study of personality as a specialty within psychology. The extent of his influence is reflected in the title of a recent intellectual biography—*Inventing Personality: Gordon Allport and the Science of Selfhood* (Nicholson, 2003).

The excerpt in this chapter is from *Personality: A Psychological Interpretation*, a famous textbook that Allport published in 1937. It is generally considered the first text in what was then the emerging field of personality psychology (Hilgard, 1987). Allport's advocacy for a research strategy focusing on the individual was evident from the start of the book, even in the opening paragraph of the Preface.

> As a rule, science regards the individual as a mere bothersome accident. Psychology, too, considers him as something to be brushed aside so the main business of accounting for the uniformity of events can get under way. The result is that on all sides we see psychologists enthusiastically at work upon a somewhat shadowy portrait entitled "the generalized human mind." Though serving well a certain purpose, this portrait is not altogether satisfying to those who compare it with the living individual models from which it is

Excerpts from: Allport, G. W. (1937a). *Personality: A psychological interpretation*. New York: Henry Holt.

drawn. It seems unreal and esoteric, devoid of locus, self-consciousness, and organic unity—all essential characteristics of the minds we know.

With intention of supplementing this abstract portrait by one that is more life-like, a new movement within psychological science has gradually grown up. It attempts in a variety of ways and from many points of view to depict and account for the manifest individuality of the mind. This new movement has come to be known (in America) as the *psychology of personality*. Especially within the past fifteen years has its progress been notable.

Since it is young, this movement finds difficulty in evaluating its first achievements. Its research is plentiful but piecemeal, its theories are numerous but conflicting. Yet every year more and more psychological investigators are attracted to it, and colleges at a rapid rate are adding the study of personality to their psychological curricula. The result of this rising tide of interest is an insistent demand for a guide book that will *define* the new field of study—one that will articulate its objectives, formulate its standards, and test the progress made thus far. (p. vii, italics in the original)

Allport's goal, then, was to provide this guidebook to personality. In his opening chapter, "Psychology and the Study of the Individual," he elaborated on his belief that psychology need not limit itself to the study of general principles. Then in Chapter 2 ("Defining Personality"), he described what he meant by the concept of personality. After an exhaustive survey of how the term had been used historically, starting with the ancient Greeks, Allport arrived at a "definition for this book" (p. 47).

From this long survey of past and present usage what may we conclude? Since there is no such thing as a wrong definition of any term, if it is supported by usage, it is evident that no one, neither the theologian, the philosopher, the jurist, the sociologist, the man in the street, nor the psychologist, can monopolize "personality." For the psychologist, to be sure, some definitions seem to be more serviceable than others. Completely unsuitable are biosocial formulations in terms of social reputation or superficial charm. . . . The distinction between reputation (social effectiveness) and the true personality is one that will be observed rigidly throughout this book. . . . More helpful are those conceptions that ascribe to personality a *solid organization* of dispositions and sentiments. Valuable likewise are definitions that refer to the *style of life*, to *modes of adaptation* to one's surroundings, to *progressive growth* and development and to *distinctiveness*.

Might we not say that, psychologically considered, personality is what a man really is? This terse expression states the essential biophysical position, and is acceptable enough in principle. The following amplification seems to serve the purpose better:

PERSONALITY IS THE DYNAMIC ORGANIZATION WITHIN THE INDIVIDUAL OF THOSE PSYCHOPHYSICAL SYSTEMS THAT DETERMINE HIS UNIQUE ADJUSTMENTS TO HIS ENVIRONMENT. (pp. 47–48, italics and upper case usage in the original)

Allport continued by elaborating and further clarifying each component of his definition. The term "organization" meant that different attributes of the personality were organizing into a coherent whole (Allport was influenced by the gestalt psychologists), and "dynamic" meant that the organization was "constantly evolving and changing" (p. 48). As for "psychophysical systems," they were

> [h]abits, specific and general attitudes, sentiments, and dispositions. . . . In later chapters these dispositions will be ordered within a theory of *traits*. The term "system" refers to traits or groups of traits in a latent or active condition. The term "psychophysical" reminds us that personality is neither exclusively mental nor exclusively neural. The organization entails the operation of both body and mind, inextricably fused into a personal unity . . .
>
> *Unique*. Strictly speaking every adjustment of every person is unique, in time and place, and in quality. In a sense, therefore, this criterion seems redundant. It becomes important, however, in our later discussions of the problem of quantitative variation among individuals in respect to so-called "common" traits . . . , and is therefore emphasized in the definition.
>
> *Adjustments to His Environment*. This phrase has a functional and evolutionary significance. Personality is a mode of survival. "Adjustment," however, must be interpreted broadly enough to include maladjustments, and "environmental" to include the behavioral environment (meaningful to the individual) as well as the surrounding geographical environment. (pp. 48–50, italics in the original)

Personality, for Allport, was composed of various "traits," attributes that a person would display with a high degree of consistency in various situations (e.g., shyness). He identified three different categories of trait—cardinal, central, and secondary.

> In every personality there are traits of major significance and traits of minor significance. Occasionally some trait is so pervasive and so outstanding in a life that it deserves to be called a *cardinal trait*. It is so dominant that there are few activities that cannot be traced directly or indirectly to its influence. The list of terms on pp. 302f., derived from the proper names of historical and fictional characters, shows clearly what is meant by cardinal traits. No such trait can for long remain hidden; an individual is known by it, and may even be famous for it. . . . (pp. 337–338, italics in the original)

The list of traits-named-for-persons that Allport referred to included such terms as Calvinistic, Falstaffian, Faustian, Napoleonic, and Machiavellian. As powerful as cardinal traits are in the life of the individual, however, they are not the whole story.

> It has been objected that the conception of a cardinal trait is essentially tautological, for, one asks, is not the cardinal trait identical with the personality itself? This objection cannot be admitted; however well integrated a life may be around the cardinal trait there remains specific habits, incidental and non-organized tendencies, and minor traits of some degree that cannot be subsumed functionally under the cardinal trait. Though pervasive and pivotal, a cardinal trait still remains within the personality; it never coincides with it.
>
> It is an unusual personality that possesses one and only one eminent trait. Ordinarily it seems that the foci of personality (though not wholly separate

from one another) lie in a handful of distinguishable *central traits*. . . . Central traits are those usually mentioned in careful letters of recommendation, in rating scales where the rater stars the outstanding characteristics of the individual, or in brief verbal descriptions of a person.

One may speak, on a still less important level, of *secondary traits*, less conspicuous, less generalized, less consistent, and less often called into play than central traits. They are aroused by a narrower range of equivalent stimuli and they issue into a narrower range of equivalent responses. Being so circumscribed they may escape the notice of all but close acquaintances.

It goes without saying that these three gradations are altogether arbitrary and are phrased merely for the convenience of discourse. There are no criteria, statistical or otherwise, by which to mark off one grade from another. In reality there are all possible degrees of organization in a trait from the most circumscribed and unstable to the most pervasive and most firmly integrated. It is useful, however, to have these distinctions at hand when one wishes to speak roughly of the relative prominence of various traits in a given personality. (p. 338, italics in the original)

Allport devoted one whole section of his book (four chapters in 126 pages) to the question of how to analyze and measure personality. He described a wide range of methods, ranging from self-report surveys to laboratory studies, but he especially advocated for in-depth case studies. In Chapter 14, "A Survey of Methods," after making the point that the study of personality was complex enough to require a diversity of methods, he detailed some guidelines for completing the case study, which he regarded as the "most comprehensive" of the methods for investigating personality.

There follows finally the preparation of the life-history or Case Study. This method is logically the last in our series, for it is the most comprehensive of all, and lies closest to the initial starting point of common sense. It provides a framework within which the psychologist can place all his observations gathered by other methods; it is his final affirmation of the individuality and uniqueness of every personality. It is a completely synthetic method, the only one that is spacious enough to embrace all assembled facts. . . .

The case study has not ordinarily been recognized as a psychological method, for, to date, psychology has had little interest in the complete person. It has been developed chiefly at the hands of clinicians and sociologists who find it valuable for the light it sheds upon maladjustments or upon the social influences surrounding the individual. Because psychologists have neglected the method it has fallen into the hands of specialists interested only in certain limited aspects of personality . . .

Suggestions for the Preparation of a Case Study

Since individuality is never twice repeated, the form of the psychological case study must vary. It is impossible to prescribe in detail the information that it shall include or the exact manner in which it shall be presented. What is significant in one life may be insignificant in another; hence a form adapted to one case is ill-suited to another. There is only one inviolable rule, and that is *fidelity* to the life that is treated, including, of course, accuracy in all detail. There are a few additional rules, which if interpreted liberally, are serviceable guides.

Deal only with a personality that is known. It is essential that a case study be based upon long acquaintance or else upon unusually complete and dependable information from a battery of auxiliary methods including the psychological interview. It is important that there be no serious gaps in the writer's knowledge, no long periods of time for which information is lacking, nor important aspects of the subject's life (such as his sexual or religious attitudes) that are totally hidden. The events of childhood are likely to be most obscure, and require special care in reconstruction. Firsthand information is preferable; that lacking, the investigator must be critical of his sources. Ideally, two or more investigators should write independent studies of the same case, thus checking the facts recorded as well as the interpretations drawn.

Except in unusual cases a similarity in cultural and racial affiliations of the writer and his subject is desirable. Likewise, the less discrepancy in age the better. It is particularly difficult for a youthful writer to evaluate the experiences and attitudes of one older than himself, and few writers are able to portray accurately and convincingly a personality of the opposite sex....

Write objectively and with directness. The less the intrusion of the personality of the writer into the case study, the better. Emotional bias is easy to detect and casts suspicion on the entire study. It is useless, for example, for a young man to attempt an objective study of his fiancée....

Although length is a wholly secondary consideration, experience shows that the most successful studies are not so short as to exclude important information, nor so long as to include repetition and irrelevancy. Many excellent studies from the psychologist's point of view are between 4,000 and 8,000 words....

Use both general description and specific illustrations. It is not effective to write entirely in general terms nor entirely by incident. The best results are secured by giving a general statement of the attitude, trait, or conflict in question, and then following this statement with a specific and altogether *typical* illustration. It is a shrewd gift to be able to select incidents that are apt condensations of traits. General statements draw attention to the dynamic organization as a whole, while specific incidents by particularizing the operation of traits make them seem more personal and life-like....

Give all essential information concerning formative influences. Since, from the genetic point of view, all causes lie in past conditions, the longitudinal stream of life must be traced with care. It is true that over-emphasis upon early events is the besetting sin of many psychologists who forget that the motive forces of the adult have undergone many transformations since childhood. Even though the importance of origins is often exaggerated, a knowledge of the course of development and of the process of transformation aids greatly in understanding....

Consider the personality also from the point of view of the future. What does the individual plan to do? Is there a Bestimmung [note: destination or destiny], or is the life undirected? What trends are unmistakable; what general prognosis might be made and what specific predictions?

Many successful case studies seem naturally to fall into three sections: (a) a description of present status, (b) an account of past influences and the successive stages of development, and (c) an indication of future trends....

The case study is the most complete and most synthetic of all methods available for the study of personality. Properly used it has the full value both of a work of science and a work of art. It can include data drawn from tests, experiments, psychographs, depth-analysis, and statistics; it can incorporate explanations derived from the general laws of psychology: genetic, comparative, abnormal. In short, it embraces both the scientific (inferential) and the intuitive aspects of understanding.

One drawback of the case study must not be overlooked. As in every activity in which intuition plays a part, there is a danger that the interpreter will write his own message across the case and obscure it. . . . This is why the case method should be employed only by those who are trained to avoid partisanship. (pp. 388–395, italics and upper case usage in the original)

In his guideline about examining the "formative influence" of childhood and early life, Allport cautioned against an overemphasis on the importance of childhood for determining the adult personality. This was a constant theme of his work, one consequence being a general skepticism of the value of the Freudian psychoanalytic strategy. Allport believed strongly that while the past was not to be ignored as a factor influencing personality, people were just as much affected by their current beliefs and immediate environment, and by their thoughts and plans for the future. For example, when examining the problem of motivation (*why* does behavior occur?), Allport proposed that motives for current behaviors need not be tied to the past. That is, he argued that current motives often stood on their own—they were autonomous. He detailed his principle of the *functional autonomy of motives* in a well-known paper (Allport, 1937b), and he repeated whole passages from the article in Chapter 7 ("The Transformation of Motives") of his personality text.

Before describing the principle of functional autonomy, its theoretical significance should stand out clearly. The stress in this volume is constantly on the ultimate and irreducible uniqueness of personality. "But how," cry all the traditional scientists, including the older dynamic psychologists, "how are we ever to have a *science* of unique events? Science must generalize." Perhaps it must, what the objectors forget is that *a general law may be a law that tells how uniqueness comes about*. It is manifest error to assume that a general principle of motivation must involve the postulation of abstract or general motives. The principle of functional autonomy, here described, is general enough to meet the needs of science, but particularized enough in its operation to account for the uniqueness of personal conduct.

The dynamic psychology proposed here regards adult motives as infinitely varied, and as self-sustaining, contemporary systems, growing out of antecedent systems, but functionally independent of them. . . .

Let us begin in a common sense way. An ex-sailor has a craving for the sea, a musician longs to return to the instrument after an enforced absence, a city-dweller yearns for his native hills, and a miser continues to amass his useless horde. Now, the sailor may have first acquired his love for the sea [incidentally to] his struggle to earn a living. The sea was merely a conditioned stimulus associated with satisfaction of his "nutritional craving." But now the ex-sailor is perhaps a wealthy banker; the original motive is destroyed; and yet the hunger for the sea persists unabated, even increases in intensity as it becomes more remote from the "nutritional segment." The musician may first have been stung by a rebuke or by a slur on his inferior performances into mastering his instrument, but now he is safely beyond the power of these taunts; there is no need to continue, yet he loves his instrument more than anything else in the world. Once indeed the city dweller may have associated the hills around his mountain home with nutritional and erotogenic satisfactions, but these satisfactions he finds in his city home, *not* in the mountains; whence then comes all his hill-hunger? The miser perhaps learned his habits of thrift in dire necessity, or perhaps his thrift was a symptom of sexual perversion (as Freud would claim), and yet the miserliness persists, and even becomes stronger with the years, even after the necessity or the roots of the neurosis have been relieved. . . .

Workmanship is a good example of functional autonomy. A good workman feels compelled to do clean-cut jobs even though his security, or the praise of others, no longer depend upon high standards. In fact, in a day of jerry-building his workman-like standards may be to his disadvantage. Even so he cannot do a slipshod job. (pp. 193–196, italics in the original)

After publishing his text, Allport continued to make important contributions to personality theory for the rest of his career, including a well-known book-length case study, *Letters from Jenny* (Allport, 1965). He also made important contributions to social psychology, including a famous book on prejudice (Allport, 1954). While he earned a number of honors (e.g., APA presidency in 1939) and awards, Allport's prized possession was a book of collected papers by fifty-five of his doctoral students that recognized the constant theme of his professional life—the study of the individual. In his autobiography, Allport (1967) wrote that the former students had "presented me with two handsomely bound volumes of their own writings with the following inscription: 'From his students—in appreciation of his respect for their individuality.' This is an intimate honor, and one I prize above all others" (p. 24).

CONCEPT REVIEW QUESTIONS

1. What was meant by the study of the "generalized human mind," what was Allport's opinion about this strategy, and what did he propose instead?

2. Allport is known for describing three different forms of "personality trait." What were they?

3. What was Allport's belief about the importance of childhood for later personality? How does the concept of functional autonomy fit in here?

DISCUSSION QUESTION

1. Allport describes the case study method as "the most comprehensive" of all the methods used by researchers in psychology? Why would he argue this? Do you agree? Explain.

KURT LEWIN (1890–1947): THE LEADERSHIP STUDIES

Kurt Lewin was a German psychologist whose early connections with gestalt psychology had an enduring effect on his research and theorizing. Like Koffka (Chapter 13), he earned a doctorate with Carl Stumpf. During the 1920s and early 1930s, Lewin held an academic position at the Psychological Institute at the University of Berlin, where he became close colleagues with the Institute's director, Wolfgang Köhler (Chapter 14), and gestalt psychology's founder, Max Wertheimer (who was at Berlin for a time). Lewin left Germany for the United States in 1933—as a Jew he was concerned (with good reason, of course) about the then-developing Nazi threat. He spent several years at Cornell University, and then went to the University of Iowa. There he worked in the Iowa Child Welfare Station, a research institute affiliated with the university, but not directly connected with the psychology department.

Lewin made important contributions to a number of subfields in psychology, especially social psychology. Along with Floyd Allport (brother of Gordon, whose writings on personality occupied Chapter 31), Lewin is considered a pioneer in the field of modern social psychology. Among his best known work is a series of studies examining different styles of leadership.

Lewin's leadership studies developed in the 1930s during the Iowa years, originating from his general interest in group dynamics, a belief in the value of democracy (after having witnessed its absence in Germany), and a specific interest in leadership expressed by one of his graduate students, Ronald Lippitt (Marrow, 1969). Ralph White, a post-doctoral student with interests in political philosophy who shared Lewin's views about government, soon joined the effort. The outcome was a series of field studies comparing the effects of different leadership styles on the group activities of pre-adolescent boys. The following excerpt is from one of these studies, published in the *Journal of Social Psychology* in 1939. Lewin started by outlining the questions he hoped to answer.

> The present report is a preliminary summary on one phase of a series of experimental studies of group life which has as its aim a scientific approach to such questions as the following: What underlies such differing patterns of group behavior as rebellion against authority, persecution of a scapegoat,

Excerpts from: Lewin, K., Lippitt, R., & White, R. K. (1939). Patterns of aggressive behavior in experimentally created "social climates." *Journal of Social Psychology*, *10*, 271–299.

apathetic submissiveness to authoritarian domination, or attack upon an outgroup? How may differences in subgroup structure, group stratification, and potency of ego-centered and group-centered goals be utilized as criteria for predicting the social resultants of different group atmospheres? Is not democratic group life more pleasant, but authoritarianism more efficient? These are the sorts of questions to which "opinionated" answers are many and varied today, and to which scientific answers are, on that account, all the more necessary. An experimental approach to the phenomena of group life obviously raises many difficulties of creation and scientific control, but the fruitfulness of the method seems to compensate for the added experimental problems. (p. 271)

Lewin next described an initiating experiment, Lippitt's masters thesis, that compared two leadership styles—authoritarian and democratic. Lippitt's study "suggested more hypotheses than answers" (p. 271), and led to a second study, the main focus of the paper excerpted herein. The second experiment had improved controls and tried hard to match the groups on a variety of factors. Like the first experiment, it also compared authoritarian and democratic leaders, but a third type was added.

Four new clubs of 10-year-old boys were organized, on a voluntary basis as before, the variety of club activities was extended, while four different adult leaders participated. To the variables of authoritarian and democratic procedures was added a third, "*laissez-faire*" group ... without adult supervision. Also the behavior of each club was studied in different "social climates." Every six weeks each group had a new leader with a different technique of leadership, each club having three leaders during the course of the five months of the experimental series. The data on aggressive behavior summarized in this paper are drawn from both series of experiments.

Some of the techniques used for the equating of groups ... will be summarized here with the improvements in method of the second experiment. Before the clubs were organized the schoolroom group as a whole was studied. Using the sociometric technique developed by Moreno the interpersonal relations of the children, in terms of rejections, friendships, and leadership were ascertained. Teacher ratings on relevant items of social behavior (e.g., teasing, showing off, obedience, physical energy) were secured, and observations were made on the playground and in the schoolroom by the investigators. The school records supplied information on intellectual status, physical status, and socio-economic background. From the larger number of eager volunteers in each room it was then possible to select from each schoolroom two five-member clubs, which were carefully equated on patterns of interpersonal relationships, intellectual, physical, and socio-economic status, in addition to personality characteristics. The attempt was made not to equate the boys within a particular club, but to ensure the same pattern in each group as a whole. (pp. 271–272, italics in the original)

Lewin and his team used what today would be called a repeated measures design—each group of boys experienced all three leadership styles. The activities used included such tasks as making masks, painting a mural, carving soap, and building model airplanes. To insure that authoritarian and democratic groups worked the tasks equally, once a democratic group had selected a particular task (e.g., mural painting), a corresponding authoritarian leader would choose that same task for his group. Leaders in the laissez-faire groups, because they exerted no serious influence on their groups, were not able to insure their groups would work on a corresponding task; consequently, for this condition, "the activity factor could not be completely controlled" (p. 274).

Long before psychologists adopted an ethics code, Lewin was aware of the potential danger of his study and took steps to insure minimal harm to his participants.

> It should be clear that due to the voluntary nature of the group participation, and the cooperation of the parents and school systems, no radically autocratic methods (e.g., use of threats, instilling fear, etc.) were used. Fairly congenial extra-club relationships were maintained with each member by the leader.

In a table, the researchers summarized the three different leadership styles.

Authoritarian	Democratic	Laissez-faire
All determination of policy by the leader.	All policies a matter of group discussion and decision, encouraged and assisted by the leader.	Complete freedom for group and individual decision, without any leader participation.
Techniques and activity steps dictated by the authority, one at a time, so that future steps were always uncertain to a large degree.	...where technical advice was needed the leader suggested two or three alternative procedures from which choice could be made.	Various materials supplied by the leader, who made it clear that he would supply information when asked.
The leader usually dictated the particular work task and work companions of each member.	The members were free to work with whomever they chose and the division of tasks was left up to the group.	Complete non-participation by the leader.
The dominator was personal in his praise and criticism of the work of each member, but remained aloof from active group participation except when demonstrating. He was friendly or impersonal rather than openly hostile.	The leader was "objective" or "fact-minded" in his praise and criticism, and tried to be a regular group member in spirit without doing too much of the work.	Very infrequent comments on member activities unless questioned, and no attempt to participate or interfere with the course of events.

(p. 273)

Once the experiment began, the data-collection process was exhaustive, including:

a. A quantitative running account of the social interactions of the five children and the leader, in terms of symbols for directive, compliant, and objective (fact-minded) approaches and responses, including a category of purposeful refusal to respond to a social approach.

b. A minute by minute group structure analysis giving a record of: activity subgroupings, [whether] the activity goal of each subgroup was initiated by the leader or spontaneously formed by the children, and ratings on degree of unity of each subgrouping.

c. An interpretive running account of significant member actions, and changes in dynamics of the group as a whole.

d. Continuous stenographic recordings of all conversation.

e. An interpretive running account of inter-club relationships.

f. An "impressionistic" write-up by the leader as to what he saw and felt from within the group atmosphere during each meeting.

g. Comments by guest observers.

h. Movie records of several segments of club life. (p. 274)

In addition, several "extra-club" pieces of information were collected—each child was interviewed, both during transition times from one leader to another, at the end of the study, and later during "two summer hikes" (p. 275); parents were interviewed about home life; teachers were asked whether the club activities affected in-school behaviors; and the boys were given the Rorschach inkblot test.

Given the complexity of the data collection, the description of the results was understandably extensive. Lewin, Lippitt, and White indicated that a more comprehensive analysis would be forthcoming, and that the current article would focus on aggression. They started by referring back to the first study, Lippitt's 1937 masters thesis, highlighting three findings—in the autocratic group, compared to the democratic group, there was a higher level of aggressiveness among club members, a persistent need for the attention of the leader, and a tendency for four of the five members to join together and denigrate the efforts of the fifth member (i.e., scapegoating occurred). They then moved to the second study, starting with what today would be called a manipulation check, before describing their main results.

> In the second experiment ... there were five democratic [note: in fact, there were only four democratic groups in the second study], five autocratic, and two *"laissez-faire"* atmospheres. The fact that the leaders were successful in modifying their behavior to correspond to these three philosophies of leadership is clear on the basis of several quantitative indices. For instance, the ratio of "directive" to "compliant" behavior on the part of the autocratic leaders was 63 to 1; on the part of the democratic leaders it was 1.1 to 1. The total amount of leader participation was less than half as great in *"laissez-faire"* as in either autocracy or democracy. (p. 278, italics in the original)

Lewin's team presented their data (from both studies combined) in several graphs. The figure below was the critical one.

> The data on aggression averages in these three atmospheres are summarized in the graph below. [The data] indicate average amounts of aggression per 50-minute, five-member club meeting[s]. They represent behavior records, as recorded by the interaction observer, and include all social actions, both verbal and physical, which he designated as "hostile" or "joking hostile." The figure shows especially the bimodal character of the aggression averages in autocracy; four of the five autocracies had an extremely low level of aggression, and the fifth an extremely high one. For comparison, a sixth bar has been added to represent aggression in Lippitt's 1937 experiment, computed on the same basis. It is obviously comparable with the single case of exceptionally aggressive behavior in the 1938 experiment. For comparison, also, four lines have been added which indicate the aggression level in the two *laissez-faire* groups, in the four 1938 democracies, and in Lippitt's 1937 democracy. It can be seen that two of the autocracies are above the entire range of democracies, and are in this respect comparable with the two *laissez-faire* groups. The other four autocracies are at the opposite extreme, below the entire range of the democracies. . . .

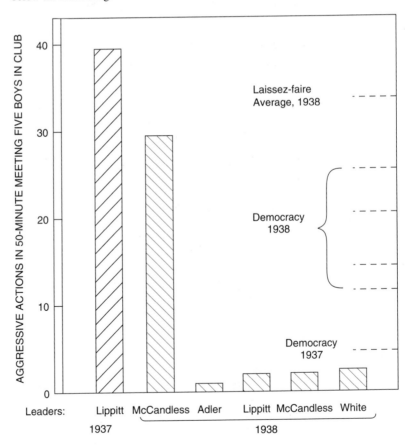

The average number of aggressive actions per meeting in the different atmospheres was as follows:

Laissez-faire	38
Autocracy (aggressive reaction)	30
Democracy	20
Autocracy (apathetic reaction)	2

(pp. 278–281, italics in the original)

These results were puzzling to Lewin and his co-authors. In the 1937 study, the result was straightforward—autocracy led to more aggression than democracy. In the 1938 study, however, autocratic leadership produced two completely opposite results—either a lot of aggression (one group), or virtually none (four groups). How could this disparity be resolved? Lewin believed that despite the different reactions, all the autocracy groups experienced frustration—they just responded to it differently.

In the interpretation of these data it is natural to ask: Why are the results for autocracy paradoxical? Why is the reaction to autocracy sometimes very aggressive, with much rebellion or persecution of scapegoats, and sometimes very nonaggressive? Are the underlying dynamics in these two cases as different as the surface behavior? The high level of aggression in some autocracies has often been interpreted mainly in terms of tension, which presumably results from frustration of individual goals. Is it, then, an indication of non-frustration when the aggression level in some other autocracies is found to be extremely low?

Four lines of evidence in our experiments indicate that this is not the case, and that the low level of aggression in the apathetic autocracies is not due to a lack of frustration.

First of all, there are the sudden outbursts of aggression which occurred on the days of transition from a repressed autocratic atmosphere to the much freer atmosphere of democracy or *laissez-faire*. . . . The boys behaved just as if they had previously been in a state of bottled up tension, which could not show itself overtly as long as the repressive influence of the autocracy was felt, but which burst out unmistakably when that pressure was removed.

A second and very similar type of evidence can be obtained from the records on the days when the leader left the room for 10 or 15 minutes. In the three other atmospheres (*laissez-faire*, aggressive autocracy, and democracy) the aggression level did not rise when the leader left the room. In the apathetic autocracies, however, the level of aggression rises very rapidly to 10 times its former level. . . . [T]he rapid disappearance of apathy when the leader goes out shows clearly that it was due to the repressive influence of the leader rather than to any particular absence of frustration. In this connection it should also be added that the autocratic leader never forbade aggression. His "repressive influence" was not a prohibition created by explicit command but a sort of generalized inhibition or restraining force.

In the third place, there are the judgments of observers who found themselves using such terms as "dull," "lifeless," "submissive," "repressed," and "apathetic" in describing the nonaggressive reaction to autocracy. There was little smiling, joking, freedom of movement, freedom of initiating new projects, etc.; talk was largely confined to the immediate activity in progress, and bodily tension was often manifested. Moving pictures tell the same story. . . .

The fourth and perhaps the most convincing indication of the existence of frustration in these atmospheres is the testimony of the boys themselves. They were individually interviewed, just before each day of transition to a new atmosphere, and again at the end of the whole experiment. The interviewing was done by an adult who had not served as a leader in the boy's own group. . . . With surprising unanimity the boys agreed in a relative dislike for their autocratic leader regardless of his individual personality. Nineteen of the 20 boys liked their leader in democracy better than their leader in autocracy. . . .

As between leaders in autocracy and "*laissez-faire*," the preference was for the "*laissez-faire*" in seven cases out of ten. (pp. 282–285, italics in the original)

Lewin, Lippitt, and White reported several other results, including outgroup hostility, manifested by two "wars," that included much name-calling and, in one of the events, throwing soap pieces back and forth (the task was carving soap bars into statues). The researchers also observed examples of scapegoating (as in Lippitt's 1937 study), and aggression against "substitute hate objects" (p. 288). In their discussion, they returned to the question of "tension in the field," a typical Lewinian concept, and reflected on the question of why the autocracies produced aggression at times, but submission more often. After identifying a number of factors that related to aggression (e.g., tension, group rigidity, restricted freedom of movement), they warned against a simple solution.

The factors named are sufficient to warn against any "one-factor" theory of aggression. Here, as in regard to any other behavior, it is the specific constellation of the field as a whole that determines whether or not aggression will occur. In every case one has to consider both the driving and restraining forces and the cognitive structure of the field. On the other hand, only in this way will one be able to understand the paradox of behavior that autocracy may lead either to aggression or to apathy. It was stated that aggression is partly to be viewed as an emotional outbreak due to tension and that this tension, in turn, is due to pressure and restraining forces (lack of space of free movement). We have apathy when the pressure and the restraining forces from without are kept stronger than the forces . . . within the person which lead to the emotional expression, and are due to the tension. Whether or not the forces from without or those from within are stronger depends upon the absolute amount of pressure and also on the "willingness" of the person to "accept" the pressure. (p. 297)

The paper concludes by addressing an issue common to laboratory research—the extent to which its results generalize to the world outside of the lab.

The field theoretical approach also provides indications for the circumstances under which one might generalize the results of such experimental group studies. One must be careful of making too hasty generalization, perhaps especially in the field of political science. The varieties of democ-racies, autocracies, or "*laissez-faire*" atmospheres are, of course, numerous. Besides, there are always individual differences of character and background to consider. On the other hand, it would be wrong to minimize the possibility of generalization. The answer in social psychology and sociology has to be the same as in an experiment in any science. The essence of an experiment is to create a situation which shows a certain pattern. What happens depends by and large upon this pattern and is largely although not completely inde-pendent of the absolute size of the field. This is one of the reasons why experiments are possible and worthwhile.

The generalization from an experimental situation should, therefore, go always to those life situations which show the same or sufficiently similar general patterns. (p. 297, italics in the original)

In 1944, Lewin moved from Iowa to Massachusetts, after receiving funding for a project that he had long desired. Under the sponsorship of the Mas-sachusetts Institute of Technology (MIT), he established a Research Center for Group Dynamics the following year. Unfortunately, just three years after arriv-ing in Boston, he suffered a fatal heart attack. In the following year (1948), the Research Center moved to the University of Michigan, where it resides today.

CONCEPT REVIEW QUESTIONS

1. Methodologically, how did the 1938 study improve over Lippitt's 1937 mas-ters thesis?

2. What was the major difference in outcome between Lippitt's 1937 masters thesis, and the more extensive study completed by Lewin, Lippitt, and White in 1938?

3. Lewin, Lippitt and White argued that the boys in the autocratic-apathetic groups were just as frustrated as those in the autocratic-aggressive groups. What were their arguments?

DISCUSSION QUESTION

1. Near the end of their paper, the authors address the question of generaliz-ability. What was their argument? Do you agree or disagree? Explain.

CHAPTER 33

FREDERICK C. BARTLETT (1886–1969): CONSTRUCTIVE MEMORY

Frederick Bartlett was born in the rural Cotswold district in England, and educated at the University of London and Cambridge University. He became Director of the Cambridge psychology laboratory in 1922, and by 1930, he had created a world-class research operation. As a result, he became the first professor at Cambridge named to the position of professor of psychology (Roediger, 2000).

Bartlett's research interests were wide-ranging, including topics in anthropology as well as psychology. His research in memory began during World War I, while he was a student, and it eventually produced *Remembering: A Study in Experimental and Social Psychology* in 1932. The following excerpt is from a 1967 reprinting of that landmark book.

Bartlett opened his memory book by raising serious questions about the usefulness of research in the Ebbinghaus (Chapter 6) tradition, with its emphasis on the effects of rote repetition on the memorization of highly artificial stimuli, the famous nonsense syllables, and its theoretical basis in associationism. Bartlett believed that all stimuli had meaning for the individual, so that the Ebbinghaus strategy was flawed from the start.

> In reality, the experiments are much less easy than was assumed by Ebbinghaus. Any psychologist who has used them in the laboratory knows perfectly well that lists of nonsense syllables set up a mass of associations which may be very much more odd, and may vary more from person to person, than those aroused by common language with its conventional meaning. It is urged that this is no serious drawback, since it may be countered by a routine uniform exposure of the syllables and the inculcation of a perfectly automatic attitude of repetition in the learner; so that, with time and patience, each subject learns to take the nonsense syllables solely for what they are in themselves.
>
> Once more the remedy is at least as bad as the disease. It means that the results of the nonsense syllable experiments begin to be significant only when very special habits of reception and repetition have been set up. They

Excerpts from: Bartlett, F. C. (1967). *Remembering: A study in experimental and social psychology*. Cambridge, UK: Cambridge University Press. (Original work published 1932) may then, indeed, throw some light upon the mode of establishment and the control of such habits, but it is at least doubtful whether they can help us to see how, in general, memory reactions are determined.

The psychologist, of all people, must not stand in awe of the stimulus. Uniformity and simplicity of structure of stimuli are no guarantee whatever of uniformity and simplicity of structure in organic response, particularly at the human level. . . .

So far as the stimulus side of his method goes, Ebbinghaus's work is open to the following criticisms:

a. It is impossible to rid stimuli of meaning so long as they remain capable of arousing any human response.

b. The effort to do this creates an atmosphere of artificiality for all memory experiments, making them rather a study of the establishment of maintenance of repetition habits.

c. To make the explanation of the variety of recall responses depend mainly upon variations of stimuli and of their order, frequency, and mode of presentation, is to ignore dangerously those equally important conditions of response which belong to the subjective attitude and to predetermined reaction tendencies. (pp. 3–4)

Instead of the Ebbinghaus strategy, Bartlett argued that research on memory should focus more on the attributes of the memorizer and less on the nature of the stimulus materials, and that memory must be understood in the context of realistic situations using everyday materials, rather than artificial nonsense syllables. He also believed that the memorizer, rather than passively accumulating associative strength as the result of practice and repetition, *actively* organized the material into meaningful wholes that he referred to as *schemata* (plural form of "schema"). Bartlett defined these schemata as "active organisation[s] of past reactions, or of past experiences, which must always be supposed to be operating in any well-adapted organic response" (p. 201). For example, as a result of our experiences, we will develop a schema relating to the concept of death. This schema will in turn influence our current and future perceptions of death and dying and affect our memory of these experiences. People with different experiences and from different cultures will have different schemata about death.

To provide empirical support for his arguments, Bartlett developed a series of tasks on perception, imagination, and memory. The memory experiments are the best known and two of them will be excerpted here. Bartlett called the first the *Method of Description.*

I endeavored, in this series of experiments, to avoid as far as possible the artificiality which hangs over laboratory experiments in psychology. I therefore discarded the use of nonsense syllables and throughout employed material a part of which, at least, might fairly be regarded as interesting and sufficiently normal for the subjects concerned not to force upon them ad hoc modes of observation and of recall. Moreover, the type of material used obviates the necessity for long practice before the results of experimentation can begin to be seriously considered. . . .

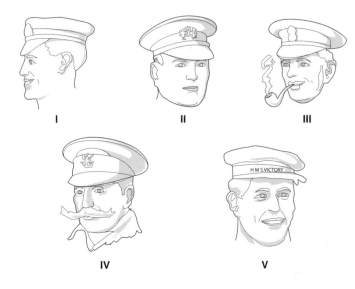

I   II   III

IV   V

A series of five picture post-cards was used. On each card was a represen-
tation of the face of a navy, or military, officer or man. The experiments
were carried out during the early days of the Great War [World War I], when
there was a very widespread interest in the fighting services. The particular
cards were chosen because the faces ... were sufficiently alike to render
their grouping easy, while at the same time each face had definite individual
peculiarities. (pp. 47–48)

Bartlett placed the five cards face down in front of each of 20 participants,
always arranged in the same sequence. The volunteers were given ten seconds
to examine each of the five cards, and when studying a particular card, the
other four remained face down. Bartlett then let 30 minutes pass, during which
he engaged participants in conversation unrelated to the experiment. After the
interval, participants were asked to describe the details of the pictures in the same
order they studied them, and they were asked a series of questions. You will note
in Bartlett's description that except for an occasional frequency count, his results
are described in narrative form, not as summary statistics, and his descriptions
of methodology are often vague. As one reviewer pointed out, Bartlett's studies
are better conceived of as "controlled demonstrations, rather than true experiments" (Roediger, 1997, p. 489). Bartlett himself was unapologetic about the
absence of statistical analysis in the book: "In this book there will be no statistics whatever" (p. 9). Also, Bartlett's rather casual attitude toward experimental
control is evident as he described the questions he asked of participants.

It is not necessary to give the questions in detail, particularly as I did not
hesitate to adapt them or to supplement them in accordance with what I
judged to be the psychological needs of the moment. They could all be
grouped very well under the following four headings:

a. those dealing with position or with direction of regard;
b. those dealing straightforwardly with particular detail;

   c. those suggesting detail not present in the case in question, but found else-
     where in the series
   d. those suggesting detail not present anywhere in the series (p. 49)

What did Bartlett find? First with regard to "position," by which he meant the ability to recall the pictures accurately in sequence, he found something similar to a modern serial position effect. Perfect recall of the first face, and better recall for the beginning and end than the middle faces. By "direction of regard," he meant whether the faces were turned to the left or right; here he found chance performance—the wrong choice was made more than half the time. As for accuracy of detail, transposing detail ("transferring") from one picture to another, and reporting detail not in the cards ("importation"), Bartlett found numerous mistakes.

> All but six of the twenty subjects transferred detail, and in nearly every case this was done at the very outset. . . .
>   Four cases concerned the pipe, four the mustache and four the badge. That is to say, the detail most frequently transferred was generally of an outstanding character, for at that time military cap badges were matters of considerable interest among my subjects.
>   Detail was transferred from an earlier to later card in the series almost twice as often as in the reverse direction. . . .
>   In the first free description of the faces, nineteen cases occurred of details being introduced into the series from outside, and thirteen of the subjects were involved. The influence of questions—even of straightforward ques-tions of fact—in inducing this kind of importation of detail may be very strong. . . . (pp. 57–58)

Bartlett identified a subgroup of his subjects that he referred to as visu-alizers, and he spotted a tendency for them to be more likely to import addi-tional detail into their descriptions than those who relied less on visualization. He also hinted at a phenomenon well known to researchers of eyewitness memory—confidence in one's memory and accuracy are not always highly correlated.

> The subject easily at the head of the list for importations in each of the trials was the most definite visualizer of the whole group. He remarked that he has cultivated a habit of visualizing, and practiced himself in it constantly. He was completely confident throughout.
>   The subject next on the list for number of importations introduced after an interval was also a pronounced visualizer. He, too, appeared well satisfied with his work. . . .
>   It is perhaps most curious that importation seemed definitely most liable to occur in relation to salient detail. However, when we consider that salience of detail in the main is determined by specialized interest, we can see that this is after all just what might be expected. For example, one subject, an Army officer, was especially interested in military cap badges. In his descriptions he changed these into badges of regiments with which he was most familiar on active service. (p. 58)

Bartlett's results with his method of description, although not described in very great detail, sound remarkably like modern studies of memory—the lack of accuracy, the addition of detail not originally seen, the damaging effects of leading questions, the lack of correlation between accuracy and confidence. The study also illustrates one of the main themes of his book, an emphasis on the interests and attitudes of the memorizer (e.g., the officer interested in badges) rather than the nature of the stimulus material itself.

The most famous of Bartlett's memory studies used what he called the *Method of Repeated Reproduction*. Participants were given a 328-word story to read through twice at their own speed. The story was a Native American folk tale called "The War of the Ghosts." Thus, the story reflected a culture quite different from that of early twentieth century England, and the story had certain elements that would not seem to "make sense" from the standpoint of a typical Britisher. Here is the story in its entirety.

> One night two young men from Egulac went down to the river to hunt seals, and while they were there it became foggy and calm. Then they heard war-cries, and they thought: "Maybe this is a war-party." They escaped to the shore, and hid behind a log. Now canoes came up, and they heard the noise of paddles, and saw one canoe coming up to them. There were five men in the canoe, and they said:
>
> "What do you think? We wish to take you along. We are going up the river to make war on the people."
>
> One of the young men said: "I have no arrows."
>
> "Arrows are in the canoe," they said.
>
> "I will not go along. I might be killed. My relatives do not know where I have gone. But you," he said, turning to the other, "may go with them."
>
> So one of the young men went, but the other returned home.
>
> And the warriors went on up the river to a town on the other side of Kalama. The people came down to the water, and they began to fight, and many were killed. But presently the young man heard one of the warriors say: "Quick, let us go home: that Indian has been hit." Now he thought: "Oh, they are ghosts." He did not feel sick, but they said he had been shot.
>
> So the canoes went back to Egulac, and the young man went ashore to his house, and made a fire. And he told everybody and said: "Behold I accompanied the ghosts, and we went to fight. Many of our fellows were killed, and many of those who attacked us were killed. They said I was hit, and I did not feel sick."
>
> He told it all, and then he became quiet. When the sun rose he fell down. Something black came out of his mouth. His face became contorted. The people jumped up and cried.
>
> He was dead. (p. 65)

Unless you are a member of this particular culture, I suspect that you found the passage to be a bit odd. So did Bartlett's twenty participants (seven women, thirteen men). Fifteen minutes after reading the story, they were asked to reproduce as much of it as they could. Additional reproductions were elicited at later intervals ranging from hours to months. Bartlett even found one former participant *six years later* and asked him to recall the story. Bartlett reported the results by reproducing dozens of the actual recalled stories, then summarizing the kinds of errors found. Total recall declined with the passage of time, of course, but what was more intriguing to Bartlett was the quality of the reproductions. Participants did not just recall less; what they recalled was shaped by their need to form a coherent, understandable story within the context of their own knowledge systems (i.e., schemata). Thus, "something black coming out of his mouth," was transformed to "foaming at the mouth" for one participant and the soul leaving the body for another. Also, the ambiguity about the ghosts (if they are already ghosts, how come they can be killed?) led one participant to decide that "Ghosts" was just a label for a particular tribe; that transformation (or "rationalisation," as Bartlett called it) "made the whole thing more comprehensible" (p. 68). Others recalled erroneously but logically, that the "ghosts" appeared only after some Indians were killed in the battle. In all, then, subjects recalled the story within the framework of their own cultural ideas and understanding about battle and death. On the basis of the Ghosts study and other studies reported in the book, Bartlett drew some general conclusions about memory. First, he made the point about the need to make the story meaningful.

> In these experiments rationalisation was applied sometimes to the stories as a whole and sometimes to particular details. In the first case, the process expressed the need, felt by practically every educated observer, that a story should have a general setting. Hardly ever, at the outset, was there an attitude of simple acceptance. Every story presented had to be connected, certainly as a whole, and, if possible, as regards its details also, with something else. This is ... the factor which I have ... called "effort after meaning." ... It could be said that there is a constant effort to get the maximum possible of meaning into the material presented. ...
>
> A very common remark made about the folk-stories used, for example, was: 'That is not an English tale.' Sometimes the narrative was rendered satisfactory by being called a 'dream.' 'This,' said one observer, 'is very clearly a murder concealment dream.' She proceeded to an interpretation along the lines of modern symbolism, and the story was, with no further trouble, comfortably accepted. ...
>
> The rationalisation which gives to material as a whole its appropriate [meaning] is only part of the total process. Details must also be dealt with, and every chain of reproductions illustrated how the rationalising process was applied to particular items. ... Rationalisation in regard to form found its main expression in the linking together of events within the stories; rationalisation as concerned with details of material was usually carried out by connecting the given items with something outside the story and supplied by the observer himself. This is analogous to what I have called "importation" [and] it was of three main types:
>
> First, there was the process, in all instances witting during its early stages, but later producing unwitting transformations, by which presented material was connected with other matter outside the story, but having the same general nature. For example, in *The War of the Ghosts* the "something black" was frequently interpreted as a materialisation of the dying man's breath.
>
> The second process of rationalisation ... was unwitting from start to finish. The transformation of "something black" into "foamed at the mouth"

was a case in point. So was the introduction of an "island" into *The War of the Ghosts* by several subjects.

The third type of rationalisation is very closely related to the second. It is the case in which some particular, and maybe isolated detail, is transformed immediately into a more familiar character. Thus "canoe" became "boat;" "paddling" became "rowing;" . . . and so on in a very large number of cases.

The general function of rationalisation is in all instances the same. It is to render material acceptable, understandable, comfortable, straightforward; to rob it of its puzzling elements. As such it is a powerful factor in all perceptual and [memory] processes. (pp. 84–89)

In Chapter 10 of his book, Bartlett outlined a theory of memory. As implied by the description of "effort after meaning," memory was not merely an act of reproducing intact memory traces; rather, it was an active process of *construction*.

We must, then, consider what does actually happen more often than not when we say that we remember. The first notion to get rid of is that memory is primarily or literally reduplicative, or reproductive. In a world of constantly changing environment, literal recall is extraordinarily unimportant. . . .

In the many thousands of cases of remembering which I collected, a considerable number of which I have recorded here, literal recall was very rare. With few exceptions, . . . re-excitement of individual traces did not look to be in the least what was happening. . . . In fact, if we consider the evidence rather than presupposition, remembering appears to be far more decisively an affair of construction rather than one of mere reproduction. . . . [C]ondensation, elaboration and invention are common features of ordinary remembering, and these all very often involve the mingling of materials belonging originally to different "schemata." (pp. 204–205)

Bartlett borrowed the term schema from a British neurologist, Henry Head. After saying that he did not like the term ("It is at once too definite and too sketchy"—p. 201), Bartlett proceeded to rely on it for his theory. As described earlier, schemata (plural of schema) can be thought of as general concepts that make up our understanding of the world, and memories are constructed with reference to them. So, for instance, when Bartlett's subject recalled "foaming at the mouth" instead of the more obscure "something black came out of his mouth," that person's schemata about illness and death contributed to the construction of the memory.

Bartlett's ideas about memory did not make much of a stir in the United States, appearing during the height of neobehaviorism. In fact, one American reviewer of the book was dismissive, writing that the book would "find a place upon the shelves of those who study remembering, but it will not be in the special section reserved for those investigators whose writings have become landmarks (Jenkins, 1935, p. 715). By landmarks, the reviewer presumably was thinking of Ebbinghaus. It was only in the 1960s, after cognitive psychology had emerged from multiple sources, that the significance of the work began to be appreciated. His notion of memory as constructive is now widely accepted and central to the understanding of such phenomena as false memory (e.g., Roediger & McDermott, 1995) and eyewitness memory (e.g., Loftus, 1979).

After the remembering book, Bartlett turned to other interests, including the thinking process in general, and produced another classic book in the history of cognitive psychology, *Thinking: An Experimental and Social Study*, shortly after his retirement in 1952 (Bartlett, 1958).

CONCEPT REVIEW QUESTIONS

1. Consider Bartlett's "method of description." What was the method and what were the results?
2. Describe the *War of the Ghosts* study and what can be concluded from it about memory.
3. Bartlett described memory as being constructive. What did he mean?

DISCUSSION QUESTION

1. Think back to the Ebbinghaus excerpt (Chapter 6). Describe Bartlett's criticism of memory research in the "Ebbinghaus tradition." Had Ebbinghaus lived, what might have been his criticism of the "Bartlett tradition?"

JOHN JENKINS (1901–1948) AND KARL DALLENBACH (1887–1971): INTERFERENCE AND MEMORY

If you open almost any introductory psychology text to the chapter on memory, it is likely that you will encounter a description of retroactive interference, and the example used will be a study by Jenkins and Dallenbach (1924) about the different effects of interference for those sleeping and those remaining awake. *Retroactive interference* occurs when one learns some material, then encounters some interfering activity (e.g., learning some other material), and then has difficulty recalling the initially learned material. In the interval between studying and recalling, there is presumably more opportunity for interference if one is awake than if one is asleep. Testing this idea was the purpose of the study excerpted here. Obliviscence (also spelled oblivescence), derives from the Latin word (*oblivisci*) for forgetting, and so the article's title makes clear its purpose.

At the time of the study, John Jenkins was an undergraduate, a senior at Cornell University, and Karl Dallenbach was on the psychology faculty and directing the project. Jenkins and Dallenbach opened their article by making reference to the famous Ebbinghaus (Chapter 6) forgetting curve. The Ebbinghaus (1885/1964) study included retention intervals that must have included sleep, but Ebbinghaus did not examine differences among intervals involving either sleep or waking.

> Ebbinghaus found that forgetting is a function of time: it is very rapid at first, but becomes progressively slower as time elapses. According to the results of his experiments, 41.8% of a series of nonsense syllables, as measured by the Method of Savings, is forgotten after an interval of 20 min.; 55.8% is forgotten after 1 hr.; 64.2% after 8.8 hrs.; 66.3% one day; 72.2% after 2 days; 74.6% after 6 days; and 78.9% is forgotten after 31 days.

Excerpts from: Jenkins, J. G., & Dallenbach, K. M. (1924). Obliviscence during sleep and waking. *American Journal of Psychology*, *35*, 605–612.

The results for the 8.8 hr. and 1 day periods are the least satisfactory; for, as Ebbinghaus himself points out, the difference between the values for these successive periods is not of the same order as the differences between the values of the other successive periods. Between 8.8 and 24 hr. periods the difference is 2.1% [i.e., 66.3 — 64.2], whereas between the 24 and 48 hr. periods the difference is 6.1% [note: the difference is actually 5.9%: 72.2 — 66.3]; that is, in the later interval of 24 hrs. about three times as much is forgotten as during the earlier period of 15 hrs. . . .

Ebbinghaus did not think the figures credible even under the plausible assumption that sleep—which formed the greater part of the 15 hr. interval and proportionately a much smaller part of the following 24 hrs.—materially retarded forgetting. He sought an explanation among the accidental errors of his experiments and thus neglected the investigation of obliviscence during sleep. . . . We have consequently taken it as the object of the present Study. It is our purpose to compare the rate of forgetting during sleep and waking. (p. 605)

Most of the research on memory that occurred in the latter half of the twentieth century, during the time of the so-called (but see Leahy, 1992) cognitive revolution, used different groups of participants for the different experimental conditions of the study, and employed large numbers of participants. And when the Jenkins and Dallenbach study is presented in most introductory textbooks, the reader gets the impression that there were two "groups" of participants, some in the "sleep" group, and some in the "awake" group. Such was not the case, however. Using a strategy that was common in the 1920s, there were very few participants, and a great deal was asked of each of them. In fact, Jenkins and Dallenbach collected data on just two persons in their main study, and each person participated in each and every experimental condition. As was the custom at the time, research participants were referred to as "observers," or "Os"—this derived from the introspective studies of the day, in which the participants would be "observing" and reporting on their mental processes during the experiment.

Procedure. Two *Os*, L. R. Hodell (H) and J. S. McGraw (Mc), served throughout the course of the experiments. Both were seniors at Cornell University; neither had any previous experience in memory experiments. Both worked without knowledge of the nature or object of the problem.

The *Os* were required to learn nonsense syllables which were typewritten on slips of paper and presented, by means of the Spindler & Hoyer memory apparatus, in series of ten. Exposure was made at the rate of 0.7 sec. The syllables were read aloud by the *Os* as presented. . . .

An adaptation of the Method of Retained Members was employed. The series was repeated by the *Os* until learning had come to the first correct recitation and then, after 1, 2, 4, or 8 hrs., a free reproduction was called for. The amount lost was taken as a relative measure of the amount forgotten. . . . (pp. 605–606, italics in the original)

In modern terms, then, one of the independent variables was retention interval, and it had four levels (1, 2, 4, and 8 hours). The second variable was whether a period of sleep or waking intervened during the retention interval. Here's how this factor was handled methodologically.

> The *Os* and the junior author [i.e., Jenkins], who acted throughout as *E*, lived in the laboratory during the course of the experiments, and regulated their lives, as far as possible, in accordance with the requirements of this Study. The times of learning at night [i.e., the "sleeping during the retention interval" condition] varied between 11:30 p.m. and 1 a.m.; and the times of learning at day [i.e., the "awake" condition], with single exceptions for each *O* for every time interval, varied between 8 and 10 a.m. The exceptions mentioned were for purposes of comparison and check, and the times of learning for them varied between 2 and 4 p.m. . . .
>
> The following general instructions were given to the *Os*: "I am going to show you, with the aid of this apparatus, a series of nonsense syllables which I wish you to learn as rapidly as possible. The syllables will appear successively and will be visible through the little window in front of you. Give each syllable full and equal attention and pronounce every one aloud as it appears. All the vowels are to be pronounced short unless a long vowel is indicated by the dash over the letter. The syllables are without meaning. Do not attempt to read meaning into them. Do not use a mnemonic system in memorizing. When you can repeat the series in its correct order report the fact to me. Do not on any account repeat the series after you have left the experimental room."
>
> The experimental room was adjacent to the improvised dormitory, and the experiments at night were not begun until the *O* was undressed and ready for bed. *O* retired immediately after learning the series; and, as the rule of the sleeping quarters was quiet, distractions and retroactive inhibitions were reduced to a minimum. *O*, after learning at day, went about his routine affairs. (pp. 606–607, italics in the original)

After the retention interval had passed, the Os returned to the experimental room and attempted to recall the list of nonsense syllables learned earlier. Some of the shorter retention intervals at night meant that the Os were awakened in the middle of the night, which led to an interesting outcome.

> Recall was always made in the experimental room with *O* seated before the apparatus in the position held during learning. During the experiments at night the *Os* were separately waked, after the appropriate interval, by *E*, who was himself waked by an alarm clock, and they were taken one at a time to the experimental room where their reproductions were received. After a few experiments *E* found it difficult to arouse the *Os* and difficult to know when they were awake. The *Os* would leave their beds, go into the next room, give their reproductions, and the next morning say that they remembered nothing of it. Unfortunately, it did not occur to *E* to apply special tests; he judged by the behavior of the *Os*, and assumed they were awake. (p. 607, italics in the original)

The study had one confound, which was that during the day, the Os were told when they were to report back to the lab; that is, they knew the retention interval. At night, however, they did not know when they would be wakened. Jenkins and Dallenbach considered several ways to correct the problem, but decided in the end that the difference would not be critical to their results.

> The length of the interval between learning and reproduction was not known to the Os at night; but during the experiments at day the following sentence was added to the instructions: "You will please report in this room for the reproduction at x o'clock."—the hour depending upon the time of learning and the interval desired. We did not attempt to eliminate this difference between the experiments during waking and sleep. We might have done so by requiring the Os to report at the laboratory at every one of the intervals used in the experiment until the particular one desired was reached, or by informing the Os at night that they would be waked for their reproduction at such and such a time; but we thought both methods more objectionable than the existence of difference. The first was objectionable because it would keep the experiment constantly in the Os mind; because it would only partially accomplish the desired end—if the reproduction was not received at the 1, 2, or 4 hr. interval O would definitely know that it would be received at the 8 hr. interval; and because the effect of the blank appointments would probably be more disturbing than specific knowledge of the actual time of the reproduction. The second was objectionable because the attitude of the Os toward going to sleep differed according as they knew whether the reproduction would be given after a long or a short interval. The only way of equalizing the experiments during sleep was to keep this knowledge from the Os. Since E and the Os were not together during the day, the time of the reproduction could not similarly be kept from the Os during the day-time experiments. (p. 607, italics in the original)

A modern memory researcher would solve this problem by having eight different groups of subjects—one for each condition in the study (four retention intervals times the two different types of retention interval). Having each O participate in each of the eight conditions, by necessity, meant that the experiment took place over an extended period of time. Sure enough, these two volunteers (not to mention Jenkins) gave up the better part of the end of their senior year to the study, an extraordinary commitment of time. Imagine asking students today to spend the last two months of their senior year memorizing nonsense syllables and sleeping in a lab every night, for no benefit other than contributing data for the research project of another senior college student!

> After a short practice series the experiments began on April 14, 1923 and continued until June 7. With but few exceptions, on days when the Os were indisposed, experiments were conducted every night and every day. Particular care was taken to see that the Os' physical condition was constant, and the experiments were postponed whenever it was apparent that a fluctuation had occurred.

The time-intervals between learning and reproduction were varied at haphazard. We planned to have eight experiments for every interval during both sleep and waking. The series were completed for the experiments during sleep; but H failed to complete two of the waking series, and Mc failed to complete one. (p. 607, italics in the original)

As was typical of research during this era, when extensive data were collected from a small number of participants (Os), the results included lengthy tables with raw data for each participant. This was true of the Jenkins and Dallenbach study, but they also included a summary table and a graph. I have redesigned their Table III and included it here. The numbers in the table are the average number of syllables (out of 10) recalled for each condition and for all conditions combined.

	H		Mc	
	sleep	**waking**	**sleep**	**waking**
1 hr.	7.1	4.4	7.0	4.8
2 hr.	5.4	2.8	5.4	3.4
4 hr.	5.3	2.4	5.8	2.1
8 hr.	5.5	.4	5.8	1.4
totals	5.8	2.4	6.0	2.8

These data show that there is a marked difference in the rate of forgetting during sleep and waking. On an average, as is shown in Table III under the caption "Totals," more than twice as many syllables are reproduced by both *Os* after intervals of sleep than after intervals of waking. On an average, 5.8 and 6.0 syllables were reported by H and Mc respectively in the sleep experiments, and only 2.4 and 2.8 syllables in the waking experiments. The superiority of reproductions after intervals of sleep is also shown at every one of the experimental intervals. At the end of 1 hr. of sleep an average of 7.1 and 7.0 syllables was reproduced, whereas an average of only 4.4 and 4.8 syllables was reproduced after a like interval of waking. At the 2 hr. interval, both sleep and waking, there is a corresponding drop in the averages of each *O*; but the reproductions after sleep still maintain a decided superiority. This superiority becomes more and more pronounced as the length of the intervals increases; for the average number of reproductions for both *Os* continues to decline at the 4 hr. and 8 hr. intervals of waking, whereas after like intervals of sleep the average of the 2 hr. interval is maintained.

Comparative curves are shown in [the graph below], in which the average number of syllables reproduced after the various time-intervals is plotted separately for each *O* and for the sleep and waking experiments. The curves of the waking experiments take a familiar form: a sharp decline which becomes progressively flatter. The form of the curves of the sleep experiments, however, is very different: after a small initial decline the curves flatten and a high and constant level is thenceforth maintained. (pp. 609–610, italics in the original)

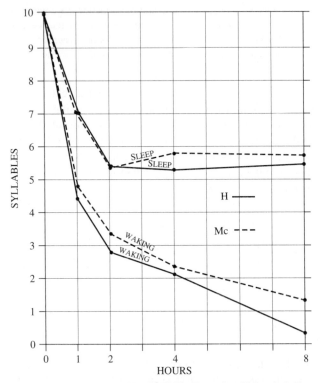

Fig. I. Average Number of Syllables Reproduced by each *O* after
the Various Time-Intervals of Sleep and Waking

When Jenkins and Dallenbach referred to the curves for the waking experiments as taking a "familiar form," they are referring to the form of the Ebbinghaus forgetting curve, which you can examine by turning back to Chapter 6. They
also argued that their results could not be attributed to any differences in initial
learning. If that had been the case, then there would have been more repetitions
needed to learn in the sleeping condition than in the waking condition. In fact, the
opposite was true—slightly more repetitions needed during the day than at night.

Incidentally, for research published in journals today, it is not considered
appropriate to include both a table and a graph of the same data in the same
article (mainly to save valuable page space), but this practice was commonplace
during the time of the Jenkins and Dallenbach study. Thus, in addition to their
Table III, they included the graph above. Some years later, Dallenbach, much
to his embarrassment, discovered that he had made a small error in plotting the
graph (Evans, personal communication, March 13, 2008). If you examine the
table and graph closely, you can see that at the four-hour retention interval,
the points for the waking condition are reversed on the graph. In a note on the
relative merits of tables (more precise) and graphs (better for getting the gist
of a study quickly), published nearly forty years after the original study,
Dallenbach (1963) made note of the error and published both the original and
the corrected graph.

Before concluding their article, Jenkins and Dallenbach reported two additional brief experiments. The first was a partial replication using an instructor in the department (H. G. Bishop), "to see how closely the results of an experienced *O* would agree with those of H and Mc" (p. 611, italics in the original). The results were the same. The second followed upon the observation that both H and Mc sometimes couldn't remember being awakened and asked for recall. The experimenters recruited another student (C), who was put through the experiments while hypnotized (presumably analogous to sleep). C's performance was quite good, but there was not much data for Jenkins and Dallenbach to be very certain of a conclusion. They did write, however, that the results suggested "that a similar condition of retention and forgetting exists in the hypnotic and in normal sleep" (p. 612).

Jenkins and Dallenbach did not write an elaborate analysis of their results. They did, however, refer back to the initial question about the Ebbinghaus data, for his retention intervals of 8.8, 24, and 48 hours, and believed their results accounted for the problem noted by Ebbinghaus. They also concluded in their study that forgetting was due more to the effects of interference than decay.

> The difference in the rate of forgetting during sleep and waking is sufficiently large to account for the variation in Ebbinghaus' investigation. His figures for the 8.8 hr., 1 and 2 day intervals are not only credible but are confirmed by this Study. (p. 611)
>
> The results of our Study as a whole indicate that forgetting is not so much a matter of the decay of old impressions and associations as it is a matter of interference, inhibition, or obliteration of the old by the new. (p. 612)

In sum, then, during sleep there is little to interfere with or "obliterate" the memories formed during the initial studying of the syllables. When H and Mc were awake in the retention intervals, however, presumably they engaged in a number of cognitive activities that had the effect of interfering with what had been memorized.

Three years after their "sleep" study, Jenkins and Dallenbach (1927) published a second study using the same data, in which they examined the effect of serial position on recall. As in studies that later became common in the 1960s and 1970s, they found some evidence of both primacy (better recall for syllables at the start of the list) and recency (better recall for syllables at the end of the list) effects. However, their results were somewhat ambiguous. Mc showed both primacy and recency for both sleep and awake conditions; H, on the other hand, showed primacy but no recency in the sleep conditions, but neither primacy nor recency in the awake conditions.

As for the authors, John Jenkins eventually earned a Ph.D. at Cornell, under the direction of Madison Bentley, a colleague of Dallenbach's, and he served on the faculty at Cornell for a time during the 1930s. In 1938 he became the psychology department chair at the University of Maryland, where he remained until his early death in 1948. He was respected among his peers as a leading applied psychologist and, during his Cornell years, wrote a well-received text on industrial psychology (Jenkins, 1935). Karl Dallenbach was a

Ph.D. student of E. B. Titchener (Chapter 11), earning his doctorate at Cornell with an introspective study on attention (Dallenbach, 1913). After brief stays at Oregon and Ohio State, he returned to Cornell at Titchener's invitation as a member of the faculty, and there he remained until 1948, when he went to the University of Texas as department chair. He remained at Texas as chair for ten years and then professor, until his retirement in 1967 (at age 80!).

CONCEPT REVIEW QUESTIONS

1. What was the anomaly in the Ebbinghaus forgetting curve that led Jenkins and Dallenbach to design their study?

2. Describe the study's methodology and explain why it might be difficult to recruit research participants for a replication today.

3. With reference to the graph, describe the results of the study and explain them in terms of interference.

4. In addition to the main experiment, Jenkins and Dallenbach briefly reported on two follow-up studies. Why did they do the studies and what did they find?

DISCUSSION QUESTION

1. Consider the method you currently use to study for exams. What does this article suggest as a possible alternative?

ABRAHAM MASLOW (1908–1970): A HIERARCHY OF NEEDS

Students normally encounter Abraham Maslow in the motivation chapter of their general psychology text, when they learn about his "hierarchy of needs," the narrative usually accompanied by a sketch of a pyramid with the needs arranged horizontally from the bottom (physiological) to the top (self-actualization). The excerpt that you will read here is from the first published description of this familiar model, an article that appeared in the prominent journal *Psychological Review* in 1943.

Maslow's name is associated with *humanistic psychology*, an approach that emerged in the 1960s and was a powerful force in American psychology for at least two decades. It is known for its rejection of what it believed was the dogmatic and deterministic pronouncements of psychoanalysis and behaviorism, and it came to be known as psychology's "third force," in contrast to these other two. Ironically, given Maslow's passion for humanistic psychology, his initial enthusiasm for psychology was triggered by his discovery, while an undergraduate, of John Watson's (Chapter 18) version of behaviorism. Furthermore, long after he had abandoned behaviorism, he still valued the precision and rigor of scientific thinking, hoping to bring a scientific attitude to the topics of interest to humanistic psychologists (Coon, 2006).

Maslow's graduate training was at the University of Wisconsin, in the laboratory of Harry Harlow, famous for his research in primate behavior (e.g., the adverse effects of depriving infant rhesus monkeys of attachment needs). Maslow earned a Ph.D. in 1932 with a dissertation on the relative influence of sexual needs and power in rhesus pairs. After completing some post-doctoral research under the direction of Thorndike (Chapter 8) at Columbia, he gained a faculty position at Brooklyn College and then (1951) at Brandeis University in Massachusetts, where he remained for the rest of his career.

Maslow's shift away from behaviorism began in the 1930s and, by the end of the decade, his interests had become focused on human motivation. By the early 1940s, he was ready to try out some of his new ideas and in 1943, he published his paper on the hierarchy of needs with the ambitious title of "A

Excerpts from: Maslow, A. (1943b). A theory of human motivation. *Psychological Review*, *50*, 370–396.

Theory of Human Motivation." He began the article by summarizing the points he had just made in another 1943 paper called "A Preface to Motivational Theory" (Maslow, 1943a). There he stressed that any theory must be grounded in the idea of the person as an integrated whole, that motivation should go far beyond simple biological drives (e.g., hunger), that a mere listing of drives would not be very helpful, and that a theory of motivation should be person-centered and not derived from animal research. Then he began with an indication of some of the influences on his own thinking.

> The present paper is an attempt to formulate a positive theory of motivation which will satisfy these theoretical demands and at the same time conform to the known facts, clinical and observational as well as experimental. It derives most directly, however, from clinical experience. This theory is, I think, in the functionalist tradition of James and Dewey, and is fused with the holism of Wertheimer, Goldstein, and Gestalt Psychology, and with the dynamicism of Freud and Adler. This fusion or synthesis may arbitrarily be called a 'general-dynamic' theory.
>
> It is far easier to perceive and to criticize the aspects in motivation theory than to remedy them. Mostly this is because of the very serious lack of sound data in this area. I conceive this lack of sound facts to be due primarily to the absence of a valid theory of motivation. The present theory then must be considered to be a suggested program or framework for future research and must stand or fall, not so much on facts available or evidence presented, as upon researches to be done, researches suggested perhaps, by the questions raised in this paper. (p. 371)

Given humanistic psychology's rejection of psychoanalytic theory, it might seem surprising to see Maslow include Freud and Adler on his list of influences. The inclusion undoubtedly reflects the lingering effects of Maslow's doctoral dissertation, which contrasted the relative influence of sexual motivation (Freud) with a motive for power (Adler's idea of striving for superiority and to overcome inferiority).

After these introductory remarks, Maslow then described what he considered a person's five most critical needs. First, the basic biological needs. Note Maslow's criticism of the usefulness of drawing conclusions about humans on the basis of animal research.

> *The 'physiological' needs.*—The needs that are usually taken as the starting point for motivation theory are the so-called physiological drives . . .
>
> Undoubtedly these physiological needs are the most pre-potent of all needs. What this means specifically is, that in the human being who is missing everything in life in an extreme fashion, it is most likely that the major motivation would be the physiological needs rather than any others. A person who is lacking food, safety, love, and esteem would most probably hunger for food more strongly than for anything else.
>
> If all the needs are unsatisfied, and the organism is then dominated by the physiological needs, all other needs may become simply non-existent or be pushed into the background. It is then fair to characterize the whole organism by saying simply that it is hungry, for consciousness is almost completely preempted by hunger. . . .

It cannot possibly be denied that such things are true but their *generality* can be denied. Emergency conditions are, almost by definition, rare in the normally functioning peaceful society. That this truism can be forgotten is due mainly to two reasons. First, rats have few motivations other than physiological ones, and since so much of the research upon motivation has been made with these animals, it is easy to carry the rat-picture over to the human being. Secondly, it is too often not realized that culture itself is an adaptive tool, one of whose main functions is to make the physiological emergencies come less and less often. In most of the known societies, chronic extreme hunger of the emergency type is rare, rather than common. In any case, this is still true in the United States. The average American citizen is experiencing appetite rather than hunger when he says "I am hungry." He is apt to experience sheer life-and-death hunger only by accident and then only a few times through his entire life.

Obviously a good way to obscure the 'higher' motivations, and to get a lopsided view of human capacities and human nature, is to make the organism extremely and chronically hungry or thirsty. Anyone who attempts to make an emergency picture into a typical one, and who will measure all of man's goals and desires by his behavior during extreme physiological deprivation is certainly being blind to many things. It is quite true that man lives by bread alone—when there is no bread. But what happens to man's desires when there is plenty of bread and when his belly is chronically filled?

At once other (and 'higher') needs emerge and these, rather than physiological hungers, dominate the organism. And when these in turn are satisfied, again new (and still 'higher') needs emerge and so on. This is what we mean by saying that the basic human needs are organized into a hierarchy of relative prepotency.

One main implication of this phrasing is that gratification becomes as important a concept as deprivation in motivation theory, for it releases the organism from the domination of a relatively more physiological need, permitting thereby the emergence of other more social goals. The physiological needs, along with their partial goals, when chronically gratified cease to exist as active determinants or organizers of behavior. They now exist only in a potential fashion in the sense that they may emerge again to dominate the organism if they are thwarted. But a want that is satisfied is no longer a want. The organism is dominated and its behavior organized only by unsatisfied needs. If hunger is satisfied, it becomes unimportant in the current dynamics of the individual. (pp. 372–375, italics in the original)

The second level of Maslow's hierarchy includes what he referred to as "safety" needs. If basic physiological needs (e.g., hunger, thirst) have been satisfied, then needs for safety and security rise to the forefront. Maslow pointed out that safety needs are most obvious in young children, but also evident in certain adult behaviors.

The safety needs.—If the physiological needs are relatively well gratified, there then emerges a new set of needs, which we may categorize roughly as the safety needs. All that has been said of the physiological needs is equally true, although in lesser degree, of these desires. The organism may equally well be wholly dominated by them. They may serve as the almost exclusive organizers of behavior, recruiting all the capacities of the organism in their service, and we may then fairly describe the whole organism as a safety-seeking mechanism. . . .

Although in this paper we are interested primarily in the needs of the adult, we can approach an understanding of his safety needs perhaps more efficiently by observation of infants and children, in whom these needs are much more simple and obvious. One reason for the clearer appearance of the threat or danger reaction in infants, is that they do not inhibit this reaction at all, whereas adults in our society have been taught to inhibit it at all costs. Thus even when adults do feel their safety to be threatened we may not be able to see this on the surface. Infants will react in a total fashion and as if they were endangered, if they are disturbed or dropped suddenly, startled by loud noises, flashing light, or other unusual sensory stimulation, by rough handling, by general loss of support in the mother's arms, or by inadequate support. . . .

The healthy, normal, fortunate adult in our culture is largely satisfied in his safety needs. The peaceful, smoothly running, 'good' society ordinarily makes its members feel safe enough from wild animals, extremes of temperature, criminals, assault and murder, tyranny, etc. Therefore, in a very real sense, he no longer has any safety needs as active motivators. Just as a sated man no longer feels hungry, a safe man no longer feels endangered. If we wish to see these needs directly and clearly we must turn to neurotic or near-neurotic individuals, and to the economic and social underdogs. In between these extremes, we can perceive the expressions of safety needs only in such phenomena as, for instance, the common preference for a job with tenure and protection, the desire for a savings account, and for insurance of various kinds (medical, dental, unemployment, disability, old age).

Other broader aspects of the attempt to seek safety and stability in the world are seen in the very common preference for familiar rather than unfamiliar things, or for the known rather than the unknown. The tendency to have some religion or world-philosophy that organizes the universe and the men in it into some sort of satisfactorily coherent, meaningful whole is also in part motivated by safety-seeking. . . . (pp. 376–379, italics in the original)

Once secure, and having been fed, humans next feel the needs for love (which Maslow differentiates from sex) and belongingness, then self-esteem (note the reference to Adler again), and finally, self-actualization.

The love needs.—If both the physiological and the safety needs are fairly well gratified, then there will emerge the love and affection and belongingness needs, and the whole cycle already described will repeat itself with this new center. Now the person will feel keenly, as never before, the absence of friends, or a sweetheart, or a wife, or children. He will hunger for affectionate relations with people in general, namely, for a place in his group, and he will strive with great intensity to achieve this goal. . . .

One thing that must be stressed at this point is that love is not synonymous with sex. Sex may be studied as a purely physiological need. Ordinarily sexual behavior is multi-determined, that is to say, determined not only by sexual but also by other needs, chief among which are the love and affection needs. Also not to be overlooked is the fact that the love needs involve both giving *and* receiving love.

The esteem needs.—All people in our society (with a few pathological exceptions) have a need or desire for a stable, firmly based, (usually) high evaluation of themselves, for self-respect, or self-esteem, and for the esteem of others. By firmly based self-esteem, we mean that which is soundly based upon real capacity, achievement and respect from others. These needs may be classified into two subsidiary sets. These are, first, the desire for strength, for achievement, for adequacy, for confidence in the face of the world, and for independence and freedom. Secondly, we have what we may call the desire for reputation or prestige (defining it as respect or esteem from other people), recognition, attention, importance or appreciation. These needs have been relatively stressed by Alfred Adler and his followers, and have been relatively neglected by Freud and the psychoanalysts. More and more today however there is appearing widespread appreciation of their central importance.

Satisfaction of the self-esteem need leads to feelings of self-confidence, worth, strength, capability and adequacy of being useful and necessary in the world. But thwarting of these needs produces feelings of inferiority, of weakness and of helplessness. . . .

The need for self-actualization.—Even if all these needs are satisfied, we may still often (if not always) expect that a new discontent and restlessness will soon develop, unless the individual is doing what he is fitted for. A musician must make music, an artist must paint, a poet must write, if he is to be ultimately happy. What a man *can* be, he *must* be. This need we may call self-actualization.

This term, first coined by Kurt Goldstein, is being used in this paper in a much more specific and limited fashion. It refers to the desire for self-fulfillment, namely, to the tendency for him to become actualized in what he is potentially. This tendency might be phrased as the desire to become more and more what one is, to become everything that one is capable of becoming.

The specific form that these needs will take will of course vary greatly from person to person. In one individual it may take the form of the desire to be an ideal mother, in another it may be expressed athletically, and in still another it may be expressed in painting pictures or in inventions. It is not necessarily a creative urge although in people who have any capacities for creation it will take this form.

The clear emergence of these needs rests upon prior satisfaction of the physiological, safety, love and esteem needs. We shall call people who are satisfied in these needs, basically satisfied people, and it is from these that we may expect the fullest (and healthiest) creativeness. Since, in our society, basically satisfied people are the exception, we do not know much about self-actualization, either experimentally or clinically. It remains a challenging problem for research. (pp. 380–383, italics in the original)

Maslow's concept of self-actualization was not well developed in this 1943 paper, but it soon became the center of his research (Coon, 2006). Over the next few years, he tried his best to identify the defining features of "self-actualizers," using as models two colleagues he came to know during his years in New York—the anthropologist Ruth Benedict and the gestalt psychologist Max Wertheimer. He later wrote that when studying these individuals, that "their two patterns could be generalized. I was talking about a kind of individual, not about two incomparable individuals. . . . I tried to see if this pattern could be found elsewhere" (Maslow, 1971, pp. 41–42). Maslow began compiling a journal that he called the "Good Human Being Notebook," in which he noted the attributes of both acquaintances and historical individuals that he considered self-actualized (Lowry, 1973). Then in 1950, he wrote "Self-Actualizing People: A Study of Psychological Health," in which he tried to sum up the characteristics of self-actualized people. They were, he believed, emotionally mature, creative, humorous, passionate about some cause (e.g., their work), and relatively unconcerned about gaining the approval of others (Maslow, 1950).

For the remainder of his 1943 paper, Maslow elaborated on his hierarchy and recognized that there could be exceptions to the sequencing of needs that he had specified. He also recognized that his model largely neglected what could be called "cognitive" needs.

> *The desires to know and to understand.*—So far, we have mentioned the cognitive needs only in passing. Acquiring knowledge and systematizing the universe have been considered as, in part, techniques for the achievement of basic safety in the world, or, for the intelligent man, expressions of self-actualization. . . . True though these formulations may be, they do not constitute definitive answers to the question as to the motivation role of curiosity, learning, philosophizing, experimenting, etc. . . .
>
> Rather tentatively, then, and largely in the hope of stimulating discussion and research, we shall postulate a basic desire to know, to be aware of reality, to get the facts, to satisfy curiosity, or as Wertheimer phrases it, to see rather than to be blind.
>
> This postulation, however, is not enough. Even after we know, we are impelled to know more and more minutely and microscopically on the one hand, and on the other, more and more extensively in the direction of a world philosophy, religion, etc. The facts that we acquire, if they are isolated or atomistic, inevitably get theorized about, and either analyzed or organized or both. This process has been phrased by some as the search for 'meaning.' We shall then postulate a desire to understand, to systematize, to organize, to analyze, to look for relations and meanings. (pp. 384–385, italics in the original)

Maslow also elaborated on his earlier criticism of the usefulness of animal research, although he made an exception for the research of Edward Tolman (Chapter 19). Like Maslow, Tolman had been influenced by the gestaltists and saw behavior not as driven by unsatisfied needs, but pulled toward future goals.

> *Animal- and human-centering.*—This theory starts with the human being rather than any lower and presumably 'simpler' animal. Too many of the findings that have been made in animals have been proven to be true for animals but not for the human being. There is no reason whatsoever why we should start with animals in order to study human motivation. The logic or rather illogic behind this general fallacy of 'pseudo-simplicity' has been exposed often enough by philosophers and logicians as well as by scientists in each of the various fields. It is no more necessary to study animals before

one can study man than it is to study mathematics before one can study geology or psychology or biology.

We may also reject the old, naive, behaviorism which assumed that it was somehow necessary, or at least more 'scientific' to judge human beings by animal standards. One consequence of this belief was that the whole notion of purpose and goal was excluded from motivational psychology simply because one could not ask a white rat about his purposes. Tolman has long since proven in animal studies themselves that this exclusion was not necessary. (p. 392, italics in the original)

Maslow's ideas, and those of the other humanistic psychologists, began gaining currency during the decade of the 1960s. The "rebellion against prevailing authority" motif, a central message of the third force's rejection of behaviorism and psychoanalysis, meshed with the historical context, a decade of turmoil in the United States. With Maslow providing the main impetus, a *Journal of Humanistic Psychology* was started in 1961; the American Association of Humanistic Psychologists began a year later. Maslow was elected APA president in 1968, and the APA created a division for humanistic psychology (Division 32) in 1972. As for Maslow, while at Brandeis he suffered a heart attack in December of 1967. Another one three years later killed him at age 62.

CONCEPT REVIEW QUESTIONS

1. Describe Maslow's attitude about the relevance of animal research for increasing our understanding of human behavior.
2. Early in his article, Maslow argued that "gratification becomes as important a concept as deprivation in motivation theory." How does that idea fit with his notion of "hierarchy?"
3. What did Maslow have to say about "cognitive needs," which are lacking in the hierarchy?

DISCUSSION QUESTION

1. Can you think of circumstances that might serve as arguments against the validity of Maslow's hierarchy of needs theory?

CHAPTER *36*

CARL ROGERS (1902–1987): THE THERAPEUTIC ENVIRONMENT

Along with Abraham Maslow (Chapter 35), Carl Rogers is known as a leader in the humanistic psychology movement. His original goal in life was to be a minister, and he studied at the Union Theological Seminary in New York. In an environment where students were encouraged to think for themselves, however, Rogers (1961b) "thought [himself] right out of religious work" (p. 8) and into psychology. He earned a doctorate from Columbia in 1931 and, while working as a psychologist at a child guidance clinic in Rochester, New York, began developing a unique form of therapy that came to be known as "client-centered" or "person-centered" psychotherapy. It was grounded in the humanistic psychology principle that people should take responsibility for their lives; it also rejected the Freudian principle that what has happened to us in the past is a critical determinant of our present and future lives.

In 1961, Rogers published a series of essays and lectures under the general title, *On Becoming a Person.* Among other essays, it includes a brief auto-biographical chapter, and an essay entitled "Some hypotheses regarding the facilitation of personal growth" (Rogers, 1961a). This chapter, excerpted here, makes clear the Rogerian dictum that therapeutic change will follow from the creation of the proper therapeutic environment.

Rogers opened his essay by describing the challenge of psychotherapy, and some of the influences on him as he developed his client-centered strategy.

> To be faced by a troubled, conflicted person who is seeking and expecting help, has always constituted a great challenge to me. Do I have the knowl-edge, the resources, the psychological strength, the skill—do I have whatever it takes to be of help to such an individual?
>
> For more than twenty-five years I have been trying to meet this kind of challenge. It has caused me to draw upon every element of my professional background: the rigorous methods of personality measurement at Teacher's College, Columbia; the Freudian psychoanalytic insights and methods of the Institute for Child Guidance where I worked as an intern; the continuing developments in the field of clinical psychology, with which I have been

Excerpts from: Rogers, C. R. (1961a). Some hypotheses regarding the facilitation of personal growth. In C. R. Rogers (Ed.), *On becoming a person* (pp. 31–38). Boston: Houghton-Mifflin.

252

closely associated; the briefer exposure to the work of Otto Rank, to the methods of psychiatric social work, and other resources too numerous to mention. But most of all it has meant a continual learning from my own experience and that of my colleagues at the Counseling Center as we have endeavored to discover for ourselves effective means of working with people in distress. Gradually I have developed a way of working which grows out of that experience, and which can be tested, refined, and reshaped by further experience and by research. (pp. 31–32)

Rogers then described his philosophy of therapy, one that shows how he gradually distanced himself from the psychiatric model of the expert physician directing the course of treatment for a subservient patient. The second paragraph also gets at a theme that runs through much of Rogers' writings—although he developed his therapy approach in the context of a therapy trying to help a client, he believed that his process was equally useful for any type of human relationship. As you will see, he expanded on this theme later in the essay.

One brief way of describing the change which has taken place in me is to say that in my early professional years I was asking the question, How can I treat, or cure, or change this person? Now I would phrase the question this way: How can I provide a relationship which this person may use for his own personal growth?

It is as I have come to put the question in this second way that I realize that whatever I have learned is applicable to all of my human relationships, not just to working with clients with problems. It is for this reason that I feel it is possible that the learnings which have had meaning for me in my experience may have some meaning for you in your experience, since all of us are involved in human relationships.

Perhaps I should start with a negative learning. It has gradually been driven home to me that I cannot be of help to this troubled person by means of any intellectual or training procedure. No approach which relies on knowledge, upon training, upon the acceptance of something that is *taught*, is of any use. These approaches seem so tempting and direct that I have, in the past, tried a great many of them. It is possible to explain a person to himself, to prescribe steps which should lead him forward, to train him in knowledge about a more satisfying mode of life. But such methods are, in my experience, futile and inconsequential. The most they can accomplish is some temporary change, which soon disappears, leaving the individual more than ever convinced of his inadequacy. (pp. 32–33, italics in the original)

The main point of the essay is stated first as a general hypothesis. Rogers then elaborated on each of the three components of the hypothesis.

I can state the overall hypothesis in one sentence, as follows. If I can provide a certain type of relationship, the other person will discover within himself the capacity to use that relationship for growth, and change and personal development will occur.

The Relationship

But what meaning do these terms have? Let me take separately the three major phrases in this sentence and indicate something of the meaning they have for me. What is this certain type of relationship I would like to provide?

I have found that the more that I can be genuine in the relationship, the more helpful it will be. This means that I need to be aware of my own feelings ... rather than presenting an outward facade of one attitude, while actually holding another attitude at a deeper ... level. Being genuine also involves the willingness to be and to express, in my words and my behavior, the various feelings and attitudes which exist in me. It is only in this way that the relationship can have *reality*, and reality seems deeply important as a first condition. It is only by providing the genuine reality which is in me, that the other person can successfully seek for the reality in him. I have found this to be true even when the attitudes I feel are not attitudes with which I am pleased, or attitudes which seem conducive to a good relationship. It seems extremely important to be *real*.

As a second condition, I find that the more acceptance and liking I feel toward this individual, the more I will be creating a relationship which he can use. By acceptance I mean a warm regard for him as a person of unconditional self-worth—of value no matter what his condition, his behavior, or his feelings. It means a respect and a liking for him as a separate person, a willingness for him to possess his own feelings in his own way. It means an acceptance of and regard for his attitudes of the moment, no matter how negative or positive, no matter how much they may contradict other attitudes he has held in the past. This acceptance of each fluctuating aspect of this other person makes it for him a relationship of warmth and safety, and the safety of being liked and prized as a person seems a highly important element in a helping relationship.

I also find that the relationship is significant to the extent that I feel a continuing desire to understand—a sensitive empathy with each of the client's feelings and communications as they seem to him at that moment. Acceptance does not mean much until it involves understanding. It is only as I *understand* the feelings and thoughts which seem so horrible to you, or so weak, or so sentimental, or so bizarre—it is only as I see them as you see them, and accept them and you, that you feel really free to explore all the hidden nooks and frightening crannies of your inner and often buried experience. This *freedom* is an important condition of the relationship.... There is also complete freedom from any type of moral or diagnostic evaluation, since all such evaluations are, I believe, always threatening.

Thus the relationship which I have found helpful is characterized by a sort of transparency on my part, in which my real feelings are evident; by an acceptance of this other person as a separate person with value in his own right; and by a deep empathic understanding which enables me to see his private world through his eyes. When these conditions are achieved, I become a companion to my client, accompanying him in the frightening search for himself, which he now feels free to undertake. (pp. 33–34, italics in the original)

These three attributes are the essence of client-centered therapy. The therapist's job is not to diagnose and treat, but to create a healthy atmosphere in which the client can begin to change. First, therapists must be genuine, which implies that therapists must be emotionally healthy themselves. Although Rogers doesn't say it, this genuineness also enables the therapist to act as a model for the kind of emotional health being sought in the client. Second, therapists must show what Rogers elsewhere called *unconditional positive regard*. This means accepting a person as having value by virtue of simply being a human being. In practical terms, this can mean avoiding labels. For example, I once heard a tape of Rogers talking with a teenager who had been in various kinds of trouble. The boy, very defensively, opened the conversation by saying that he imagined Rogers must have had a lot of experience dealing with delinquents. Rogers, very calmly, simply responded that he would prefer to think of the boy as "Mike." The message—the boy was a person, not the label "delinquent." The third component of an effective therapist-client relationship, *empathy*, follows from the humanistic philosophy proposing that reality is the reality as perceived and experienced by a person. Hence, understanding someone else requires trying to understand how that person views things. Rogers recognized that a complete understanding of another person was impossible, but it was the effort that counted. This effort included the major therapeutic technique used by Rogers, called *reflection*. This meant taking something said by the client and rephrasing it in a way that leads the client to think "this therapist understands what I'm saying." To illustrate, consider this exchange from a transcript of a therapy session with Rogers.

C: I suppose from the practical point of view it could be said that what I ought to be doing is solving some . . . day-to-day problems. And yet, . . . what I'm trying to do is solve . . . something else that's a great . . . deal more important than little day-to-day problems.

T: I wonder if this will distort your meaning, that from a hard headed point of view you ought to be spending time thinking through some specific problems. But you wonder if perhaps maybe you aren't on a quest for this whole you and perhaps that's more important than a solution to the day-to-day problems.

C: I think that's it. I think that's it. That's probably what I mean. (Rogers, 1961c, p. 90)

If the therapist succeeds in establishing the proper therapeutic environment, good things will happen, according to Rogers, and he did not mince words about the certainty of a good outcome. This passage also illustrates another central component of the humanistic message—everyone has the potential for growth and the opportunity to move in the direction of self-actualization.

I would say that when I hold in myself the kind of attitudes I have described, and when the other person can to some degree experience these attitudes, then I believe that change and constructive personal development will *invariably* occur—and I include the word "invariably" only after long and careful consideration.

The Motivation for Change
So much for the relationship. The second phrase in my overall hypothesis was that the individual will discover within himself the capacity to use this relationship for growth. . . . Gradually my experience has forced me to conclude that the individual has within himself the capacity and the

tendency, latent if not evident, to move forward toward maturity. In a suitable psychological climate this tendency is released, and becomes actual rather than potential. It is evident in the capacity of the individual to understand those aspects of his life and of himself which are causing him pain and dissatisfaction.... It shows itself in the tendency to reorganize his personality and his relationship to life in ways which are regarded as more mature. Whether one calls it a growth tendency, a drive towards self-actualization, or a forward-moving directional tendency, it is the mainspring of life, and is, in the last analysis, the tendency upon which all psychotherapy depends. It is the urge which is evident in all organic and human life—to expand, extend, become autonomous, develop, mature—the tendency to express and activate all the capacities of the organism, to the extent that such activation enhances the organism or the self. This tendency may become deeply buried under layer after layer of encrusted psychological defenses; it may be hidden behind elaborate facades which deny its existence; but it is my belief that it exists in every individual, and awaits only the proper conditions to be released and expressed. (p. 35, italics in the original)

The third part of Rogers' hypothesis concerns the outcome of successful therapy (keep in mind that Rogers was writing at a time when the phrase "gender-neutral language" did not yet exist).

We know that individuals who live in such a relationship even for a relatively limited number of hours show profound and significant changes in personality, attitudes, and behavior.... In such a relationship the individual becomes more integrated, more effective. He shows fewer of the characteristics which are usually termed neurotic or psychotic, and more of the characteristics of a healthy, well-functioning person. He changes the perception of himself, becoming more realistic in his views of self. He becomes more like the person he wishes to be. He values himself more highly. He is more self-confident and self-directing. He has a better understanding of himself, becomes more open to his experience, denies or represses less of his experience. He becomes more accepting in his attitudes toward others, seeing others as more similar to himself.

In his behavior he shows similar changes. He is less frustrated by stress, and recovers from stress more quickly. He becomes more mature in his everyday behavior as this is observed by friends. He is less defensive, more adaptive, more able to meet situations creatively.

These are some of the changes which we now know come about in individuals who have completed a series of counseling interviews in which the psychological atmosphere approximates the relationship I described. Each of the statements made is based upon objective evidence. Much more research needs to be done, but there can no longer be any doubt as to the effectiveness of such a relationship in producing personality change. (p. 36)

These last two sentences hint at another important contribution made by Rogers. He was among the first to systematically evaluate therapy outcomes, completing a series of studies comparing individuals before and after undergoing therapy, and even including control groups not receiving therapy (e.g., Rogers, 1961d). Rogers concluded his essay by returning to a point he mentioned briefly at the outset—what he had to say about a therapeutic relationship applied to *all* human relationships.

> To me, the exciting thing about these research findings is not simply the fact that they give evidence of the efficacy of one form of psychotherapy, though that is by no means unimportant. The excitement comes from the fact that these findings justify an even broader hypothesis regarding all human relationships. There seems every reason to suppose that the therapeutic relationship is only one instance of interpersonal relations, and that the same lawfulness governs all such relationships. Thus it seems reasonable to hypothesize that if the parent creates with his child a psychological climate such as we have described, then the child will become more self-directing, socialized, and mature. To the extent that the teacher creates such a relationship with his class, the student will become a self-initiated learner, more original, more self-disciplined, less anxious and other-directed. If the administrator, or military or industrial leader, creates such a climate within his organization, then his staff will become more self-responsible, more creative, better able to adapt to new problems, more basically cooperative. It appears possible to me that we are seeing the emergence of a new field of human relationships, in which we may specify that if certain attitudinal conditions exist, then certain definable changes will occur. (p. 37)

As an alternative to Freudian-based insight therapies, in which the therapist played the controlling role, client-centered therapy (first called nondirective therapy), along with a number of similar humanistic therapies, quickly became popular among clinical psychologists in the 1960s and 1970s. In contrast with analytic approaches, it was easier to grasp conceptually and it actually seemed to help people. It was also based on a more optimistic assessment of human potential for change, reflecting Rogers's own ability to take control of his life and a general faith that things can be improved if one works hard enough. And research on therapy effectiveness has consistently shown that the quality of the therapeutic environment is an important predictor of a successful therapy outcome (e.g., Wampold, 2001).

Rogers held academic positions at Ohio State University (1940), the University of Chicago (1943), and the University of Wisconsin (1955), where he developed his client-centered therapy further and conducted some of the outcome research. He was elected president of the American Psychological Association in 1946. He left academia in the early 1960s for the peaceful environment of La Jolla, California, where he founded the Center for the Study of the Person. There he extended his ideas into the area of group psychotherapy and helped develop the "encounter group" movement.

CONCEPT REVIEW QUESTIONS

1. How did Rogers' approach to therapy differ from a more traditional psychiatric strategy?

2. What three essential attributes must exist before a relationship can be effective, according to Rogers?

3. What is the relationship between empathy, reflection, and the general philosophy of a humanistic psychology?

DISCUSSION QUESTION

1. Rogers believed that his model for therapeutic relationships held for all relationships. Do you agree? Explain.

REFERENCES

Allport, G. W. (1937a). *Personality: A psychological interpretation*. New York: Holt.

Allport, G. W. (1937b). The functional autonomy of motives. *American Journal of Psychology, 50*, 141–156.

Allport, G. W. (1954). *The nature of prejudice*. Cambridge, MA: Addison-Wesley.

Allport, G. W. (1965). *Letters from Jenny*. New York: Harcourt, Brace, & World.

Allport, G. W. (1967). Gordon Allport. In E. G. Boring & G. Lindzey (Eds.), *A history of psychology in autobiography. Vol. 5* (pp. 3–25). New York: Appleton-Century.

Angell, J. R. (1907). The province of functional psychology. *Psychological Review, 14*, 61–91.

Babkin, B. P. (1949). *Pavlov: A biography*. Chicago: University of Chicago Press.

Bartlett, F. C. (1958). *Thinking: An experimental and social study*. London: Allen & Unwin.

Bartlett, F. C. (1967). *Remembering: A study in experimental and social psychology*. Cambridge, UK: Cambridge University Press. (Original work published 1932)

Benjamin, L. T., Jr. (2000). Hugo Münsterberg: Portrait of an applied psychologist. In G. A. Kimble & M. Wertheimer (Eds.), *Portraits of pioneers in psychology, Vol. 4* (pp. 113–129). Washington, DC: American Psychological Association.

Benjamin, L. T., Jr. (2003). Harry Hollingworth and the shame of applied psychology. In D. B. Baker (Ed.), *Thick description and fine texture: Studies in the history of psychology* (pp. 38–56). Akron, OH: University of Akron Press.

Benjamin, L. T., Jr., Rogers, A. M., & Rosenbaum, A. (1991). Coca-Cola, caffeine, and mental deficiency: Harry Hollingworth and the Chattanooga trial. *Journal of the History of the Behavioral Sciences, 27*, 42–55.

Binet, A., & Simon, T. (1916). *The development of intelligence in children* (E. S. Kite, Trans.). Baltimore, MD: Williams and Wilkins.

Blodgett, H. C. (1929). The effect of the introduction of reward upon the maze performance of rats. *University of California Publications in Psychology, 4*, 113–134.

Bjork, D. W. (1993). *B. F. Skinner: A life*. New York: Basic Books.

Blumenthal, A. L. (1975). A reappraisal of Wilhelm Wundt. *American Psychologist, 30*, 1081–1088.

Boring, E. G. (1950). *A history of experimental psychology* (2nd ed.). Englewood Cliffs, NJ: Prentice-Hall.

Boring, E. G. (1961). Edward Bradford Titchener, 1867–1927. In E. G. Boring (Ed.), *Psychologist at large: An autobiography and selected essays* (pp. 246–265). New York: Basic Books. (Original work published 1927)

Broca, P. (1965). Paul Broca (1824–1880) on the speech center, 1861. In R. J. Herrnstein & E. G. Boring (Eds.), *A sourcebook in the history of psychology* (pp. 223–229). Cambridge, MA: Harvard University Press. (Original work published 1861)

Brotemarkle, R. A. (Ed.) (1931). *Clinical psychology: Studies in honor of Lightner Witmer*. Philadelphia: University of Pennsylvania Press.

Buckley, K. W. (1989). *Mechanical man: John Broadus Watson and the beginnings of behaviorism*. New York: Guilford Press.

Calkins, M. W. (1894). Association I. *Psychological Review, 1*, 476–483.

Calkins, M. W. (1896). Association II. *Psychological Review*, *3*, 32–49.

Calkins, M. W. (1896). Association: An essay analytic and experimental. *Psychological Review Monograph Supplement*, *1*, No. 2.

Carr, H. A., & Watson, J. B. (1908). Orientation in the white rat. *Journal of Comparative Neurology and Psychology*, *18*, 27–44.

Cattell, J. M. (1890). Mental tests and measurements. *Mind*, *15*, 373–381.

Clark, K. B., & Clark, M. P. (1939). The development of consciousness of self and the emergence of racial identification of Negro preschool children. *Journal of Social Psychology*, *11*, 591–599.

Clark, K. B., & Clark, M. P. (1940). Skin color as a factor in racial identification of Negro preschool children. *Journal of Social Psychology*, *11*, 159–169.

Clark, K. B., & Clark, M. P. (1958). Racial identification and preference in Negro children. In E. E. Maccoby, T. M. Newcomb, & E. L. Hartley (Eds.) *Readings in social psychology* (3rd ed.) (pp. 602–611). New York: Holt, Rinehart, Winston.

Cloninger, S. C. (2004). *Theories of personality: Understanding persons* (4th ed.). Upper Saddle River, NJ: Prentice-Hall.

Coon, D. J. (2006). Abraham Maslow: Reconnaissance for eupsychia. In D. A. Dewsbury, L. T. Benjamin, Jr., & M. Wertheimer (Eds.), *Portraits of pioneers in psychology*, *Vol. 6* (pp. 255–271). Washington, DC: American Psychological Association.

Cottingham, J. (1986). *Descartes*. New York: Basil Blackwell.

Dallenbach, K. M. (1913). The measurement of attention. *American Journal of Psychology*, *24*, 465–507.

Dallenbach, K. M. (1963). Tables vs. graphs as means of presenting experimental results. *American Journal of Psychology*, *76*, 700–702.

Decker, H. S. (1975). "The Interpretation of Dreams": Early reception by the educated German public. *Journal of the History of the Behavioral Sciences*, *11*, 129–141.

Descartes, R. (1960). *Discourse on method* (L. J. Lafleur, Trans.). Indianapolis: Bobbs-Merrill. (Original work published 1637)

Descartes, R. (1969). Passions of the soul. In E. S. Haldane & G. R. T. Ross (Trans.) *The philosophical works of Descartes*, *Vol. I* (pp. 329–427). New York: Cambridge University Press. (Original work published 1649)

Dewsbury, D. A. (1984). *Comparative psychology in the twentieth century*. Stroudsburg, PA: Hutchinson Ross.

Ebbinghaus, H. (1964). *Memory: A contribution to experimental psychology* (H. A. Ruger & C. A. Bussenius, Trans.). New York: Dover. (Original work published 1885)

Evans, R. B. (1990). William James and his *Principles*. In M. G. Johnson & T. B. Henley (Eds.), *Reflections on 'The Principles of Psychology'* (pp. 11–31). Hillsdale, NJ: Erlbaum.

Evans, R. B. (2008, March 13). Email from R. B. Evans to C. J. Goodwin.

Fancher, R. E. (1985). *The intelligence men: Makers of the IQ controversy*. New York: W. W. Norton.

Fancher, R. E. (1987). Henry Goddard and the Kallikak family photographs. *American Psychologist*, *42*, 585–590.

Fearing, F. (1930). *Reflex action: A study in the history of physiological psychology*. New York: Hafner.

Fechner, G. (1966). *Elements of psychophysics*. New York: Holt, Rinehart and Winston. (Original work published 1860)

Fernberger, S. W. (1931). The history of the psychological clinic. In R. A. Brotemarkle (Ed.), *Clinical psychology: Studies in honor of Lightner Witmer* (pp. 10–36). Philadelphia: University of Pennsylvania Press.

Ferster, C. B., & Skinner, B. F. (1957). *Schedules of reinforcement*. New York: Appleton-Century-Crofts.

Finger, S. (2000). *Minds behind the brain: A history of the pioneers and their discoveries*. New York: Oxford University Press.

Flourens, P. (1978). Phrenology examined (C. D. Meigs, Trans.). In D. N. Robinson (Ed.), *Significant contributions to the history of psychology. Series E. Vol. II.* Washington, DC: University Publications of America. (Original work published 1846)

Forrest, D. W. (1974). *Francis Galton: The life and work of a Victorian genius.* New York: Taplinger.

Freud, S. (1938). The interpretation of dreams. In A. A. Brill (Ed. & Trans.), *The basic writings of Sigmund Freud* (pp. 179–549). New York: Random House. (Original work published 1900)

Freud, S. (1938). The psychopathology of everyday life. In A. A. Brill (Ed. & Trans.), *The basic writings of Sigmund Freud* (pp. 33–178). New York: Random House. (Original work published 1901)

Freud, S. (1938). Three contributions to the theory of sex. In A. A. Brill (Ed. & Trans.), *The basic writings of Sigmund Freud* (pp. 551–629). New York: Random House. (Original work published 1905)

Freud, S. (1957). *Five lectures on psychoanalysis* (J. Strachey, Trans.). New York: W. W. Norton. (Original work published 1909)

Freud, S. (1959). *The ego and the id* (J. Strachey, Trans.). New York: Bantam Books. (Original work published 1923)

Furumoto, L. (1979). Mary Whiton Calkins (1863–1930): Fourteenth president of the American Psychological Association. *Journal of the History of the Behavioral Sciences, 15,* 346–356.

Furumoto, L. (1991). From "paired associates" to a psychology of self: The intellectual odyssey of Mary Whiton Calkins. In G. A. Kimble, M. Wertheimer, & C. L. White (Eds.), *Portraits of pioneers in psychology* (pp. 56–72). Washington, DC: American Psychological Association.

Galef, B. G., Jr. (1998). Edward Thorndike: Revolutionary psychologist, ambiguous biologist. *American Psychologist, 53,* 1128–1134.

Galton, F. (1874). *English men of science: Their nature and nurture.* London: Macmillan.

Galton, F. (1950). *Hereditary genius.* London: Watts & Co.. (Original work published 1869)

Galton, F. (1965). Galton on mental capacity, 1883. In R. J. Herrnstein & E. G. Boring (Eds.), *A sourcebook in the history of psychology* (pp. 421–423). Cambridge, MA: Harvard University Press. (Original work published 1883)

Gay, P. (1988). *Freud: A life for our time.* New York: W. W. Norton.

Gillham, N. W. (2001). *A life of Sir Francis Galton: From African exploration to the birth of eugenics.* New York: Oxford University Press.

Goddard, H. H. (1912). *The Kallikak family: A study in the heredity of feeblemindedness.* New York: Macmillan.

Goodenough, F. L. (1950). Edward Lee Thorndike: 1874–1949. *American Journal of Psychology, 63,* 291–301.

Goodwin, C. J. (2008). *A history of modern psychology* (3rd ed.). New York: Wiley.

Gould, S. J. (1981). *The mismeasure of man.* New York: Norton.

Grmek, M. D. (1972). François Magendie. In C. C. Gillespie (Ed.), *Dictionary of scientific biography. Vol. IX.* New York: Scribner.

Hale, M., Jr. (1980). *Human science and social order: Hugo Münsterberg and the origins of applied psychology.* Philadelphia, PA: Temple University Press.

Hannush, M. J. (1987). John B. Watson remembered: An interview with James B. Watson. *Journal of the History of the Behavioral Sciences, 23,* 137–152.

Harris, B. (1979). Whatever happened to Little Albert? *American Psychologist, 34,* 151–160.

Hilgard, E. R. (1948). *Theories of learning.* New York: Appleton-Century-Crofts.

Hilgard, E. R. (1964). *Introduction to Dover Edition of "Memory: A contribution to experimental psychology."* New York: Dover.

Hilgard, E. R. (1987). *Psychology in America: A historical survey.* San Diego: Harcourt Brace Jovanovich.

Hollingworth, H. L. (1916). *Vocational psychology: Its problems and methods.* New York: D. Appleton and Company.

Hollingworth, L. S. (1914). Functional periodicity. *Teachers College Contributions to Education*, No. 69. New York: Columbia University Press.

Hollingworth, L. S. (1926). *Gifted children: Their nature and nurture*. New York: Macmillan.

Horney, K. (1937). *The neurotic personality of our time*. New York: Norton.

Horney, K. (1939). *New ways in psychoanalysis*. New York: Norton.

Horney, K. (1945). *Our inner conflicts: A constructive theory of neurosis*. New York: Norton.

Horney, K. (1950). *Neurosis and human growth: The struggle toward self-realization*. New York: Norton.

Hornstein, G. A. (1992). The return of the repressed: Psychology's problematic relations with psychoanalysis, 1909–1960. *American Psychologist*, *47*, 254–263.

Hothersall, D. (1995). *History of psychology* (3rd ed.). New York: McGraw-Hill.

Jackson, J. P., Jr. (2000). The triumph of the segregationists? A historiographic inquiry into psychology and the *Brown* litigation. *History of Psychology*, *3*, 239–261.

James, W. (1950). *Principles of psychology*. *Vol. 1* & 2. New York: Dover. (Original work published 1890)

James, W. (1961). *Psychology: The briefer course*. New York: Harper & Row. (Original work published 1892)

Jenkins, J. G. (1935). *Psychology in business and industry: An introduction to psychotechnology*. New York: Wiley.

Jenkins, J. G., & Dallenbach, K. M. (1924). Obliviscence during sleep and waking. *American Journal of Psychology*, *35*, 605–612.

Jenkins, J. G., & Dallenbach, K. M. (1927). The effect of serial position on recall. *American Journal of Psychology*, *38*, 285–291.

Jones, M. C. (1924a). The elimination of children's fears. *Journal of Experimental Psychology*, *7*, 382–390.

Jones, M. C. (1924b). A laboratory study of fear: The case of Peter. *Pedagogical Seminary*, *31*, 308–315.

Jones, M. C. (1926). A development of early behavior patterns in young children. *Pedagogical Seminary*, *33*, 537–585.

Klein, A. G. (2002). *Forgotten voice: A biography of Leta Stetter Hollingworth*. Scottsdale, AZ: Great Potential Press.

Koffka, K. (1922). Perception: An introduction to the Gestalt-theorie. *Psychological Bulletin*, *19*, 531–585.

Lal, S. (2002). Giving children security: Mamie Phipps Clark and the racialization of child psychology. *American Psychologist*, *57*, 20–28.

Landy, F. J. (1993). Early influences on the development of industrial/organizational psychology. In T. K. Fagan & G. R. VandenBos (Eds.), *Exploring applied psychology: Origins and critical analyses* (pp. 83–118). Washington, DC: American Psychological Association.

Leahey, T. H. (1992). The mythical revolutions of American psychology. *American Psychologist*, *47*, 308–318.

Lewin, K., Lippitt, R., & White, R. K. (1939). Patterns of aggressive behavior in experimentally created "social climates." *Journal of Social Psychology*, *10*, 271–299.

Locke, J. (1963). *An essay concerning human understanding*. Germany: Scientia Verlag Aalen. (Original work published 1690)

Loftus, E. F. (1979). *Eyewitness testimony*. Cambridge, MA: Harvard University Press.

Lowry, R. J. (1973). *A. H. Maslow: An intellectual portrait*. Monterey, CA: Brooks/Cole.

Madigan, S., & O'Hara, R. (1992). Short-term memory at the turn of the century: Mary Whiton Calkins's memory research. *American Psychologist*, *47*, 170–174.

Magendie, F. (1965). François Magendie (1783–1855) on spinal nerve roots, 1822. In R. J. Herrnstein & E. G. Boring (Eds.), *A sourcebook in the history of psychology* (pp. 19–22). Cambridge, MA: Harvard University Press. (Original work published 1822)

Marrow, A. J. (1969). *The practical theorist: The life and work of Kurt Lewin*. New York: Basic Books.

Maslow, A. H. (1943a). A preface to motivational theory. *Psychosomatic Medicine*, *5*, 85–92.

Maslow, A. H. (1943b). A theory of human motivation. *Psychological Review*, *50*, 370–396.

Maslow, A. H. (1950). Self-actualizing people: A study of psychological health. In *Personality symposia: Symposium #1 on values* (pp. 11–34). New York: Grune and Stratton.

Maslow, A. H. (1971). *The farther reaches of human nature*. New York: Viking.

McReynolds, P. (1997). *Lightner Witmer: His life and times*. Washington, DC: American Psychological Association.

Miles, W. R. (1930). On the history of research with rats and mazes: A collection of notes. *Journal of General Psychology*, *3*, 324–337.

Mill, J. S. (1869). *The subjection of women*. London: Longmans, Green, Reader, and Dyer.

Mill, J. S. (1987). *A system of logic, ratiocinative and inductive, being a connected view of the principles of evidence, and the methods of scientific investigation*. LaSalle, IL: Open Court Classics. (Original work published 1843)

Mill, J. S. (1989). *Autobiography*. London: Penguin. (Original work published 1873)

Miller, G. A. (1956). The magical number seven, plus or minus two: Some limits on our capacity for processing information. *Psychological Review*, *63*, 81–97.

Montague, H., & Hollingworth, L. S. (1914). The comparative variability of the sexes at birth. *American Journal of Sociology*, *20*, 335–370.

Morison, S. E. (1965). *The Oxford history of the American people*. New York: Oxford University Press.

Münsterberg, H. (1908). *On the witness stand*. New York: The McClure Company.

Münsterberg, H. (1909). *Psychotherapy*. New York: Moffat, Yard.

Münsterberg, H. (1913). *Psychology and industrial efficiency*. New York: Houghton Mifflin.

Nicholson, I. A. M. (2003). *Inventing personality: Gordon Allport and the science of selfhood*. Washington, DC: American Psychological Association.

Pavlov, I. P. (1906, November). The scientific investigation of the psychical faculties or processes in the higher animals. *Science*, *24*, 613–619.

Pavlov, I. P. (1960). *Conditioned reflexes* (G. V. Anrep, Trans.). New York: Dover. (Original work published 1927)

Quin, S. (1988). *A mind of her own: The life of Karen Horney*. Reading, MA: Addison-Wesley.

Roediger, H. L. III. (1985). Remembering Ebbinghaus. *Contemporary Psychology*, *30*, 519–523.

Roediger, H. L. III. (1997). Remembering. *Contemporary Psychology*, *42*, 488–492.

Roediger, H. L. III. (2000). Sir Charles Frederick Bartlett: Experimental and applied psychologist. In G. A. Kimble & M. Wertheimer (Eds.), *Portraits of pioneers in psychology. Vol. 4* (pp. 149–161). Washington, DC: American Psychological Association.

Roediger, H. L. III, & McDermott, K. B. (1995). Creating false memories: Remembering words not presented in lists. *Journal of Experimental Psychology: Learning Memory, and Cognition*, *21*, 803–814.

Rogers, C. R. (1961a). Some hypotheses regarding the facilitation of personal growth. In C. R. Rogers (Ed.), *On becoming a person* (pp. 31–38). Boston: Houghton-Mifflin.

Rogers, C. R. (1961b). This is me: The development of my professional thinking and personal philosophy. In C. R. Rogers (Ed.), *On becoming a person* (pp. 3–31). Boston: Houghton-Mifflin.

Rogers, C. R. (1961c). Some of the directions evident in therapy. In C. R. Rogers (Ed.), *On becoming a person* (pp. 73–106). Boston: Houghton-Mifflin.

Rogers, C. R. (1961d). Personality change in psychotherapy. In C. R. Rogers (Ed.), *On becoming a person* (pp. 225–242). Boston: Houghton-Mifflin.

Rosenzweig, S. (1992). *The historic expedition to America (1909): Freud, Jung, and Hall the king-maker*. St. Louis: Rana House.

Ross, D. (1972). *G. Stanley Hall: The psychologist as prophet*. Chicago: University of Chicago Press.

Rutherford, A. (2006). Mother of behavior therapy and beyond: Mary Cover Jones and the study of the "whole child." In D. A. Dewsbury, L. T. Benjamin, Jr., & M. Wertheimer (Eds.), *Portraits of pioneers in psychology*, *Vol. 6* (pp. 189–204). Washington, DC: American Psychological Association.

Ryalls, J. (1984). Where does the term "aphasia" come from? *Brain and Language*, *21*, 358–363.

Samelson, F. (1981). The struggle for scientific authority: The reception of Watson's behaviorism, 1913–1920. *Journal of the History of the Behavioral Sciences*, *17*, 399–425.

Samelson, F. (1985). Organizing for the kingdom of behavior: Academic battles and organizational policies in the twenties. *Journal of the History of the Behavioral Sciences*, *21*, 33–47.

Schiller, F. (1979). *Paul Broca: Founder of French anthropology, explorer of the brain*. Berkeley, CA: University of California Press.

Scott, W. D. (1903). *The psychology of advertising in theory and practice*. Boston: Small & Maynard.

Scott, W. D. (1908). *The psychology of advertising*. Boston: Small & Maynard.

Scott, W. D. (1911). *Increasing Human efficiency in business*. New York: Macmillan.

Sechzer, J. A., (1983). The ethical dilemma of some classical animal experiments. *Annals of the New York Academy of Sciences*, *406*, 5–12.

Shakow, D. (1930). Hermann Ebbinghaus. *American Journal of Psychology*, *42*, 505–518.

Skinner, B. F. (1953). *Science and human behavior*. New York: Macmillan.

Skinner, B. F. (1990). Can psychology be a science of the mind? *American Psychologist*, *45*, 1206–1210.

Small, W. S. (1900). Experimental study of the mental processes of the rat. I. *American Journal of Psychology*, *11*, 133–165.

Small, W. S. (1901). Experimental study of the mental processes of the rat. II. *American Journal of Psychology*, *12*, 206–239.

Sokal, M. M. (Ed.). (1981). *An education in psychology: James McKeen Cattell's journal and letters from Germany and England, 1880–1888*. Cambridge, MA: The MIT Press.

Sokal, M. M. (1984). The Gestalt psychologists in behaviorist America. *American Historical Review*, *89*, 1240–1263.

Spillman, J., & Spillman, L. (1993). The rise and fall of Hugo Münsterberg. *Journal of the History of the Behavioral Sciences*, *29*, 322–338.

Strack, F., Martin, L., & Stepper, S. (1988). Inhibiting and facilitating conditions of the human smile: A nonobtrusive test of the facial feedback hypothesis. *Journal of Personality and Social Psychology*, *54*, 768–777.

Strong, E. K., Jr. (1955). Walter Dill Scott: 1869–1955. *American Journal of Psychology*, *68*, 682–683.

Titchener, E. B. (1898). Postulates of a structural psychology. *Psychological Review*, *7*, 449–465.

Titchener, E. B. (1909). *A text-book of psychology*. New York: Macmillan.

Titchener, E. B. (1914). On "psychology as the behaviorist views it." *Proceedings of the American Philosophical Society*, *53*(213), 2–3.

Thorndike, E. L. (1898). Animal intelligence: An experimental study of the associative processes in animals. *Psychological Review Monograph Supplements*, *2* (4, Whole No. 8).

Thorndike, E. L. (1900). Comparative psychology. *Psychological Review*, *7*, 424–426.

Thorndike, E. L. (2000). *Animal intelligence: Experimental studies*. New Brunswick, NJ: Transaction Publishers. (Original work published 1911)

Tinker, M. A. (1980). Wundt's doctoral students and their theses, 1875–1920. In W. G. Bringmann & R. D. Tweney (Eds.), *Wundt studies: A centennial collection* (pp. 269–272). Toronto: Hogrefe.

Tolman, E. C. (1932). *Purposive behavior in animals and men*. New York: Appleton-Century-Crofts.

Tolman, E. C. (1948). Cognitive maps in rats and men. *Psychological Review*, *55*, 189–208.

Tolman, E. C. (1959). Principles of purposive behavior. In S. Koch (Ed.), *Psychology: A study of a science. Study 1. Vol. 2* (pp. 92–157). New York: McGraw-Hill.

Tolman, E. C., & Honzik, C. H. (1930). Introduction and removal of reward, and maze performance in rats. *University of California Publications in Psychology, 4*, 257–275.

Tolman, E. C., Ritchie, B. F., & Kalish, D. (1946). Studies in spatial learning. I. Orientation and the short-cut. *Journal of Experimental Psychology, 36*, 13–24.

Wampold, B. E. (2001). *The great psychotherapy debate: Models, methods, and findings*. Mahwah, NJ: Erlbaum.

Watson, J. B. (1907). Kinesthetic and organic sensations: Their role in the reactions of the white rat to the maze. *Psychological Review Monograph Supplements, 8* (#33).

Watson, J. B. (1913). Psychology as the behaviorist views it. *Psychological Review, 20*, 158–177.

Watson, J. B. & Morgan, J. J. B. (1917). Emotional reactions and psychological experimentation. *American Journal of Psychology, 28*, 163–174.

Watson, J. B., & Rayner, R. (1920). Conditioned emotional reactions. *Journal of Experimental Psychology, 3*, 1–14.

Watson, J. B. (1928). *Psychological care of infant and child*. New York: Norton.

Wertheimer, M. (1967). Gestalt theory. In W. D. Ellis (Ed.), *A source book of Gestalt psychology* (pp. 1–11). London: Routledge and Kegan Paul. (Original talk delivered 1924)

Windholz, G., & Lamal, P. A. (1985). Köhler's insight revisited. *Teaching of Psychology, 12*, 165–167.

Wissler, C. (1965). Clark Wissler (1870–1947) on the inadequacy of mental tests. In R. J. Herrnstein & E. G. Boring (Eds.), *A sourcebook in the history of psychology* (pp. 442–445). Cambridge, MA: Harvard University Press. (Original work published 1901)

Witmer, L. (1907). Clinical psychology. *Psychological Clinic, 1*, 1–9.

Wolpe, J. (1958). *Psychotherapy by reciprocal inhibition*. Palo Alto, CA: Stanford University Press.

Wundt, W. (1897). *Outlines of psychology* (C. H. Judd, Trans.). Leipzig: Wilhelm Engelmann.

Wundt, W. (1904). *Principles of physiological psychology* (5th ed.) (E. B. Titchener, Trans.). New York: Macmillan. (Original work published 1873–1874)

Wundt, W. (1912). *An introduction to psychology* (R. Pintner, Trans.). London: Allen & Co.

Yerkes, R. M., & Morgulis, S. (1909). The method of Pawlow in animal psychology. *Psychological Bulletin, 6*, 257–273.

Zenderland, L. (1998). *Measuring minds: Henry Herbart Goddard and the origins of American intelligence testing*. New York: Cambridge University Press.

INDEX